MAX WEBER, RATIONALITY AND MODERNITY

MAX WEBER, RATIONALITY AND MODERNITY

Edited by

Scott Lash
University of Lancaster

Sam Whimster
City of London Polytechnic

London
ALLEN & UNWIN
Boston   Sydney

Allen & Unwin (Publishers) Ltd,
40 Museum Street, London WC1A 1LU, UK

Allen & Unwin (Publishers) Ltd,
Park Lane, Hemel Hempstead, Herts HP2 4TE, UK

Allen & Unwin, Inc.,
8 Winchester Place, Winchester, Mass. 01890, USA

Allen & Unwin (Australia) Ltd,
8 Napier Street, North Sydney, NSW 2060, Australia

First published in 1987

British Library Cataloguing in Publication Data

Max Weber, rationality and modernity.
1. Weber, Max
I. Lash, Scott   II. Whimster, Sam
301'.092'4   HM22.G3W4
ISBN 0–04–301234–5
ISBN 0–04–301235–3 Pbk

Library of Congress Cataloging-in-Publication Data

Max Weber, rationality and modernity.
Bibliography: p.
Includes index.
1. Weber, Max, 1864–1920.   2. Sociology – Germany.
3. Rationalism.   4. Modernism.   I. Lash, Scott.
II. Whimster, Sam 1947–
HM22.G3W454735   1986   301'.092'4   86–13991
ISBN 0–04–301234–5 (alk. paper)
ISBN 0–04–301235–3 (pbk.: alk. paper)

Set in 10 on 12 point Bembo by
Computape (Pickering) Limited, North Yorkshire
and printed in Great Britain by
Mackays of Chatham

Contents

Contents

Notes on the Contributors

Martin Albrow is Professor of Sociological Theory and Director of the Population Centre at University College, Cardiff. He is editor of the new journal *International Sociology* and is President of the British Sociological Association. He is the author of *Bureaucracy*.

Jeffrey Alexander is Professor of Sociology at the University of California, Los Angeles. He is author of the four-volume work *Theoretical Logic in Sociology* and has published a number of articles on sociological theory in the leading sociological journals.

Roslyn Bologh lectures in Sociology and Philosophy at the College of Staten Island and the Graduate Center, City University of New York. She has developed feminist ideas within a Marxian and phenomenological tradition and has published *Dialectical Phenomenology: Marx's Method*.

Pierre Bourdieu is Professor of Sociology at the Collège de France, Paris, and is Director of Studies at the École des Hautes Études. He is the author of numerous articles on culture, power and society; his books that have been translated into English include *Outline of a Theory of Practice, Reproduction in Education, Society and Education* and *Distinction: A Social Critique of the Judgement of Taste*.

Luciano Cavalli is Professor of Sociology at the University of Florence. He is the author of a number of studies on Max Weber, and his books include *Il capo carismatico* and *Carisma e tirannide nel XX secolo. Il caso Hitler*. His current work concerns the crisis of leadership in contemporary democracy.

Regis Factor is Professor of Political Science at the University of South Florida. He is co-author of *Max Weber and the Dispute over Reason and Value* (with Stephen Turner).

Colin Gordon is a freelance writer and translator and lives in Oxford. He has translated and edited a number of Michel Foucault's writings, including *Power/Knowledge: Selected Interviews and Other Writings*. He is an editor of the journal, *Ideology and Consciousness*.

Wilhelm Hennis is Professor and Director of the Institute of Political Science at the University of Freiburg. He is the author of *Politik und praktische Philosophie* and he is in the course of finishing a series of articles on Max Weber that are soon to be published in English under the title *Max Weber: Essays in Reconstruction*.

Barry Hindess is Professor of Sociology at the University of Liverpool. He is author of *The Decline of Working Class Politics*, *Pre-Capitalist Modes of Production* (with P. Q. Hirst), a co-author of *Marx's Capital and Capitalism Today* and author of *Parliamentary Democracy and Socialist Politics*.

Scott Lash is Lecturer in Sociology at the University of Lancaster. His articles have appeared in such journals as *Theory and Society*, *Sociology*, *Telos* and *Theory, Culture and Society*. He is author of *The Militant Worker, Class and Radicalism in France and America*. He is co-author of the forthcoming *The End of Organized Capitalism* (with J. Urry).

Wolfgang Mommsen is Professor of Modern History at the University of Düsseldorf, West Germany. He has published extensively in the fields of imperialism, modern German history and historiography and on Max Weber. His books include *Max Weber and German Politics 1890–1920, Theories of Imperialism* and *The Age of Bureaucracy*. He is a senior editor of the *Max Weber Gesamtausgabe*.

Guenther Roth is Professor of Sociology at the University of Washington, Seattle. He is the author of *The Social Democrats in Imperial Germany*, *Scholarship and Partisanship* (with Reinhard Bendix) and *Max Weber's Vision of History* (with Wolfgang Schluchter). He has recently written on the Peace Movement for *Theory and History*.

Wolfgang Schluchter is Professor of Sociology at the University of Heidelberg, West Germany. He is the author of *The Rise of Western Rationalism* and *Max Weber's Vision of History* (with Guenther Roth) and senior editor of the *Max Weber Gesamtausgabe*. He has recently edited a cycle of studies: *Max Webers Studie über das antike Judentum, Max Webers Studie über Konfuzianismus und Taoismus, Max Webers Studie über Hinduismus, Max Webers Sicht des antiken Christentums*, with a further volume on Islam forthcoming.

Ralph Schroeder is completing a Ph.D. on Max Weber's sociology of religion at the London School of Economics.

Bryan Turner is Professor of Sociology at Flinders University, South Australia. He is the author of *Weber and Islam, For Weber: Essays on the Sociology of Fate, Marx and the End of Orientalism* and *The Body and Society: Explorations in Social Theory*.

Stephen Turner is Professor of Sociology at the University of South Florida. He has published a number of articles in sociology and philosophy journals and is author of *Sociological Explanation as Translation, Max Weber and the Dispute over Reason and Value* (with Regis Factor) and *The Search for a Methodology of Social Science*, and is co-editor of *Sociological Theory in Transition*.

Johannes Weiß is Professor of Sociology at the University of Kassel, West Germany. He is the author of *Weber and the Marxist World* and *Max Webers Grundlegung der Soziologie*, and co-editor of *Soziologische Revue*.

Sam Whimster is Senior Lecturer in Sociology at City of London Polytechnic. He has published on Max Weber and German historians for the *British Journal of Sociology* and the forthcoming volume *Max Weber and his Contemporaries*. He has recently written on the sociology of decision-making.

Editions and Abbreviations of Weber Texts

AJ   *Ancient Judaism*, trans. and ed. Hans Gerth and Don Martindale (New York: Free Press, 1952).

ES   *Economy and Society. An Outline of Interpretive Sociology*, ed. Guenther Roth and Claus Wittich (New York: Bedminster Press, 1968).

FMW   *From Max Weber: Essays in Sociology*, trans. and ed. H. H. Gerth and C. Wright Mills (London: Routledge & Kegan Paul, 1948).

GASS   *Gesammelte Aufsätze zur Soziologie und Sozialpolitik* (Tübingen: J. C. B. Mohr [Paul Siebeck], 1924).

GASW   *Gesammelte Aufsätze zur Sozial-und Wirtschaftsgeschichte* (Tübingen: J. C. B. Mohr [Paul Siebeck], 1924).

GEH   *General Economic History*, trans. Frank H. Knight (London: Allen & Unwin, 1927).

GPS   *Gesammelte Politische Schriften*, ed. Johannes Winckelmann (Tübingen: J. C. B. Mohr [Paul Siebeck], 1971).

MSS   *Methodology of the Social Sciences*, trans. and ed. Edward A. Shils and Henry Finch (New York: Free Press, 1949).

MUS   *The Rational and Social Foundations of Music*, trans. and ed. D. Martindale, J. Riedel and G. Neuwirth (Carbondale: Southern Illinois University Press, 1958).

MWG   *Max Weber Gesamtausgabe*, ed. Horst Baier, M. Rainer Lepsius, Wolfgang J. Mommsen, Wolfgang Schluchter and Johannes Winckelmann (Tübingen: J. C. B. Mohr [Paul Siebeck], 1984–).

PESC   *The Protestant Ethic and the Spirit of Capitalism*, trans. Talcott Parsons (London: Unwin University Books, 1930).

RC   *The Religion of China*, trans. and ed. Hans Gerth (New York: Free Press, 1951).

RI   *The Religion of India*, trans. and ed. Hans Gerth and Don Martindale (New York: Free Press, 1958).

R&K   *Roscher and Knies: The Logical Problems of Historical Economics*, trans. Guy Oakes (New York: Free Press, 1975).

RS   *Gesammelte Aufsätze zur Religionssoziologie*, 3 vols. (Tübingen: J. C. B. Mohr [Paul Siebeck], 1920–1).

WL   *Gesammelte Aufsätze zur Wissenschaftslehre*, ed. J. Winckelmann (Tübingen: J. C. B. Mohr [Paul Siebeck], 1973).

WS   *Weber, Selections in Translation*, ed. W. G. Runciman and trans. Eric Matthews (Cambridge: Cambridge University Press, 1978).

WuG   *Wirtschaft und Gesellschaft. Grundriß der verstehenden Soziologie*, ed. Johannes Winckelmann (Tübingen, J. C. B. Mohr [Paul Siebeck], 1972).

For reasons of exactitude and consistency of usage quotations of Max Weber's writings used throughout this reader may differ from the existing, standard translations.

Acknowledgements

We would like to thank Professors John Rex and Gianfranco Poggi for their advice and support at an early stage of this book; thanks are also due to Mr Ralph Schroeder for his knowledgeable help and interest in the preparation of the manuscript; finally to record that Mr Gordon Smith at Allen & Unwin has been an unfailing source of encouragement, courtesy and intelligence throughout this, at times, complex enterprise.

Introduction

SAM WHIMSTER and SCOTT LASH

As we enter the closing decades of the twentieth century there is a growing recognition that Max Weber is our foremost social theorist of the condition of modernity. His pre-eminence, which is only now beginning to be truly appreciated, stems from the scope, the depth and the intensity which he brought to this project. Simply put, Weber sought to explain the place of the modern individual in the world. Behind this deceptively simple formulation lay a gigantic enterprise.

Max Weber pursued three sets of questions: first, how Western civilization came to modernity, why other civilizations progressed in different directions, and the consequences of the attainment of modernity for the world as a whole – what Weber referred to as its 'universal historical significance'. A second set of questions relate to the nature and character of modernity; for Weber these turned on the special place of science and rationality within society. Third, there is a set of questions about living in the modern world; here Weber's position comes down to recognizing modernity for what it is and thereby placing limits on our expectations as to what is and what is not possible in a modern, rationalized world. These three sets of questions – one might say Weber the comparative historian, Weber the social theorist of rationality and Weber the social philosopher – can be seen to be interlinked when they are addressed through the concept of modernity.

It is as well to be clear that approaching these questions from an interest in the phenomenon of modernity represents a substantive change within Weber studies. This is not a particularly sudden shift, for the signs of the re-orientation of our interest in Weber have been building up over the last ten years. The process has been signalled by the emergence of a new Weberian scholarship that places culture and religion as the primary explanatory concepts in Weber's account of *both* the religious and the modern age. Friedrich Tenbruck's seminal article (translation, 1980) argued that we had to understand Weber's theory of societal change as deriving from a developmental logic rooted in a society's religious and cultural world-view. In a similar vein Wolfgang Schluchter demonstrated

1

that growth in cognitive capacity, seen as a kind of quotient of civilizational rationality, was interdependent with the developmental stage of society (1979, pp. 11–64). Apart from tapping an overlooked side of Weber's work, these studies had significant implications for the modern world and underlined Max Weber's assertion that we study other cultures in order to make intelligible our own position in the world (Mommsen, 1974, pp. 1–21). These analyses have placed the emphasis of study upon world-views and the ways in which they provide a coherent structuring of the social world and man's place within it. As a comparative sociologist of religion Weber outlined the distinctive features of the great cultural religions: Confucianism, Buddhism and Hinduism, Islam, Judaism and Christianity. This enabled him to point up the distinctive difference of the Protestant world-view. But the story does not end with the translation of this world-view into the rational and practical attitude to the world that formed the basis for the modern institutional practices within the state, the bureaucracy and the enterprise, for Weber also charted the transition of this relatively well unified world-view to its dissolution in a secularized culture. Here the trajectory of Weber's analysis moves from a Protestant society, through the Enlightenment to the post-religious, 'rationalistic' world with its characteristic plurality of 'gods and demons'.

Interpretations of Weber on the secular age are diverse and mutually conflicting; a situation that reflects the state of Weberian scholarship and the reception of his thought. While we attempt in this Introduction to provide an overview of these debates, it has to be recognized that ultimately the reception of his ideas relates to the current, and at the moment, unintegrated state of contemporary social theory. As a starting point, it is instructive none the less to consider the way in which Max Weber since the Second World War came to epitomize a 'value-free' social science. Much of sociology was based on the need to know and chart the demographic dynamics of the people – their age distribution, their family size and housing patterns, their changing occupational and class structure, their educational and leisure needs and their political affiliations. The role of Max Weber in this model was peripheral, but he was due to play a more central role. Weber represented the humanities input into the social sciences and was associated with the 'new' interpretive approach (and in addition was germinal for historical sociology). It was the political and campus struggles of the late 1960s, however, that brought Weber centre stage. The investigative/social-trends model of social science was never properly equipped to defend itself to its students and practitioners as a legitimate science of social reality, and in the intellectual and moral panic consequent upon the campus disturbances Max Weber was crudely appropriated to enforce the axiom of 'value-free' social science.

This led to a situation where Weber was presented as a founding member of 'positivist' sociology and a defender of intellectual orthodoxy, whereas Marx and, for example, Lukács and Gramsci stood for the radical, the humanistic and the committed. Max Weber's subtle and long dialogue with the ghost of Marx was turned into a stick to beat the claims of radicalism (see Antonio and Glassman, 1985). What is now evident, however, is that the wrong end of the stick was picked up. Weber did have a very clear stance on the relation of science, politics and culture. Moreover it was radical and not orthodox, and towards the end of his life was addressed not so much against Marxists as against two enemies: a positivistic conception of science that threatened to 'behaviourize' the problems of man as a cultural being, and, secondly, the irrationalist nature of cultural movements that demanded authenticity and immediacy in opposition to the 'objectivizing' character of science (see Turner and Factor, 1984a). This legacy is not solely a sophisticated methodology of social science, but has rightly been perceived as a more general, existential stance to questions of knowledge, values, truth and commitment in a world where modern science and rationality should signify the elimination of illusion (Löwith, 1982).

In order to bring out the complexities and paradoxes of this stance a further change in social and political theory needs to be registered. Whereas Marxism had held an exclusive monopoly on radicalism, moral conviction and the certainties of collective action, by the late 1970s this role had been appropriated by a new liberalism that propounded a theoretical radicalism and the demand for its social and political implementation and by a new conservatism and its associated moral fundamentalism. Socialism and liberalism were compared and assessed in terms of their liberating potential and their oppressive practice of power rather than in terms of exploitation and its supersession. This signified more than a realignment in politics; it opened up a set of issues that never received adequate airing in the old left-versus-right debates, of Marx against Weber, of capitalist irrationality versus formal rationality.

Grasping this new scenario places us in a far better position to consider the full range and power of Weber's thought. Instead of a formalized sociology that stressed the ideal type, insisted on the separation of 'fact' and 'value', tended to an ahistorical usage of Weberian typologies and took the Protestant-ethic thesis as a model of modernization for societies whose cultures neither were Christian nor shared many of the social structural principles of Western Europe (see Hall, 1985), we now have possession of a Weber who does not simplistically exclude values, who offers a number of versions as to how societal change is to be conceived and is far less Eurocentrist in its account of the processes of rationalization.

Accompanying this reorientation is a new interest in the role of culture in a post-religious world and a polemicization of the question whether contemporary industrial civilization will advance to a secular, rational (and implicitly progressive) culture. An examination of recent trends in social theory reveals Weber's presence but as yet has not given proper recognition to his nodal position. Critical social theory has been marked by a more appreciative evaluation of Weber. Whereas the old Frankfurt project sought to berate capitalist society for its irrationalities and superficialities (Marcuse, 1971) and made its assessment from a putative canon of aesthetic rationality, Jürgen Habermas now seeks out not so much a Weber who is the theorist of instrumental rationality and its implicit subservience to the dominant interests of capitalist society but rather a Weber whose concept of substantive rationality can be refashioned by the instruments of an interpretive tradition of social theory.

In French social theory Weber's prophetic insights into the deadening effects of bureaucratic, economic and cultural rationalization have had echoes in both structuralist and post-structuralist thought. The idea that the autonomy of the individual is fatally compromised by the processes of rationalization received expression in the structuralists' critique of the moral-rational ego. But it was in the figure of Michel Foucault that the implications of the emergence of modern institutions for the autonomy of the person, both psychic and physical, became most apparent. This was more than an affinity between the Weberian analysis of rationalization and the Foucauldian analysis of power and institutions, but marked a deeper concern about the genealogies of rationality in the modern era and how the modern citizen could best respond to assert the integrity of his or her person.

The restitution of the moral integrity of the individual is the prime concern of the cultural conservatives who sought to build an absolutist standpoint for morality and conduct amidst the *malaise* of what they regard as today's value-pluralism and rootlessness. In social theory this concern was signalled by Daniel Bell, who saw contemporary popular, mass culture as undermining the old disciplines of work, family and cultural enjoyment. Bell's at times apocalyptic analysis ended in a call for the resurrection of traditional Judaeo-Christian values; a call echoed by other analysts of the discontents of modernity such as Christopher Lasch and Alistair MacIntyre. Bell's theme was in part the Weberian one of the secularization of the Protestant ethic. But where Weber sounded the arrival of modernity with the elegiac notes of cultural disenchantment, for Bell modernist culture signified the rage against order and the search for the new and the immediate of the European avant-garde. This in its turn became the popular, but disintegrative, culture of capitalism from the generation of Bob Dylan onwards.

The pathways of all these analyses lead back to Max Weber, for he sought to make intelligible the social grounding of rationality. It was under the impact of modernity that Weber queried the nature of reason and rationality which Enlightenment thinkers had taken to be sovereign and self-evidential. For Weber the histories and trajectories of reason and rationality had to be traced, their effects upon the social world pursued; most especially, he pressed the need to come to terms with the findings of those investigations. These issues take Weber studies beyond the old debates as to who had the 'correct' concept of science and whether capitalism was 'rational' or 'irrational'. Instead there is now a much more earnest concern about how best to live in advanced industrialized societies and about the extent to which science and rationality can be a resource for directing our lives. In other words, we are faced with the technological and political problems about where to draw the line beyond which science cannot advise and of determining the possibilities of freedom and control in a world of rationalized structures of government, technology and work.

To be armed with such questions and to return to Max Weber along the different pathways of contemporary social theory are of course no guarantee that the questions will be answered satisfactorily. In Weber's contradictory persona these questions ultimately give rise to a number of antinomies: the ability to act and control our lives vs the objectifying consequences of action; material causality vs cultural meaning; the directionality of historical development vs the contingency of history; the objectivity of truth vs the relativism of knowledge; and the commitment to values and beliefs vs the responsibility to the consequences of one's actions. In the consideration of these antinomies one has to decide whether Weber needlessly or erroneously complicates the analysis of social reality or whether he properly warns us away from easy solutions. These antinomies recur in different ways and in different guises throughout the four parts of this book. But attention has first to be given to a brief exposition of Weber's understanding of modernity, so that these antinomies may be more precisely located. Pertinent here, drawing on the recent Weber scholarship, are the topics of (1) man's relation to the world and its periodization (Schluchter, 1979, pp. 11–64), (2) the processes of rationalization (Kalberg, 1980) and (3) the world of many spheres (Brubaker, 1984, pp. 61–90).

A Threefold Periodization of Man's Relation to the World

The analytic of Weber's thinking about the relation of man to the world turns on the account of how the world is interpreted by the great world religions, each one of which is treated as a separate unit of civilization. The accomplishment of world religions is to conceptualize a dualistic relation between humankind and the physical universe. There is another world beyond the mundane world of human, corporal existence. The religions of the major civilizations provide cohesive, systematic accounts of man's place in the cosmos, where the notion of the cosmos, whatever the religion, implies the existence of a world beyond the mundane. These 'other worlds' are epitomized by salvation religions, making maximal promises of another life after death. Irrespective of the content of the promise, the important characteristic of these religions is that they create a new level in people's consciousness – that there is another realm beyond mundane existence. For this reason these religions are said to introduce a 'cognitive duality': how one thinks about everyday human existence and how one thinks of the beyond, of material causality and supra-mundane purpose and meaning. It is the role of priests, the first intellectuals, to provide religious legitimations that hold this duality together and make sense of it. While priests are never wholly successful in this endeavour – because of the irreconcilable disparity between the experience of earthly existence and religious cosmology – the religious legitimation does ensure a secure world-view. The great world religions, then, are cosmocentric and as such are cognitively dualistic.

Either side of this great plateau of civilizational experience, if one views it in universal historical terms, is the primitive and the modern. The primitive and modern periods in certain key respects have more in common with each other than they do with the vast middle period of world religions. This interpretation does not square with the view of a gradual evolutionism through the three periods which, as Weber never tired of repeating, should not be taken for linear, progressive stages. The crucial respect is man's relation to the world. For the primitive there is no 'other' world or afterlife, and hence religion cannot be structured through cosmocentric accounts. The psychic needs of people are met through magic, tribal cults, ritual, and primitive charismatic communities such as warrior bands. Instead of an ordered cosmology there is a plurality of beliefs, none of which are able to go beyond the world as it is immediately experienced. And instead of the universality of a religious ethic, for example brotherly love, there is the particularism of village and sib.

In the modern period the order of religious legitimation is certainly peripheralized, if not eliminated. Further, the cognitive dualism is not only bereft of an over-arching religious and metaphysical belief system but undergoes a process of differentiation. Science displaces religious legitimation in the modern era, but science is singularly ill-suited to explaining the ultimate questions. The problem of finding an under-pinning for the ultimate questions of meaning is intensified because the modern individual now has to cope with more than just the two major spheres – the worldly and the religious. Instead human existence is divided up into an increasing number of realms which Weber terms 'life orders'. In the 'Intermediate Reflection' (FMW, pp. 323–59) these life orders comprise the economic, the political, the aesthetic, the erotic and the intellectual. Historically these have divided off from a religiously bound universe, and by the modern era, as the end of *The Protestant Ethic* makes clear, religion has become an outworn shell. The modern individual has access to a scientific cognitive understanding of the physical world and the life sciences, but this entirely lacks the integrative structure of the old religious legitimation. Arguably the differentiation of the life orders makes the need for such an underpinning more necessary, for science can provide no ultimate meanings; moreover human existence is cruelly split between the public realm of the economic and political and the private realm of the erotic and the aesthetic. In Weber's account each life order has its own set of values, the 'value-spheres'. This means that the modern individual always has to confront an irrevocable value-pluralism. For Weber this is the price of science dislodging religion.

The similarity of the modern to the primitive is the absence of a coherent structuring through a unified and usually systematized set of religious and metaphysical beliefs. In this sense both have to live with the inevitability of a plurality of beliefs. The modern, as Weber says in 'Politics as a Vocation', has like the ancient Greeks to live with a plurality of gods and demons. The modern espouses one set of values rather than another, just as the ancients might sacrifice at one altar rather than another. The other similarity of the modern and the primitive is the lack of structuring of psychic needs. Both the primitive and the modern are forced back on to their own, self-referential resources. The psychic needs of the primitive cannot go unmet for there is too much to be accounted for: pain, victory, defeat, the rigours of the physical world. The needs are met through rite, cult, magic and a polytheism of spirits. They are not met through a mediating structure of belief but by whatever localist sorcery is at hand. In a similar manner the modern-era psychic needs are vulnerable to exploitation and the precariousness of placing the self as the only point of reference. The needs are not so great in that science and reason have created a materially more secure world and have provided rational forms of explanations for what occurs in the physical and social world; nevertheless the absence of ultimate meanings does not eliminate the search for such meanings. Weber's advice on this is to come to terms with this predicament, though he realized just as clearly that in the modern era there developed strong tendencies to re-enchant the world and to champion values that stood beyond any reasoned scrutiny.

7

The Processes of Rationalization

A thorough and extensive reading of Weber's writings shows it to be impermissible to assume that rationalization is specific to modern, Western civilization. The modern West is of course the major exemplification of rationalization, especially as it is portrayed in *The Protestant Ethic*. Christian asceticism, allied to a notion of calling, led to an attitude of rational conduct in the world and as a result was diffused throughout economic and political behaviour. Rationalization in the modern world, a phenomenon with which we are only too familiar, is in fact an effect of a prior process of rationalization. In the first instance it is religious beliefs that are rationalized. Here priests attempt to provide an internally consistent and coherent account according to a cosmocentric viewpoint. So Puritanism represents a radicalization of salvation beliefs which, despite its irrationalist premises, the foremost being predestination, offers a clearer and more consistent account than the preceding notions of salvation. The unintended consequence of this radical salvation religion is to effect a rationalization of practical conduct, and this accounts for its momentous consequences for Western European history.

Once it is understood that rationalization is not confined to the concrete example of rational action within Western institutions but rather refers to a process that is common to all religious belief systems – the drive to consistency, coherence and greater applicability – then it is possible, indeed necessary, to take a less Eurocentrist view of this process. At a more general level, to use Weber's terminology, there exist propensities to rationalize both material and ideal interests, both those of want satisfaction and those of beliefs and ideas. All the major world religions undergo an internal process of rationalization. While the contents of the ideas of the major religions may be very different this should not obscure the point that the process of rationalization is not unique to any one civilization. Nor should it be assumed that because of its rationalistic compulsions rationalization is a continuous process. The histories of the world religions are all characterized by major eruptions which break the mould of the previous systems of belief and establish entirely new ideas. In their turn these new religious ideas are subject to routinization; that is, they lose their extraordinariness. In Max Weber's historical sociology there are numerous references to this dialectic of charismatically inspired eruptions and their routinization (Mommsen, Chapter 1). The point to note here is that the rationalization process is frequently disrupted, and there is no inevitability of the internal development of a set of beliefs.

There is the further question as to whether a rationalization process has an effect on the direction of development of a civilization. The crude answer is yes, but it is very hard to specify the nature of the interaction between religiously derived views of the world and a civilization's development. In part the difficulty concerns the number of factors involved – religious ideas, their agents of dissemination, the reception of religious ideas in people's attitude to the world, and the economic and political stratification of rulers and masses. Clearly this is a complex equation and in many ways *Economy and Society* can be regarded as an enormous factorial analysis of these interactions. These problems indicate that rationalization should not be identified with the direction taken by Western civilization and that other civilizations are not static and forge their own lines of development.

If rationalization is accepted as a phenomenon of the pre-modern world, should rationalization in the modern world also be regarded as non-continuous and subject to reverses and changes of direction? Is Weber making more than a rhetorical point in the closing pages of *The Protestant Ethic* where he suggests that after material civilization has run its course – fondly imagining this will occur when the last ton of fossil fuel has been burnt – new prophets and new or even old ideas and ideals will emerge? Should the process of rationalization in the West also be regarded as subject to charismatic eruption that will signal new sets of values and even changes in the direction of industrial civilization? If one does interpret Weber as holding out that possibility, then this raises questions about the degree of control that modern scientific industrial-based civilizations have over the course of societal development. Undoubtedly this is a central question, and Weber gives us a number of answers: (1) It is irreversible, and the future is bleak – a disenchanted, bureaucratized world with no autonomy for the individual. (2) It is a world characterized by instrumental action; i.e. people choose their goals for cogent reasons and seek the best way of achieving them. This issue is specifically addressed in Part 2 of the book.

A World of Many Spheres

The outcome of the break-up of a world unified by a cosmocentric legitimation is the world of competing value-spheres. Although Weber enumerates five life orders and value-spheres in the 'Intermediate Reflections', he focuses on the interrelation of three spheres: those of science, politics and culture. One needs to follow the full train of Weber's reasoning to understand how he seeks to provide a way of coming to terms with a pluralism of value-spheres. On science Weber sought to disabuse the notion that it could provide a new over-arching legitimation in the modern world. Science cannot provide ultimate meanings as to how we should conduct our lives, pursue our politics, or order our societies. This is often formulated as the demand for value-freedom: that science can explain what is, but not what ought to be. Yet it is more than a methodological protocol, for in saying that science cannot provide some absolute underpinning to our values and beliefs, Weber was fully aware that this radicalized the question of how the modern person is to seek order, meaning and control in his or her life. Let us take science, politics and culture separately and then assemble the whole picture.

Science is a set of rational procedures for the investigation and explanation of the physical and social world. The rationality of its procedures consists of correct reasoning (of which logic and mathematics are the examplars), hypothesis formation and empirical and experimental forms of verification. These procedures are applied to selected areas of investigation; for example, cellular biology or price movements. It is for the scientist to decide what object to study in the social or physical world. The emphasis on science as procedures and selection of objects defines the limits of science for Weber. Science provides answers only in relation to what is asked and is never enabled to provide overall answers as to the nature of the physical world or the social world. Likewise the procedural character of science means that it can have no illusions that it is somehow privileged to explore ultimate questions. Any 'scientific' enterprise that claims to be able to explain the whole of the world and to provide a comprehensive *Weltanschauung*, as did positivistic monism or forms of Marxism in Weber's day, has to be regarded as bogus. Weber clearly considered that the claims of the Enlightenment for science and human reason were over-pitched. His sociological explanation for this was that the Enlightenment philosophers in the first flush of the discovery of a post-religious age represented a charisma of reason. This sociological reductionism, bringing the philosophers down to earth again, does not mean that Weber denied the capacity of human reason, nor that Weber was a relativist. He was simply delimiting the claims of science. Weber's position here anticipates what today is termed critical rationalism.

In the political sphere the modern citizen has to form opinions about what he or she wants to see effected. Weber believed that no science of ethics or of politics would come to the citizen's aid and tell them what the right or the good thing was. This was a matter for the individual to decide. Weber not only blocks off the way to scientific justification, so intensifying the dilemmas of choice and commitment for the citizen, but also radicalizes the distinction between ethics and power. This might seem to lead to an irrationalism of blind choice and commitment in politics. Weber's response to this was to say that we have to be responsible for the consequences of our political beliefs. Being responsible is the opposite to blind choice. One has the obligation and, more so in modern society than in any other, one has the means and ability to think through the consequences that will flow from the implementation of a particular set of political values. If one is politically speaking a 'monetarist' – to take a recent example – the choice of those values is the individual's alone. Having chosen that course of action, the individual is responsible for its effects. Not to think through the consequences of one's value is a form of blind commitment, or what Weber termed a fundamentalist conviction ethic. Conversely one cannot hide behind a stance of responsibility and evade value-choice; in the matter of politics at some point commitment is required. As will be seen, Weber's position on politics is open to contention; in particular the distinction between responsible commitment and blind commitment has a clarity that is sometimes difficult to apply.

On culture we have to distinguish between culture as arts and literature, and man as a cultural being. The latter is a general assumption of Weber's sociology. Man is to be treated as a social and cultural being possessing values and beliefs. No social science can neglect this condition, and Weber is absolutely venomous towards forms of behaviourism and positivism that seek to efface the cultural nature of humankind (our word; Weber's was *Kulturmensch*). As regards the arts and literature Weber regarded this as a walled-off area, private to the individual and to his or her intimates. It is not clear whether Weber subscribed to an aesthetic theory. However, it is certain that the canon of the aesthetic was not to be applied outside its own sphere. Art and literature cannot inform politics, and Adorno and Horkheimer's claim that the aesthetic was the sole remaining source of substantive rationality and the last bastion from which to reconstitute an irrationalist society would have been dismissed out of hand.

The transposition of a set of values from one sphere into another is inadmissible. Two major implications of this stance have attracted comment: its sparseness and the strength of character required to sustain it. The separation of politics, science and culture radicalizes rather than minimalizes the rationalization of the life orders and its attendant value-conflicts. Weber's message is that you have to be tough to survive and the weak go to the wall, or more precisely cower within the protection of church and sect or simply flee the world. This stance has generally been interpreted as élitist, which it is; Weber candidly admitted that science was an affair of the intellectual aristocracy. Politics was a special calling, and only few individuals were suited to its joint demands of rational responsibility and commitment to freely chosen beliefs. On the arts Weber was decidedly highbrow.

The accompaniment of this tough-minded approach is Weber's reluctance to sociologize or psychologize the predicament of the modern individual. Talcott Parsons's project, for instance, was devoted precisely to the problem of the conflicting demands on the individual and how these are accomplished satisfactorily for individual and society. Parsons's sociological correlate to the plurality of the life orders is the model of the role-playing social actor. Weber's social actor may be split seven ways, but Weber never relinquishes the integrity of the personality – either sociologically or psychologically.

The sparseness of Weber's position has always attracted comment, from the delivery of 'Science as a Vocation' onwards. As we have already noted, this was crudely characterized as 'value-freedom'. Current thinking has gone beyond this precept. Not only do we not pass value-judgements, but science and philosophy cannot provide the grounds for us to formulate such judgements. This leads to the paradoxical situation that the science of cultural man (*Kulturmensch*) cannot provide a science of personality; nor may it speculate on the basis of social existence; nor can it constitute a moral theory of society or political philosophy. This refusal to ground a science of social reality in any substantive predicate is today referred to as anti-foundationalism.

In its unelaborated form this is also a difficult position to live with. Its end-point is usually taken to be nihilism: there are no values other than what the individual chooses to assert and there are no social-scientific or moral universals, but only the cognitive relativism of science and the moral relativism of action. The nihilist position has been attributed to Nietzsche, and Weber's anti-foundationalism is seen to borrow from Nietzsche (see Chapter 10). Social scientists and social philosophers have been anything but complacent about this issue. In relation to Weber – but also independently of him (Rawls, 1972; Rorty, 1980; MacIntyre, 1981) – there now exists a lively debate on the limits and the grounding of a liberal moral and political philosophy. The options are various, but one can note two tendencies: (1) to restore or, if necessary, reconstruct a value-rationality (Winckelmann, 1952), or substantive rationality (Habermas, 1984), or classical political philosophy tradition to Weber (Strauss, 1953; Eden, 1983; Hennis, 1983 and Chapter 2); (2) to celebrate the Nietzschean and to escape the 'prison house' of rationality and science – in its turn celebrated to various degrees by French post-structuralists (see Dews, 1984; Lash, 1984b; Gordon, 1986).

These two options are radically divergent responses to the problems of modernism, by which is meant the experience of living in an era (post-Enlightenment) in which the linkages to a unified *Weltanschauung* have been uncoupled. Intellectually this is analysed as a destructuring of the individual from an integrated world, as the absence of universals in morality, as the changed relation between agency and structure in social theory, and the difficulty of grounding knowledge in unshakeable certainty. One option is pessimistic as to the chances of reintegrating personality and culture (see Hennis, Chapter 2), whereas another option based in critical cultural studies seeks to turn this uncoupling into an energy for resistance and freedom (see Turner, Chapter 11 and Lash,

12

Chapter 17). In this volume there is a reluctance by contributors to become ensnared in the extremes of this debate. Instead the need is stressed to find new ways of gaining control over our lives, institutions and destiny. This may be taken to indicate that Max Weber was pointing out the fragility of the Enlightenment project but not its denial, and to the fact that if we are going to attribute autonomous agency to the individual in the modern world we have to analyse its limits and possibilities (Giddens, 1985).

Part 1 is taken up with the theme of rationalization and focuses on two issues: how we should interpret Weber's theory of rationalization as an account of historical change, and what significance we should place on the effects of rationalization in the modern world. As will be seen, the answer given to the one question has implications for the other, and we have therefore to be very clear that Max Weber's views on modernity itself are to be arrived at only through his comparative historical sociology. Wolfgang Mommsen opens Chapter 1 with a survey of current interpretations of rationalization and draws out the lines of disagreement that have become increasingly apparent over the last ten years or so. Mommsen is opposed to an interpretation that in historical or developmental terms would place charisma as an essentially pre-rationalist phase of human history and make rationalization into the central explanatory concept for the rise of the West and its decisive break with traditional forms of societies. While the older parts of Weber's writings do permit the reading of such a directional logic – from traditional and charismatic societies to that of modern, rational society – Mommsen argues that in the later versions of the three types of legitimate domination charisma no longer pertains to 'early forms of human social order, but stood instead for a universal type of social organization' (page 46).

Accordingly in universal historical terms rationalization does not come to replace charisma, but rather history is always – in both its traditionalist and modern phases – characterized by an antinomy between rationalization and charisma. Whatever the specific society, it is the existence of material and ideal interests that provides the starting-point for the processes of rationalization; equally there is always the possibility that the orderly processes of rationalization will be disrupted by charismatic personalities and movements that will introduce entirely new values. Weber's final position envisioned a dialectic between the forces of charisma and rationalization. This dialectic extended to the modern world. Charisma and routinization are mutually and necessarily interactive. Charismatic movements require a succeeding period of rationalization to consolidate the new value-ideal, and rationalization with its danger of becoming over-ordered and ossified is vulnerable to charismatic eruptions. From the perspective of this view of history the modern world is not immune to the forces of charisma, which are, as Mommsen writes, 'the fount of all creative activity that took its orientation from personal value ideals of non-everyday character' (page 46). The consequences of this are a theme that recurs throughout this book.

Wilhelm Hennis (Chapter 2) interprets the rationalization process as one producing a disciplined, disenchanted and depersonalized modern world. It is the world of the 'iron cage' in which the modern individual is imprisoned. What is qualitatively different in Hennis's analysis of this process is his comparison of the effects of rationalization on the life orders and value-spheres in modernity with those of a pre-modern era, in particular the estates society of old Europe. What this reveals, argues Hennis, is that the unification of the conduct of one's life, on the one side, and the powers and orders of society, on the other, is an impossibility in the modern world. This is primarily because the very anthropology of man – his unity as a thinking, feeling and political being – has been fatally fragmented by the rationalization of the life orders and value-spheres in conditions of modern capitalism. Using the example of the break-up of the old patriarchal system of rural labour and life on the Elbian estates under the impact of crude capitalistic methods, Hennis argues that Weber's concern lay with the integration of personality and life orders in the old system. Max Weber's analysis of the cultural conditions of man is predicated on an older tradition of political science stretching back to Aristotle and Plato. The demand for a complete freedom from value-judgements in today's science is an ironic statement of the rationalization of science itself and its dismemberment of the integrity of cultural man of a previous era. Hennis's essay is an eloquent plea for the revival of the old questions: about the place of man in the natural order and the possibility of determining one's conduct in the world. The plea is made despite, indeed because of, Weber's unflinching analysis of the impoverishment of man as a cultural being in the modern, rationalized world.

Guenther Roth (Chapter 3) argues that Weber's views of modernity can be arrived at only through the full understanding of Weber's treatment of societal change. The question of how we have come to modernity has to be answered in all its dimensions before gauging the significance of modernity. Through a scholarly analysis of the various kinds of developmental history written on the grand scale, particularly the work of Lamprecht, Breysig, Sombart and Bücher, Roth shows the range of models Weber could draw on and, more significantly, Weber's critical distance from any *one* model. Roth acknowledges an overall similarity between Weber and his contemporaries: that they all conceived of a general evolutionary process from an undifferentiated primitive society through to the mature cultural civilizations. For Weber this is expressed through the process of rationalization which is as much a cultural imperative to consistency and rigour as are the material processes of modern civilization. Hence its favoured ground is religion with its drive to an ethical unification of man's place in the world; but equally rulership, administration, the household and the enterprise are the sites of the rationalization process. For Roth, however, this does not amount to a general process of evolution propelled by the force of rationalization, because against such holistic account Roth stresses the particularity of rationalization. While rationalization may be a universal compulsion – to consistency, order and rigour – the institutional sites of rationalization are as likely to pull apart from each other as to work and combine together. The developmental process is the fortuitous result of combinations, breakdowns and recombinations of the economic, the religious, the legal and the political. Roth concludes that 'Weber disaggregated developmental history into evolutionary, historical and typological dimensions . . . on a worldwide scale, modernity has become just one element in a mix of historical forces' (pages 88–9), and he goes on to suggest that post-modernity will see new combinations of tradition, different elements of charisma as well as rationalization. Roth's essay is a powerful reminder that the question of how we have come to modernity can never be definitely answered, for we are ourselves still part of that story.

Wolfgang Schluchter has been associated with the project of reconstructing the full trajectory of the rise of the West through an analysis of the rationalistic kernel of Western religion and how this was worked through – rationalized – into the realms of work, law, politics and culture. This rationalistic kernel was epitomized by the Calvinist 'solution' to the need for certainty as to whether one would be saved or not. The unintended consequences of this search for certainty led to a methodical, rational attitude to the world. In his essay in this volume (Chapter 4) Schluchter extends his analysis of this rationalist kernel to the other cultural, salvation religions. All religions when regarded solely in terms of belief have a compulsion to consistency. This operates as a dictate upon human thought and action and is the basis of religious rationalism. The subjectivism of religious belief, however, has to coexist with an objective material world, the world of the other life orders and their values. So, for instance, Christianity 'demands brotherliness and love from a "world" that is violent, brutal, egoistic and lacking in compassion' (page 97). Schluchter suggests that Weber's insight that this was a condition of all religions was reached through the analogy of the theory of musical harmony. The pure, mathematical rationalism of harmony cannot be fully realized in practice; it is difficult for the instruments to reproduce it exactly, and harmonically it doesn't sound 'right'. The Western practice of keyboard tuning, temperament, is an example of the empirical fudging that takes place. Acoustical theory stipulates that the tonal distance between each note is the same for all notes; yet the twelve-note scale, the diatonic scale, of the modern piano does not observe this mathematical exactitude. Certain notes are closer together than others; the gap between E flat and E natural is larger than between B flat and B natural. The working out of logical rationalism in the world is the process of rationalization, and this is a feature common to all the world religions.

Because this is universal, we should not, argues Schluchter, regard rationalism as peculiar to Western religion alone. The idea of 'logical or teleological "consistency" of one's intellectual-theoretical or practical-ethical standpoint' (FMW, p. 324) may, says Schluchter, express a rationalist prejudice, but certainly not a Western one. While Weber probably did adhere around the time of 1904–5 to a Western prejudice that inner-worldly asceticism was a far more 'rational' religion than the irrationalities of mysticism and world-flight of Eastern religions, the later Weber in the 'Sociology of Religion' chapter of *Economy and Society* and in the 'Intermediate Reflections' had come to see that there were a variety of ways of working out the specific salvation beliefs of a religion. From the perspective of the universalism of rationality, Confucianism was the most rational form of adjustment to the world, Protestantism the most rational form of domination of the world and Indian salvation religions the most rational form of world-flight. In a sometimes intricate analysis of Weber's writings Schluchter reconstructs the full analytic range of Weber's model. The comparative sociologist is not enabled to pass judgements as to which way of working out the rationalist core of religion in society – and so determining the direction of rationalization in those societies – was the more successful. Yet as Schluchter shows there is more than a hint of value-judgement at the end of the 'Intermediate Reflections' where Weber opines that the organic social ethic of the Indian religions not only retained a 'consistent' solution to salvation but effected a reconciliation with the practical demands of the other life orders. Such a judgement recalls Roth's observation that the post-modern world will be shot through with elements of tradition, charisma and forms of rationalization, an observation that could be usefully extended to seeing modern life orders co-existing with Islamic world-affirmation or Confucian world-adjustment.

Part 2 extends the analysis of rationalization and inquires into its relation to the typology of social action, the last statement of which is made in Chapter 1 of *Economy and Society*. The question here is how the action types of instrumental rationality (*Zweckrationalität*) and value-rationality (*Wertrationalität*) relate to the processes of rationalization. For Weber this relation appears not to have been problematic. Rationalization is simply the overall effect of the extension of either instrumental or value-rationality. The growth of value-rationality within the religious sphere that includes moves to a more ordered, coherent and applicable religious doctrine would have been an example of religious rationalization. The extension of instrumental rationality in the modern world, for instance Weber's account of bureaucratic rationality, would be another example of rationalization. There is an obvious problem here of the varieties of content of the behaviour that can be typified as either value- or instrumentally rational, and in this sense Weber's usage of the term 'rationalization' is not clear-cut. But the idea that there was a jump from the action types to processes of rationalization is something that Weber eliminated through the pronounced nominalism of his final sociology as laid down in Part 1 of *Economy and Society*.

Contemporary sociology seems less satisfied with this 'seamless' extension of social action types to the processes of rationalization which in their own way can be said to constitute the process of societal change. Many of these theories of societal change, moreover, as Mommsen points out in Chapter 1, are neo-evolutionary social theories, and, very simply, these cannot be derived from the action types of the social actor. Instead these neo-evolutionary theories talk in a language of systems, sub-systems, steering mechanisms and inherent logics pertaining to the cognitive structures of specified systems. What the works of Parsons, Luhmann and Habermas all share is a clear separation of the action level from the system level and a belief that the complexity of societal change is intelligible only through an analysis at the level of system.

These matters are not the esoteric preserve of sociological theorists, for they are pertinent to a crucial issue already raised: to what extent does the individual have control over his life and to what extent do individuals in society have control over the directionality and nature of change of their societies? Modern societies were given up to the inexorable processes of rationalization – a new bureaucratization of the world, a new petrification, *ein stahlhartes Gehaüse*; yet on the other hand the growth of instrumental rationality meant that the fixing and attainment of goals were possible in a way that simply could not have been imagined in a pre-modern world. Making sense of these ambivalences necessitates a close and critical look at Weber's sociological theory.

Barry Hindess (Chapter 6) seeks to grasp the issue at its root and regards Weber's project as invalidated because of its ineradicable humanist pretension. This assumes that the individual is capable of acting rationally; that is, choosing ends and means of action according to the actor's own evaluation and assessment. Hindess in effect takes Hennis very much at his word; modern capitalist society is not a tableau within which the *Kulturmensch* can lead his life according to his own values. Accordingly it is erroneous to postulate, as Weber does, the individual as the starting-point for decision and action. For Hindess the so-called rational actor is circumscribed by 'the discursive conditions of action'; further, it is often *collective* actors – institutions such as the capitalist enterprise, the organization, the state – that define the basis as to what will constitute a rational assessment. It is to these collective agencies and their discursive conditions that sociology has to turn. Sociology has to reject the 'spurious unity' between the individual rational actor and the rationalizing tendencies of the modern world.

In a similar vein Pierre Bourdieu (Chapter 5) rejects Weber's method of typifying religiously oriented behaviour. Covering very much the same ground as Schluchter in this volume, Bourdieu suggests that the ideal determination of religious interests in terms of the purity or the coherence of doctrine – essentially what Schluchter understands as religious rationalism and the processes of its rationalization – should be dropped in favour of the material determination of religious ideas and interests. While there might exist demands for coherent and satisfying theodicies to situate the place of man in relation to his natural and social surroundings, the nature of religion and magic is best regarded as a process of symbolic interaction, through which is enacted a competition for religious power over how the needs of the laity are ministered to. This competition is structured through its relation to the 'determinate social positions' of key social agents: on one side priests, prophets and magicians and, on the other, the social stratification of the laity. The notion of competition indicates a market theory of 'producers' and 'consumers' of religious/magical ideas. In no sense is this a free market; at a structural level it is the position of agents within a society's overall stratification that counts. This enables Bourdieu to distinguish between religious legitimation – in the widest sense of how religion cognitively structures the world – from, for him the more important concept, the *legitimacy* religion bestows upon significant social agents whether priests or laity. Readers of Bourdieu's work on contemporary culture will recognize, in this interpretation of Weber's sociology of religion, the place culture occupies in providing the legitimacy as well as strategies for maintaining defined positions within a social structure. In this approach culture is never self-legitimating – for example, a pure aesthetic of art – just as there is no pure doctrine of religion.

The contributions by Johannes Weiß and Martin Albrow are likewise aware of the disjuncture between the action level, the level of determination by the individual or by sets of individuals, and the overall level of society and its processes of change. Both authors make reference to the work of Niklas Luhmann and suggest that the concept of rationality in system terms may require a different treatment to that of rationality of the individual social actor. However, both authors are prepared to work within Weber's framework once certain obstacles are removed. For Weiß (Chapter 7) an apparent paradox has to be resolved. On the one side Weber's methodology as well as social theory indicates that the future cannot be predicted by reference to objective laws of history, yet on the other hand Weber makes a number of apodictic and often extreme statements about the irreversible nature of rationalization in the modern world. Instrumental rationality signifies control over the ends one wishes to pursue, whereas the effects of rationally chosen decisions give rise to complexes of actions, for instance those embodied in the development of a technology, that are seemingly beyond our control and recall. Weiß affirms the theme of control; rationality, science and technology give humankind the ability to control the destiny of its society. Drawing on the work of Prigogine in the philosophy of science, he asserts that irreversibility is a feature of the openness and spontaneous nature of the historical process. It is because people choose to embark on a course of action, such as an energy diversification programme, that it is irreversible. The modern material and technological world is the result of choices. If we are to fulfil the Enlightenment project that material security and the pursuit of culture are something that can be created for all, then the 'realization of these moral and political goals requires not a lesser but rather a greater amount of technological rationality' (page 161).

Martin Albrow (Chapter 8) approaches the same issue, arguing that the full Kantian measure of Weber's usage of rationality has been insufficiently appreciated. The growth of rationality, he notes, 'was as obvious as the growth of industry or the rise of the modern state' (page 165). While Max Weber evidenced the distrust and pessimism of the products of an intellectualized and rationalized society typical of many German intellectuals, Albrow firmly cautions against over-emphasizing this trait in the understanding of Weber's concept of rationality. Anglo-Saxon philosophy has interpreted *Zweckrationalität* exclusively in terms of a means-end rationality to the detriment of the evaluation of the ends themselves. Similarly Habermas has stressed the individualistic and instrumentalist side of *Zweckrationalität*, denying the concept any footing in value-rationality. In part Habermas is justified to the extent that Weber's sociology of the life orders under conditions of modern and progressive rationalization suggests the separate development of rationalization in the societal, cultural and personal spheres. In this the unity of Kant's system with its distinction between pure reason, practical reason and the aesthetic judgement under modern conditions suffers a fragmentation. Concepts of values and ideals in the sphere of morality or art are sealed off from societal rationality, a field predominated by instrumental rationality. Albrow, however, suggests that the concept of *Zweckrationalität*, which

19

he prefers to translate as 'purpose rationality', partakes of both practical reason and pure reason, of both the categorical imperative and the hypothetical imperative. When we choose an end we make a moral evaluative choice as well as a means-end assessment of probable outcomes. The former process has been crowded out of the picture by the latter, but Weber, argues Albrow, would have taken the former for granted. It would have been an assumption held by any *Gymnasium*-educated person and something that did not have to be spelt out.

Albrow goes on to show 'the interplay between technical progress and reasoned argument'. Taking two recent examples, the UK Data Protection Act and the Warnock Committee of Inquiry into Human Fertilization and Embryology, Albrow demonstrates the interaction between rationalization (of information and data, and of research and medical practice in human fertility) and values (the rights of individuals and the safeguarding of our ideas as to what constitutes life itself). In passing legislation controlling what can only be regarded as spectacular examples of rationalization in the modern world – the computerization of information and *in vitro* fertilization – we are able to insert our own values into the process of rationalization: in these cases that of the right of the individual to have access to information and the need to affirm our almost instinctual notions of what constitutes life. Albrow continues that it would be premature to assume that causality displaces meaning in the modern world. However, on a more sombre note he concludes that the interrelation between rationality and freedom is dependent on control of and access to positions of power.

Part 3 and Part 4 of the book turn to the issues raised by living in a non-religiously legitimated world and its consequent conflict between the value-spheres. The Enlightenment project – the attempt of an age to free itself from the fetters of tradition and religion and to realize the dream of man's control over nature and society – again represents the optimistic perspective. But in the last two parts of the book this theme is pursued in its implications for individual personality, culture and politics. Culture and personality were of course the great topics of attention in the human sciences and arts of the late nineteenth and early twentieth centuries. They represented a counterpoint to the optimistic vision of the Enlightenment; first the investigation and unravelling of personality, especially that of man (as male of the species), indicated that the free citizen, the beneficiary of the enlightened and politically emancipated age, was not a benign maximizer of the opportunities newly presented; secondly, the field of culture and the arts far from becoming the creative property of all citizens appeared to be progressively devalued as the new machine age became established. The point and counterpoint of progress and cultural disenchantment were a study and practice that Weber made uniquely his own.

Weber commentators are at something of a disadvantage when they come to interpret the ambivalences of Weber's position. We have already seen in Part 2 that instrumental rationality seemingly places goal attainment in the hands of the modern individual, yet the consequence of multiple actions is to create a complex beyond the control of any group within society. On culture and meaning Weber asserts that individuals in their social interaction create and construct their own meaning, but he then elsewhere asserts emphatically that the processes of rationalization in the modern world negate and devalue the cultural resources available. Unsurprisingly commentators may thus be split into two camps. On the one side are the secular optimists whose maximal position asserts that control over society, the construction of meaning and the integrity of personality are all prizes attainable and within reach. On the other side are the cultural pessimists who see the breakdown of the post-Puritan personality and the associated work ethic, and the replacement of a once aesthetic culture with a mass consumption culture whose one insistent motif is hedonistic enjoyment.

The contributions to Part 3 make a number of differing assessments of cultural and social existence in the post-religious era. Jeffrey Alexander (Chapter 9) sees these possibilities as finely balanced between the chance of freedom and the forces of domination. Modernity has signalled the release of the individual from the constraints of religion, but it is precisely this freedom of the modern to construct meaning and impose his or her cultural significance upon the world that has become the central focus of existentialist thought. The major figure to realize the problems inherent in a totally free choice of values was Friedrich Nietzsche, and it is from his legacy that twentieth-century existentialist thought derives. In Chapter 10 Ralph Schroeder demonstrates that Weber and Nietzsche came to the problems of modernity through an analysis of *both* the age of the major religions and that of the primitive. Nietzsche, like Weber, regarded the primitive era as being one of a pluralism of values, unordered by any over-arching ethico-religious systems, and as existing in a natural state of conflict. Again for both thinkers Judaeo-Christianity denoted an inner orientation towards a transcendent goal. The modern era retains inner-directed behaviour but without retaining the rigour of religiously specified goal attainment. Hence the modern era presents the challenge of electing or committing oneself to freely chosen goals and values in combination with the ability to carry through the challenge derived from the psychological strength of inner-directed behaviour. Analysts from Nietzsche onwards have been quick to appreciate the 'other side' of this legacy. First, few individuals measure up to realizing this concept of

21

freedom. For Nietzsche it was only the superior, the cultural élite, who were able to rise above the mire of everyday existence and create new values. Secondly, the legacy of inner-directed behaviour only too easily falls back into the unreflective and habitual. Nietzsche and Weber were very much concerned with the first aspect, the need to create and uphold goals. Nietzsche adopted a solipsistic solution that the individual should respond only to the imperative of his (for it was rarely 'her') own will to power. Weber held that only certain individuals were capable of display-ing the commitment to freely chosen or created values. However, as Schroeder points out, he counterbalanced this Nietzschean ethos by his insistence that in the world of politics and science there was an equal commitment respectively to the consequences of one's actions and to truth and objectivity.

Twentieth-century thought has been more exercised by the second aspect: people's preference to deny freedom (the fear of freedom) and their willingness to conspire with those structures – work, politics, family – that impose discipline. Turning to Weber's sociology of religion, Alexander notes that the 'Puritan objectification of the spirit promoted not only economic individualism but the subjective conditions for the methodical domination in business and factory' (page 194). Historically this individualism was in part formative for citizenship, equality and the notion that man could master his environment. Yet the counterparts of those achievements, stemming from the objectification of the spirit, are the phenomena of discipline and depersonalization that represent, so to speak, an awesome opportunity-cost for those achievements. The objec-tive side of depersonalization is realized in bureaucracy and technology, but just as importantly its subjective side, stemming from the depersonal-ization of self and other, is capable of producing man's inhumanity to man. Even the inner core of personality, which as Ralph Schroeder shows in Chapter 10 was so prized by Nietzsche and Weber, is surrendered. Referring to Sartre, Alexander notes the propensity of the modern individual to escape the possibility of his or her own freedom and to subject him- or herself to the given, contingent constraints of society. Alexander concludes on a Durkheimian note that the see-saw of freedom and its denial can be stabilized only through institutional structures and values that are themselves the embodiments of people's will to control and direct their lives and society.

The social theorist who has recently done most to promote a critical understanding of the forces of discipline and depersonalization is Michel Foucault. By taking the actual practice of power as his starting-point, Foucault has provided an interesting parallel to Weber's studies of domination and rulership. Whereas Weber saw subjects as being on the receiving end of structures of power, Foucault has posited the idea of the individuating processes of power that facilitate subjugation. And whereas Weber originates discipline from the inner-directed sources of Puritanism, Foucault has been concerned to demonstrate how the interests of power-holders have generated discourses and technologies to make subjects complicit in their own subjection. These affinities have been drawn on in the contributions by Alexander (Chapter 9) and Bryan Turner (Chapter 11). Alexander notes that the technology of discipline, deriving from warfare and exemplified in the following of the charismatic leader, has been as important as inner-worldly asceticism in the creation of the individuation that has formed a lethal resource for subjection and domination. Taking the human body as a focus of interest, Bryan Turner charts the transitions from the rationalizing tendencies of Puritanism to the rationalizing discourses of recent biopolitics. While inner-worldly asceticism provided a code of control over the body, strictly limiting display, indulgence and sensuality, there exists now a medical discourse that operates from *without*, prescribing how the body should be kept and how it should look. The message here is that being healthy is looking good. The new externally imposed cosmetic of the body has an elective affinity with the consumerist orientation of contemporary capitalism (as opposed to the ascetically attuned disciplines of an earlier, production-oriented capitalism). The consumerist capitalism in the advanced nations today is of course a turn of events unanticipated by Weber. Behind this lies a critique of Weber as being so wedded to the old order and cultural values that the pessimistic analysis of disenchantment – the loss of naïveté consequent upon a rationalizing scepticism – meant Weber was blind to the possibilities of the innocent enjoyment of leisure and consumer capitalism.

Innocent enjoyment is not a trait normally associated with Max Weber, yet Roslyn Bologh's probing account (Chapter 12) of the interpersonal dynamics of erotic love shows that perhaps Weber was not such a stranger to the pleasures of the body. Although the major intellectual thrust of Weber's analysis of erotic love in the 'Intermediate Reflections' is to point up the value-conflicts between religious brotherhood and the disregarding behaviour of lover and beloved, it is clear that the detail and sensitivity with which Weber treats the physical passion between two lovers suggest a less stern (but no less committed) Weber than the one to whom we have been accustomed – not least through the photographs of Weber himself. Bologh notes that Weber with great prescience observes the unconscious coercion of lover upon beloved. Passion involves an unavoidable brutality of one soul to another. If we take the beloved to be a woman, there can be no straightforward feminist response to this situation, for the beloved acts complicitly with this coercion. This relates to the more general issue of how desire is to be reconciled with ethical behaviour, and self-expression with social relations. Puritan-based cultures imposed internal discipline and looked upon the world of expression or sociable communion with a 'loveless clarity' whose origins lie in a theology that placed man as the instrument of God's will. Drawing on Simmel's analysis of social forms, Bologh proposes that desire can be reconciled with sociability if we acquire the social grace to recognize that the presence of the other is in itself pleasurable and that the other is therefore desirable.

Bologh's analysis outlines two quasi-pathologies of a post-Puritan culture: either inner-directed behaviour becomes self-denying and ritualistic in expression, or, following Weber's sociology of religion, the alternative is mysticism and the search for oneness with the world (see Carroll, 1977). In the modern world this alternative course may take a number of forms; the socially disregarding behaviour may be the oneness of erotic love, the fanaticism of sect or political faction, or mystic and aesthetic flights from the world. These are Weber's categories, yet in many ways they correctly belong to the religious age proper, as Schluchter's typology of salvation religions indicates. There is perhaps a way of redescribing the vicissitudes of the self and personality in the modern world. As Hennis demonstrates, the coupling of personality and life orders truly makes sense only in an estates society that provides the means for the direction of life.

Whimster and Lash (Chapters 13 and 17) propose that the concept of modernism provides a more direct access to the experience of urbanism and advanced capitalism (*Hochkapitalismus*) from the late nineteenth century onwards. Artistically first portrayed by Baudelaire and Manet and turned into a sociological aesthetic by Weber's friend and contemporary, Georg Simmel, modernism provides a probing account of both the psychic distress of coping with the multiple stimuli of urbanized existence as well as the sense of the new, the exciting, the pleasurable and those avenues totally denied in the old static social order of the village community. Daniel Bell, who took a censorious line on these phenomena, first introduced modernism as a sociological concept in *The Cultural Contradictions of Capitalism* (1976). In this work the self is portrayed as no longer structured by innerly driven motives becoming accommodated to an externally given society, but is instead composed of the immediate gratification of desire. Narcissistically the self is unmindfully projected on to the world and demands a continuous gratification; under the sole impulsion of desire it is prepared to destroy an order built on work and delayed gratification.

Whimster shows that Weber was not unaware of the destabilizing forces of modernism (the term favoured by Wilhelmine intellectuals was *Impressionismus*) and that in many ways the major dangers to Weber's vision of a commitment to *Beruf* were the modernistic currents of anarchism, free love, *Lebensphilosphie*, expressionism and the fanatical cult of the personality. Through an analysis of the external and internal dimensions of personality in the religious age, the major threat to the integrity of structured personality in the secular age is the collapse of self. This theme is brought into relief through a comparison of Weber's position with that of the young Lukács and especially Simmel. Both of these men favoured an aesthetically rooted inner realm in the face of a reified external world. For Simmel the forms of the external world had to be broken down allowing the authenticity of the inner soul expression. Weber is generally regarded as having little sympathy for the claims of what in this volume is termed aesthetic modernism. Hence in 'Politics as a Vocation' and 'Science as a Vocation' Weber denounces the aestheticization of politics and the search for authenticity in everyday life; such tendencies amounted to a miscegenation of the value-spheres, whereas the mature person should recognize the separation of the value-spheres as a condition of the modern world that has to be lived with. Despite this hostility, Whimster argues that Weber's pointed interest in such modernist movements indicates that he was very well aware of the affectual forces of modernism. The insights of modernism reinforce the notion in the sociology of religion that the cosmic structuring of self is one of the major forces behind the religious rationalization of the world, and behind that need lurks the danger of a collapse into an acosmic oneness with the world – a myth that signifies a return to a pre-primitivist world.

Part 4 turns to the world of modern politics, the state and law. Weber's position on these questions have of course been debated before and, one has to note, with some passion. The debates of the 1960s were occupied on the one side by the Left and liberal Left, who asserted the justification for socialist democracy and liberal parliamentary democracy respectively. Weber's espousal of formal rationality favoured a technicism in politics and an endorsement of 'rational' capitalism (Habermas, 1972), and his call for a plebiscitary leadership democracy was seen to open the door to future charismatic leaders and signalled a rejection of the liberal values of parliamentary democracy and debate (Stammer, 1971, pp. 83–132). These critiques clearly caused an outrage in the intellectual establishment for whom Weber stood as the embodiment of a cultured liberal tradition that propounded rationality in the conduct of politics and offered a cautious prognosis of the advance of institutions embodying liberal, progressive values. Reviewing these debates today one is left wondering whether Weber's political utterances are so deserving or can bear the weight of such partisanship.

Besides, the configuration of the debate has now altered and is perhaps better positioned to make a more fruitful use of Weber's legacy. The old axis of Left and Left liberals versus old liberals and conservatives has now been overlaid with new divides. In the West socialism has weakened, and the truth of its emancipatory slogans is far more hesitantly proclaimed. Meanwhile neo-liberals in France, Britain and the United States have claimed the radical ground, replacing emancipation from capitalist exploitation with a libertarianism that would free the citizen from the stifling oppression of welfarism and the corporatist state.

Echoing some of Alexander's thoughts on the two sides of citizenship – freedom yet regimentation – Colin Gordon (Chapter 14) opens Part 4 with a re-examination of the liberal tradition. Gordon confronts an issue that has always caused perplexity: Weber's national liberal complexion. This should not be understood as a politicized *raison d'état* superimposed on the profession of market freedoms of modern capitalism, argues Gordon, but as two axes, disparate yet intersecting, that all capitalist societies contain. The one axis, the older tradition, is that of pastoralism of the state for its subjects. As Foucault noted with reference to the church, pastoralism is a practice of power in the name of welfare for the soul and body. In the European state tradition this is represented by cameralism and localist administration (*Polizei*). This gave way to, but was not displaced by, the second axis, that of the autonomous economic subject who remains inscrutable to the totalizing function of the state. The rationality of economic agents is not assimilable to the rationality of government and as such represents a problematic disjuncture in the modern art of government. The way out of this, Gordon suggests, is the fostering of a citizenship that would resist the instrumentalism of government yet make the field of economic behaviour less of a mystery to the state. Turning to the work of Wilhelm Hennis and the nineteenth-century traditions of German political economy (*Nationalökonomie*), Gordon looks at the possibility for an economic doctrine of economic units as social entities that would give sufficient space for the control of life conduct, and at the same time would foster citizenship as institutionalized within intermediate strata of a society's population. The basis for such a doctrine, as Foucault himself noted with approval, lies with the school of the German *Ordoliberalen* who were in part responsible for the institution and success of the social market economy in the Federal Republic in the 1950s.

Turner and Factor (Chapter 16) turn their attention to the ways in which the academics sought to define a liberalism that would accommodate interest representation, constitutional forms and party politics. In Weber's day the certainties of a conservative *Rechtsstaat* were challenged by the younger academics who rejected the elder generation's belief that the state had a benign monopoly of both right and might. In its place developed an analysis of the particularism and the conflict of interest groups and classes within modern society as a realist analysis of the exercise of power. Ihering was the jurist who challenged the Kantian assumptions that lay behind the *Rechtsstaat* that held that people and groups act from ethical intent. Adapting utilitarianism, Ihering argued that action proceeded from the more immediate will of the individual or group and the desire to fulfil its interests. Once the particularism of interest demands was recognized, the problem then became one of reconciling the differences of interest within a higher association and seeking a constitutional form which would reflect intermediate ends to which all parties would be able to agree. Radbruch argued that, though there was a need to square the particularism of interest within a higher association like the constitutional state, it did not follow that this was practically achievable. The best that could be done was to assert the value of one's own interests and then to seek some prioritization of those values. Because no absolute value standard exists, this prioritization could be effected only by what Radbruch termed 'decisionism'. Radbruch's position can be seen to be proximate to Weber's stance on values; we choose and commit ourselves to ultimate values even though we know, and expect others to know, that these values cannot be canonized through an absolute underpinning.

Decisionism was given a far more dubious slant by the Weimar jurist Carl Schmitt. Radbruch and Weber still adhered to a conception of a political community. Despite the fact that they pointed to the conflict of interests and values, it may be argued their position assumed a tolerance, namely, that to be committed to one's own values is to accept that others are committed to theirs but that neither party can claim absolute legitimation. Carl Schmitt saw no reason to assume such tolerance. Classes, religious groups and political factions made absolutist demands on the state which threatened one of its primary functions: to be able in its external relations with other states to recognize friend from foe and act accordingly. Schmitt's response was simply to sweep aside any internal constitutional solution and to proclaim the need for a strong leader who was able to pursue the power interests of the nation state. For Schmitt the advent of mass democracy signalled the demise of the internal realm of public debate; instead the masses would acclaim their leader through a plebiscite. Turner and Factor regard Weber's decisionism as closer to Schmitt than to that of Radbruch. Weber relegated the idea of a constitutional and democratic forum as a way of achieving some common ground between different interest groups, political parties and value-positions in favour of electoral, plebiscitary competition between strong, potentially charismatic leaders.

Although acclamation may appear to have an almost medieval tinge about it, Luciano Cavalli (Chapter 15) argues that the giving of trust to a leader by the masses is a prominent feature of twentieth-century politics.

27

At first sight Weber's political sociology would suggest otherwise. Charismatic domination in Weber's typology belongs to traditional societies, and rulership through party machines, state civil service and political élites would seem to be the more apt Weberian analysis. Against this Cavalli draws on two themes already mentioned in this volume. The secular age shows a startling ability to produce mass movements of a quasi-religious nature; secondly, in a world that is less structured and less coherent because of the waning of class, religion and community there occurs a constant, and exploitable, level of dissatisfaction in a mass materialist society. Weber's ideas on charismatic leadership, when allied to work in social psychology, provide the basis of a model that can explain both dictatorship as well as plebiscitary leadership. Cavalli schematizes the conditions of charismatic leadership according to three conditions: the existence of an extraordinary situation or crisis in which a breakdown of crucial cultural expectations of a people has occurred; secondly, the resurgence of popular secular religions; thirdly, the emotionality of the masses, who in conditions of breakdown are capable of exhibiting regression. Under these circumstances a leader is able to integrate the ego and the ego ideal of the masses.

Cavalli demonstrates the applicability of this schema to the case of Hitler and German fascism. He also extends it to the analysis of the contemporary trend to plebiscitary leaderships. In the latter case an uncoerced vote occurs (unlike in fascism), and trust is freely placed in the leader. In contrast to Carl Schmitt's view that strong leadership was required in order to combat parties that held to a total world-view, Cavalli notes instead that the decline of the class-based political party has given rise to a 'catch-all' party in which the personality of the leader is more important than the party's particular ideological programme. This tendency has been further facilitated by the move within the mass media from text to television, which has greatly helped the projection of the figure of the leader.

The implications of Cavalli's political sociology are far reaching. It is that the sociological and social psychological conditions are moving increasingly towards the probability of the emergence of leaders who stand beyond party and who represent a new principle of governability. Leaders are conferred extensive powers and in the case of Hitler even the right to make law. Clearly one of the themes in the political analysis of this situation is the Tocquevillian observation that power becomes centralized in those mass societies which do not have the restraints of intermediate strata that protect and foster political citizenship and democratic culture. Equally insistently, throughout this reader the further argument is developed that, to understand the peculiar lability of power and the psychic instability that occurs in modernized twentieth-century societies, one needs to take account of the effects of rationalization in a world where the psychic, the scientific, the economic and political are no longer pinioned together.

In the concluding chapter (Chapter 17) Scott Lash calls for a clearer awareness of the modalities of modernity, precisely in order to come to terms with the changed character of twentieth-century society. Social sciences generally have conceived of modernity as an era that is dated from the Renaissance and comes of age in the Enlightenment and the emergence of bourgeois democracies. Lash claims, however, that we require an additional concept to describe and begin to explain the experience of living in today's advanced capitalist societies. He argues that these societies underwent a set of qualitative changes at the turn of the twentieth century which can best be rendered by the concept of 'modernism'. In support of these claims Lash scrutinizes the notion of the modern in three prominent contemporary social theorists – Daniel Bell, Foucault and Habermas – and then in Weber. He argues that the understanding of the modern in each of these four theorists has at least as much in common with modern*ism* as it does with received notions of modernity.

This second phase can best be summed up by pointing to the two faces of citizenship. As an Enlightenment concept it is the assurance of individualism, freedom and the cognitive and political will to create man's political society; this is the promise of modernity. But its other face is individuation and subjection to the instrumentalities of power and the surrender of an autonomous will to some higher, protecting agency. Combining elements of contemporary social theory, Lash searches for a possible reconciliation between these antinomies.

Lash turns first to the arguments of Daniel Bell that the Enlightenment project has been subverted by the pervasion of individual and social behaviour by aesthetic modernism. For Bell the modern sensibility is like a pale carbon copy of the artistic avant-garde of the early twentieth century; it rages against all notions of order and places the direct and immediate expression of self as paramount. The social self cuts loose from any anchoring in norms of behaviour – sociality, ethics, aesthetics, reasoned argument – that in the era of the Enlightenment were underpinned by certain philosophically enunciated universals. This change is replicated in the operation and practice of power, especially that of law and state. As Foucault has noted, reason is devalued into a resource for the exercise, not of the citizen as sovereign, but of a new demography that he terms biopolitics. In this both the soul and the body of the citizen become an object to be controlled by the state. This represents an assault upon the integrity of the citizen as a rights-bearing subject who has control of the conduct of his or her own life and personality. This new instrumentalism of power, Lash argues, is to be dated at the end of the nineteenth century and corresponds with the emergence of an 'organized capitalism' and the bureaucratic Welfare State. This would appear to have effectively undermined the Enlightenment project. Instead Lash suggests, through a discussion of Habermas, a possible recognition of a new autonomy of self whose reason is immanent within the self and not referential to some outside body of foundationalist 'truths', who realizes the possibilities that have accompanied the modernist aestheticization of everyday social reality (at least as a way of resistance to the instrumentalism of power) and whose by no means fully constrained subjectivity provides the starting-point for an open and disclosing consensual community able to revivify the idea of substantive rationality. As Schluchter (1981) and Habermas (1984) have shown, substantive rationality, exemplified in the belief of natural law predicated on reason, became a casualty of the evolution of advanced industrial societies. Lash points out that Habermas has been able to resurrect this concept through a reformulation of Weber's theory of rationalization. It is precisely because the modern world has experienced the separation of a once integrated life-world of the legitimations of knowledge, morality and culture that we are able self-reflexively to apply the contents of those spheres to the social production of substantive rationality. Lash observes, however, that Habermas's severe criticisms of aesthetic modernism are in some measure misplaced. It is partly due to the modernist sensibility of the self as immanent and as self-referential that Habermasian communicative rationality can indeed be realized in practice.

Here Weber's analysis and categories are to some extent being used against him. Weber believed that in the future it would be formal rationality, not so different from what the Foucauldians refer to as the instrumentalism of power, that would predominate in the spheres of politics, state and work, and that furthermore those who stood up for their beliefs and convictions would be outflanked by the superiority of formal rationality and its technical efficiency. Equally we know that Weber was never ready to renounce the importance of substantive values to the full drive of rationalization whose end-point would be complete formal rationality. In a final section Lash shows how these tensions characterize Weber's sociology of law. On the one side, predictability and efficiency lead to the demand for formal rationality. On the other hand, for Max Weber the institution of the nation state embodied substantive values. Weber's solution, though it can hardly be admitted as a reconciliation, was decisionism. The nation state is the ultimate arbiter of decisions within the public realm. It is the unmediated, unsocialized and therefore ultimately unreasoned nature of 'decisionism' that requires a further scrutiny of the claims of substantive rationality in the field of state and law.

This introduction, we hope, will have given an indication of the many aspects of Weber's analysis of the emergence and nature of modernity. Weber himself lived through a sea-change in which the cultural, social, economic and political sides of modernity revealed a deeper, less optimistic hue. Today's social science, likewise, appears to be coming to the end of a phase in which an optimistic model of society, based on a liberal progressive vision of modernization, held sway. And today's modernity – lest we forget, a story far from over – promises to be unforgiving of any optimism or pessimism that is falsely posed. In seeking to make our modern, global social reality intelligible we will seek reassurance and guidance from Weber's insights and intellectual integrity. But it should also be clear from the scope and breadth that Weber introduced to such a project, embracing as it did the prospects for human conduct, knowledge and belief, that such endeavours are not necessarily graced by comfort, certainty, or satisfaction.

PART ONE

The Processes of Rationalization

1

Personal Conduct and Societal Change

Towards a Reconstruction of Max Weber's Concept of History

WOLFGANG MOMMSEN
Translated by Rainhild Wells

For some years now Max Weber's sociological work has been attracting a new kind of attention, not just of the social sciences and historiography but from the wider public as well. His programme of constructing ideal type concepts oriented towards history, which had been neglected as a relic of historical thinking, has now become topical again. Ever since the 'end of ideology' thesis has been revealed as both rash and erroneous, and ever since technological, economic and social progress has appeared to be increasingly problematic, the need has arisen once again to reassure ourselves of our place in relation to history. In this situation going back to Max Weber's work presents itself as an obvious choice for it provides an unrivalled combination of the macro-sociological, on the one hand, and on the other a precise definition of the field together with concrete historical research.

Max Weber was probably the last of the line of great liberal thinkers of the nineteenth and twentieth centuries and he endeavoured to formulate his political views on the basis of the whole of Western history as it was known. Faced with an industrial mass society that transformed the conditions within which Western man was to live his life, he sought, at a time of enormous constraint, new answers to the old question of the scope of personal freedom. At a time when the materialist philosophies of history and their associated ideologies had called into question the notion of individual freedom, Max Weber's 'interpretive sociology' offered the possibility for the individual to orientate him or herself to the world in a rational way. 'We cannot read off the meaning of the world from our investigation of it however perfect, rather we have to create this meaning

35

ourselves' (MSS, p. 56); for Weber this was a state of affairs beyond which one could not go. This did not mean a return to irrationalism, but instead formed the starting-point for developing a system of 'interpretive sociology' that would enable the individual to calculate as rationally as possible the basis for his action in relation to his own situation. The decision as to which ultimate ideal one chose from other competing and, in formal terms, equally valid ideals should be made in complete knowledge of other possible ways of leading one's life. In the last analysis interpretive sociology of a universal historical compass could serve to indicate the optimal form of conducting one's life according to one's own ultimate ideals. This required that our entire knowledge of the past be put into systematic order at any given time according to specific perspectives. His works on the history of ancient society, the development of the Occidental city and the sociology of the world religions are far more than narrative history; they represent ideal-typical and systematic treatment of defined segments of historical reality in their significance for modern man. Likewise the theory behind ideal types, which in *Economy and Society* is a systematization of all known history, was in the first instance meant as an aid for conceptually orienting the individual in the face of the infinite diversity of the past, even though it also serves as a specific aid for the historian to make 'the causal explanation of some historically and culturally important phenomenon' (ES, p. 20).

Max Weber always warned against the misconstruing of the ideal-typical reconstruction of segments of the past that appear to 'hold a meaning' as elements of a materialist philosophy of history; instead he emphasized time and time again the merely hypothetical and perspectival character of the ideal type as it is applied to the historical process in his work. So, for instance, Puritanism as the ground from which sprang the spirit of capitalism was one such hypothesis. Admittedly his investigations into the sociology of religion can be interpreted in some measure as a grandiose attempt at a substantive reconstruction of Occidental history in terms of the origins of the 'specific and peculiar "rationalism" of Western culture' (PESC, p. 26). In the 'Author's Introduction' to the 'Collected Essays on the Sociology of Religion' Weber himself emphasized with the utmost clarity the 'singularity' of Western civilization; *it alone* has produced rational science and rational harmonic music; *it alone* has brought to perfection the bureaucratic principle of rule through the organization of trained officials; *it alone* had fully developed capitalism as the rational, capitalistic organization of (formally) free labour (PESC, p. 21) in its specific form as a production-intensive, continuous and market-oriented system of industrial production for the maximization of profit, which would determine the life of every individual in the foreseeable future. It would be a mistake, however, to conclude from this that the reconstruction of this irreversible secular process was the specific object of his historical sociology. Of course Weber himself invited this misunderstanding to some degree by allowing his analyses of the other great world religions and their influence on societies to appear merely as a contrast to the specific character of Western civilization and as an indirect corroboration of the hypothesis of modern capitalism and the spirit of Protestantism. And equally there is no lack of remarks suggesting that Western civilization had reached its 'end-point' of development. In at times almost apocalyptic formulations he evoked again and again the impending petrification of Occidental civilization based on the principles of individuality and competition, albeit in a hypothetical manner as for instance in his treatise, 'Parliament and Government in a Reconstructed Germany' of 1918: 'Together with the inanimate machine it [bureaucracy] is busy fabricating the shell of future servility which men will perhaps be forced to inhabit some day, as powerless as the fellahs of ancient Egypt.' This would occur if the German people were determined to put a technically good civil service higher than everything else (ES, p. 1402).

Influenced by these and other similar remarks previous research has been prepared to adopt the rationalization thesis as the axis of his work without too much deliberation. Accordingly history is reconstructed as a process of the rationalization of social relations and of increasing disenchantment, in which all world-views become progressively devalued. Two different strategies of interpretation offered themselves and were, indeed, adopted: first, the teleological reconstruction of the history of the Occident as an essentially linear process of disenchantment and as the rationalization of the predominating world-views and orders of society; second, an *evolutionist interpretation* of world history as an evolutionary process of selection, in the course of which the present rational order of the world had developed as one among many other historically possible patterns of society and was reached through a historical progression of previously attained levels of rationalization.

Günter Abramowski's study, *Das Geschichtsbild Max Webers*, which closely follows the texts themselves, shows with remarkable clarity the extent to which the teleological interpretation with rationalization as its central thesis is possible and makes sense (Abramowski, 1966). But readings like this, when measured against the originality and richness of his ideal-typical interpretation of the past, lead inevitably to a narrowing of Weber's questions and to a dilution of his theories. And in the process the tensions in Weber's work quite frequently are unacceptably harmonized and the chronological order of his *oeuvre* is disregarded. But most of all the antinomy within the structure of his thought is excised to be replaced by a largely uniform model of interpretation. The newer evolutionary theories, in particular that of Wolfgang Schluchter, are an improvement in this respect (1981). Schluchter has suggested transferring the rationalization thesis, as it is to be found pre-eminently in the writings on the sociology of religion, into a model of a 'societal history of the West', which avoids the pitfalls of a straightforward evolutionary theory. In a similar manner Stefan Breuer has recently attempted to distil from Weber's writings on the history of the classical world an evolutionary model of historical development (1982). The advantage of this approach is that it does not lead to a conception of world history as directed towards a single goal and hence to a mono-linear, teleological and material recon-struction. Instead it is able to do justice to the variety of sociological formations and to the breaks in the continuity of societal development as they have occurred in the course of over a millennium of Western history. All the same this approach seeks to show that according to Max Weber world history is a directional and irreversible process in which the principle of rationalization has triumphed out of an inner necessity. Despite the countless relapses and the repeated interruptions in the continuity, the history of the West is a process of man's increasing domination over the world due to the progressive rationalization of world-views and a corresponding development in the steering capacities of social systems. Decisive importance is given to the formally rational methods of science, the rational institutions of the capitalist industrial system and the bureaucratic and institutional state that developed solely in the West. From this perspective Weber's sociology appears as the apo-theosis of the principle of rationality and modern rational science with progressive disenchantment and the end of ideology as its logical corre-lates. It is unarguably the case that Max Weber's writings, at least up to 1913, allow one such interpretation of his whole work. Nevertheless the question arises whether this really gets to the heart of Weber's intentions, or only – as we believe – touches on one, admittedly important, aspect.

The recent interpretations of Wolfgang Schluchter and Arnold Zingerle are in some ways attempts to refute the view that the evolutionary dynamic of religious world-views was at the core of Weber's sociology. Friedrich Tenbruck doubts whether evolutionist interpretations that opt one-sidely in favour of a rationalistic world-view and a world 'freed from enchantment' do in fact correspond to Weber's own view (1975; 1980). While Schluchter and Tenbruck agree that the question 'What is ration-ality?' lies at the centre of Weber's work, they arrive at different conclusions. Tenbruck rightly points out that Weber emphasized repeatedly that the rationalization of world-views, which were originally determined by religion, could develop in a great variety of directions and not solely in the direction of a reduced religious orientation to the world and a corresponding increase in instrumentally rational forms of conduct guided by modern 'value-free' science. Therefore rationalization should not, he claims, merely be understood as a self-propelling process of progressive disenchantment of religious world-views, but rather as a step leading precisely to the intensification of the effects of religious values on society. This is something that may be observed in all world religions. The ability of religious and ideological world-views – which were supposed to have disappeared as it were into the obscurity of the past – to set the course of societal development is a feature, says Tenbruck, that has to be rehabilitated in the present time as well.

Wilhelm Hennis has taken a much stronger position against neo-evolutionist interpretations of Weber's work and the supposition that the rationalization process is its apotheosis (1983). Hennis disputes that the development of Western 'rationalism' in the hitherto described sense – as a process of increasing disenchantment or, rather, as an increasingly purely rational and functional order of all social relationships – was really Max Weber's theme. Instead, argues Hennis, the primary concern was the 'development of mankind' (*Entwicklung des Menschentums*) as such. In Weber's work the analysis of social structures is always carried out with respect to one main consideration: what type of person is granted the optimal chances? As support for his thesis Hennis refers to an illuminating remark of Weber's concerning the intentions that guided him when writing *The Protestant Ethic and the Spirit of Capitalism*: 'it was not the furtherance of capitalism in its expansion which formed the *centre* of my interest, but the development of the type of mankind that was brought about by the conjunction of religiously and economically conditioned factors' (Hennis, 1983, p. 148). Hennis therefore regards the entire recent research to be erroneous in concluding that Weber wanted to write 'the universal history of the establishment of occidental rationalism' (Hennis, 1983, p. 150). In contrast to this Hennis takes up an older tradition, that of Löwith, Jaspers and Landshut, who had mainly emphasized the anthropological basis of human existence in Weber's thinking. The dangers to individuality and the increasing 'alienation of man' as a result of the advance of bureaucratic forms of social organization had already been singled out by Löwith as the central idea in Weber's work (Löwith, 1982). In the investigations into the sociology of religion and sociology in general, Weber was primarily interested in the following question: under what conditions and in what forms has a rationalization of the conduct of life (*Lebensführung*) come about for the individual in pursuit of his or her ideals, whether those ideals are religious in origin or not? It is no accident that Weber demands that sociology has ultimately to relate all social processes to the active or passive individual and that any sociology that does not place the individual person as the essential point of reference in its analysis and interpretation is not fulfilling its task. Whether we have to follow Hennis and conclude that Weber's 'interpretive sociology' was

39

primarily directed towards an anthropological understanding may be left
open at this juncture (Hennis, 1983, p. 158).

We need to put the flesh on Hennis's proposals. The questions – how
the directionality of a certain world-view, influenced by material and
institutional factors, gives rise to the rationalization of the conduct of life
of particular social groups – occupies a central position in his work
because it is closely related to his conception of historical change. The
rationalization of the conduct of life in a specific direction precipitates
change in society each time it affects a significant social group. What is
meant by the 'rationalization of the conduct of life' (*Lebensführung*)? It
means the orientation of the individual's way of life in the light of certain
ultimate values that are regarded as absolutely binding irrespective of
whether these do or do not come into conflict with everyday life. Because
of this the individual, or the group to which he belongs, accumulates a
capacity for action whose force under certain conditions can have revolutionary consequences for the existing social system of which he is a part.
Two examples may serve to illustrate this. Precisely because the Puritan
seeks confirmation of the fact that he has been 'chosen' in the success of his
career, he puts everything into the maximization of his professional
success; this requires a conduct of life of extreme frugality and the
observation of a strict work ethic. Secondly, precisely because the
charismatic leader is deeply convinced of the correctness of the ultimate
ideals that move him, so there emanates from his charisma impulses of a
far-reaching character. If he succeeds in convincing his followers of the
absolute stringency of the ideals or aims professed by him, so these
deploy, as it were, a concrete social effect. As a result the followers feel
obliged to shape their own personal conduct of life in the same direction,
so that an optimal realization of those ideals and goals is brought about in
society.

Here we encounter a general model of societal change that is in principle
equally valid for all epochs of historical change. Consequently those
interpretations that regard the process of progressive rationalization of all
spheres of life as the central matter of Weber's work reveal themselves to
be one-sided generalizations of a particular aspect of his work. It cannot
simply be said that for Weber rationalization is a process resulting from
the interaction of ideal and material factors and proceeds in a mechanical
and autonomous fashion, without allowing for the possibility of opposing forces that could give yet another direction to the course of events. In
his own day Weber diagnosed the dangers of ossification, but held that a
break-out from this situation was conceivable; indeed he pleaded for
economic and political conditions that would make this a possibility. In
principle he adhered to a pluralistic model of societal change. Formal
rationalization – that is to say, the instrumentally rational perfection of the

existing system – could be, but did not have to be, the ultimate objective of the historical process. The dichotomy within the concept of rationalization itself, with its opposition of formal and substantive rationality, shows this to be the case. There can occur 'substantive' rationalizations proceeding in the most different directions and that run counter to 'formal' rationalization.

Admittedly this is often obscured by Weber's own way of expressing himself, in particular in his earlier writings. Even in the later writings there are residues of an 'objectivistic' use of language in regard to rationalization that give rise to misinterpretations. In Max Weber's conception of universal history, disenchantment and rationalization play a decisive role, and their potential termination is the often referred to 'shell of future servility'. But wherever he gives such a gloomy perspective, he emphasizes the hypothetical nature of such trends. This also applies to the altogether more pointed remarks that are to be found at the end of *The Protestant Ethic and the Spirit of Capitalism*:

> No one knows as yet who will live within these confines [created by modern industrial capitalism] in future, and whether, at the end of this vast development, totally new prophets will emerge or there will be a powerful revival of old ideas and ideals, or, if neither of these, whether there will be a state of mechanised petrification, embellished by a kind of frenzied self-importance. In that case it might indeed become true to say of the 'last men' of this cultural development: 'specialists without soul, hedonists without heart: this cipher flatters itself that it has reached a stage of humanity never before attained'.
>
> (WS, p. 171)

The reader's attention is immediately drawn to the fact that at this point one is entering the field of value judgement and opinions based on belief, with which 'this purely historical presentation should not be encumbered'. Despite this caveat a central element of Weber's philosophy of history is addressed, namely, the fear that the modern world could become ossified in the same way as the historical pattern of late Antiquity. Elsewhere he expressed this fear even more directly: 'The bureaucratisation of society will in all probability *one day* gain control over capitalism in our society, just as it did in Antiquity' (1976, p. 365). But we are not dealing here with statements of a materialist philosophy of history, rather with hypothetical remarks, which should not be understood in either a teleological or evolutionary sense and least of all as a material reconstruction of actual history; in some sense we are dealing with a 'self-denying prophecy'. In other words these statements were intended to mobilize counter-forces in order to arrest those trends.

Following on from this, we need to observe that there are two partly competing and overlapping outlines of world history in Max Weber's work. In the earlier phases of his work, and the oldest stage of *Economy and Society* in particular (probably written between 1911–13), a model of the historical process predominates that can be termed 'directional' and is presented in a quasi-objectivistic manner – though to be sure it is qualified with *rebus sic stantibus* clauses. According to this model at the beginning of Occidental history there existed magical world-views and charismatic forms of political, ideological, or religious rulership, which in the course of their development are increasingly subjected to routinization and subsequently the 'demagicalization' of their ideological bases. Over the course of time these older forms of social organization are constantly exposed to new thrusts of rationalization. The latter are produced and carried through by social strata who, as a result of the conjunction of specific religious movements and particular constellations, have submitted to a process of the 'rationalization of the conduct of life'; they submit for the purpose of the maximization of the religious and social norms that they champion. One such phenomenon was Jewish prophecy, which was enormously successful in inducing a certain 'rationalization of the conduct of life' in respect to specific religious ideals of life and political values. But of course the most important example is furnished by the impact of Puritanism on world history. This, says Weber, not only produced the continuously functioning industrialism of modern capitalism with its division of labour, but also the basis of the modern democratic order with its principle of the representation of individuals having equal rights. Capitalism, and the bureaucratization that inevitably accompanies it, had finally called forth a mesh of material interests that dispensed with the ideal motivations that had originally governed the behaviour of actors and henceforward progressed according to its own dynamic of interests. The danger that societies of the Western type would become ossified in the same way as that of late Antiquity appeared increasingly real. It seemed to Weber that there was a negative end-point embedded within the schema of Occidental history, and that this cast a shadow, a sense of finality, across the uniqueness of Western civilization.

In *The Protestant Ethic* Weber sometimes uses an almost objectivistic form of expression to describe the irreversible nature of this process, particularly in respect to the capitalist system, which appears to operate according to its own autonomy. But increasingly he endeavoured to correct the apparently deterministic feature of this hypothetical schema of Western history. In his early writings rationalization usually applies to the conduct of life in the service of particular religious ideals or, alternatively, to the maximization of the effectiveness of action in the pursuit of predetermined goals, thereby drawing on the apparatus of rational science and technology to the full. Although he distinguished in principle between different types of rationalization, formal-rational rationalization was absolutely predominant. In his late works, however, notably in the new version of *Economy and Society* written in 1920 (comprising the *Kategorienlehre*), he strongly emphasized the fact that the conduct of life could be rationalized in altogether different directions, depending on the particular world-view. He now distinguished in principle between 'formal' and 'material' rationality; by 'formal rationality' is meant the strategy of adapting one's own conduct of life to the predetermined purposes of the kind that the capitalist system has imposed on modern man, whether he wanted it or not. Under 'material rationality' on the other hand, he meant the rationalization of the conduct of the life of the individual in respect to ultimate value positions, which could under certain historical conditions lead to far-reaching changes of society. Therefore the principles of formal and material rationality as a rule are always in sharp contrast with one another. While in the earlier writings the propensity was for formal rationality eventually to get the better of material rationality, Weber now considered them dichotomous principles inherent in the historical process at all times.

Here we encounter a conception of historical change that stands in a relationship of initially only latent tension to the previously mentioned teleological plan of world history, which culminated in the modern rationalistic civilization and terminates in a society of bureaucratic servitude. Accordingly the rationalization of the conduct of life with respect to ultimate values that are regarded as unalterable constitutes the real substratum of any dynamic of societal change. Consequently there can be rationalizations of entirely different kinds, proceeding in entirely different directions, depending on the ideal basis that is their starting-point. In the 'Author's Introduction' to the 'Collected Essays on the Sociology of World Religions' it states, 'Rationalizations have occurred in the various departments of life in a great variety of ways in all cultural areas' (PESC, p. 26). For the further course of events in actual historical reality, it had been decisive 'which spheres were rationalized and in what direction'. The previous view that implicitly held that there was one kind of rationalization absolutely dominant – namely, that which took material shape in Western civilization – was repudiated. Unfortunately it has to be admitted that this was not done sufficiently clearly with the result that Weber research for a long time has been able to pass over this change without giving it sufficient attention.

So it is not rationalization that is peculiar to the Occident but only a specific sort of rationalization: the progressive accumulation of formal and so technical rationality. Probably in the endeavour not to have to rewrite all his earlier investigations, Weber contented himself with this unclear and somewhat ambiguous conceptual dichotomization, and in this way left unresolved the contradictions in his argument that have given rise to repeated misunderstandings right down to the present day.

Behind the plan of a teleological history of the Occident, whose climax was modern rationalistic culture and whose latent and negative end-point was the 'shell of future servility', we can therefore discern a deeper layer of historical reality. Here there are in principle a plurality of competing rationalizations, each of which is dependent upon a different value position, and these value positions are, in their turn, in constant conflict with one another. Historical change occurs in the form of thrusts of rationalization of admittedly different quality and having different objectives; these are induced by the articulation of new world-views. Of course not all forms of rationalization that are realized in the personal conduct of life and the related social group lead to societal change of far-reaching extent. Some world-views, such as the doctrine of Confucianism, which comes to terms with the world and its injustices, had quietistic consequences for society. Another case was Hinduism in which social action was ultimately oriented towards a search for salvation that found its solution in a form of contemplation that fled from the world. Whereas wherever thrusts of rationalization resulted in the direction of inner-worldly activity, they had, in Weber's view, revolutionary effects on the surrounding society.

It is always the extraordinary powers that give the impetus to such rationalization, through first the conduct of life of the group primarily affected, and then the restructuring of social institutions in a corresponding direction. 'The direction of the entirety of the conduct of life, wherever it was rationalized in a thorough manner, was always determined in the deepest sense by final values, to which this rationalization was oriented' (FMW, p. 287). The probability that such ultimate values will initiate far-reaching societal changes increases with the degree of opposition between ultimate ideals that are given to, and are binding upon, the individual and the everyday reality. Precisely because the individual sees himself confronted with extraordinary challenges, which are in sharp contrast to the traditional conditions and customary ways of life, he is forced to change radically 'from within' the way he conducts his own life. In this way there arise accumulations of energies in society that have a capacity to innovate and to break up the established order and to restructure it fundamentally.

As is well known, Max Weber developed this model of societal change using the example of the 'inner-worldly asceticism' of Puritanism, from which he directly derived the process of the rise of the modern rationalistic civilization of the West. Then, in the course of his writings on universal historical sociology, he generalized this approach step by step. In his studies on the sociology of religion he looked above all for comparable phenomena in cultures determined by other world religions. He found essentially two variants of such religiously determined behaviour: first a tendency towards flight from the world and contemplation, as in Hinduism and Confucianism and in a more mitigated form Buddhism; second, an inner-worldly tendency that in the first instance included Jewish prophecy, and Protestantism in its Calvinist or Puritan varieties, but not so much Lutheranism with its orientation to authority and readiness to adapt to the prevailing conditions of the time.

The religious movements that had a profound effect on society were, according to Weber, those characterized by powerful eschatological prophecy and saviour figures, which provided the stimulus for the ethical rationalization of everyday life. In the 'Introduction' to 'The Economic Ethics of the World Religions', which is a key text for the understanding of Max Weber's work, this finding is summarized succinctly:

> The Occidental sects of religious virtuosi have been the ferment for the methodical rationalization of the conduct of life, including economic conduct. These sects have not become outlets for the longing to escape from the senselessness of inner-worldly activity, as did the Asiatic communities of contemplative, or orgiastic or apathetic ecstatics.
>
> (FMW, p. 291)

This was a step forward in the generalizing of the concept of societal change. With it Weber arrived at a new evaluation of the concept of charisma. This was no longer a sign of an archaic or early formation of society; rather it was the key concept that allowed all religious, intellectual, or political movements of an other-worldly provenance to be understood as phenomena of essentially the same character. The numerous known forms of the influence on the historical world of typically other-worldly attitudes had one thing in common, namely, their origin in highly personal behaviour of a charismatic quality. Accordingly Weber now increasingly combined them under the concept of the *charisma* of the religious founder, prophet, politician, thinker, or leader.

Initially Weber had regarded the foundation of charismatic allegiances, and the revolutionary change in the relationships constituting society that occurred with the aid of charismatic forms in the establishment of authority, allegiance and rulership, as a typical phenomenon of the early history of mankind, since magic and charisma seemed to be virtually interchangeable phenomena in the initial stages of human society. Gradually however he felt compelled to reinterpret and extend the concept of charisma. This advanced from being merely a historical category for the purpose of describing certain archaic forms of rulership or allegiance to becoming a structural category of historical reality. Of course here too one can observe an overlapping of the earlier and later usage of the term in his writings. The different significances of the concept were never really clearly separated, although in the late work the second variant definitely superseded the earlier one.

This goes hand in hand with the fact that Weber increasingly lost interest in reconstructing defined segments of historical reality in the form of ideal-typical models of processes of quasi-teleological character, as in the classical case of *The Protestant Ethic* – especially as it was not possible to formulate these processes in such a way as to encompass the whole of history. In this respect it was true that an objective reconstruction of world history did not seem possible in any case. Very early on Weber had concluded: 'The continuum of Mediterranean–European civilizational development has known neither an enclosed cyclical movement, nor an unequivocally mono-linear evolution' (Weber, 1976, p. 366). Weber rejected the possibility of a material theory of world history for methodo-logical reasons as well; after all any interpretation of history depended on changing perspectives. Instead he turned to the major attempt at an ideal-typical reconstruction of history, which permitted an interpretation of history from whatever perspective was adopted, and thus could be regarded as 'value free' in a specific sense.

Weber's new aim is most easily demonstrated using the example of the different stages that the theory of the 'three pure types of legitimate domination' went through during the period 1913 to 1920. Initially it was still a thoroughly historical construction, that is, a succession in real history from charismatic, via traditional to legal and bureaucratic forms of societal and political organization, although these were presented in the form of ideal types. This changed radically from about 1916–17 onwards. Then the 'three types of legitimate domination' were presented as 'directional', but it was emphasized that especially the charismatic type could in principle appear in the most varied historical formations and in different epochs, including the modern one. In the later versions of the 'three pure types of legitimate domination' Weber reversed the sequence of the three types of domination. Charisma was now no longer inter-preted as merely an ideal-typical pattern for the establishment of spiritual, religious, or political rule peculiar to early forms of human social order, but stood instead for a universal type of social organization. Charisma was also the fount of all creative activity that took its orientation from personal value ideals of non-everyday character.

However, this new level of systematic conceptualization, replacing the processual form of ideal type, never attained a complete development in Max Weber's work. The overlapping nature of the texts, in the form they are available to us today, makes it difficult to gain a clear appreciation. Here an outline of the usage of the concept of charisma will have to suffice; this detaches itself from being a part of a specific phase in universal history and instead advances to be the antinomic counter-concept to that of 'rationality'. At the end of the chapter on political and hierocratic rule, written even before 1913 and dealing exclusively with the historical manifestations of religiously charismatic forms of domination, Max Weber speaks of the Age of Enlightenment; the 'reason' of the individual, if it were allowed to develop freely by virtue of divine providence and because the individual knew his own interests best, would inevitably result in the best of worlds – at least in relative terms: 'The charismatic apotheosis of reason is altogether the last form that charisma adopted on its eventful path' (ES, p. 1209). Charisma appears here as a phenomenon of the past that has definitely been superseded in the modern age. In other, chronologically later texts, this verdict is mitigated; instead the import-ance of charisma is diminished through the bureaucratization and rationalization of all areas of life. In the later parts of *Economy and Society*, particularly the chapter on the 'types of domination', charisma as a type of political or religious rulership is admittedly still assigned to predomin-antly pre-rationalistic epochs, but at the same time a new quality is attributed to it, namely, that of being an innovative force, especially in the field of politics.

In the end charisma and rationalization are interpreted as forces dichotomously related to one another, both of which bring about societal change but in differing ways and with opposing tendencies. Charisma (which in Weber's later sociological theory had come to replace both Jewish prophecy and Puritan asceticism in the early history of the modern world) marks the place where personality forces its way into the empirical processes of history. Rationalization on the other hand begins to take effect either as an adaptation to existing value ideals or as an adaption to material interests or institutional conditions; beyond this rationalization is also effective indirectly via the intellectualization of the perception of reality.

This antinomic model of historical change is the theoretical quintess-ence of Max Weber's historical sociology. But it still requires an inter-pretation that differentiates out its particularity. Charisma, especially in its pure form, is a typically ephemeral phenomenon and as such is unstable, because it is essentially if not exclusively dependent on the personal aura of an individual great personality. It works only in a limited measure (although with great intensity), but above all is effective only in a mediated form. Charisma generally transfers itself into world-views that are carried, and if necessary are further developed, by a charismatic following. The great theological eschatologies of the various world religions can be regarded as world-views of this sort in the field of religion. In the field of politics they are ideologies, and in the field of economic action, as in the case of Puritanism, religious doctrines can result in the development of, for example, a specific economic ethic and, as a consequence, the interpretation of the world in terms of success. Looked at sociologically as a rule it is specific groups of intellectuals who tend to monopolize the 'administration' of the ideology of a specific mission, whether it be of a religious or a non-religious kind. They become, as it were, the trustees of 'ideal interests' that are embodied in world-views and their derivatives.

Whether and how far such world-views manage to assert themselves in the empirical world in the above fashion, depends to a considerable degree on the constellation of material interests. In 1920 Weber expressed this interplay of ideal (ultimately founded on charisma) and material factors and their effect on societal change in the following concise formula: 'Interests (material and ideal), not ideas, govern man's actions directly. But the world-views created by ideas have very often set the points and so determined the course of action propelled by the dynamics of interest' (FMW, p. 280). World-views become transformed into historical reality only through the operation of several intermediaries. They are given permanent existence through the routinization of charisma. How far they actually proceed in history depends to a large extent on the 'external, social and the inner, psychological defined interest-situation' of those strata 'who were the bearers of the respective methodical conduct of life at the crucial time of its formation'. This means however that the existing political, economic and institutional conditions, which each movement encounters, essentially help to decide its ultimate fate, since these usually channel the 'material interests' of the actors to a high degree and so limit their ideal options.

Max Weber came to hold, as we have seen, an antinomic model of historical change, whose poles are charisma and rationalization; this in its turn is interlocked in a most concrete way with the respective constellation of material and ideal interests. Charisma is the source of value-oriented and creative action, whereas rationalization is guided by the need for the maximization of whatever particular goals are striven after and therefore operates in the directions of the goal-oriented and formally rational organization of all conditions of life and social relations. In the early period of history, charisma and routinization are the great antipodes; under modern conditions it is charisma and formal (i.e. bureaucratic) rationality that are the antipodes. This interpretation is clearly part of the design of the final version of *Economy and Society*, although it does not receive its full development. So we read at the end of the systematic presentation of the types of charismatic domination:

In traditionalist periods charisma is *the* great revolutionary force, in contrast to the equally revolutionary force of 'ratio' which works from *without*, either by changing the conditions of life and daily problems and so changing men's attitudes to those conditions, or else through intellectualization. Charisma on the other hand *can* effect a remoulding from within, which, born out of necessity and enthusiasm, signifies a change in the central convictions and actions accompanied by a complete re-orientation to all individual forms of life and to the 'world' in general.

(ES, p. 245, italics in original)

Charisma and rationalization appear here as antagonistic forces of great historical import, both of which can have an equally revolutionary force even though this works in different directions. Even at this stage Weber held to the idea that manifestations of charismatic rulership and revolutions were to be found principally in the earlier periods of history, while the modern world belonged essentially to the type of legal, formally rationalistic order, and that any prognosis essentially would have to favour the latter. But in no way could it be argued that charisma had in principle lost its significance in modernity as a basic source of social action.

Quite the contrary, for he saw charismatic movements in his own day, especially in the field of politics, and this to such an extent that he had intended for some time to deal with the type, 'charismatic revolutions', in a separate chapter, which however never got written. (This relates to the chapter on 'Theories of Revolution', which also was never written. See ES, pp. 254, 264–6.) In 1919 Weber commented: 'Revolutions under a charismatic leader, directed against hereditary charismatic powers or the powers of office, are to be found in all types of organizations, from states to trade unions (especially at the present time!)' (ES, p. 252). Equally he now paid particular attention to the phenomenon of the routinization of charisma and the 'transformation of charisma in an anti-authoritarian direction' (ES, pp. 266–71). Charisma was no longer a phenomenon that appeared in the early phases of history, but his interest concerned how charisma could establish itself in the political realm under modern conditions. The 'anti-authoritarian transformation of charisma', in which the legitimacy of the charismatic leader depends formally on the recognition by voters within the framework of a constitutional system but without restricting his responsibility to his own ultimate convictions, appeared to Weber as the only form of democratic government still possible under modern conditions that did not lead towards a lack of leadership and the reduction of government to mere routine and inefficiency. Here Weber has definitely renounced that interpretation, predominating throughout his earlier writings, which regards charismatic phenomena as ways of establishing religious, ideological, or spiritual rulership peculiar to the early phases of Western history. Charisma appears as a source of personal leadership regardless of the specific area of society. Although it has to be considered a 'typical initial phenomenon' of religious, political, or some other kind of rule, it is still the form in which individual creativity makes its mark in the reality of society. It alone – at least at certain points – is able to break through the great forces of routinization and rationalization that are always at work within society.

In this by no means unqualified way charisma and rationalization appear in Weber's work as the contrary poles of historical change. They need not necessarily be opposing forces. Under certain circumstances charisma may call for phases of rationalization, when these serve the best way of achieving its professed ideals. Equally it can form an alliance with the techniques of formal rationality, in order to perpetuate its own rule. The anti-authoritarian transformation of charisma, Weber frequently stressed, normally led 'into the path of rationality' (ES, p. 269). All the same the type of charismatic rule due to personal dedication, to extraordinary value-ideals, or 'gifts of grace' and the type of legal rulership with its formal rationalization of all areas of life together represent the antinomic basic principles of society. Actual history takes place in the area of conflict between these two poles. It is a constant competition between the originally charismatically induced movements and the existing political, economic and religious institutions, the latter having formal rationality on their side.

In this respect the gloomy prognostications on the future petrification of the Western world, which are to be found so often in Weber's work, are not really to be understood as material statements about the finite nature of history, but rather as prophetic warnings designed to call forth forces to counter what seemed under given circumstances to be the greatest danger for Western man. The predictions are part of a pluralistic model of societal change that considered history as open-ended in principle and regarded development as not unidirectional. The triumphal march of rationalization in the West, which Weber described and analysed as a secular phenomenon, was not the last word. For in as much as formal rationality was embodied in modern capitalism and bureaucracy, it was irrational when looked at from different perspectives or alternative models of rationalization. To this extent Max Weber could write as early as 1917 that despite the 'magnificent rationalism of an ethically methodical conduct of life', which had originated from Jewish prophecy and had been victorious in its development, the problems of a rational orientation to the world had still not been solved: 'The old, numerous gods deprived of their magic and so in the form of impersonal powers risen again from their graves, strive for power over our lives and recommence their eternal battle with each other' (FMW, p. 149). In the light of this perception Weber undertook to formulate his programme of an ideal-typical reconstruction of Occidental history in a new way. The dialogue between rationalization that originally had been charismatically induced and its embodiment in the form of impersonal institutions and economic structures, which constitute the reality of history, is one that is fundamentally infinite and can never be concluded.

2

Personality and Life Orders:

Max Weber's Theme

WILHELM HENNIS

Translated by Keith Tribe

Principal insight: ultimately everything is ethical.
(Goethe, Autobiographical Schema of 1810)

Weber described his work up until around 1910 in terms of 'cultural science', and while there occurred a shift towards the use of a sociological terminology this changed nothing with regard to the *intent* of his central question: the 'cultural problems of man'; this is the object of his work. This means: the problems arising from the insertion of man (*Mensch*), a being capable of social action, into social constellations that in their turn mould these persons, develop their capacities, or alternatively deform them to the extent of 'parcellicizing the soul'. In the last analysis this is the cultural problematic of his times and it is from here that we must look for Weber's central theme. We will investigate it at three levels: (1) at a substantive level, the 'structural' relation between humanity and the social orders and powers; (2) the anthropological and ethical values interwoven with Weber's empirical findings; (3) the special cultural problems of 'modern' cultural humanity (*Kulturmenschentum*) (see Hennis, 1983, pp. 156, 171), which will be dealt with briefly).

The Personality and the Life Orders

Marianne Weber, reporting on Weber's participation in the debates of the Frankfurt Sociological Congress during the autumn of 1910, recounts the manner in which he sought to delimit the tasks of the Society: 'above all a purely scientific and "value free" treatment of all the problems: "the question should be put as to what is and why something is exactly the way it is, but there shall be no judgment as to its desirability or undesirability", ' (Marianne Weber, 1975, p. 422). What is at stake in this 'what is'? Marianne reports how Weber developed and worked on the problem of the survey of associations and newspapers whose investigation 'could be fruitful', and he formulated a possible framework for questions that 'ultimately should relate to the universal point of view: How do those phenomena influence the formation of modern man?' Even for the sociology of associations (ranging from bowling-clubs to political parties and religious sects) 'the most important question would be the extent to which a person's whole make-up (*Gesamthabitus*) is influenced by the various aspects of club activity' (Marianne Weber, 1975, p. 422). What, in a previous essay, has been called Weber's anthropological and characterological principle (in part, at least, with reference to the surveys of the press and associations) is described here by Marianne as the 'universal point of view' directing his questions (Hennis, 1983, pp. 158–60).

This raises the question whether there exists in his writings an external feature – for instance, in the title of one of his works which could be directly ascribed to this 'universal point of view'. Quite clearly this is not the case; none of the printed texts allows such an ascription. How much easier everything would have been if Weber's most famous study could be attributed to this 'universal point of view', if in its title it referred to the capitalistic *Gesamthabitus* instead of to the 'spirit' of capitalism.

However Marianne provides us with help. Searching for the link to the 'universal point of view' in this still invaluable biography, we come across a topic whose theme is recorded but not its contents. This is the lecture that Weber delivered at Burg Lauenstein in the autumn of 1917. Marianne gives a vivid picture of the intellectual mood, and the famous photograph of Weber in conversation with Ernst Toller and Erich Mühsam brings the situation to life for us (Knoll, 1957, p. 190; Marianne Weber, 1975, pp. 597–8; Krüger, 1983, pp. 234–6). It is quite obvious that Eugen Diederichs, publisher of *Die Tat* and sponsoring organizer of the conference, had the same problem deciphering Weber's letter announcing his theme that the works as a whole have created until today. Weber was not prepared to talk on 'The Personality and its Influence on Life' but on something far more specific. 'The Personality and the Life Orders' (*Die Persönlichkeit und die Lebensordnungen*).

The lecture is not known to us, and the available reports do not tell us very much about it, but one may guess that Weber did not give the audience (who were mainly youthful students and expecting some sort of guidance) what they wished to hear (Diederichs, 1925, pp. 294–6). 'Be who you are. In any case you live in "orders" which have their own law-like autonomy, they make their demands. Gentlemen, only he who knows how to live up to the demands of the day has "personality".' He may have expressed himself in this way. The tension between an external order and demands of inner personality – fate, chance – that will have been the theme. I think it is worth raising the question whether the tension between the human person, the endless malleability of human nature on the one hand, and on the other hand the 'orders of life' – the orders of society and its powers cited in the actual title of *Economy and Society* – are not in truth the lifelong theme running throughout his works.

I will first attempt to establish this thesis on the basis of two texts from the later works, in which 'the universal point of view' is worked out in a way that is unquestionably ideal-typically pure.

The texts are 'Science as a Vocation' and 'Politics as a Vocation'. Here the theme of 'personality and life orders' is developed in a by no means general fashion, but is instead spelt out in a classroom manner on the basis of concrete 'life orders'. Such an interpretation is made plausible by the fact that only five weeks separated the Lauenstein address and the delivery of 'Science as a Vocation', and it is thus permissible to assume that the 'general' and the 'particular' themes in Weber's preparation overlay each other (Mommsen, 1984, p. 268 n. 292). It is hardly accidental that today we have only the 'particular' version in a finished form; the lectures were delivered by 'request', and in the case of 'Politics as a Vocation' he accepted only from the fear that an unsuitable speaker might otherwise seize the opportunity.

How does Weber approach the two topics? In the driest fashion imaginable: 'Now we economists have a pedantic custom, which I should like to follow, of always beginning with external conditions. In this case we begin with the question: what are the conditions of science as a vocation in the material sense of the term?' (FMW, p. 129). Of the twenty-six pages of the lecture more than six are devoted to the external conditions of the academic profession. German conditions are compared with American, and it is shown how even in this field the separation of the worker from the means of production has become the 'fate' of all. He finally comes to the expectations of his listeners (probably quite different to his own): 'But I believe you actually wish to hear something else, namely the *inward* calling for science' (FMW, p. 134). The lecture proceeds to the question as to who has 'personality' in the field of science. And the answer is given, 'only he who is devoted *solely* to the work at hand'; 'An inner devotion to the task' is decisive; only this can raise the scientist 'to the level and dignity of the subject' he pretends to serve (FMW, p. 134).

But 'this holds not only for the field of science'. 'Politics as a Vocation' follows the same pattern. Weber depicts in an even more disillusioned fashion the external workings of modern politics. In the English trans- lation more than forty of the fifty-one pages are given over to sociological considerations: the definition of politics, of the state, of the bases of legitimation, the distinction between living 'from' politics as opposed to 'for' politics, of officials and politicians, and finally a comparative sociology of political parties. In the last dozen pages he finally comes to the issues that the listeners presumably came to hear: 'Now, what inner enjoyments can this career offer and what personal conditions are presupposed for one who enters this avenue?' (FMW, p. 114). What goes to make up the 'genuine man' who is able to pursue the 'vocation of politics'? Once again at root it is the capacity of devotion to the matter at hand 'if action is to have an inner strength' (FMW, p. 117).

It is not necessary to say anything more about these famous texts. The point is this: when asked to deliver lectures on politics and science as a vocation, Weber addressed the topics in a manner that can, if we are not mistaken, throw light on all his work. The point of departure is the 'external' given conditions. The life orders do however possess a kind of inner regularity of their own, an organized form of rationality, which has to be confronted by all those who become involved in them. The tension between the regularities of these orders – 'spheres', 'values' – becomes the third major element in Weber's theme; for the *Kulturmensch* it is an unavoidable fact that 'we are placed within life orders, each of which is governed by different laws' (FMW, p. 123).

There is a fundamental problem that precedes the tensions produced from the respective life orders; each of these orders involves demands, claims, moulding, impositions, or alternatively the possibilities of chances in the direction of life and the formation of personality. What becomes of the person who enters one such order, or is caught up in the power of it – whether this is a matter of free choice or whether one is born into it through family, status, linguistic community, state and religion? What 'fate' do the orders dictate, open up, or deny to the person placed in their power through the conditions of time and place? Is this Weber's theme?

The Empirical Findings: Rural Labour Organization in East Elbia

There is a passage in the 'Objectivity' essay (1904) that has always played a key role in the consideration of Weber's intentions:

> The social science that *we* wish to pursue is a *science of reality*. We want to understand the reality of life as it surrounds us, and into which we are placed, in its individuality (*Eigenart*): the interrelation and the cultural *meaning* of its individual phenomena in their contemporary framework and the historical reasons for their becoming so-and-not-otherwise.
>
> (MSS, p. 72, italics in original)

The reason why Weber wishes to pursue social science in this way has been shown in a previous essay (Hennis, 1983). He is concerned with the fate of man, and hence the problematic is anthropological, characterologi-cal and ethical in nature, and this draws Weber and his universal historical researches into a differentiating illumination of the culture in which *we* are placed. The material through which the questions are developed is the 'reality of life' as it has historically 'become'; as Weber put it in the prospectus for the founding of the German Sociological Society, 'the structural relations of our culture', and as it is elaborated in an exemplary way in the sections on the external conditions in the two lectures on science and politics.[1] Not only there, however: the 'structural relations of culture', viewed from the aspect of the cultural significance they have for cultural beings, alive to such impressions, lead to the isolation of the questions that for the scientist are worth posing. They are factually embodied in the reciprocal relations of people and external relations, and neither one of these by themselves are the subject of Weber's work.

Can this be seen in Weber's work? I will try to demonstrate this in outline and then go on to show how Weber's diagnosis of the cultural problematic of his time, his notion of the 'destiny of mankind', defined his conceptualization down to the last detail.

The specifically Weberian theme of personality and the life orders is fully present and dominating in the two surveys of rural labour. They have always been read in general as texts that provide some understanding of the young political academic, of the nationalist and imperialist. These surveys certainly do involve political judgements and proposals, and it is possible to evalute them biographically from the political aspect (Mommsen, 1984, pp. 21–34). Nevertheless these writings of the 27- to 30-year-old Weber have a much greater, simply 'fundamental' signifi-cance for the way in which he posed his problems (Tribe, 1983, pp. 181–226; Scaff, 1984, pp. 190–215).

The scope of what is addressed and covered by Weber in the surveys into rural labour is apparent only to those who are prepared to consider everything that appeared between 1892 and 1899 on this theme, and if possible in the light of his writings on ancient agrarian history. *Only then does the impulse and aim of these investigations become apparent*, and an enormous field opens up before the reader. It is possible to see here how the young academic gives free rein more or less for the first time to his scientific imagination, which was historically and empirically saturated and was disciplined by the tasks assigned to him and by the critical regard of his more experienced colleagues. In the surveys and the related lectures, in the contributions to debates and newspaper articles, we can see the first measured and considered analysis of 'life order'. It is already a contri-bution to an 'interpretive sociology' and is oriented to 'social action' – or more concretely, to the conduct of life of man as he lives in a community (in an almost Aristotelian sense). This 'life order' is the rural labour organization or, defined more broadly, the social and economic ensemble 'within which the working population finds itself' and as that ensemble determines 'fate and the overall situation' (Weber, 1894a, p. 64). Everything that he had learned from Meitzen's school of agrarian statistics and from his study of Roman agrarian law is developed here in a clear and vivid fashion. His craving for material is insatiable: Vinogradoff's work on the medieval English village is dealt with alongside a study of the agrarian organization of the Argentinian pampas.

In order to make as clear as possible a differentiating clarification of the conditions in eastern Germany, he employs the most extreme 'typical' cases: the example of the total lack of freedom of the slave in Antiquity, who lived in barracks without any family, and the Argentinian gaucho as a counter-example of total but just as 'barbaric' freedom. The differences of labour organization in the south, west, north-west and east of Germany are introduced, and it is shown that labour plays a completely different role in these areas, especially in respect to smallholdings and wage-labour. In the west, wage-labour

is considered to some extent to be a neighbourly act of helping out . . . these people distinguish quite unconsciously the concept of labour from that of duty or obligation. Here individualism in labour organizations finds its most extreme form . . . He labours perhaps because he actually has to, but in his mind it is because he likes to. He is not familiar with the kind of labour that we know in the east, this rigid, obligatory form of labour that yokes the whole life together.

(GASW, pp. 444–5)

The political implications for the German Reich of this kind of social organization are immediately drawn. The southern and west German labourers lack the 'characteristic Prussian concept of "damned duty and obligation". This frequently overlooked psychological moment is of great importance for the question: would such a reorganization of the [east German] labour organization, and by implication the radical break-up of all the large estates, be a politically desirable objective?' Weber rejects the idea categorically. 'It is no accident that the regions of Germany where this organization prevails [west Germany] have not been endowed with the political organizations and political sensibility which made possible the unity of the *Reich*' (GASW, p. 445).

Disregarding the fragmentary form in which Weber's studies on rural labour organization have come down to us, we are strongly reminded of Tocqueville's analysis of the moral consequences of the transition from the personal servitude of Ancien Régime to the individualistic epoch of unfettered equality.[2] 'The historically developed social stratification of the population' is decisive; it is the point at which the 'general situation' of the labourer is determined (Weber, 1894a, p. 65). Weber carried out his rural survey at the time that the process of destruction of the old patriarchal labour organization was in full swing. 'The irretrievable disintegration of this labour organization has in part already begun, in places is under way and is ultimately only a question of time' (GASW, p. 449). There was no way back. In places the older patriarchal organization was still intact but was increasingly losing its people, and they were being replaced by Polish and Russian migrant workers. At the same time the ruling stratum was changing; in place of the older aristocracy there appeared a class of agricultural entrepreneurs who in terms of their social characteristics were no different in principle to commercial capitalistic entrepreneurs. Patriarchal relations – defined by Weber in his questionnaire of 1892 as 'fatherly concern on the one side, true loyalty on the other' (Baumgarten, 1964, p. 383) – lost their foundation, and the 'free' labourer replaced the *Instmann* who had lived within an economic community of interest *vis-à-vis* his landlord. The transformation of the labour organization 'brought about by the modern reorganization of the enterprise' changed 'the face of the permanent labour force as much as that of casual labour. The "free labour contract" thus arrived in the countryside with the worker paid in money and living either on his own or in rented property. *Let us consider the consequences*' (Weber, 1979, p. 185, italics in original).

This emphatic 'let us consider the consequences' is typical of Weber's approach. The consequences for what? As the survey states – for the situation, the relationships of the rural labourers. Not least among the objectives of the survey is a consideration of the 'inner', 'human' effects that the shift to the enterprise form had on the people concerned. The changing face of the masters is likewise important. They too owe their character, their 'personality', to the life orders: that of the old and that of the emergent new. The old estate owner was no mere common employer 'but rather a political autocrat, a miniature territorial ruler who personally dominated the labourer' (Weber, 1979, p. 180). In his report to the fifth Evangelical–Social Congress, Weber deployed his sociology of domination to the full, although this was hardly appreciated by his public. The old landed aristocrat lived in the naïve belief

> that he was predestined to be ruler and that the others likewise were destined to live on his land in obedience. Why? This was something he did not think about. Such absence of reflectiveness was indeed one of the material virtues of his domination (Laughter). *I am completely serious.* The absence of pure commercial considerations was characteristic and from the point of view of the state quite valuable. This class of

our landed aristocracy, precisely because of this lack of real commercial intelligence, was suitable as a political ruling class, is now on the wane, and in its place there is emerging a class of rural entrepreneurs, a class with a different social and economic physiognomy.

(Weber, 1894a, p. 70, italics added)

It is also the leading aristocrats – Kanitz is meant here – who are no longer cast in the same mould. 'Their foreheads have lost the crimson shade of passion and taken on the pallor of thought. They are agrarian meditators, a combination of scholar and noble' (Weber, 1894a, pp. 70–1). And the rural labourer? As a class they have become proletarianized (Weber, 1894a, p. 71).

The bases of social organization of the eastern landed estates crumbled. Weber is far from playing down the merits of the eastern aristocracy. But he does not consider that it can be claimed 'that we owe an especial thanks to a large landed property as such. Above all, I do not believe that any due recognition is owing to individual persons, rather than to the social organizations of which these people are a product' (GASW, p. 456). This is an almost 'materialistic' formulation of the relation between 'personality and life order'.

A social organization that moulds people like 'products' and does so independently of the motives that might be attributed to them as merits is an aspect of Weber's work that in my opinion cannot be overstated; this goes far beyond the dichotomy of 'values' and 'facts', which is always associated with Weber's method. This insight derives directly from his perception of the agrarian world – both its upper and lower levels.

A well-known passage from 'The Economic Ethics of the World Religions' is employed by every interpretation of Weber that aspires to be of some significance: 'Not ideas, but (material and ideal) interests directly command human action. But "images of the world" created by "ideas" have often been the switchpoint determining the future course according to which the dynamic of interest conditioned action' (FMW, p. 280). Weber thus recognized 'ideal' interests. But the question is: can this concept be used to render intelligible 'social action', which is not religiously motivated, in the old social orders, whether it be burgher, peasant, or noble? We have already seen that *the* central concept in Weberian sociology is that of conduct of life (*Lebensführung*). In *Economy and Society* it is absolutely clear that this belongs completely to the world or orders – of estates (*Stände*),[3] whereas classes have no particular conduct of life. They do have a standard of living – in Weber's precise formulation, the typical probability for obtaining 'consumption goods', gaining an 'external' position in life and an 'inner' destiny, and, lastly, there exists in general an interest in the maintenance of this standard (ES, p. 302). The upholding of conduct of life appropriate to an estate (*Stand*) in terms of the conduct of life (and Weber of course defines *Stand* in terms of conduct of life) is conditioned by factors other than 'interests'. The 'image of the world' and conduct of life belong together in a society still governed by 'orders'; this cannot be explained on the basis of the mediation of 'ideas' and 'interests' alone – not even 'ideal' interests. What is the place of this sense of appropriate dignity (*Würdegefühl*) that is such an important concept for Weber?[4] Undoubtedly one could force this concept in somewhere, but it would not be a very good fit. His ideas on the constitution of the social orders ('social organization', the 'structural relations of cultures') are still conditioned by considerations – both learned from history and directly experienced – that are not covered by that typical nineteenth-century dichotomy, the conceptual couple of ideas and interests.

It is well known that Weber was influenced by Rodbertus's theory of the *oikos* (ES, pp. 99, 124; 1976, pp. 42–3). He saw in the almost autarchic eastern estates the persistence of the 'fragments of the isolated household economy' (Weber, 1979, p. 179). The estate owner now had to become involved in cash transactions if he was to maintain his standard of living at the level of the upper bourgeoisie and not become a peasant; and this standard was no longer sustainable on the old economic basis of production for local markets. In the east it became evident to Weber that capitalism displaced the standards of a traditional way of life at all *social* levels. Instead of way or conduct of life the related concept of 'standard of life' assumed a central place. But it is only the way of life and its related 'social action', open as it is to the influence of the whole spectrum of possible orders and powers, that require interpretive understanding and are in fact capable of it. The standard of living can be established by a single measure: that of income or wage compared with the price of the means of subsistence. While paying due regard to the lines cited from the 'Economic Ethics of the World Religions', it is the conditions for the way and conduct of life *prior* to interests and ideals that direct human conduct; throughout the Ancien Régime these conditions were not 'reflected', that is, 'rationalized' by either ideas or interests. Affect and *ratio* were not set separately distinct. The ties holding old communities together were not woven out of ideas and interests; instead these ties were constituted in ways that elude modern concepts.

What is it that separates Weber from us and makes an understanding of him so worthwhile? No 'modern' sociologist (a) would be able to conceive these conditions, the foundations or 'store' is exhausted; (b) would be unconsciously influenced by the principles of liberty and equality to be able to locate the way of life – in its specifically *ständisch* cast – in any special place in the system of the social scientific categories.

Estate-orders (*Stände*) have a marginal status and cannot be accommodated by the usual social indicators.

Person and Cause

The sociologist, oriented to empiricism and value-freedom, might be content when considering personality and life order (i.e. 'personality profile' and the corresponding empirical 'life orders') with the demonstration of Weber's theme in terms of the empirical constellations indicated above. But the political scientist wants to go further, wants to know whether this is Weber's final word on the theme of 'personality and life order'. It is the authority of Weber himself that binds modern social science to a freedom from value judgements. The proper understanding of this stipulation is of the greatest significance for all the social sciences. For political science it is something more: it is a question crucial to our lives. Weber's authority seems to recommend that the old central question of political science (what is the best political order?) be abandoned as insoluble, and that the discipline henceforth direct itself to 'empirical' political sociology and at long last begin to practise it. For the one point of view Weber is the end-point of decline from the classical political science that began with Plato and Aristotle; for the other, he stands as the solid point of departure for every scientific form of investigation in political science.

Now if it is true that the question of the modern way of life occupies the centre of Weber's problematic, lending the whole work an anthropological intentionality, then one is permitted to ask whether it is possible to deal with the conduct of life, with the 'fate' of modern man, without becoming involved in questions of value. He had himself, if cryptically, attributed questions of that which is imposed (*Zumutung*) from outside – e.g. political communities, convention – to the sphere of values (*Wertsphären*).[5] Nevertheless behind the empirical-historical investigations of the correlation between personality and life order, might there not be an idea of a 'proper' way and conduct of life – even in Weber? Leo Strauss, one of Weber's sharpest critics, said of Hobbes's political science that it was the first specifically *modern* attempt to give a coherent and comprehensive answer to 'the question of the proper life of man' that was at the same time the 'question of the proper arrangement of human life together' (Strauss, 1966, p. 5). The question of the proper life of man, *simultaneously* a question of the proper ordering of the human community (we should say of personality *and* life order), is indeed the classical theme of political science, and Hobbes only elaborated this in a 'modern' fashion. The question of the proper conduct of life of man as human being and the ordering of social relations according to the correctness of this idea is in fact the central question of *natural law*; this is a problematic that has become unfamiliar to us today. To have abandoned this question, indeed to have betrayed it, is the bitter accusation levelled by Stauss and some others against Weber.

The demonstration offered above – that on the empirical level it is the relation of personality and life order that thematically determines the substance of Weber's work – compels us, I believe, to go further and see if this question might not also have a determining effect on the 'normative' level of the work. Put more precisely, is there not an idea of man, an anthropology, at the basis of his cultural scientific investigations and his interpretive sociology? This is meant not in the sense of measuring crania that was so fashionable in his time, but in the tradition of Western thought and reflection on man. And are not the social orders and powers arrayed by him covertly directed by this idea?

Only the outlines of this question can be indicated here. The problematic of the mode of modern life – disenchanted, rationalized and disciplined – became clear for Weber with capitalism. The latter has only a need for the partial use of human beings. It isolates for itself specific utilizable qualities. In comparison to this what is the whole human person? We might recall Weber's distinction between the effects of prophecy, one of which operates from within on the 'whole', and the other working only externally and effecting the cultivation of a form of conduct of life as in the Confucian ethic of propriety. 'An optimally adjusted person, rationalizing his conduct only to the degree requisite for adjustment, does not constitute a unity but only a complex of useful and particular traits' (RC, p. 235). The striving from within for a unity that we associate with the concept of personality did not occur in China. 'Life remained a series of occurrences and did not appear as a whole that was methodically arranged with respect to a transcendent goal' (RC, p. 235).

How does this systematic unity, a whole, emerge in the human person? If I am correct, this occurs by the fact that such a person is capable of a complete and inwardly motivated personal devotion to a cause that transcends individuality. The conditions of the modern world do not force human subjects to such devotion through tradition, or a deep sense of necessity, or prophetic force; nevertheless it is possible to cultivate the ability of decisively 'taking a position', even if this is a weaker form of devotion. Devotion to a cause is directed by ethical imperatives only under quite specific circumstances. The more 'natural', more 'original' form of ethical devotion is to a person not to a cause. In each case the relation of the human subject either to persons or to a cause must be ethical, and so be interpreted from within and be *individually* realizable. That is relatively straightforward if the 'cause' or 'cultural value' is something out of the ordinary. What happens then if it is everyday life, which for Weber is synonymous with the modern world of specialism (*Berufswelt*), that exclusively lays claim to man yet at the same time withholds an ethical construction of this claim? *For Weber this state of affairs comes about with capitalism.* Modern capitalism entered the world because of the historically unique potentiality for the completely ethical interpretation of the everyday; this is why ascetic Puritanism so fascinated him. Since that time capitalism has come to rely on a 'mechanical' foundation and can dispense with the spiritual support of religion. The 'distant and impersonal "objectivity"' of modern capitalism, the 'calculability' and rational consistency, the seriousness of labour stripped of its naïve simplicity, the specialist 'narrowing' of modern life that calls forth the challenge of the 'pathetic opposition of the artistically oriented, as well as the ethical and purely human point of view, and which lacked for serious-minded people a contained unity of ethical self-justification': they would be 'replaced, if at all, by surrogates which would easily be seen as such'. Thereby it was 'self-evident that capitalism could exist quite easily; either this was fatalistically accepted as inevitable, as increasingly the case today, or, as in the Enlightenment and the modern style of liberalism, it would be legitimated as somehow using the *relatively* best of worlds, through the *relatively* optimal means, to make the *relatively* best possible' (italics in original). 'For serious-minded people however capitalism could no longer appear to form the external expression of a style of life based upon an ultimate finished and demonstrable unity of personality' (Weber, 1982, pp. 296–7). *Once* things had been different; once vocation and the innermost ethical form of personality (this is decisive!) had formed an unbroken whole. In the Middle Ages this 'spiritual bond' between the innermost core of personality and vocation had been absent. Today on the other hand 'the inner dissolution of this unity is quite tangible' (Weber, 1978, p. 1124). At one time however the Puritans had brought the two together: 'the innermost core of personality' and the necessity of vocation in the everyday. What consequences follow for humanity once the rationalized ordering of the everyday no longer permits this? I believe that this is the central question that Weber, following on from Marx, posed to the world in which we are 'placed'.

I also believe that this question leads us for the second time to the 'theme' that runs throughout Weber's writings, a theme that emerges in a recognizable form long before Weber's involvement in religious problems. The theme is already in evidence in the initial empirical writings and in the very first writings on medieval trading companies and the agrarian history of Antiquity. Again it is in the years of engagement with the survey of rural labour that we find the first, quite precise and easily ascertainable formulation of the problem.

63

In 1892 immediately before publication of his own major contribution to the *Verein* survey, Weber published an essay in *Christliche Welt* rebutting criticism that had been directed by an orthodox Consistory councillor against Paul Göhre's book of his experience as a factory worker (Weber, 1892, cols. 1104–9; Marianne Weber, 1975, p. 133). He wrote of Göhre's book, *Three Months as a Factory Worker*: the reader has the impression that the workers depicted by Göhre 'are people of one's own flesh and blood, having much the same intellectual and sociable needs, pursuing the material and internal interests *assigned to them by the organization of human society* with roughly the same degree of comprehension and stupidity as those of the reader' (italics added). He commended the depth of Göhre's studies for the way in which they made plain what the bare figures of the usual statistical investigations could not – 'the ultimately decisive feature: that reflex deep in the human body which determined mood and attitude'. 'No statistic, no discussion no matter how painstaking and didactic, can signify so tangibly the psychological moment, the inner-life condition of the worker.' The 28-year-old Weber makes clear in the same essay how significant the concept of profession (*Berufsbegriff*) is even at this time; Göhre's critic contends that this book 'falls outside the God-given path of profession', and Weber asks in reply whether this critic is aware 'of the anachronism involved in this canonization of man to the confines of profession, one serving human ends, at a time when a steadily increasing section of the population were losing contact with the idea of profession in this sense, an idea moreover that had to be lost in the course of economic changes' (Weber, 1892, col. 1108). He wrote this thirteen years before the famous passage stating that the idea of 'vocational duty' merely circulated in our lives 'as the ghost of former religious beliefs', and, with few exceptions, individuals usually dispensed with an ethically meaningful interpretation of their vocational fulfilment (PESC, p. 182). In the closing passage of *The Protestant Ethic* Weber neglected to mention why this was so. He had however done so more than a decade before, and with a pungency that in my opinion is unmatched in all of the later writings.

We find this explication in the essay of 1894, once again in the *Christliche Welt*, that analyses the work of his friend and political compatriot Friedrich Naumann (Weber, 1894b). Naumann, argued Weber, had not sufficiently recognized the reality of the capitalist economy and its tendency to promote the formation of large enterprises. Weber writes (and I consider this passage to be central to the *foundation* of Weber's work):

The leading characteristic of modern development is the demise of *personal relationships of domination* as the basis of labour organization and with it the subjective, psychological conditions of dependency of the dominated classes that allowed the imprint of religious and ethical views. In artisanal production, in agricultural labour organization, and especially in the large agricultural enterprise, the psychological basis for a relationship of subordination, which is a condition of every labour relation, is present in the *personal* relationship to the master. Hence I believe Naumann's – quite unconsciously – slight interest in the agricultural worker's struggle for emancipation. A similar situation exists in the *personally* managed industrial enterprise which Naumann seems forced to recognize as a product of evolutionary development. Modern developments however replace this form of enterprise increasingly with one founded on *impersonal* domination of the *class* of proprietors. It puts purely commercial relationships in place of personal ones, and payments of tribute to an unknown, unseen and intangible power in place of personal subordination, removing in this way the possibility of comprehending the relationship of rulers and ruled in ethical and religious terms. The individual entrepreneur is merely a class-type. It is this which is the problem from a religious viewpoint, and not some form of social and economic harm arising from the distribution of property.

(Weber, 1894b, col. 475, italics in original)

So Weber sees the central problem of the modern economic order as the lack of possibility of regulating the relationship between owners of capital and labourers in any conceivable ethical–psychological manner; it is a question of the absence of ethics (*Nichtethisierbarkeit*).

The logic of this course of development followed by the specifically modern mode of class formation will force Naumann, if his programme is to be realized, into an *opposition to every form of private capital*; for it is no longer individual persons with individual psychological relationships who confront one another, and here moral and religious influences do not have at the present any power over the individual.

(Weber, 1894b, col. 475, italics in original)

For the present? In any case the idea of the impenetrability of apersonal relationships to ethical interpretation runs through the entire work. It is to some extent the second time we come across the theme under investigation, which is *inseparably* bound up with the empirical circumstances of personality and life orders.

During the same year, 1894, Weber published at Naumann's request his small book on the Stock Exchange that even today is perhaps the most intelligible German-language introduction to the subject (GASS, pp. 256–322). He describes interest on capital as tribute payments. Once interest was a sign of lack of freedom. 'Among brothers' loans were made without interest. 'Interest was levied by the foreign conqueror from both people and as a rent from land; or the lord and owner of land levied it from the propertyless who were therefore not completely free persons who rented land from him.' Ownership of land is the oldest form of interest-bearing rights. It still exists today, as is shown by the rental rates in cities. The difference today is that it is another lord who demands tributes, namely the owner of capital.

> It is his peculiar quality to be 'impersonal'. The tax farmer taxed the lord and ruled over him personally, as well as being known to him; today the owner of interest-bearing bonds has no idea of whose income is taxed on his behalf, and the landowner who has taken up credit does not know the original lender of the money that the bank places at his disposal. The *impersonal* nature of the relationship between those paying and those receiving interest is the most characteristic feature of the contemporary obligations of tribute. Therefore one speaks of the domination of 'capital' and not that of 'capitalists'.
>
> (GASS, p. 267, italics in original)

The modern payer of tribute confronts not only a stranger but an unperson. Weber constantly returns to this basic point. Shareholders likewise do not know one another.

> A socialist organization would bind all together with a single thread. Present day organization binds everyone through countless threads to each other. Each hauls on the network of threads so that he might attain the place that he desires and which he believes to be his; but even if he is a giant and holds many threads within his grasp, he is far more pulled by others to the position that is open to him.
>
> (GASS, p. 273)

That could come from *Capital*, but Weber sees deeper and further than Marx, for whom one must always provide the ethical dimension. Weber on the other hand elaborates this dimension with a precision that a professor of ethics could scarcely better.[6]

> Every purely personal relationship of man to man, of whatever kind and inclusive of the most complete enslavement, is open to ethical regulation; ethical demands can be made of them since their constitution depends on the individual wills of the parties concerned, hence making space for the development of charitable virtue. Rational relationships of business are not like this and the more rationally differentiated they are, the less they are susceptible to such regulation.

There is no possibility in practice or even in principle of any charitable regulation of relationships arising between the holder of savings and the holder of a mortgage from a loan bank, between the holder of government bonds and the taxpayer, between the shareholder and factory worker, between the tobacco importer and the foreign plantation owner, and between an industrial consumer of raw materials and a miner. The objectification (*Versachlichung*) of the economy through the process of market association follows its own material regularities; to ignore them is to court economic failure and in the long run economic ruin. Rational economic association always brings about objectification and it is impossible to direct a cosmos of objective-rational social action by charitable appeals to particular individuals. The objectified cosmos of capitalism certainly offers no support for any such charitable orientation. The demands of religious charity founder here not only because of the refractoriness and weakness of particular individuals, as happens everywhere, but because they lose their meaning altogether. The religious ethic is confronted by a world of associational relationships which for fundamental reasons cannot submit to its original norms.

(ES, p. 585)

This completes our presentation of the second level at which Weber's theme emerges: the ethical consequences of this kind of cosmos, of this materially fully rationalized life order. It is not merely its rational autonomy that renders it immune to ethical domination. More important is the fact that it holds out to those persons bound up within it the possibility of an 'ethicization' of their 'location' in this order. No foothold is offered to an 'inwardly oriented' interpretation; every position adopted on the grounds of ethical principles becomes mere declamation. It is no longer possible to determine the way and the conduct of life individually, other than as a simple disciplined functioning in a process of association that is completely objectified and impersonal. Here we approach the question as to why the 'process of Occidental rationalization' – which has to be related to each life order if we are to perceive the significance it has in his work – was in fact so central for Weber.[7]

Weber repeatedly expresses the idea, of which the *Christliche Welt* essay outlined above is an early instance, that ethical demands can be made of every *personal* relationship, even if this relationship involves force; it is the personal bond that counts. But it is not only 'masterless slavery' (as Adolf Wagner dubbed the modern proletariat) but rather the 'cosmos of the rational state machine (*Staatsanstalt*) which no longer has the character, in any form' of an order to which one can make ethical demands, 'as will be discussed in due course' (ES, p. 600). *Homo politicus* 'like the *homo*

67

oeconomicus discharges his responsibilities most ideally when he does so according to the rational rules of the modern order based on compulsion'; that is, 'without regard to person, *sine ira et studio*, without hatred and so without love, without discretion and so without mercy, and as impartial vocational duty and not by virtue of a personal relationship'. The personalistic estate order recognized that one had to proceed differently according to the status and prestige of the person concerned, and was aware of the instances when problems might occasionally arise. This is not the case with the modern state: 'The modern judiciary passes judgement on the life of the criminal not out of personal anger or a need for vengeance, but quite detachedly and for the sake of objective norms and ends and simply according to the working of its rational autonomy.' Internal political violence becomes increasingly objectified into the 'order of a state based on rule of law – from the religious point of view this is merely the most effective mimicry of violence' (ES, p. 600).

There is no doubt that for Weber the depersonalization of the modern world, whose kernel is always the rationalizing process of objectification, in the 'inexorable power over our lives', has unfolded in modern capitalism. Nothing is more erroneous than the still common opposition of Weber and Marx. The former lacks a philosophy of history based on hope and any sort of revolutionary promise, including the myth of the proletariat. It was none the less a matter of simple intellectual candour that any 'objective', yet culturally oriented, assessment of the state of the world in which we live would begin with Marx and Nietzsche.[8]

Even in Weber's dissertation we can detect a conception of the modern world as defined by Marx. Its theme is the contrast between forms of legal contract determined on the one hand in a purely objective, capital-oriented fashion and on the other through personal ties. The lawyer finds his way from law to social economics. He finds the paradox of formally free labour under conditions of capitalism a striking one, specifically the way in which 'freedom' is associated with the complete objectification of the person of the employee and is subjected to the market by the ethically *neutral* conditions of the capitalist economic form. In 1902, his darkest year, Weber published a review of the first extensive scientific investigation of the labour contract that had appeared in German, a contract that even in hire and lease was purely objective, and this was of especial interest to him (Weber, 1902, pp. 723–34).

It was in these years that the 'theme' of Weberian sociology received its fullest development. A cascade of conceptual polarities locate the theme, and they all turn on the contrast between the possibility of personal contract and objective-impersonal properties that deny such possibilities. First comes 'church' and 'sect', fully present in *The Protestant Ethic*; then, and related to this, 'institution' and 'association'; 'associational and communal relationships',[9] domination by personal authority or through constellation of interests and so on; each of these couples is ultimately determined by the question of the 'ethical' inward consequences that these orders and powers have on the person.[10] There can be no doubt that we also have here the basis for Weber's establishment of sociology as an interpretive (*verstehende*) sociology concerned with the meaning for *individual* action *but which remained a cultural science*. The restricted conception of 'his' sociology is consistently related to the actual material involved; where there is nothing 'personal' to register Weber falls silent and gets no further than unfulfilled intentions. Throughout the entirety of the writing it is ultimately the great 'cultural problems' of the age to which his work is directed; more specifically it is the elaboration of the 'subjective particularity of modern man', the manner of his 'fitting in' with or adaptation to modern society – life orders in the widest sense or, put differently, the '*objective* properties of modern *culture*' – the concept he consistently favours over that of society. Weber's specific sociological problematic is located in the relation between 'the property of man' (personality) and 'the property of culture' (life order), and this remained constant throughout his work, even when he shifted his discussion from a 'cultural-scientific problematic' to that of a 'sociological' one. It should be quite evident by now what is disclosed by the term, the great 'cultural problems' of the time; we have not found anything new here, but have simply confirmed the old suspicions; namely, it is the fate of man to endure the human and psychic consequences of the 'non-obligatory character of public life'.[11] The 'ultimate and most sublime values' that people make to each other have been forced out of the public realm into 'the distant realm of mystic life or into the brotherliness of unmediated relationships of one to another'. It is the 'depersonalization' of all the life orders that determine man's life – from the organization of labour in East Elbia, through the rational institutional state, to the modern enterprise of scientific organization; in these the great cultural problems of the time are realized. If Weberian sociology revolves upon the conduct of life on the one side, and on the other the orders and powers that condition life, then the culmination of rationalization is the destruction of this connection. 'To lead one's life', to have the possibility of doing so, always implies that some degree of freedom is left for the conduct of one's life. Complete rationality denies this free space. A completely rationalized order gives no chance for conduct of life in the sense defined by Weber. There is no space for conduct of life within 'the iron cage'; it is rationalized away, and discipline alone is enough. Likewise each completely rationalized 'power' and 'cultural value' wholly defined by rationality is unsuitable to direct one's life, except where technical decisions have to be made. Weber's postulate of the value-freedom of the sociological and economic sciences likewise purport to nothing more; with the claims to lead one's life it has nothing to do, as in the first sentence of the 1913 *Logos* essay: 'By value judgements are to be understood practical evaluations of the unsatis- factory or satisfactory character of phenomena subject to the influence of our action' (MSS, p. 1) – i.e. conduct of life. Here and only here do we find the core of the well-known postulate: anger at the demands of a power, which science had doubtless become, in relation to the central point of all his thought, *the conduct of life of the free individual*. Here science had nothing to say, at least in the form that it had adopted.

Weber was not in a position to approach the objectified life order of the modern world directly. Any of today's moderately competent social scientists is able to do this with the assistance of functional and systems models. Weber did not get as far as this. All the instances of clearly objectified life orders are based on contrasts – with traditional Europe – and he had more or less exhausted the theme of life orders that concerned him in the sociology of bureaucracy, namely, the rule 'of "formalistic impersonality", *sine ira et studio*, without hatred or passion, and so without "love" or "enthusiasm" – this is the way the official directs his affairs' (ES, p. 225). It was not Weber's early death that prevented the development of the sociologies of the state,[12] the factory and the army beyond conceptual definitions, but rather the limitations of his intentions and the possibilities of his problematic. When today's organizational sociology makes free with Weber, as it frequently does, it does so in the spirit of Wagner.

Prospect

We break off here, even though we have not reached the third level of our theme, personality and life order. It is not just the opacity of the individual life orders in their rationalized and objectified form, starting with the vocational world, that becomes an ethical problem; rather it is a secondary consequence of rationality, namely, the struggle of the life orders one with another and the setting down of the modern *Kulturmensch* within this. The tensions and conflicts of the life orders – this is how Weber formulated it at the start of the 'Intermediate Reflections' – become more intense and gain force the more each is exposed to the 'obligation of consistency'. Orders and spheres collide with increasing force, but only in the 'individual human breast' to the extent that it remains sensitive at the ethical level to these conflicts. The third and most sublime level of Weber's theme is simultaneously the most 'historic' and deeply rooted in the sensibility of his age – and his person. Where Weber saw the possibility of cultural goods 'being hastily made to serve valueless ends, moreover ends which were completely contradictory and mutually antagonistic', where an uneasiness 'with a culture becoming ever more senseless in its further differentiation and development' shapes his theme, today instead there prevails a mood of contentment with 'pluralism' and pleasure in the excitement of role change. I will leave this aspect of the theme for a more relaxed and 'historical' treatment.

We must recall the reserve with which we began our study of Weber's theme. If we have succeeded in exposing some part of it, it should not prevent further work in this direction but rather stimulate new and impartial readings of the *oeuvre*. This is the sole intention of the arguments put forward here.

Following on from the explication of Weber's problematic, we have sought to make a case for a theme leading through the work from the survey on rural labour to the famous lectures on science and politics from Weber's final years. This theme, the question of the relation between life order and the development of personality, is not taken up merely at the empirical level, but is dealt with as a question concerning the destiny of the human species; the question of the possibility of living a life in a manner that, under the prevailing conditions, can be interpreted ethically. One might remember the ideal motives that, according to Weber, drove the best and most virtuous of the East Elbian rural workers away from their homes.

We often encounter in Weber's work the curious word 'ethically neutral' (*anethisch*) – not unethical or anti-ethical, but ethically *neutral*. A prime concept of an ethically neutral institution was for Weber the market. Domination through a constellation of interests had an ethically neutral character, that is, was not susceptible to ethical interpretation. This resistance, opacity, of the world in which we are 'placed' to ethical interpretation is the 'fate' with which Weber's work struggles.

What would be on the agenda if the claimed basic theme in Weber were proved to be correct? Initially a much more precise analysis of the entire body of writing would be called for, beyond anything that might be possible in one essay. It is not to be hoped that the theme can be defined with complete exactitude. In a central passage in the Inaugural Address, which is of central importance for the understanding of the *oeuvre*, Weber mentions the 'forces of selection' acting upon the inhabitants of East Elbia through the historically influenced conditions, and he 'willingly concedes' that he is in no position to

develop theoretically the significance of the various general points which may be derived from them. The immensely difficult question, certainly insoluble at the present, of *where to place the limit* of the variability of physical and psychological qualities in a population under

71

the influence of its given conditions is something I will not even venture to touch on.

(Weber, 1980, p. 435, italics in original)

Weber, a lover of exact concepts, never turned the immense topic of 'anthropology and history and sociology' (for this is what the question of personality and life order implies) into a 'theory' of this relation, despite amassing materials and his conviction of the cultural importance of this theme. He never sought to develop a 'reconstruction' of this relation. The general viewpoints lie – for the most part implicitly – at the basis of his concepts.[13] We have sought here, within the limits imposed upon us, only to establish as far as is possible what was made explicit.

A search for 'theoretical' clarity is quite foreign to the spirit of Weber's work. It seems to me more important to prove that his questions were by no means eccentric, but rather corresponded in the closest possible way to those questions that related to the new 'place of man in the world' that occupied his contemporaries from Dilthey to Scheler. We shall have to examine the concepts hitherto employed in the comprehension of Weberian science. On the basis of which scientific context and tendencies is the work to be understood? In my opinion in the disappearing tradition of the moral sciences, and especially the tradition of the German Historical School, as a student of which Weber was to some extent baptized three times: as a student of the Historical School of Law, as a young representative of the Historical School of Economics, and finally as a major representative of German neo-idealism.

In our first essay (Hennis, 1983, pp. 135–80) we began with the question of whether Weber is correctly placed in the shrine of modern 'value-free' social science. Desecration was not intended, but neither was misplaced devotion. Weber belongs to the late tradition of practical science, and he finds a place in the prehistory of modern science only if his central questions and concerns are neglected.

What kind of provocation does this image of Weber present to current social science, if any at all? For me this is the real question. It could be that Weber would then lose interest for contemporary science. 'The torch of cultural problems has moved onward.' Social science has for a long time (we write in 1984) sought 'to shift its location and change its conceptual apparatus so that it might regard the stream of events from the heights of reflective thought' (MSS, p. 112). Who could dare to doubt this? Nevertheless it could be the case that Weber's work, centred on the question of human destiny in the modern world, could make *us* aware of the questions that *we no longer pose*, and thereby provide an impulse for the posing of new questions.

Notes

This is a shortened version of an article, 'Max Webers Thema. "Die Persönlichkeit und die Lebensordnungen"', that appeared in the *Zeitschrift für Politik*, vol. 31, no. 1 (1984), pp. 11–52.

1 Published in September 1910 as an appendix to the *Archiv für Sozialwissenschaft und Sozialpolitik*.

2 Weber was certainly well acquainted with Tocqueville, even if he relied more on Bryce for his views on American politics. Both Tocqueville and Weber are liberals – but of a very particular kind. They are not interested in 'rights' and 'freedoms' but rather in the moral constitutions that correspond to them. As yet this has not been studied in any detail. Cf. Freund (1974) and Hennis (1982, pp. 403 ff.).

3 Cf. ES, pp. 305–7, 937; on the problem of the free-floating intellectual's conduct of life see ES, p. 506. Where the chances of individual life conduct vanish, the domain of discipline begins (ES, pp. 729–31).

4 For Weber conduct of life and sense of dignity (*Würdegefuhl*) were intimately related; in the world of 'naked rationality' this relation is dissolved. If one can forgive the play on words: Weber's work is a 'farewell-symphony' to yesterday's world that is continually interrupted by a 'nevertheless'. He cannot think of anything to characterize modernity apart from conceptual definition, as in rational institutional state (*Anstaltsstaat*). Weber's analytic force is intelligible only with respect to the *limits* of *interpretive* sociology.

5 The concept of imposition (*Zumutung*) is related to value-spheres (ES, pp. 901–4, 922). [Hennis relates the concept, *Zumutung*, back to an earlier part of his article, which has not been included here. See his original (Hennis, 1984, pp. 38–9) – eds.]

6 One of the most interesting new works on ethics begins with the sentence, 'Ethics is the theory of human *Lebensführung*' (Rendtdorff, 1980, Vol. 1, p. 11). The central concept of Weber's work is thus also the central concept of ethics. However much he liked tangling with the 'ethical culture' people (e.g. Friedrich Wilhelm Foerster and his circle, 'from which I am distanced in many respects as much as possible': FMW, p. 145) – from the Inaugural Address, in the text on the Stock Exchange and at regular intervals up to the two great lectures at the close of his work – he did in fact remain under the influence of these most intimate of contemporary opponents. One of the most widely read books of Foerster, republished several times, was simply called *Lebensführung* (1901). This also belongs to a biography of the *oeuvre*. On Toennies's relation to the 'Society for Ethical Culture' see Mitzman (1973, pp. 117 ff.).

7 Walter saw in a much clearer fashion than modern-day evolutionary interpreters (Habermas, Schluchter and in important respects also Tenbruck):

> His ideal developmental types do not possess the genuine properties of 'development'. Even his central concept of rationalisation does not really mean a necessary form of development unravelling in the form of human destiny, as Alfred Weber insisted. Max Weber is much more concerned with specific individual causes, here furthering and there hindering the realisation of rationalisation. (1926, p.26)

8 The best summary of the relation to Marx and Nietzsche is still Baumgarten's

(1964, pp. 554, 571 ff.). More detailed and written with sympathy and understanding, which has no parallel in the German literature is Fleischmann (1964, pp. 190–238).

9 Since Toennies is out of fashion, recent German sociology has tried to put as much space as possible between his famous conceptual couple and Weber's usage. There is no need of this. In doing so one only denies oneself one of the most important sources for the understanding of Weber. Weber's formulation corresponds only to the orientation of *his* sociology towards 'social action'. In contrast to such distancing, I see in Weber more of a radicalization and universalization of Toennies's view. Moreover Toennies was a socialist and basically an optimist, whereas Weber was neither. See Cahnmann (1973, pp. 257–83; 1981, pp. 154–7).

10 When examined more closely it becomes apparent that the most well known of Weber's conceptual series, the threefold types of legitimation, is in fact arranged in a rigorously polar manner: obedience with respect to 'legally established, objective *impersonal order*' or with respect to 'the *person* of the *master* appointed by tradition' or the 'charismatic leader by virtue of *personal* trust' (ES, pp. 215–16, italics in original). This is the typology in its final form, but it is the same for all other versions.

11 As put by Landshut (1929, p. 130) in relation to the closing passages of 'Science as a Vocation'.

12 Both sets of students' notes from the Munich lectures – announced as 'Sociology of the State' – demonstrate that nothing more was to be expected from this quarter. Weber's last letter to Marianne (19.5.1920) underlines this: 'nothing new here; lectures overflowing – follow my nose to begin with (all the same stuff, charisma etc.)' (Baumgarten, 1964, p. 635).

13 Thus the task for the future does not consist in the reconstruction of Weber's anthropology. It does not exist, and would be a creation of the reconstructor. It is more a question of specifying closely the radius of the concepts – not least *Mensch*, *Persönlichkeit*, *Kulturmensch* – that Weber used to identify the relation of personality and life order. Important here are Henrich (1952) and Portis (1978).

3

Rationalization in Max Weber's Developmental History

GUENTHER ROTH

For Max Weber the modern world was a product of a long rationalization and intellectualization. As heir to the tradition of Progress he spoke of 'the process of intellectualization to which we have been exposed for millennia' and, he added disapprovingly, 'to which it has become customary to react in an exceedingly negative fashion' (FMW, p. 138). Weber approached the outcome with matter-of-factness in the spirit neither of *Wertfreiheit* nor of *Kulturkritik*. Thus, science as a vocation appeared to him part of 'the inescapable condition of our historical situation. We cannot evade it so long as we remain true to ourselves.'[1] He never doubted that we should remain true to ourselves as modern human beings. Scientists must specialize; capitalists must follow the rules and ethic of the market economy or fail; politicians must accept public responsibility. Only the religious virtuosi can continue to live as they had before the coming of modernity; their world-view was rationalized long ago in a different direction. As a political man Weber was passionately involved with the present and the shaping of the future. But as a scholar he looked mostly backward and formulated only a partial theory of modernity, which emphasized impersonal authority and subjectivist culture. While the political writings necessarily treat constitutional aspects of modernity, mainly in the context of the nation state, the scholarly work deals more with rationalization and intellectualization throughout history than with the nature of modernity. To be sure, Weber often looked back from the vantage-point of modernity, but he spent more effort on studying its genesis than on diagnosing it. Since historical awareness is part of modernity, studying the past constitutes an affirmation of the modern world-view.

I consider it paradoxical that Weber's work continues to be scrutinized for a theory of modernity that has only a narrow textual base, when the bulk of his historical analysis has attracted much less attention. Weber's specific views on modernity must be reconstructed from a few dozen

75

pages in a very large *oeuvre*. A few paragraphs at the end of *The Protestant Ethic and the Spirit of Capitalism*, a few pages in the two speeches on science and politics as a vocation, a few remarks in the 'Introduction' and the 'Intermediate Reflections' of 'The Economic Ethics of the World Religions', the brief 'Author's Introduction' of 1920, some passages in *Economy and Society*, some scattered observations elsewhere – all these have carried an enormous burden of interpretive weight. Not surprisingly, a whole library has been filled with competing interpretations, for the fragmentary character of Weber's theory of modernity lends itself to greatly divergent reading.[2]

In this essay I would like to consider the larger part of Weber's work that deals with rationalization in history. Weber turned rationalization into a crucial constituent of developmental history (*Entwicklungsgeschichte*), a notion neglected in the Weber literature and usually in the English translations. He had no simple 'rationalization thesis' linking previous periods with modernity in the manner of the older and newer developmental history of his teachers and peers. He modified the tradition of unilinear progress by viewing socio-cultural evolution as rationalization along various dimensions and directions. At the same time he also rejected the 'scientific' developmental history of his day with its application of historical laws. Working in the mould of developmental history, he broke it into several pieces. He responded to the crisis of evolutionism with a disaggregation of developmental history into a multi-dimensional mode of analysis. Herein lies the significance his work gained decades later for the comparative study of modernization, for neo-evolutionary theory and for historical sociology. Depending on the dimension selected or emphasized, Weber could be made useful for the comparative sociology of Reinhard Bendix, the neo-evolutionary interests of Talcott Parsons and Jürgen Habermas, or the 'developmental' concerns of Wolfgang Schluchter.[3]

I will first touch upon the intellectual and institutional context in which Weber worked and then sketch his own efforts at resolving some of the problems of developmental history. I will conclude with some observations on his view of modernity and on the continued utility of his work for understanding a 'post-modern' world.

Developmental History and Stage Theory in the Works of Weber's Contemporaries

The old *Entwicklungsgeschichte* had idealist and romanticist origins. It contained a metaphysical teleology of world history and in various combinations addressed both the self-realization of the world spirit through the ages and the unfolding of the spirit of the individual peoples. By the 1890s a mood of political and intellectual realism seized a new generation, mixing positivist and historicist impulses. Karl Lamprecht (1856–1915), Kurt Breysig (1866–1940) and Werner Sombart (1863–1941) began to advance a new programme of empirical developmental history. In 1896 Lamprecht and Breysig published programmatic statements in the *Deutsche Zeitschrift für Geschichtswissenschaft*. Lamprecht defended his vast project of the *Deutsche Geschichte* (which came to comprise eighteen volumes) with the best of his many polemical essays: 'Was ist Kulturgeschichte?' (Lamprecht, 1896, pp. 75–150). Ten years younger than Lamprecht and eager to stake his own claim, Breysig announced his apostasy from Prussian political and administrative history with his essay 'Über Entwicklungsgeschichte' (Breysig, 1896, pp. 161–174, 193–211). Their notions of developmental history showed similarities as well as differences. On the most general level, they both promoted cultural history over political history, the comprehensive and long-range study of cultures and civilizations over the study of great men and the state. They differed primarily in that Lamprecht chose a psychological approach and Breysig a structural one.

Lamprecht, who had begun his career as an economic historian of the Middle Ages, replaced political periodization and the older economic stage theories with a theory of psychologically defined *Kulturzeitalter*. Every people (or nation) underwent progressive differentiation through the stages of animism, symbolism, typologism, conventionalism, individualism and subjectivism. These stages were paralleled, but not determined, by economic ones. The psychological stages transfused all aspect of life, and therefore Lamprecht attempted a complete German history in all its political, economic, social and cultural manifestations throughout the conventional three ages, which spanned two millennia. He chose German history as the case that could best be documented, from the Roman sources onward, but in later years he also studied the sequence of art styles in Chinese history in support of the universal applicability of his *Kulturzeitalter*.

In contrast to Lamprecht, Breysig recognized three ages (Antiquity, medieval and modern times) as the developmental pattern of world history. Although most peoples did not develop through all stages, he thought the most successful had done so. Apart from this overall scheme Breysig presented twenty-four historical laws in *The Stages and Laws of World History* (1905). Differing from Lamprecht's preoccupation with German history, he drew on ethnographic and historical data from all over the globe. His most ambitious enterprises were the 1,600 pages of *The Cultural History of Modern Times*, subtitled: *A Comparative Developmental History of the Leading European Peoples and of Their Social and*

Intellectual Life (1900–01), and the 1,800 pages of *The History of Mankind* (1907–55), the last two volumes of which appeared posthumously; the first one dealt with the 'peoples of primeval eternity', a study of the American Northwest and Northern Indians (1900, 1907). As early as 1896 Breysig planned a book that anticipated in some respects Weber's studies in the economic ethics of the world religions and parts of *Economy and Society*. In March of that year he sketched in his diary a programme combining sociology and universal history, the 'systematic cross-cut and the historical longitudinal section' (1962, pp. 91 ff.).

In contrast to Lamprecht and Breysig, Werner Sombart was for a time one of Weber's allies. He was first and foremost a historian of modern capitalism and a critic of modernity. His first programmatic statement appeared in 1893 in the introduction to 'Studies on the Developmental History of the Italian Proletariat'. In 1905 followed 'Studies on the Developmental History of the North American Proletariat', which became famous under the later title 'Why Is There No Socialism in the United States?' In 1913 he began publishing his 'Studies on the Developmental History of Modern Capitalism' with *Luxury and Capitalism* and *War and Capitalism*.[4] Sombart enlarged the scope of comparative research by including 'undeveloped areas as long as they belong to the same culture' (*Kulturkreis*). Just as the biologist studies the lowest organism in order to clarify the basic features of the Darwinian theory of evolution, 'so the sociologist will prefer to turn to those countries in which social development – let us say right away: capitalism – is just beginning' (Sombart, 1893, pp. 177 ff.). Sombart argued that in the search for regularities – the primary task of the economist – observations from more advanced countries could be tested by application to less developed ones. At the same time the exemplary influence of an advanced country on a less developed one could be studied. For Sombart the most important scientific problem was the relation between ideas and the facts of economic and social development. He made a striking suggestion; in the advanced countries it is easier to see how social and economic facts influence the shape of ideas, whereas in follower countries 'the impact of dominant ideas on the actual development' can be more clearly seen. Sombart had in mind especially the relation between capitalism as a social system and proletarian socialism as a system of ideas. He advanced a theory of developmental history that contrasts the national peculiarities of a people with the typical elements of capitalist development.

It is characteristic of the work of Lamprecht, Breysig and Sombart that it claimed to be scientific in a threefold sense: (1) it was meant to be purely empirical, not a philosophy of history; (2) it was for this reason value-neutral; and (3) it was theoretical, imposing lawful order on the flow of events. Weber's thinking was in part a critical response to these three very successful, if highly controversial proponents of developmental history. He ignored the 'national' historiographers' poor opinion of them, but observed the vigorous critique advanced by economic and 'universal' historians of the calibre of Georg von Below (1858–1927) and Eduard Meyer (1855–1930). This critique was in part directed also against the economic stage theories that were the core of economic historism.

Among Weber's contemporaries, Sombart and Karl Bücher (1847–1930) endeavoured to improve on the older stage theories that filled the textbooks in economics, ranging from those of Friedrich List, Karl Rodbertus, Bruno Hildenbrand and even Marx and Engels to those of Gustav Schönberg, Gustav Schmoller, Richard Hildebrand and Adolph Wagner. In 1894 Bücher first presented his very popular scheme of a sequence from the closed household to the urban economy and national economy (1894); in 1899 Sombart proposed his own scheme of a movement from individual economy through transitional economy to social economy (1899, pp. 368, 405). Both Bücher and Sombart emphasized that they were dealing with logical stages, not historical periodization, but this did not save them from Below's and Meyer's severe strictures.

Eduard Meyer was no less critical of Bücher and Sombart than of Lamprecht and Breysig, against whom he wrote 'On the Theory and Method of History' (1902).[5] It was this essay to which Weber devoted the first half of his 'Critical Studies on the Logic of *Kulturwissenschaft*' (1906), the second part of which stated his views on historical causality in terms of 'objective possibility' and 'adequate causation'. Previously, Weber had treated the problems of historical economics in his essay on Roscher and Knies, the older representatives of developmental history, and there he had also shown his disdain for Lamprecht, which was echoed again in the Ostwald critique of 1909 (WL, p. 417). Breysig did not fare much better in the essay on Eduard Meyer. Weber accused Lamprecht of equating causality with the operation of laws, of reifying the nation in the form of a social psychological entity and of hiding philosophical assumptions behind the false exactness of allegedly psychological categories; he took Breysig to task for confusing the difference between historical causality (*historischer Realgrund*) and cognitive ground (*Erkenntnisgrund*) and for sharing the error of some 'modern' historians that historical particularity and uniqueness can be identified by first establishing what is common in historical developments (R&K, pp. 105, 111, 214, 224; MSS, pp. 129, 133).

This, then, was an important part of the setting for Weber's approach to developmental history. His critique was advanced in his methodological writings, which to a significant extent addressed the old and new developmental history. Many scholars have pointed out that Weber's alternative, advanced in the substantive writings, involved the substitution of metaphysical and positivist laws with historical typologies and theoretically constructed stages. It is less well known that Weber offered his solution within the established mode of intellectual organization of knowledge in economics and *Staatswissenschaft*. Unlike Lamprecht and Breysig, Weber stayed close to the systematic handbook and textbook tradition in economics and public administration, then an important part of a scholar's legitimation. Weber's 'doctor father', Levin Goldschmidt, had bridged the legal and economic textbook literature with his three-volume *Handbook of Commercial Law*, the first volume of which comprised a 'universal history of commercial law' (3rd rev. ed. 1891). The older generation of historical economists (Roscher, Knies, Rausch) had written texts that remained influential for a long time, and the leader of the younger school of historical economics, Gustav Schmoller, presented his evolutionary views in his famous *Grundriss der Volkswirtschaftslehre* (1900–4). In between appeared Gustav Schönberg's *Handbook of Political Economy* (1882, 4th ed. 1897), which Weber encountered as a student and was destined to affect the composition of *Economy and Society*.[6] In 1909 Weber took over the editorship of a new *Handbook of Political Economy*, which was intended to replace Schönberg's opus and was finally named *Grundriss der Sozialökonomik*. The *Grundriss* was a very ambitious effort to change the whole field of economics broadly understood. It aimed at treating 'the development (*Entfaltung*) of the economy above all as part of the general rationalization of life (VII) and at elucidating the operation of capitalism, in all its complexity, within the modern state.[7] Weber's own massive contribution, 'The Economy and the Normative and de facto Powers', known today as *Economy and Society*, became the mature statement of his developmental history and historical sociology. It was preceded by a political stage theory in another handbook 'article', the 288 pages on 'Agrarian Conditions in Antiquity' for the famous third edition of the *Handwörterbuch der Staatswissenschaften* (Weber, 1976). In emulating this handbook and textbook tradition Weber too tried to legitimate himself as a major contributor to a synthetic effort.

Weber's Disaggregation of Developmental History

Instead of retaining a unitary conception – historical entities following laws of development in lawful stages – Weber in effect disaggregated developmental history into several parts or dimensions. Writing in a formal, impersonal handbook and textbook style, he did not use the author's voice to explain the reasons for his dissatisfactions with the modes of developmental history. He simply presented his alternative. It was, however, not only multi-dimensional but also ambiguous. I recognize four dimensions in Weber's alternative, which I will label (1) general socio-cultural evolution with theoretically constructed stages; (2) specific developmental histories as special cases of rationalization; (3) the specific historical explanation of Mediterranean and European history; and (4) historical sociology: socio-historical models and rules of experience. In the textual exposition of *Economy and Society*, especially its older part (II), these dimensions overlap and cannot always be successfully disentangled, but they can be separated analytically. I will pay more attention to the first and second dimension than to the other two dimensions, which present less difficulty and are more familiar. I will restore Weber's terminology of *Entwicklungsgeschichte* and *Eigengesetzlichkeit* in the English translations, even if some awkwardness cannot be avoided.

General Socio-Cultural Evolution and Rationalization In the absence of 'objective' laws, the general 'development of culture' (WuG, p. 226; ES, p. 375), as Weber called it, must be reconstructed through a 'subjective' interest. Modern people have an inherent interest in how the components of a complex modern society – law, religion, economy, polity – came into being over many centuries. The 'most general developmental features' (WuG, p. 505; ES, p. 883 omitted) of these spheres can be ordered into 'theoretical stages of development' (WuG, p. 504; ES, p. 882) from a given vantage-point, such as 'the general rationalization of life' (WuG, p. 250; ES, p. 407). In *Economy and Society* Weber constructed, for all four spheres, stages that transcended the Western *Kulturkreis* (civilization) but were oriented, in one way or another, towards the problem of rationalization.

For the field of law, Weber drew up the following scheme of rationalization:

> Divided into theoretic 'developmental stages', the general development of law and procedure may be viewed as passing through these stages . . . arising in primitive legal procedure from a combination of magically conditioned formalism and irrationality conditioned by revelation, [the formal qualities of the law] proceed to increasingly specialized juridical and logical rationality and systematization, sometimes passing through the detour of theocratically or patrimonially conditioned substantive and informal expediency. Finally, they assume, at least from an external viewpoint, an increasingly logical sublimation and deductive rigor and develop an increasingly rational technique in procedure.
>
> (WuG, p. 504; ES, p. 882)

Weber cautioned the reader that he was 'here only concerned with the most general lines of development' and hence ignored 'the fact that in

81

historical reality the theoretically constructed stages of rationality have not everywhere followed in the sequence which we have just outlined, nor have they occurred everywhere, even in the Occident' (WuG, p. 505; ES, p. 882). But as was true of the older evolutionist theories, his scheme remained here Euro-centric, since law had reached its highest degree of rationalization only in nineteenth-century Europe. Weber reminded the reader, however, that law 'can be rationalized in various ways and by no means necessarily in the direction of the development of its "juristic" qualities' (WuG, p. 456; ES, p. 776).

In contrast to law, highly rationalized religion was for Weber not a constitutive part of modernity. Significant religious rationalization had occurred in both Asia and Europe. All religions had begun with and retained a 'sober rational' motive in warding off this-worldly evil, but this quality was transcended by a 'specific developmental process of a peculiarly dualist kind. On the one hand, the idea of god was increasingly rationalized ... on the other, the original practical rationalism receded' (WuG, p. 259; ES, p. 424). Nowhere did Weber come closer to the older evolutionary stage theories than in the early sections of his chapter on religion in *Economy and Society*; religion emerged out of magic and passed through the stages of local and functional deities and political gods before achieving the level of the ethical world religions. Several times Weber made judgements about what was of primary or of secondary importance for developmental history (cf. WuG, p. 246; ES, p. 402; see also FMW, p. 327). But he diverged from the older evolutionism by analysing the ways in which the world religions reached a high degree of rationalization in different times and places. Thus, the most consistent rational solutions to the problem of theodicy were found in Zoroastrianism, Buddhism and Calvinism. Only the latter was the end-point of a long religious strand of rationalization that paradoxically helped bring the modern secular world into being.

In the economic realm, too, Weber took off from older theories of social differentiation. In treating the 'evolution of the household' – one of the few times Weber used the term 'evolution' (WuG, p. 230; ES, p. 381) – he described the bifurcation of the household into enterprise and *oikos*. In the fullness of time both evolved into modernity. The development of the enterprise culminated in the large-scale and bureaucratized capitalist enterprise. The *oikos* developed into patrimonialism and ultimately into the bureaucratic public administration of the modern state.

In his evolutionary scheme of domination Weber traced the progression not only from patriarchalism through patrimonialism to the modern state, but also from the multiple holders of legitimate authority to the monopolization of the legitimate use of force within a defined territory. Traditional and charismatic domination originated in the very 'early past'

(WL, p. 483; Weber, 1961, pp. 11–12). Even enacted or imposed domination (*gesatzte Herrschaft*) – usually translated as 'legal-rational' – was not completely absent in early history, just as traditional domination and charismatic domination have persisted into modernity: 'Charisma is found by no means only at primitive stages of development, just as the three types of domination cannot simply be put into a line of development. They in fact appear together in the most diverse combinations.' Charisma has been ubiquitous: 'Exercised by prophets and military leaders of all periods, it has persisted through the centuries' (WuG, pp. 669–70; ES, p. 1133). But in the course of its depersonalization and intellectualization, 'the last [developmental] form that charisma assumed in its fateful course [was] the charismatic glorification of reason' in the eighteenth century (WuG, p. 726; ES, p. 1209). Correspondingly, modern democracy was the product of an anti-authoritarian transformation of charisma into the principle and practice of popular sovereignty. Here again the interests in the nature of political modernity shaped the theoretically constructed 'evolutionary' schemes.

General socio-cultural development was propelled by rising needs and expectations, which lead to the emergence of the various value and institutional spheres. The more these spheres followed a logic and 'law of their own' (*Eigengesetzlichkeit*), the greater the historical dynamics because of the tensions arising among them. In particular, the more religion was ethically systematized and the more the secular spheres developed in their own spirit, the more did religion constitute 'a strong dynamic component of development' (WuG, p. 350; ES, p. 579).[8]

If developmental stages are theoretical constructs, the notion of *Eigengesetzlichkeit*, which has been obscured in most translations as a technical term, is an explanatory device. Weber adopted it in large part for the sake of his positive critique of historical materialism and its monocausal assumptions: 'We shall see time and again that the structural forms of social action have an *Eigengesetzlichkeit*. In a given case, they can always be codetermined by other than economic causes' (WuG, p. 201; ES, p. 341). The autonomy of the market is juxtaposed with the 'very pronounced autonomy of the religious sphere' (WuG, p. 264; ES, p. 433). 'The rationalization of the religious sphere has an autonomy in relation to which economic conditions can only act as "developmental paths"' (WuG, p. 704; ES, p. 1179). Here the connection between the concepts of *Eigengesetzlichkeit* and rationalization is clear. 'Autonomy' has a directional logic. Its consistency is partly cause and partly product of rationalization.

For Weber, then, as for his peers, the general development of culture from relatively undifferentiated conditions (WuG, p. 219; ES, p. 365) to the level of the *Kulturvölker*, the major civilizations, was the basic framework for his analysis. General socio-cultural evolution amounted to rationalization. The resulting social differentiation created spheres with a rationalized 'autonomy'. In turn, the world-views and institutions arising within these spheres had a developmental history of their own. This brings me to a more restrictive sense in which Weber employs the concept of developmental history. This usage, too, was not particular to him, but well established at the time, especially among constitutional historians.[9]

Specific Developmental Histories: Special Cases of Rationalization   Developmental history in the restricted sense is not identical with the natural history of a 'historical individual', which has a beginning and an end. A rationalized world-view or organization may remain 'fully developed' long after it has achieved its characteristic articulation or configuration. In principle, every historical structure has a developmental history in so far as it develops from some beginning into a distinct configuration. Of course, many historical developments prove abortive. But if the circumstances permit a structure to follow its directional logic to a culminating point, the stage of full development has been reached. Thus, Weber can speak of the 'full development' (*Vollentwicklung*) of symbolism (WuG, p. 249; ES, p. 406) or of the ancient Israelite city (AJ, p. 20) and of the ancient and medieval city (WuG, p. 744; ES, p. 1241) no less than the *Vollentwicklung* of legal domination in modern times (cf. FMW, p. 295) and 'fully developed modern bureaucracy' (*moderne Vollbürokratisierung*) or the fully developed political community.[10] He can refer to 'an historically important special case, the developmental history of early church authority', which Rudolf Sohm unintentionally elaborated into a sociological type of charismatic domination (WuG, p. 655; ES, p. 1112), and also write of the developmental history of the modern state and of modern *Hochkapitalismus*.

In view of Weber's interests in the distinctiveness of Western rationalism it makes sense that he pays particular attention to the great rationalized institutions of church, state and capitalism. As far as I can see, he indeed uses the noun 'developmental history' mainly in regard to these three 'autonomous' phenomena. Since the autonomy of religion depends largely on the degree of its organizational independence (cf. WuG, p. 700; ES,p. 1174), Catholicism and Calvinism are the two outstanding positive cases. The Catholic Church has persisted over many centuries as a continuous organization, reaching its full hierocratic development as early as the days of Innocent III and John XXII in the thirteenth and fourteenth centuries with an independent system of officials and taxation (WuG, p. 271; ES, p. 298). The church was the first successful Western bureaucracy, followed only much later by the modern state and the modern enterprise. For Weber the developmental history of the modern state is identical with the history of modern officialdom and the bureaucratic office, just as the whole developmental history of modern *Hochkapitalismus* is identical with the increasing bureaucratization of the economic enterprises. Everywhere the bureaucratic forms of domination are in the ascendancy.   (WL, p. 477; Weber, 1961, p. 6; see also ES, p. 224)

Most specific developmental histories belong to the past, but some are part and parcel of modernity. Since they are not historically completed, they are open to projection and tempt the observer, who in this case can also be an historical actor, to make hazardous predictions. If the 'developmental chances' (WuG, p. 578; ES, p. 1002) of a historical phenomenon depend on the interplay of economic and political conditions with its *Eigengesetzlichkeit*, a situational analysis can lead to the prognosis that there is strong likelihood of further development, although not any historical inevitability. Confident of their grasp of a specific developmental dynamic, both Weber and Sombart sometimes made historical extrapolations that were disproven by the course of events. When Sombart asked his famous question, 'Why is there no socialism in the United States?' he concluded that all the retarding factors are 'at the point of disappearing or of being turned into their opposite, so that socialism will in all probability reach its full flowering in the next generation' (Sombart, 1906, p. 142). Thus, he did not really invent the theory of American exceptionalism that has been attributed to him and has since become popular among United States historians and social scientists. Weber turned out to be wrong about the future of US party organization, which has not become bureaucratized. In general, however, he was correct in his belief that 'a bureaucracy of the European kind would inescapably arise' in the United States because 'purely technical, irrefragable needs of administration determine this development' (ES, p. 1398; FMW, p. 88; Roth, 1985, pp. 215–33). He recognized that as a frontier society – subject to a set of generalizations of its own – 'the United States still bears the character of a polity that, at least in the technical sense, is not fully bureaucratized. But the greater the zones of friction with the outside and the more urgent the needs of administrative unity at home become, the more this character is inevitably and gradually giving way formally to the bureaucratic structure' (ES, p. 971). The key word is 'formal'. When Weber states that 'everywhere the bureaucratic *forms* of domination are in the ascendancy', he does not assert that the *power* of bureaucracies is increasing everywhere.

Development and Devolution in Mediterranean–European History In contrast to the levels of socio-cultural evolution and specific developmental history, we find development and devolution intersecting on the 'purely historical' level of analysis. Here the developmental category of rationalization is largely absent. Weber did not construct typologies or models of disintegration and of declining rationality parallel to rationalization. Instead the actual rise and decline of historical entities came into view. As against the unilinear and cyclical interpretations of history Weber held that 'the continuum of Mediterranean–European *Kulturentwicklung* has up until now known neither completed "cycles" nor an unambiguously "unilinear" development. Elements of antiquity which had disappeared completely re-emerged later in a world alien to them.' The same phenomena could be viewed as part of an evolution or of a devolution. Thus, we find purely historical judgements such as the following: 'The cities of late antiquity, especially the Hellenist ones, and the manorial estates of the period were preliminary stages (*Vorstufen*) of the Middle Ages, the former in the realm of artisan production (*Gewerbe*), the latter in the agrarian sphere' (Weber, 1976, p. 366). Conversely, Occidental feudalism appeared to Weber as a 'product of disintegration' (*Verfallsprodukt*) of a patrimonial world empire. At the same time Greece and Rome showed more typological affinity with 'our Middle Ages' than with the irrigation cultures and urban centres of the Near East.

In so far as Weber treated Western history as a continuous whole, he limited himself to enumerating the distinctive historical factors within the multi-dimensional structure of *Economy and Society* and of 'The Economic Ethics of the World Religions'. This particular historical dimension is indicated by the many sentences (in both works) that contain the phrase 'only in the Occident', which often becomes a refrain. For example, after outlining his stages of legal rationalization – the general 'evolutionary' dimension mentioned above – Weber lists phenomena unique to the West:

> Only the Occident has witnessed the fully developed justice of the folk-community (*Dinggenossenschaft*) and the status-stereotyped form of patrimonialism; only the Occident has witnessed the rise of the rational economy, whose agents first allied themselves with the princely powers to overcome the estates and then turned against them in revolution; and only the West has known 'natural law' . . . Nowhere else, finally, has there occurred any phenomenon resembling Roman law and anything like its reception.

In Weber's eyes, these phenomena had 'to a very significant extent concrete political causes' rather than economic ones, and the very presence in Europe and absence elsewhere in the world of these causes 'explained' that the evolutionary 'stage of law characterized by the existence of specialized legal training had been fully reached only in the

Occident' (WuG, p. 505; ES, p. 883). Weber tended, however, to couch even his specific historical explanations in typological terms. This brings me to his historical sociology proper.

Historical Sociology: Socio-Historical Models and Rules of Experience In 'Agrarian Conditions in Antiquity' Weber offered not only an economic theory but also a politico-military typology that provided a longitudinal scheme at the same time that it permitted comparisons within the ancient realm. This typology was a first systematic effort, within a bifurcated sequence of stages, to treat patrimonialism, feudalism, charisma (as military communism), hierocracy and the independent city.[11] In *Economy and Society* and 'The Economic Ethics of the World Religions' Weber added to the developmental and historical dimensions his historical sociology proper; now systematic concept formation, socio-historical model-building and historical generalization become prominent and sometimes dominant, although the general historical theme of the distinctiveness and uniqueness of Western rationalism emerges more clearly than before as the underlying interest. Next to developmental stages appear logical stages, as when we read: 'The prophet is connected through transitional stages with the ethical teacher' (WuG, p. 271; ES, p. 444); or 'There are "stages" in the qualitative distinctiveness of the belief in belonging to a "national" community' (WuG, p. 242; ES, p. 395). At the same time historical judgements such that the *oikos* reappeared as a 'developmental product of late antiquity' (Weber, 1976, p. 46) are supplemented by the generalization that 'bureaucracy is everywhere a late product of development' (WuG, pp. 567, 578; ES, pp. 983, 1002), in Antiquity no less than modern times. To this generalization is added the rule of experience – sometimes misinterpreted in the literature – that 'a fully developed (*durchgeführte*) bureaucracy belongs to the social formations that are most difficult to destroy', a rule that also includes hierocracy (WuG, p. 569; ES, p. 987).

Weber's decision to look beyond the developmental history of Europe towards Russia, China, India and Islam for comparative illumination required that he elaborate a terminology and typology that would be applicable to all these different civilizations over two and a half millennia.[12] Historical sociology came into its own as the conceptual apparatus for comparative study.

Rationalization and Post-Modernity

Rationalization has been a constituent part of socio-cultural evolution, if not its core. The differentiation into value and institutional spheres began with the earliest development of ethical religion and with the earliest 'general rationalization of life'. For Weber history is unpredictable not only because there are no laws in the naturalist sense or because of the endless clash of human wills, but because developmental histories can overlap with, or counteract, one another. The history of Western rationalism was a history of various 'factors' coming together in an unlikely but reinforcing concatenation.

Modernity, then, is an era in which several lines of rationalization have met. But just as the past was not predetermined, so the future remains open. Bureaucratization does not obey an 'iron law' of the kind proposed by Weber's friend Robert Michels, who was another proponent of a 'scientific' developmental history. Much confusion about Weber's theory of modernity could have been avoided if the dialectical nature of his perception of bureaucratization and democratization had been properly understood. It is true that Weber guessed wrong about the bureaucratization of the United States party system, but this does not vitiate his reminder: 'It must remain an open question whether the power of bureaucracy is increasing in the modern states in which it is spreading . . . Hence, one must in every historical case analyze in which particular direction bureaucratization has developed' (WuG, p. 572; ES, p. 991).

Statements such as these indicate clearly that Weber was no developmental determinist or cultural pessimist, who assumed the inevitability of decline. He did not consider bureaucratic rationalization to lead inexorably into an iron cage, although he liked to warn of the dangers of 'Egyptianization'. In fact, his political struggle for democratization was based on the belief that it was possible to take 'responsibility before history'.[13] Political analysis involves the identification of 'developmental tendencies' in a given situation, but they have no prescriptive value; there is an 'absolute logical disparity between developmental prognosis and what we ought to do' (Weber, 1977, p. 85). When Weber studied the 'developmental tendencies' in the conditions of the East Elbian rural workforce, he dealt with an aspect of the developmental history of modern agrarian capitalism, but his proposed political solution ran counter to its developmental trends. He wanted to prevent the spread of agrarian capitalism and the influx of Polish labour through a state-supported settlement programme for German peasants. When Weber scrutinized the first Russian Revolution in 1905 he declared that 'we individualists and partisans of democratic institutions are swimming against the stream of material constellations. Whoever desires to be the weather vane of a developmental tendency may abandon those old-fashioned ideals as quickly as possible' (WS, p. 282).

The very fact that Weber disaggregated developmental history into evolutionary, historical and typological dimensions gives his work continued applicability in a historical reality that itself is multi-dimensional and multi-directional. On a worldwide scale, modernity has become just one element in a mix of historical forces. Tradition and modernity are being amalgamated in various ways that open new directions of rationalization. Weber's typologies can help us study the new combinations at the same time that we can look for new developmental histories. For Weber, the 'charisma of reason' was the logical end-point of the developmental history of charisma. It was its last form. Ever since, the various kinds of charisma, which can be ordered into a typological scheme, have continued to compete with one another, magical, institutional, personal and ideational. The question, then, becomes: which *kinds* of charisma and rationalization will shape the 'post-modern' world?[14]

At the end of his essay on 'objectivity' in the social sciences Weber pointed to the historical moments when routinized research becomes disrupted: 'The significance of the unreflectively utilized viewpoints becomes uncertain and the road is lost in the twilight. The light beam of the great cultural problems moves on. Then science too prepares to change its standpoint and its conceptual apparatus' (MSS, p. 112). We must assume that at some point the utility of Weber's work will be exhausted in the face of new analytical interests and historical problems. In my view, this point has not yet been reached. I believe that one major intrinsic reason is the very manner in which Weber struggled to come to terms with the complexities of developmental history. He tried hard to avoid the weaknesses and errors of his teachers and peers. Above all, he kept his distance from both the nomothetic and the idiographic approach – the latter, Heinrich Rickert recalled Weber saying, too easily invited an aesthetic contemplation of history. He did not want to write narratively in the manner of the political historiographers, nor did he venture to describe the flow of history as a continuous psychological process in Lamprecht's mode; he neither searched for empirical stages and laws of world history in Breysig's sense or looked for a viable meaning of Western history in a cultural synthesis, as Ernst Troeltsch and Alfred Weber endeavoured to do. Instead, he linked developmental history and historical sociology in an intricate fashion, in a combination of horizontal and vertical typologies that could be applied everywhere. The older developmental history of Weber's day had been basically philosophical; the new developmental history of his peers imitated the natural sciences. But the harder Lamprecht and Breysig strained to be 'scientific', the more idiosyncratic they became. Although Weber's combative temper made him disdain any notion of the scholarly virtue of taking the middle ground, this is what he in fact provided in the great methodological controversies of the time. The other combatants have been well-nigh forgotten together with their works, but Weber's position has been well established among those who hold that there are no naturalist laws but that developmental sequences and structural ideal types can be formulated.

In my judgement, Weber's *oeuvre* became fruitful for posterity not only because it was a path-breaking and pioneering contribution, but also because it took a relatively common-sensical and well-balanced stance that eschewed the inordinate ambitions and grand designs of his elders and contemporaries. Weber was, however, not shy about his achievement. He knew that with the first manuscript of *Economy and Society* he had brought off an innovation: 'Since Bücher's treatment of the "developmental stages" is totally inadequate, I have worked out a complete theory and exposition that relates the major social groups to the economy ... I can claim that nothing of the kind has ever been written, not even as a precursor.'[15] But if he had written more of a grand developmental history in just one key, he might have ended up looking as idiosyncratic as Lamprecht, Breysig, Spengler and Toynbee appear to us today. Although *Economy and Society* and 'The Economic Ethics of the World Religions' are as unreadably long as the works of these other historians, they have lent themselves, through their very openness, to manifold scholarly uses. Weber offered us a fragmentary theory of modernity from the viewpoint of his evolutionary theory of rationalization and his specific developmental histories. The socio-historical models were meant to facilitate the comparative study of world history in search of the distinctiveness of Western rationalism. All of these dimensions should be kept in mind even if we want to utilize only parts of the work. Otherwise the piecemeal uses of Weber's *oeuvre* will suffer from ignorance of the whole, as has happened so often before. As a historical synthesis the whole of Weber's work remains larger than the sum of its parts, in spite of their uneasy combination.

Notes

1 FWM, p. 162. This passage has often been misread. Weber does not speak 'from precisely the standpoint that hates intellectualism as the worst devil, as youth does today'; he affirms the value of science 'as against' the standpoint that hates intellectualism.

2 For the *Grundriss der Sozialökonomik* Weber had originally intended to write also on contemporary issues of capitalist society. The 1910 projected table of content listed the following themes later taken on by other contributors: checks and set-backs to capitalist development; the internal transformation of capitalism; the social impact of monopolistic and bureaucratic tendencies; the nature and social conditions of the proletariat; the so-called new middle classes; the modern state and capitalism; the general significance of modern mass communication for the capitalist economy; agrarian capitalism and

social structure; the limits of agrarian capitalism; internal colonization; and even economy and race. See 'Handbuch der politischen Oekonomie: Stoff-verteilungsplan' (Tübingen: Mohr, 1910). If Weber had written in this vein, the theme of capitalist development and the nature of modernity would have been emphasized much more strongly than it is in *Economy and Society* (as we know it).

3 See Reinhard Bendix (1984) and my review essay in *History and Theory*, vol. 24, no. 2, 1985; Talcott Parsons (1966); Wolfgang Schluchter (1981); Jürgen Habermas (1984).

4 Werner Sombart (1893, pp. 177–258; 1906; 1913).

5 Eduard Meyer (1910, pp. 86 ff.). See also Georg von Below (1926, pp. 226–7).

6 Gustav Schmoller (1900, Vol. I; 1904, Vol. II); Gustav Schönberg, ed. (1897). Carl Brinkmann once explained the novelty of Schönberg's handbook: 'Gustav Schönberg felt that the time for a mere updating of texts, such as Rausch's text by Adolf Wagner (1872, 2nd ed. 1876) was over. Therefore he published, from Tübingen, his *Handbook of Political Economy*, which imitated the legal textbooks – remember that Eugen von Philippovich's well-known *Grudriß der politischen Oekonomie* (1893) appeared first as part of Marquard-sen's *Handbook of Public Law*. Schönberg collected contributions from younger scholars on the various fields of economics, including the neigh-bouring disciplines of *Staatswissenschaft* and *Staatslehre*. As a type, the new handbook stood in between the older English and French works on economic "principles" and the older German *Staatswörterbuch'* (Brinkmann, 1937, p. 125).

7 'Vorwort' to *Grundriß der Sozialökonomik*, I, Abteilung: *Wirtschaft und Wirt-schafswissenschaft* (Tübingen: Mohr, 1914), p. VII.

8 'A large and *entwicklungsgeschichtlich* particularly important number of pro-phetic and redemptory religions have lived not only in an acute but in a permanent state of tension with the world and its orders' (FMW, p. 328).

9 See Fritz Kern, *Kingship and Law in the Middle Ages* (1970), first published 1914.

10 For 'fully developed modern bureaucracy' see WuG, p. 577; ES, p. 999. Cf. WuG, pp. 551, 563; ES, p. 956, 975. On the 'fully developed political community' see WuG, p. 516; ES, p. 904.

11 See my introduction to *Economy and Society*, pp. XLIV–LI, and Stefan Breuer (1982, pp. 174–92).

12 On the larger purposes of *Economy and Society*, see now also Stephen Kalberg, 'Max Weber's Universal-Historical Architectonic of Economically-Oriented Action: A Preliminary Reconstruction' (1983, pp. 253–88).

13 On Weber's concept of 'our responsibility before history', see my essay, 'Max Weber's Ethics and the Peace Movement Today' (Roth, 1984, pp. 491–511).

14 See my essay, 'Charisma and the Counterculture' (Roth and Schluchter, 1979, pp. 119–43).

15 See my introduction to Schluchter (1979).

4

Weber's Sociology of Rationalism and Typology of Religious Rejections of the World

WOLFGANG SCHLUCHTER

Translated by Ralph Schroeder

Forsaking all attachment to the fruit of action, always contented, dependent on none, he does nothing at all, though he engages in action.

(*Bhagavad Gita*, IV, 20)

How can you learn to know yourself? Not by observing – but by acting. Attempt to do your duty and you will soon come to know who you are.
(Goethe, *Wilhelm Meisters Wanderjahre*, Book Two, chapter 11)

Max Weber's sociology as a whole, and his sociology of religion in particular, does not aim to formulate a theory of rationality. Instead it represents a typology of religious rationalism considered from the perspective of his developmental history. This can be gathered from the 'Introduction' (to 'The Economic Ethics of the World Religions') and the 'Intermediate Reflections', among other texts. However, before considering Weber's typology of rationalism and the different ways and forms through which it has had an impact on the processes of historical development, we shall first turn, briefly, to an apparently separate text that is paradigmatic of the general relation between rationalism and the world. This text is the 'Sociology of Music', which originates from the period 1910–13.

Here Weber tries to uncover the unique conditions for the development of Occidental music. More specifically he asks:

Why did polyphonic and harmonic-homophonic music, as well as the modern tonal system, only develop in the Occident, in spite of the fact that polyvocality was fairly widespread? Why only here, and not in areas where music had been developed equally strongly – notably in Hellenic Antiquity and Japan?

(MUS, p. 83)

As is well known, Weber inquired into the specific pre-conditions for both the material and the ideal culture of the Occidental world.

As in most of his other writings, in the 'Sociology of Music' Weber divides these pre-conditions up into their 'rational', technical and social components. The 'rational' component is concerned with musical theory, whereas the technical and social factors relate to the practice of music in the widest possible sense. The development of Western music is based on a theory of music that makes use of the principles of harmony and tonality in the creation and use of notes. Everywhere else, the principle of melodic distance, which is inimical to harmony, is the most widely used. Western musical theory thus led to the development of a harmonic chord system which took the form of a 'rationally closed unity' (MUS, p. 6). Upon closer inspection, however, this rationally closed unity turns out to be a frail one. The demand for consistency that is made by musical theory simply cannot be fulfilled. This becomes the more evident, the more the theory of music tries to oblige the logic of consistency. In this manner, 'unavoidable irrationalities' come to the surface that break this rationally closed unity apart. Such breaks, in turn, can trigger new processes of rationalization. Hence the significance of these breaks for the dynamic of development.

The harmonic chord system underwent precisely this type of process. This system was inherently bound to come up against several 'irrational' obstacles. Overcoming these obstacles served to produce a 'greater variety of tonalities'.[1] The starting-point of this development was the fact that in music which was rationalized according to harmonic chords, the octave had to be physically divided up into unequal tonal steps. The result was the creation of notes and semi-tones that were different from each other. These unequal tonal steps were due to a strict application of the 'harmonic' principle of division. This situation might have remained as it was, were it not for the fact that this division led directly to other difficulties and to the 'infringement' of other 'demands' in the theory of music. One difficulty, for example, arose when the 'natural' leading note of the major scale had to be created 'artificially' for the minor scale in order to produce a dominant seventh chord for this particular key. This was achieved by raising the seventh note (transition from a pure to a harmonic major). Yet this, in turn, led to a further problem; the tonal steps adjacent to this key became too large to satisfy harmonic sensibilities. The problem was solved by a reduction of these tonal steps (melodic minor). Meeting the demands of the major scale with this construction thus 'forcibly' led to a deviation from the pure principle of harmony. A further difficulty arose because the unequal size of the tonal steps made the transposition of harmonies more difficult. Additional problems were created through these developments for the technology of instrument production, particularly with regard to keyboard instruments. Such difficulties could be avoided in systems of music that were based on the principle of melodic distance. But while the latter could, for example, facilitate transposition, they could not produce consonant chords.

These and other tensions edged the Occidental theory of music along a path towards temperament. Strictly speaking, however, such temperament means that at least some of the elements of the principle of melodic distances have to be incorporated. Yet this leads to theoretical inconsistencies. On the other hand, this secondary rationalization of the theory of music also creates entirely new possibilities, such as that of dis-harmonious displacement. Weber thinks that 'complete freedom' in Occidental chordal-harmonic music was achieved only with the arrival of temperament (MUS, p. 101). Yet temperance is at the same time a sign of the imperfection of the rationally closed unity of Western music.

What has been illustrated here by means of the development of Occidental music applies equally to teachings and ethics of salvation. The more they follow the demand for consistency, the greater the likelihood that their principles will come into conflict with the realities of life or with other principles. This conflict, in turn, will lead to compromises or to the combination of elements that contradict each other. Such an outcome seems to be an essential characteristic of historical configurations. As Weber says in his 'Introduction':

> Neither religions nor people are open and shut cases. They were historical configurations, and not logical or psychological constructions that were free of contradictions. Often times they harboured a multitude of motives which, if they were all affirmed consistently *and* at the same time, would obstruct each other or even collide head-on. That they were 'consistent' with each other was the exception, not the rule.
> (FMW, p. 291)

Yet for Weber consistency is none the less a 'dictate' of human thought and action. As such, these 'dictates' may have an historical impact, especially for religious virtuosi. That is why the 'rational' reconstruction of religious attitudes is important. They are developed by the observer in the form of ideal types, in order to understand the various attitudes of world-rejection and of conflict with the world. In doing this, the observer's heuristic imposition of order may coincide in substance with the normative orientation of the believer. It has been said that this identity represents a violation of the methodology of the ideal type, or even a Western rationalist prejudice. Neither of these criticisms hits the mark. The substantive coincidence between the heuristic imposed by the observer and the normative orientation of the participant eliminates neither the distinction between the observer and believer, nor that between the ideal type and the ideal. This remains true so long as the observer is still aware of the difference between them and proceeds accordingly; if the ideal type is *not* tacitly made to take the place of the ideal, which has an impact in history, then the coincidence between the two will be given due recognition. It must also be plausibly explained why such an overlap occurs. Either this overlap can be empirically ascertained from one case to the next, or one can assume, as does Weber, that 'what is rational in the sense of the logical or teleological "consistency" of one's intellectual-theoretical or practical-ethical standpoint' exerts at least some degree of 'power over man' (FMW, p. 324). This general assumption may express a rationalist prejudice, but certainly not a Western one. The demand for consistency is finally imposed on everyone by virtue of their participation in cultural life. Only its intensity and the relationship to other 'demands' may vary. Also this method does not predetermine which premises and pre-conditions are recognized as 'valid' by the demand for consistency.

A mere comparison between the principles of harmony and distance in the sociology of music shows that there are always several premises or pre-conditions that the demand for consistency acknowledges as being valid. Accordingly, what is 'rational' or 'irrational' for observer and the believer always depends on the viewpoint that is adopted. This discovery was recognized not only by the 'late' Weber, but is already emphasized in the earliest version of *The Protestant Ethic*.[2] Weber's sociology, and particularly the sociology of religion, is therefore not a theory of rationality as such, but rather a typology of the forms of religious rationalism within the perspective of his developmental history. Such a typology presupposes that reality can assume a variety of rational forms. Yet it is not the purpose of sociology to assert the value of any one of these forms. This is a point that is often overlooked. Perhaps it was this fundamental insight that forced Weber to reassess the status of his schematic and theoretical constructions in the third version of the 'Intermediate Reflections' and to express himself more precisely on this issue. An interesting passage that he added to this essay may be noted in this context. In 1915 he asserted that 'the schema constructed here is, of course, only intended as an ideal-typical *means of orientation*' (italics in original German). In a later version, he added that it is not intended as a philosophy in its own right. The theoretically constructed types of conflict that take place among the 'life orders' (*Lebensordnungen*) are merely supposed to show that inner conflict may be *possible* and 'adequate' in these particular situations. This schema does *not* imply that there is no conceivable standpoint from which these conflicts might not be 'transcended'. It can easily be seen that the various value-spheres have been differentiated here in order to represent a rational unity. They *rarely* appear in this form in reality. Nonetheless, they may appear in this way in reality, and they *have in fact* done so in a manner that has been historically significant.

(FMW, pp. 323–4, italics in original German)

Hence the 'Intermediate Reflections' can be thought of as being at the core of a kind of sociology of world-views after the fashion of Karl Jaspers's *Psychologie der Weltanschauungen*, a work that was strongly influenced by Weber's sociology of religion. None the less, Weber's sociology should not be interpreted as a prophetic type of philosophy.

Weber's systematic standpoint in the 'Intermediate Reflections' is therefore primarily aimed at analysing the types of value-conflict that are possible due to religious rejection of the world. As in music, the salvation religions also fail to arrive at a 'consistent type of rationalism' (FMW, p. 281). In this case, however, the conflict of values is a manifestation of the simultaneity of the creation and destruction of values. It points to the antinomic structure of human existence with its separation between objective and subjective worlds. The rejection of the world brings this antinomic structure into focus. This does not mean, of course, that a world-affirming standpoint is free of conflicts. But it *does* mean that world-rejecting religions intensify the experience of conflict by comparison with those that affirm the world. Furthermore, an 'existential' problem is created through the rejection of the world that demands a theoretical and practical solution. Such a solution may, for example, demand a certain type of theodicy and a way of life that is governed systematically by a goal of salvation.[3] In terms of this religious solution, Weber sets the religious value-sphere and life order over against the others: the economic, political, aesthetic, erotic and intellectual spheres. Just like the religious sphere, the possible demands of the non-religious spheres of life are also presented as a 'rational unity'. As with the various motives for the rejection of the world, the various religions are presented here merely in order to illustrate different conflicts and their possible solutions. The content, the social setting and especially the practical attempts at overcoming *actual* conflicts are dealt with only in Weber's individual studies of the world religions. Hence in the chapter entitled 'Religious Ethics and the "World"' (WuG, pp. 348–67) Weber describes the religious ethic of conviction in general (as opposed to that of a particular world religion), and in 'Intermediate Reflections' he talks of the ethic of brotherliness in general coming into conflict with the 'world'. Yet this 'world' is divided up into the aforementioned (non-religious) value-spheres and life orders, and hence into the basic ways of life that are bound up with them.[4] These spheres are individually – as opposed to generically – counterposed against the religious postulate. The possible conflicts among the various secular value-spheres and life orders themselves are also omitted here. The paired confrontation between the religious sphere and the worldly spheres is intended to establish both the specific and the general aspects of the conflict between 'religion' and the 'world'. Each (secular) value-sphere and life order takes certain presuppositions and pre-conditions for granted. They tie the actor to specific values and means, which may in turn result in a conflict between his religious ethic and the 'world'. The religious ethic produces the conflict because of its anti-economic, anti-political, anti-aesthetic, anti-erotic and anti-scientific rejections of the world. (Weber also uses this formulation in *Economy and Society*, pp. 581–2.) Yet these various conflicts have a common denominator; the religious demand, particularly if it is made by a salvation religion, is always aimed at just compensation. It demands brotherliness and love from a 'world' that is violent, brutal, egoistic and lacking in compassion.

This is the broader perspective or framework of Weber's sociology. His substantive analyses supplement this framework by showing historically what the ideal and social presuppositions and consequences of the world religions were. It is no accident that the section about 'Religious Ethics and the "World"' was already followed in *Economy and Society* by an (albeit incomplete) section on the 'Cultural Religions and the "World"'. Aside from its scientific or heuristic value, this broader perspective or means of orientation may be valuable in providing practical advice about how to live. The 'understanding' of historically important constellations of conflict and their 'solutions' by means of their reconstruction can in fact (in Weber's terminology) help the man of culture to find the demon who 'holds the different threads of his life together' (FMW, p. 156). It is important, however, that the creation and the choice of this demon cannot be justified by reference to this reconstruction. For such a justification would presuppose an empirical grounding of value-judgements, and this is impossible in Weber's view.

Weber's sociology of religion thus seeks to identify the various basic attitudes to the world that are motivated by religion. He tries to 'explain' how they came about and what kind of effect they have had on the various value-spheres, the life orders and religion itself. In doing this he presupposes that the structure of human existence is such that the demands of a salvation religion – if the demand for consistency is followed – will necessarily lead to an experience of the world as irrational. Indeed, he expressly declared that this type of experience was the driving-force of all religious development (FMW, p. 123). Yet it is not exclusively the fulfilment of the demands of a religion of salvation that leads to such an experience. The *hiatus irrationalis*, which is also the basis of Weber's theory of concept formation, extends beyond the confines of religion alone and it is perhaps *the* fundamental problem in life. From a systematic point of view, every 'rational' demand must come up against two obstacles: the fact that demand and reality do not always coincide, and that man must always also follow demands that are 'non-rational'. He is confronted by demands that follow the inner laws and the inner logic of certain powers over life, which are by their 'very nature non-rational or anti-rational' (FMW, p. 341). Affirmation and rejection of the world can thus be seen as the two basic standpoints that try to overcome the problem of the irrationality of the 'world' both theoretically and practically. Affirmation of the world is content with accepting this world as the best of all possible 'worlds', and it plays down the problem of irrationality. Rejection of the world, on the other hand, cannot accept the imperfection of the 'world', and therefore intensifies the problem of irrationality in theory and in practice. In order to distinguish more clearly between the various forms of this intensification and its effects, it will be necessary to differentiate further between the different attitudes that underlie the various rejections of the world. What can Weber's sociology of religion offer in this regard?

With regard to this question, an interesting shift can be noted in Weber's position between the 'Sociology of Religion' in *Economy and Society* and 'The Economic Ethics of the World Religions'. In *Economy and Society*, Weber mainly uses the concepts of adjustment to the world and flight from the world. These concepts describe the various religious attitudes to the world, and they are employed on the same level. In *Economy and Society*, the contrast between affirmation and rejection of the world (or also between adjustments to and denial of the world), which informs both the description and the systematic intent of 'The Economic Ethics of the World Religions', is not yet applied in this fashion. More-over, the attributions of various fundamental value-positions to the different world religions do not completely overlap in the two versions of this essay. The 'Intermediate Reflections' and the 'Introduction' offer more precise formulations in these terms. This can be demonstrated by looking at the different roles played by the concepts of rejection and affirmation of the world. In *Economy and Society*, for example, Weber speaks of the world-affirmation of Judaism, of accommodation to the world in Islam, of world-flight in ancient Buddhism and of the rejection of the world in early Christianity (ES, pp. 611–30). In 'Intermediate

Reflections' and in the 'Introduction', on the other hand, world-rejection is a term that applies to the attitude of religious élites to the world in *all* religions of salvation.

If the difference between the various attitudes to the world of the religions of salvation is thus to be understood within a schematic framework, the matter cannot rest with the contrast between world-affirmation and world-rejection. Instead, the various possible types of 'contrasts in terms of world-rejection must be more thoroughly distinguished'. This, too, takes place in the 'Intermediate Reflections'.

Asceticism and Contemplation

It may be useful to precede the discussion of this aspect of Weber's writings with some more basic considerations; action is determined by the goal, means, conditions and by the normative standards that are required to co-ordinate these three components of action.[5] This teleological model of action can also be used to analyse the type of action that is required by a religion of salvation. It is a kind of action that seeks to achieve the permanent spiritual state (*status spiritualis*) that is required for salvation. This is achieved by means of the systematic application of a certain salvation technique. The natural state (*status naturalis*), which is the basis for all action, should thus be controlled by religious means.

The issue is therefore what type of influence is exerted on the believer's way of life by the various goals and paths to salvation over and above his natural state (*status naturalis*) – which also includes his social state (*status socialis*). The goals and the means (or paths) to salvation of the salvation religions are particularly important for characterizing the difference between the various forms of world-rejection. These two components of action aimed at religious salvation must now be examined.

Weber did not distinguish strictly enough between paths and means to salvation. This topic is discussed in the section on the 'Typology of Asceticism and Mysticism' in the 'Intermediate Reflections'. This section clearly refers back to the 'Introduction', since the two 'polar concepts' that were introduced there are now defined more closely, and the respective goals of salvation are more clearly distinguished.

Yet the different relations between these and other concepts over the course of Weber's writings is more complex than this. Before a systematic summing up can be attempted, these relations must be further examined. Weber already applied the concepts of 'asceticism' and 'mysticism' in the first version of *The Protestant Ethic*. Here they serve to illustrate a contrast within Protestant religiosity. The contrast is between the non-ascetic Protestantism exemplified by Lutheranism (and especially late Lutheranism) as against Calvinism as an ascetic type of Protestantism. The former consists of finding rest *within* God, a *unio mystica* that is associated with passivity, emotional inwardness and 'adapting' oneself to the orders of the 'world'. The latter consists of proving oneself *before* God and in a systematic search for salvation, both of which are associated with activity, systematic self-control (particularly of the emotions) and the demand to reshape the orders of the world in accordance with God's will by peaceful or violent means (PESC, p. 130).

It can be seen that this description makes use of the polar contrast between 'rationality' and 'emotion', and also between action and beholding or contemplating. The concept of mysticism, however, is defined only residually. Weber is primarily interested in defining the concept of 'asceticism'. This also emerges from the fact that he contrasts Calvinist asceticism with the asceticism of the medieval monk. Both are 'rational', but the former is oriented towards this world, while the latter displays an other-worldly orientation. Inner-worldly asceticism turns towards the world as the place to prove oneself, while the other-worldly path turns away from it in order to transcend it. Weber's point is to distinguish between the different religions' attitudes before and after the Reformation, which exhibit rational and methodical types of action, and to set these off against a religious attitude of non-rational and unmethodical emotionality. The contrast is between active and emotional standpoints. Among other things, Weber describes the emotional attitudes as mystical, but he does not specify what he means by this. This lack of clarity also becomes evident in the course of Weber's replies to his critics where he describes Christian emotionality without making use of the concept of mysticism. Among other things, he says, 'I expressly describe Catholic asceticism as a *rationalised* type of asceticism (most clearly illustrated in the Jesuit order) by *contrast*, for example, with an unmethodical flight from the world (in Catholicism) and a merely emotional "asceticism" (in Protestantism)' (Weber, 1982, p. 155, italics in original).

Inspired by his interest in the Russian Revolution of 1905, however, in which, among other things, he diagnosed the religious situation in Russia, Weber's concept of mysticism became more sophisticated. That, in any case, is the impression one gets from reading about his part in the discussion of Ernst Troeltsch's lecture on 'Stoic-Christian Natural Law and Modern Secular Natural Law' at the first German sociological conference in 1910. At this point he saw the Orthodox Church as being suffused with mysticism. The Orthodox Church is not merely a heterodox movement like the mysticism of Tauler, nor does it display the emotional attitude of late Lutheranism. Like early Christianity, the Orthodox Church represents a *community* bound by love, and one in which the believer devotes or gives himself to others unconditionally. Weber variously describes this devotion as purposeless, acosmistic, a denial of the realities of life, or a holy prostitution of the soul. Hence this attitude contrasts sharply with the Calvinist this-worldly asceticism, which consists of doing good works and is oriented towards *society*. Weber thus distinguishes between a 'cosmistic' rational ethic and an 'acosmistic' emotional love. With this he is adopting Troeltsch's thesis about the two sides of the gospel – its absolute universalism and its absolute individualism – to his own purposes (Troeltsch, 1931, pp. 55–7). The consistent type of cosmistic rational ethic and acosmistic emotional love may, of course, have similar results in Weber's view; the result in the first case may be an unbrotherly egoism, which is occasioned by an exaggerated matter-of-factness. In the second case, there may be an exaggerated brotherly love, which may, for this very reason, turn into self-love. It is important, however, that the concept of mysticism still remains within the framework created by the first version of *The Protestant Ethic* where an ascetic and active attitude is contrasted with a mystical and emotional one. The point is, however, that the active and ascetic attitude, whether its direction is this-worldly or other-worldly, is associated with world-rejection – whereas the attitude of emotional mysticism is associated with an (unmethodical) flight from the world. Yet world-flight also entails a devotion to every human being simply because he happens to be there. Hence Christianity may be classified as offering two extreme positions in this respect: the mystical and acosmistic love of world-fleeing devotion on the one hand, and an ascetic and methodical attitude of good works, which aims to reshape the world, on the other.

It may be surmised that Weber's interpretation of mysticism underwent a significant change through his preoccupation with India. This is because in ancient Buddhism he encountered the phenomenon of a methodical – and hence 'rational' – world-flight. It was a type of world-flight that did not, at the same time, lead to the acosmistic type of love exhibited by Christianity. This study also made it clear to Weber how important it was to distinguish between Christian and non-Christian types of asceticism. Moreover, he realized that if the differences between these historical phenomena were to be accounted for, then the definitions of the concepts of mysticism and asceticism had to be given equal consideration. It also has to be determined whether Weber developed these concepts in an analytical or an historical fashion. It could be said that Weber resolved these two problems satisfactorily only in the 'Intermediate Reflections'. The most important step along this route is the essay entitled 'The Paths to Salvation and Their Influence on the Conduct of Life'. (This title is used in *Wirtschaft und Gesellschaft*, but not in *Economy and Society* where it comprises Chaps. IX–XI of the 'Sociology of Religion'.) This essay does in fact precede the section on 'Religious Ethics and the "World"', which is the first version of the 'Intermediate Reflections'.

In this section Weber discusses the results of his comparative sociology of religion and he poses a general question concerning the relation between paths to salvation and the orientation of one's life: how can a person assure himself of salvation (the *preservantia gratiae*)? In other words, how can he achieve certainty in this regard (the *certitudo salutis*) (ES, p. 538)? In Weber's view, the answer to this question is of fundamental importance to every religious person: '*Here* lies the root of all psychological drives of a purely *religious* character (PESC, p. 228, italics in original German). This comment was later directed at the Indian salvation religions.

Salvation can be either 'dispensed' by a third party or achieved by the individual himself. If it is 'dispensed', then it occurs through either persons or institutions. If it is brought about by the individual himself, then certain 'achievements' must be attained. These may be of a ritual or cultic nature on the one hand, or display a social or ethical nature on the other. The emphasis may either be on adding up each individual act or on the overall achievement. In all cases, however, the point of these 'achievements' is to overcome the state of nature. They are supposed to lead (to a greater or lesser extent) to the methodical 'reawakening' of a person. Three paths or means are important to this end: ecstasy, asceticism and contemplation. Ecstasy, however sublimated, occupies a special place among these three because, strictly speaking, only a temporary 'reawakening' can be achieved, and not a 'reawakening' that constitutes a *permanent* state of being. The other two means of salvation *can* achieve this if they are based on a soteriology, and are thus no longer tied to the pre-conditions of magic. In this case they provide the means towards a *permanent* improvement of the self, or to a *methodical* disciplining of the self in the service of the salvation goal. Although ecstasy may still exist in religions of salvation, it is usually replaced by contemplation. This is due to the fact that contemplation is a methodical technique. Asceticism and contemplation are therefore the most important soteriological methods. Asceticism is a more practical orientation, while contemplation is rather an intellectual one. This difference can be confirmed by looking at their main results. Asceticism leads to the methodical control of psychological and physical processes, or to the 'right way of acting'. Contemplation, on the other hand, leads to an emptying of consciousness, to the 'right knowledge', or to a state of enlightenment. Weber describes these states as 'mystical'. Asceticism thus produces behaviour that is 'constant', while contemplation results in a 'constant or permanent state of consciousness'. Here lies one of the reasons for Weber's tendency to associate asceticism with ethics and contemplation with gnosis. He also associates asceticism with action and mysticism with contemplation. In this way, he combines the 'means' and the 'result' within a single category.

Yet there are still other reasons for such a classification. They are to do with the fact that specific religious traditions are integrated into the formulation of Weber's concepts. For Weber, both soteriological methods of achieving salvation (or paths to salvation) are intimately connected with the various conceptions of the divine. They decisively shape the salvation premiums. Weber is mainly interested in two of these conceptions: within the Christian tradition, the conception of a personal and transcendent God prevailed. He created the world and will destroy it again one day. The conception that prevailed among the Eastern world religions is of an immanent and impersonal order, which is not created – but is eternal. It has been seen that the goal of all types of religious striving is the achievement of 'certainty' in a person's relation to the divine. What this entails is partly determined by the conception of the divine. The Christian tradition in particular has defined this relation as one between a servant or child of God, while the Asian religions define it as the possession of the divine. The Christian 'secures' this relation by behaviour that is pleasing to God, while the follower of an Asian salvation religion achieves it through a union with the divine. As Weber puts it, in the one case man is a tool, and in the other a vessel, of the divine. Thus the ascetic attitude is active while the contemplative one is passive. It still remains unclear, however, whether this classification of attitudes is analytical or historical in nature.

Yet compared with the first version of *The Protestant Ethic*, the distinction between asceticism and mysticism has now been much more closely circumscribed: tool/vessel, struggle/tranquillity, action/non-action (or emptying oneself of thought), achieving/possessing. These are some of the contrasts employed by Weber. They show that he has advanced beyond the definition of mysticism as a residual category. Asceticism and mysticism are conceptually treated on the same level, and they are at the same time more closely defined.

Weber achieves this by analysing the various types of relation to the world. A person striving for salvation can either remain within the orders of this 'world', or he can reject them. The latter path does not mean, of course, that he can become completely independent of them. Weber chose the contrast between this-worldly and other-worldly to describe these attitudes in *The Protestant Ethic* and the subsequent replies to his critics. There he used these terms mainly to distinguish between the asceticism of the Occidental monk as against 'Protestant' asceticism (PESC, pp. 118–19). In *Economy and Society* he still retains the concept of inner-worldly asceticism, but interestingly he no longer speaks of other-worldly asceticism, but of a world-rejecting asceticism. This type of asceticism is *directly* contrasted with the world-flight of contemplative mysticism. Thus he expressly avoids speaking of an asceticism of world-flight. The main reason for this is that in comparison with contemplation, even world-rejecting asceticism may have a positive effect on the believer's behaviour. None the less, Weber thinks that the distinction between world-rejecting asceticism and the type of contemplation that engenders world-flight is 'particularly fluid in this instance' (ES, p. 545).

The matter is different with the second pair of terms; the this-worldly ascetic is contrasted with the contemplative mystic who 'remains within the world and its orders' (ES, p. 547). This difference is due to the fact that the this-worldly ascetic and the this-worldly mystic develop completely different attitudes to the world and its orders. On the one hand, there are attempts to change the world or even to dominate it; on the other, there is an acceptance of the world as it is and of providence as guiding one's fate. In this context it is worth quoting a passage extensively that is crucial to Weber's overall interpretation of the effect of the search for salvation through contemplation. In Weber's view, no motivation given to 'rationally reshaping the worldly orders' can be derived from this attitude (ES, p. 550). He describes the this-worldly ascetic's and the this-worldly mystic's attitudes to the world as follows:

Neither asceticism nor contemplation affirms the world as such. The ascetic rejects the world's empirical character of creatureliness and ethical irrationality, and rejects its ethical temptations to sensual indulgence, to epicurean satisfaction, and to reliance upon natural joys and gifts. But at the same time he affirms individual rational activity within the orders of the world, affirming it to be his responsibility as well as his means for securing certification of his state of grace. On the other hand, the contemplative mystic living within the world regards action, particularly action performed within the world, as in its very nature a temptation against which he must maintain his state of grace. The contemplative mystic minimizes his activity by resigning himself to the orders within the world as it is, and lives in them incognito, so to speak, as those 'that are quiet in the land' (Psalms, 35: 20) have always done, since god has ordained once and for all that man must live in the world. The activity of the contemplative mystic within the world is characterized by a distinctive brokenness, colored by humility. He is constantly striving to escape from activity in the world back to the quietness and inwardness of his god. Conversely, the ascetic, whenever he acts in conformity with his type, is certain to become god's instrument. For this reason the ascetic's humility, which he considers a necessary obligation incumbent upon a creature of god, is always of dubious genuineness. The success of the ascetic's action is a success of

104

the god himself, to which he has contributed. At the very least this success is a special sign of divine blessing upon the ascetic and his activity. But for the genuine mystic, no success which may crown his activity within the world can have any significance with respect to salvation. For him, his maintenance of true humility within the world is his sole warranty for the conclusion that his soul has not fallen prey to the snares of the world.

(ES, pp. 548–9)

The fact that Weber is particularly concerned in this passage with Christian attitudes is confirmed by the examples he uses to illustrate the overall effect of contemplative mysticism. None the less, these two concepts, which have now been further developed and refined, are not really used to differentiate between the attitudes within the Christian salvation religions. Instead, Weber uses them to distinguish between the Christian tradition on the one hand and the traditions of the other salvation religions on the other. In terms of this contrast, the Indian religions are particularly important. He attempts to distinguish between these two traditions according to the different attitudes to the world that are promoted by them and according to the resulting impact on social action. As Weber puts it, 'the historically decisive difference between the Middle-Eastern and Asian salvation religions on the one hand and the Occidental ones on the other is that the former result mainly in contemplation while the latter result in asceticism' (ES, p. 551).

This points to the 'fundamental differences' between these two traditions. To put it briefly: while Christianity rationally buttressed an attitude of the perfecting of the self and the world and dominating them through action, the Indian religions of salvation fostered an attitude of self-deification, world-flight and rejecting the world through contemplation.

In *Economy and Society*, Weber thus closely ties the distinction between asceticism and mysticism to the traditions of the Occidental and Indian salvation religions. Moreover, he severely limits the concept of world-rejection (or at least its meaning) by his discussion of a world-rejecting asceticism. It is true that there is not only a Christian but also an Indian variety of asceticism. Weber clearly stresses that these are historical concepts and that they always describe a very complex constellation of meaning and action. None the less, he fails to distinguish clearly between a historical and an analytical point of view. Hence the two remain interwoven. Moreover, certain fundamental similarities between the Christian and Indian salvation religions are obscured by this. This becomes clear when a stronger separation is made between the historical and analytical viewpoints and the concept of world-rejection is expanded.

The 'Introduction' only confirms a part of what Weber had already said

105

in *Economy and Society* about the means towards salvation. The three most important means to salvation are ecstasy, asceticism and contemplation. He distinguishes between active asceticism and the contemplative and apathetic-ecstatic ways of life. Each of these three methods has a certain elective affinity to its respective conception of the divine and to whether its prophecy is ethical or exemplary. Ascetic domination of the world and contemplative flight from the world constitute two extremes in terms of the attitudes that result from them (FMW, pp. 291–2). Yet this opposition is expressly seen here in terms of the different rejections of the world. Nevertheless, a sharp distinction between the historical and analytical points of view is still lacking, and no precision is added to the use of these terms. The 'Introduction' even lags behind *Economy and Society* in terms of precision.

Weber adds to this discussion in the 'Intermediate Reflections' with a clearer reformulation of the concepts and the substance of the conclusions reached in *Economy and Society*. From the substantive viewpoint, he stresses one particular insight that is otherwise not new in his writings: namely, that although there is an elective affinity between the conception of a personal and transcendent creator-god and active asceticism (or an asceticism of good works), the connection is not a necessary one. Historically this is already confirmed by the fact that this type of asceticism did not develop in Judaism or Islam although their conceptions of God were to a large extent similar to the Christian one. This independence also applies to the different kinds of prophecy and to the transmission of the doctrine of religious salvation by a prophet or saviour. Again, although Judaism and Islam were ethical prophecies, neither developed an active asceticism. What can be said about the Occidental and Near Eastern salvation religions can equally be said for Asian ones: that there is an elective affinity between an immanent and impersonal conception of the divine and contemplative mysticism, but no necessary connection between the two. Hence world-view and means of salvation must be analytically separated because the former is tied to ideal factors and the latter to institutional factors.

At this point, the concept of world-rejecting asceticism is dropped from Weber's schema. He thereby confirms through his choice of terms what has long been apparent in substance: namely, that both asceticism and contemplation, in the various forms they have assumed, are world-rejecting means of salvation. However, the further distinctions between the various 'contrasts among the types of world-rejection' are made according to a criterion that had already appeared in *Economy and Society* and earlier: the distinction between world-rejecting means of salvation that turn towards the world (inner-worldly) and those that turn away from the world (other-worldly, world-flight). As a result, Weber distinguishes between inner-worldly asceticism and an asceticism of world-flight, as well as between contemplation and mysticism that take an inner-worldly form or the form of flight from the world. By contrast with *Economy and Society*, Weber no longer distinguishes between inner-worldly asceticism and inner-worldly contemplation or mysticism, but rather between inner-worldly asceticism and contemplation or mysticism that takes the form of world-flight. This new distinction may also have to do with the direction in which the substance of his analysis is leading him. At this point he is not primarily interested in the contrast between the Christian inner-worldly asceticism of good works and acosmistic Christian love. Instead, he wants to contrast a Christian attitude of action with an Indian attitude of 'knowing' (as opposed to one of emotionality).

However important these further refinements of Weber's comparative studies of religion may be, they are still not entirely satisfactory. They do not go far enough. The typology must be constructed in such a manner that its conceptual and substantive analyses do not contradict each other. Yet this demands an even sharper separation between the analytical and historical standpoints than the one that is put forward in Weber's original definition.

Aside from this, there are still problems about the clarity of some of Weber's terms. There is still a tacit association of asceticism with action and of contemplation with mysticism. Furthermore, there is the unfortunate contrast between inner-worldliness and world-flight. The contrast between turning towards the world and turning away from the world could provide a more appropriate representation of the actual circumstances. Yet these terminological disputes are of secondary importance. What is more important is that there should be a broadening of the typology of asceticism and mysticism such that a more complex understanding of the different types of impact resulting from religious rejections of the world was made possible.

Before such an attempt is made, however, it may be useful to take a brief look at the second aspect of the behaviour resulting from the striving for salvation. This aspect concerns the goals or premiums of salvation, which have so far been mentioned only indirectly in connection with the various conceptions of the divine. In Weber's 'purely empirical observations' and 'thoroughly sober descriptions' (PESC, p. 29), these salvation premiums are regarded first and foremost as psychological states. Supposedly these psychological states are already attained in this world and they have an emotional value that is important in the here and now. This is equally true in cases where the premium of salvation lies in the 'beyond', as for the Calvinist, for example, who strives for this goal through actions willed by God and as his 'tool'. The state of grace that is experienced in this case is the feeling of being a tool of God (PESC,

p. 248, n. 142). Producing this type of feeling is part of 'securing' the relation to the divine. Hence the kind of feeling that is produced does indeed depend primarily on the conception of God.

According to Weber, salvation premiums are influenced by two basic factors: by the external interests of those striving for salvation (or their social position) and by their inner interests. At bottom there is a distinction between 'external' and 'internal' needs. Such needs are tied to the religious world-view and its norms. From this point of departure, needs undergo a development that, in Weber's famous formulation, 'determined the tracks along which action had been pushed by the dynamic of interests' (FMW, p. 250). The interpretation of the relationship between man and the divine is a part of this development. It is particularly important for an understanding of the psychological state of salvation experienced directly by the believer. Tool/vessel, distance/lack of distance, acting/possessing, struggle/peace, self-perfection/self-deification: these are some of the contrasts Weber employs more or less closely in connection with his analysis of the relation between man and the 'divine'. The first concept in each pair indicates activity, the second passivity. 'Proving oneself' and 'humble acceptance' (or feelings of activity and passivity) are psychological states of salvation that do indeed manifest an intrinsic connection with the two kinds of conception of the divine. Yet this does not mean that there is a *necessary* connection between them. In the end, Weber himself connected them in this manner, distinguishing between tool and vessel and between the attitudes engendered by these two states. Such a connection can, in any case, be inferred from a passage that he inserted into the second version of *The Protestant Ethic* in 1920. He comments that

> the most significant differences between the various ways of achieving salvation for the classification of all [!] types of religiosity may be expressed in the following manner: the religious virtuoso who tries to secure his state of salvation may see himself either as a vessel *or* as a tool of divine power. In the former case this religious attitude tends towards an emotional state of mysticism, in the latter towards ascetic *action*. Luther was closer to the first type, whereas Calvinism belonged to the second type.
>
> (PESC, pp. 113–14)

If the difference between tool and vessel is decisive for the classification of *all* practical forms of religiosity, and can even be used to mark the differences within Christianity, then these two concepts should be analytically separated not only from the conception of God (as in the quote), but also from the soteriological means of salvation. Attitudes of activity or passivity, of being a vessel or a tool, could then be the consequence both of an ascetic and a contemplative disciplining of the self.

A Typology of Attitudes to the World in the Salvation Religions

The attempt can now be made to put forward a systematic typology of attitudes or standpoints towards the world that stem from the religious rejection of the world. Such a typology constitutes a central part of Weber's sociology of religion. It applies only to religious virtuosi or élites. As Weber's remarks on lay Catholicism show, he thought that the religious 'masses' tend towards a naïve affirmation of the world even within the context of a salvation religion. In this way, the 'masses' are similar to those believers among whom magic is predominant. The typology therefore represents various forms of an 'aristocracy of salvation'.

The starting-point of the typology is the relation between the 'divine', man and the 'world'. This relation can be subdivided into two parts: into the normatively construed relation to the divine on the one hand, and the normatively construed relation to the world on the other. The relation to the divine consists of two components: the god of salvation and the salvation premium. There is, in other words, a distinction between the state of salvation and the path or means by which it can be achieved. Together with the relation to the 'world', this yields three components or dimensions for the typology. The content given to these dimensions, in turn, can take two forms; as regards the state of salvation, the attitude can be activity or being a tool on the one hand, or an attitude of passivity or being a vessel on the other. In short, the attitude is either active or passive. In terms of the means of achieving salvation, there is a distinction between asceticism and contemplation. As far as the relation to the world is concerned, the possibilities exist of turning either towards or away from the world. The various attitudes adopted by the virtuosi in salvation religions can thus be arrived at by a combination of these factors. At the same time, this schema demonstrates the various effects of world-rejection – see Figure 4.1

Several interesting observations can be derived from this schema. Cases (1) to (4) seem to be historically *and* psychologically the most 'consistent' ones. They are also the main ones discussed in the 'Intermediate Reflections'. In these cases, the salvation premium, the path to salvation and the relation to the world together form a 'rationally closed unity'. The results are, of course, different in each case. These are the types of religious conduct of life that have appeared in 'historically important forms' (see Schluchter, 1981, pp. 156–66). So, for example, they appeared in the

Attitude to the divine	active		passive	
	Asceticism	Contemplation	Asceticism	Contemplation
Attitude to the world				
Turning towards world (inner-worldly)	(1) active ascetic (world-mastery)	(5) active mystic (indifference to the world)	(7) passive ascetic (indifference to the world)	(3) passive mystic (accepting one's fate in the world)
Turning away from world (other-worldly)	(2) active ascetic (overcoming the world)	(6) active mystic (indifference to the world)	(8) passive ascetic (indifference to the world)	(4) passive mystic (world-flight)

Figure 4.1   *Typology of means to salvation of religious virtuosi*

form of active asceticism in the 'calling' of Protestantism or in the active asceticism of the monk in Catholicism (cases (1) and (2)). Another case is exemplified in the form of the Indian 'forest-dweller' who renounces all social relations and lives off berries (case (4)). All these cases merely represent various types of 'rebirth' that have been made permanent. But only the first type of rebirth had a direct impact on the orders of the 'world' and thereby created a new dynamic of development. This is due to the fact that in this case each one of the different orders of the 'world' is completely subjected to religious control (or at least they are *supposed* to be subjected in this manner in theory). Weber realized early on that the case of 'inner-worldly asceticism' was highly significant for cultural history. Hence he tries to assign a 'universal-historical' role to this case within his comparative sociology of religion. In cases (5) and (6) there is already a psychological tension between the premium and the path to salvation. This does not apply in the same sense to cases (7) and (8). For although a state of passivity or peace can be achieved by means of asceticism, a state of activity or even of struggle cannot be achieved by means of contemplation.

These 'consistencies' and 'inconsistencies' become even more clear if the two different conceptions of the divine are taken into account. Thus additional content can be given to the relation between the 'divine', man and the 'world'. The transcendent creator-god intensifies activism to the point of an instrumental activism by imposing certain commandments on the virtuoso. These commandments are imposed in a loving or a punishing manner. The immanent and uncreated divine order, on the other hand, of which the virtuoso can actually become a part, increases passivism to a point of physical inactivity which becomes almost impossible. The unique character of Occidental asceticism therefore derives from the fact that it is basically an asceticism of *work* – by contrast with

Indian asceticism. The unique character of Indian mysticism, on the other hand, is due to the fact that, by contrast with Occidental mysticism, it is basically a mysticism of *self-deification*. The Occidental mystic cannot, after all, engage in a union with God because of the particular nature of his conception of the divine. Instead, the fact that he must prove himself before God allows paradoxes and tensions to become part of this type of mysticism 'which were spared Indian mysticism' (ES, p. 553). The active and self-deifying asceticism of the Jains led to similar paradoxes and tensions within the Indian tradition. Yet this only goes to show that, apart from 'consistent' historical configurations, there are also 'inconsistent' ones. The conduct of life that is associated with these configurations tends, however, to favour an attitude of indifference to the world. Such an attitude can mean either 'devotion' to the world or an acceptance of it, depending on whether there is an active or passive colouring to it.

This more concise formulation of contrast – or, better yet, this illustration of the variety among the forms of world-rejection – can also be viewed in another light. This may also allow further insight into the systematic intent of Weber's project of a comparative sociology of religion. Despite the fact that a world religion never brings forth only one type of religious élite, and that the leading élite may change in the course of time, it is still the case that a single fundamental attitude towards the world prevails within each world religion. As shown above, Weber's studies of 'The Economic Ethics of the World Religions' are arranged in such a way that Confucianism, with its affirmation of the world, comes first. Next, the 'Intermediate Reflections' lead on to the world religions that renounce or reject the world. They all share the characteristic that they are religions of salvation. These can be 'classified', among other things, through the schema shown in Figure 4.2

In the first place, these salvation religions are divided into two large camps according to whether they turn towards the world or away from it. These, in turn, are divided according to whether an ascetic, contemplative, or apathetic-ecstatic way of life prevails. This 'method of classification' is formal in so far as the conceptions of the divine and important matters of content are not yet taken into consideration as distinguishing characteristics. In this way it becomes apparent what general criteria Weber chose for his overall project of analysing how 'acting in the world' was shaped by religion. It also shows how his various subsidiary projects, whether finished or planned, stand in relation to one another.

Thus it becomes clear what Weber means when he declares at the beginning of the 'Intermediate Reflections' that any attempt at a sociology of religion like his own is also bound to 'make a contribution to the typology and sociology of rationalism itself' (FHW, p. 324). The basic religious attitudes to the world were rarely found in such a form that they

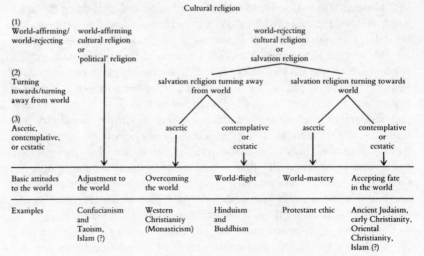

Figure 4.2   *Classification of cultural religions*

were both theoretically consistent and practically realizable. They appeared in this way only in very complex circumstances, and only in conditions that were culturally unique. Not only this, but these conditions were also selective. That is to say, the most rational forms of a certain attitude to the world did not all have a chance to develop within the *single* tradition of a world religion.

Just as Confucianism developed the most rational form of adjustment to the world, and ascetic Protestantism the most rational form of domination of the world, so the Indian salvation religions developed the most rational forms of world-flight. Moreover, Weber claims that ancient Buddhism, for example, represented the 'most radical form of striving for salvation possible' (RI, p. 206). Yet this is by no means the only religious 'achievement' or the only cultural phenomenon with which Indian culture 'surpassed' the Occident in terms of its 'universal significance and validity'. Weber makes similar claims about the Indian 'theodicy', Indian contemplation and asceticism and even Indian philosophy. These 'achievements' could well be said to compete with those of the Occident. Weber tried to list these Occidental 'achievements' in the famous 'Author's Introduction' that was written at the end of his life and preceded his series of studies in the sociology of religion.

There was, however, a second type of rationalism in India, aside from the rationalism of world-flight, which deserves a place in the typology and sociology of rationalism. It is variously called the 'rationalism of a religion with an organic social teaching', the 'organic solution to the doctrine of salvation', or the '*organic* social ethic'. Weber thought that this

teaching was the most consistently developed and practically implemented in India – even by comparison with Thomism (FMW, pp. 338–9).
This point leads to a final aspect that is illuminated by the schema in the
'Intermediate Reflections': a description of the most rational strategies for
overcoming tension and conflict produced by a rejection of the world.

Strategies for Overcoming Tension and Conflict

The religious rejection of the world produces tension and conflict in two
areas; in the first instance, they emerge through the conflict between the
status spiritualis and the *status naturalis* in the person who is 'reborn'.
Secondly, they arise because of the 'laws' to which the non-religious
spheres of life are subject – in other words, where there is a conflict in the
relation between the religious postulate and the 'world', or between the
religious 'law' and *lex naturae*. Strictly speaking, a third area that has
already been briefly mentioned should also be taken into account: the area
of conflict between the virtuosi and the 'masses'. These three areas overlap
in the person who is 'reborn' since it is he who must, in the end, overcome
the resulting tensions and conflicts.

Normally, a 'personal' solution does not suffice to overcome these
problems. Institutional solutions have to supplement 'personal' ones,
especially where the collective religious life, and not only that of the
individual, is at stake. The same applies to the ordering of the religious life
order and its relation to the non-religious orders of life. In these cases an
'individual ethic or teaching' must be supplemented by a 'social ethic' or a
'social teaching'. Similarly, religious organization must be supplemented
by the 'constitution of a church' in the widest sense, thus permitting the
institutional mediation between 'religion' and 'world'.

Weber mainly discusses two types of strategy for overcoming tension
and conflict. One may be called 'absolutization', and the other Weber
himself calls 'relativization' – or sometimes specialization or differentiation (FMW, p. 338). Absolutization consists in the radical subjection of
the *status naturalis*, the 'masses' and the 'world' to the religious demand. In
the end, this strategy only intensifies conflict instead of alleviating it. This
is because neither the natural and social inequality between people nor the
autonomy of the 'world' is accepted. If maintained consistently, this
strategy leads to violence or escapism. Otherwise, it may result in various
forms of compromise, which are – in the end – untenable in the light of the
religious postulate.

Relativization, on the other hand, allows for the coexistence of the *status
spiritualis* and the *status naturalis*, of the ethics of the virtuosi and the masses
and of religion and the other life orders. Relativization seeks to acknowl-

113

edge the validity of the different kinds of demands and to tie them together organically. It operates with a model of organic interrelation rather than strict subordination, or with a both/and rather than an either/or.

These strategies can be applied primarily to the religous life order or to the 'world' in general. The corresponding institutional 'solutions' exemplify these two directions. If absolutization applies only to the religious life order, then an aristocratic community of virtuosi is formed on the basis of 'achievement'. People are classed as either faithful or unfaithful, elect or non-elect and saved or not saved. This separation remains even if the religious institution includes both categories within its fold, as was the case in the Calvinist Church. The kind of institution that is particularly prone to this strategy, however, or that has an elective affinity for it, is the sect and the holy order. An aristocracy of salvation is already implied in their names. Protestant sects are not the only examples. Such an aristocracy of salvation is also found in the Buddhist order of monks and nuns called *sangha*, especially during its early period.

If absolutization is aimed at the world as a whole, then theocracy provides a suitable institutional solution. This solution has always appealed to the virtuosi, particularly since their goal is the domination of the world. Examples range from the Calvinists of Geneva to the New England sects.

If relativization is directed at the religious life order, then the ethic of the virtuosi and that of the laity are placed on different levels. This gradation may occur within the framework of an institution, as with the church organizations and the special religious customs of medieval Catholicism. Alternatively, there may be a loose affiliation between virtuosi and laity. Such an arrangement is typical, for example, among the various 'heterodox' salvation religions in India.

If relativization is aimed at the 'world' at large, however, the result is a dualism between hierocratic and political power – or even an organic pluralism. In this case the autonomy and the inner logic of the different value-spheres and life orders are explicitly recognized. This applies to some extent to Luther's doctrine of the two kingdoms, but even more so to Thomism and certain types of Brahmanism. However it was India, and not the Occident, that most thoroughly applied the strategy of organic relativization. Hence there are two Indian cultural phenomena that have possibly had 'universal significance and validity': striving for salvation through a flight from the world, and an organic social ethic. Both were developed along the most rational lines in India.

This is the broader perspective elaborated in the 'Intermediate Reflections', and it may also serve as a framework for the essay on Hinduism and Buddhism. The conclusion of the latter is already anticipated at the

114

end of the 'Intermediate Reflections', which finishes with a note about the extraordinary achievements of the Indian salvation religions. These achievements lie in 'the combination of the virtuoso's attainment of self-redemption through his own efforts with the universal attainability of salvation, of the strictest rejection of the world with an organic social ethic, and of contemplation as the highest path to salvation with an inner-worldly vocational ethic' (FMW, p. 359).

Notes

This is a shortened version (taken from pp. 15–43) of 'Weltflüchtiges Erlösungs-streben und organische Sozialethik. Überlegungen zu Max Webers Analysen der indischen Kulturreligionen', which appeared in *Max Webers Studie über Hinduismus und Buddhismus*, ed. W. Schluchter (Frankfurt am Main: Suhrkamp, 1984), pp. 11–71.

1   The place from which this quotation is taken (FMW, p. 281) also shows the importance of the sociology of music for the development of Weber's thought concerning rationalism. For further comments see Schluchter (1984).
2   Weber states that 'life can be "rationalized" from various ultimate standpoints and in many different directions. "Rationalism" is a historical concept that is riddled with contradictions' (PESC, pp. 77–8). When the essay (which first appeared in the *Archiv für Sozialwissenschaft und Sozialpolitik* in 1904) was published as a book in 1920, Weber prefaced this remark by saying that 'this single proposition, which is often ignored, should be placed at the beginning of any analysis of "rationalism"'.
3   Strictly speaking, only world-rejecting or salvation religions can have theodi-cies. Weber, however, uses the term 'theodicy' in a much wider sense, as shown particularly in his 'Introduction'.
4   As shown above, the lists of the value-spheres and life orders are not identical in the two texts. Weber also seems to prefer the term 'cosmos' in the earlier text (as opposed to value-spheres or life orders). This term may also explain his usage of the term 'acosmistic'.
5   See Talcott Parsons (1949, pp. 43–51).

PART TWO

Rationalization and the Limits of Rational Action

5

Legitimation and Structured Interests in Weber's Sociology of Religion

PIERRE BOURDIEU

Translated by Chris Turner

In his persistent efforts to make out a case for the historical efficacy of religious beliefs against the most reductionist forms of Marxist theory, Max Weber is sometimes led to privilege the notion of charisma in a manner that, as some writers have noted, is not without resonances of a Carlylean, 'heroic' philosophy of history – as, for example, when he refers to the charismatic leader as 'the specifically creative revolutionary force of history' (ES, p. 1117). Yet he himself provides a means of escape from the simplistic alternative of which his own least convincing analyses are a product. The alternative in question is that between the illusion of absolute autonomy, which tends to have us conceive the religious message as a spontaneously generated product of inspiration, and the reductive theory, which sees that message as the direct reflection of economic and social conditions. He himself brings out elsewhere what these two opposed and yet complementary positions both equally neglect, namely, the *religious work* carried out by specialist agents. These agents are relatively autonomous in respect of external constraints (economic constraints in particular) and invested with the institutional – or other – power to respond to a particular category of needs proper to determinate social groups by a determinate type of practice or discourse.

However, if we are to follow the line of thought indicated by Weber through to its conclusion – whilst remaining resolutely within the limits of *interpretation* (however free it may be) – we must first remove the difficulties he encounters in his attempt to define the 'protagonists' of religious action, the prophet, the magician and the priest. At the heart of all these difficulties, to which his long enumerations of exceptions bear witness, lies his conception of the 'ideal type'. This commits him either to being content with definitions that are universal in scope but extremely

119

rudimentary (for example, 'the regular exercise of the cult' as the distinguishing mark of priesthood) or to accumulating differentiating characteristics while at the same time admitting that these 'are not clearly definable', that they are not universally met with (even separately) and that one must accept the existence of all the empirically observable intermediate stages between these conceptual types, which are themselves mere summations of distinctive features:

> Applied to reality, this contrast is fluid, as are almost all sociological phenomena. Even the theoretical differentiae of these types are not unequivocably determinable ... this distinction, which is clear enough conceptually, is fluid in actuality ... Rather the distinction must be established qualitatively. (ES, p. 425)

Yet a reading of the last lines of each of the sections that make up the 'Sociology of Religion' in *Economy and Society* as something more than mere rhetorical links suffices to allow us to grasp the basic intention of Weber's programme of research.[1] At the end of paragraph 2, which is devoted to the sorcerer and the prophet we find:

> Such developments generally presupposed the operation of one or both of two forces outside the priesthood: *prophets*, the bearers of meta-physical or religious–ethical revelation, and the *laity*, the non-priestly devotees of the cult.
> Before we examine the manner in which these factors outside the priesthood influenced religion sufficiently to enable it to transcend the stages of magic, which are rather similar the world over, we must discuss some typical trends of religious evolution which are set in motion by the existence of vested interests of a priesthood in a cult.
> (ES, p. 427; italics in original)

Similarly, at the end of paragraph 3, we find:

> Prophets and priests are the twin bearers of the systematization and the rationalization of religious ethics. But there is a third significant factor of importance in determining the evolution of religous ethics: the laity, whom prophets and priests seek to influence in an ethical direction. We must now devote a brief examination to the collaboration and inter-action of these three factors. (ES, p. 439)

At the end of paragraph 4, devoted to the prophet, Max Weber insists once again on the necessity of apprehending the different agencies in their interaction: 'Hence we must now examine more closely the mutual relationships of priests, prophets and non-priests' (p. 451). Finally, in paragraph 5, devoted to the religious congregation, we find:

The three forces operative within the laity with which the priesthood must come to grips are: (a) prophecy, (b) the traditionalism of the laity, and (c) lay intellectualism. In contrast to these forces, another decisive factor at work here derives from the necessities and tendencies of the priestly enterprise as such.   (ES, p. 456)

One need only bring these various passages together and give them their full significance to derive, in a first break with Max Weber's explicit methodology, a representation of the relations between religious agents that may be termed *interactionist* (in the sense in which we speak today of *symbolic interactionism*). If this is a view of things that has to be read 'between the lines', this is because, so far as we can see, the intellectual tools Weber had at his disposal prevented him from forming a clear awareness of the principles he was applying (at least intermittently) in his research, and consequently from setting them to work in a methodical and systematic fashion. The fact that it would not be difficult to extract the explicitly stated principles of a theory of symbolic interaction from Weber's theoretical writings makes the reformulation of Weberian analyses in the language of symbolic interactionism all the easier and, it would seem, all the more legitimate.

Any analysis of the *logic* of the interactions that may develop between agents in direct confrontation with one another must be subordinated to the construction of the structure of the objective relations between the *positions* these agents occupy in the *religious field*, a structure that determines both the form their interactions may assume and the representation they may have of these interactions. The interactionist view, strictly speaking, seeks the explanatory principle of practices and representations in the logic of symbolic interactions. It more particularly scrutinizes the representations that the social actors may themselves have – in anticipation or from experience – of the action of the other agents with whom they are directly confronted. Such a view of social relations thus suffers enormously in explanatory power. It tends, in fact, to preclude any construction of the objective relations between the positions (or posts) occupied by the agents in an interactive situation; it reduces relations between positions to the level of 'inter-subjective' or 'interpersonal' relations between the agents occupying these positions. It is only by constructing the religious field as the set of all the objective relations between positions that we can arrive at the principle which explains the direct interactions between social agents and the strategies they may employ against each other. Only such a construction can rescue us from the characteristically Aristotelian logic of *typological* thought, which, being founded upon the primacy accorded to elements over relations and the bracketing out of the historical singularity of the different configurations of the religious field – and therefore of the objective relations between the protagonists competing in the religious domain – can capture the diversity of variant forms only by producing an endless list of exceptions to the realist definitions with which it operates.

Religious Interest and its Forms

The symbolic interactions that establish themselves in the religious field owe their specific form to the particular nature of the *interest* that is in play there, the *religious interest*. This interest causes lay people to expect religious specialists to carry out 'magical or religious actions', actions that are fundamentally 'this-worldly' and practical and are accomplished, as Weber has it, 'that it may go well with thee . . . and that thou mayest prolong thy days upon the earth'.[2]

Any definition of religious need will necessarily remain very rudimentary and extremely vague, so long as that need is not specified in relation to the different groups or classes concerned and their particular 'constellations of interests' in the sphere of religion.[3] (The notion of religious need or interest, as Weber defines it, remains only weakly elaborated; since they are determined by the agents' conditions of existence, religious needs belong within the systems of possible human dispositions; but they are also determined in their form and their conditions of expression by the supply of religion and the action of the religious professionals.)

Magical interests differ from properly religious interests by their *partial* and *immediate* character. Occurring more and more frequently as one descends in the social hierarchy, they are to be encountered primarily amongst the popular classes and, most particularly, amongst the peasants (whose 'lot is so strongly tied to nature, so dependent on organic processes and natural events, and economically so little oriented to rational systematization'). The greater the weight of peasant tradition within a civilization, the more popular religiosity is oriented towards magic. The peasantry, which is commonly confined within weather-ritualism or animistic magic, tends to reduce ethical religiosity to a purely formalistic ethic of *do ut des* (in relation to both god and priests) except where it is threatened by slavery or proletarianization (ES, pp. 468–71). By contrast, the town and the urban professions offer the most favourable conditions for the 'rationalization' and the 'ethicalization' of religious needs. As Weber observes:

> The bourgeois depends economically on work which is continuous and rational (or at least empirically rationalized); such work contrasts with the seasonal character of agricultural work that is exposed to unusual

and unknown forces; it makes the connection between means and ends, success and failure, relatively transparent ... The resulting rationalization and intellectualization parallel the loss of the immediate relationship to the palpable and vital realities of nature ... The forces of nature become an intellectual problem as soon as they are no longer part of the immediate environment. This provokes the rationalist quest for the transcendental meaning of existence, a search that always leads to religious speculation ... the steady professional nature of the artisan's work for his customers easily suggests the conception of duty and rewards as the basis of conduct, and ... religiosity tends to be imbued with moralistic considerations. (ES, pp. 1178–9)

The process of ethicalization and systematization, which leads from magic to religion or, if one prefers, from taboo to sin, depends not only on the interests of those 'two protagonists of systematization and rationalization, the prophet and the clergy' but also on transformations in the economic and social conditions of the laity. Thus, in Max Weber's view, progress towards monotheism is held up by two factors: on the one hand, the 'powerful material and ideological interests vested in the priests, who resided in the cultic centres and regulated the cults of the particular gods' and were therefore hostile to the process of 'concentration' that would force the small salvation enterprises out of existence, and, on the other, 'the religious need of the laity for an accessible and tangible familiar religious object ... accessible to magical influences' (ES, p. 419). Conversely, because the action of a whole set of convergent factors succeeded in removing these obstacles the cult of Yahweh ultimately triumphed over the tendencies towards syncretism, which seemed predominant in ancient Palestine. With political conditions becoming more and more difficult, the Jews, who saw conformity to divine commandments as the only possible source of hope for a future amelioration of their fate, came to regard the various traditional forms of their cult as unsatisfactory – particularly the oracles, with their ambiguous, enigmatic answers – with the result that the need was felt for more rational methods of ascertaining the divine will and for priests capable of practising such methods. In this case, the conflict was between this collective demand – which in fact coincided with the objective interests of the Levites, since it tended to exclude all the competing cults – and the individual interests of the priests of the numerous private sanctuaries. In the centralized and hierarchized organization of the priesthood the conflict found a solution that preserved the rights of all the priests without being at variance with the institution of a monopoly of the cult of Yahweh in Jerusalem.

One may properly speak of religious interests (still defined in generic terms) when there appears alongside those magical demands which continue to subsist, at least among certain classes, the expectation of a systematic message capable of giving a unitary meaning to life. Such a message would propose a coherent vision of the world and human existence to its privileged addressees and give them the means to achieve the more or less systematic regulation of their everyday behaviour. It would, therefore, at the same time be capable of providing them with *justifications of their existence* in its specific form, that is, their existence *as occupants of a determinate social position.*[4]

If religion has social functions and if it is, as a consequence, susceptible of sociological analysis, this is because the laity expect of it not only justifications of their existence that can offer them deliverance from the existential anguish of contingency or abandonment, or even from physical woes, suffering, sickness, or death. Religion has also social functions in so far as the laity expect justification of their existence as occupants of a particular position in the social structure. This definition of the function of religion is merely the most general form of the definition with which Weber implicitly operates in his analyses of the world religions. Nietzsche argues that the Christian religion performs a symbolic transmutation of the 'is' into the 'ought to be' when it offers the hope of a world turned upside-down in which the last shall be first. At the same time it transforms visible stigmata, such as illness, suffering, deformation, or weakness, into signs that the person affected is amongst the 'chosen'. For Weber, such a symbolic transmutation is at the heart of all social theodicies. It is present when they justify the established order in a direct and immediate manner – as with the doctrine of *karma*, which justifies the social status of each individual in the caste system in terms of his or her degree of religious attainment in the cycle of transmigrations. It is also present when the status quo is justified in a more indirect manner, as in the soteriologies of 'the beyond', which promise a posthumous subversion of that order (Nietzsche, 1973; ES, pp. 492–9, 934).

To the extent that religious interests have as their central principle the need for justifications of a person's or group's existence in a determinate social position, they are directly determined by the social situation. The religious message that will be most capable of satisfying a group's religious demand, and therefore of exercising its properly symbolic function of mobilization upon that group, will be the one that provides it with a quasi-systematic set of justifications for its existence as the occupant of a determinate social location. The quasi-miraculous harmony between the content of the religious message that ultimately wins out and the most strictly temporal of the interests of its privileged addressees – namely, their political interests – constitutes an essential condition of its success. Thus, for example, Weber notes that 'Concepts like sin, salvation, and religious humility have not only seemed remote from all élite

124

political classes, particularly the warrior nobles, but have indeed appeared reprehensible to its sense of honour' (ES, p. 472).

> If one wants to characterize succinctly, in a formula, so to speak, the types representative of the various strata that were the primary carriers or propagators of the so-called world religions, they would be the following: in Confucianism, the world-organizing bureaucrat; in Hinduism, the world-ordering magician; in Buddhism, the mendicant monk wandering through the world; in Islam, the warrior seeking to conquer the world; in Judaism, the wandering trader; and in Christianity, the itinerant journeyman. To be sure, all these types must not be taken as exponents of their own occupational or material 'class interests', but rather as the *ideological carriers (ideologische Träger)* of the kind of ethical or salvation doctrine which rather readily conformed to their social position.   (ES, p. 512, italics added)

Max Weber locates the central principle of the systems of religious interests in the forms in which the privileged classes and the 'negatively privileged' classes represent their positions in the social structure to themselves. Whilst for the former group their sense of dignity is rooted in a conviction as to their own 'excellence' and the perfect nature of their conduct of their lives – 'an expression of their qualitative "being", which is grounded in itself and refers to nothing beyond' – for the latter group that sense of dignity can rest only on a promise of redemption from suffering and on an invocation of Providence, which is capable of giving meaning to their present state by reference to what they are to become (ES, p. 491). It is not by chance that the *function of legitimation* finds in the great political bureaucracies both its highest expression and, at the same time, its almost totally forthright, even cynical, formulation: 'A bureaucracy is usually characterized by a profound disesteem of all irrational religion, combined, however, with a recognition of the usefulness of this type of religion as a device for controlling the people' (ES, p. 476). And Max Weber indicates elsewhere, in almost the same terms, that the great hierocratic powers (churches) are predisposed to provide political regimes with an irreplaceable 'power of legitimation' (*legitimierende Macht*) and that they constitute an 'incomparable means of domesticating the subjects' (*das unvergleichliche Mittel der Domestikation der Beherrschten*) (ES, p. 1176). By contrast, the disadvantaged classes are bearers of *demands for compensation* (salvation religions). A variable independent of the preceding one (and with which one has only to combine it to account for more highly specified forms of religious demand, such as that of the 'proletaroid intellectual') is the need for systematization; virtually absent amongst the peasantry, this reaches its maximum intensity in the intellectual strata:

125

The salvation sought by the intellectual is always based on inner need, and hence it is at once more remote from life, more theoretical and more systematic than salvation from external distress, the quest for which is characteristic of the non-privileged strata ... It is the intellectual who conceives of the 'world' as a problem of *meaning*. As intellectualism suppresses belief in magic, the world's processes become disenchanted, lose their magical significance, and henceforth simply 'are' and 'happen' but no longer signify anything. As a consequence, there is a growing demand that the world and the total pattern of life be subject to an order that is significant and meaningful.

(ES, p. 506, italics added)

Competition for Religious Legitimacy

Competition for religious power owes its specificity (particularly in relation to the competition that takes place in the political field, for example) to the fact that what is at stake is the *monopoly of the legitimate exercise of the power to modify, in a deep and lasting fashion, the practice and world-view of lay people*, by imposing on and inculcating in them a particular *religious habitus*. By this I mean a lasting, generalized and transposable disposition to act and think in conformity with the principles of a (quasi-) systematic view of the world and human existence.

The nature and form of the direct interactions between the agents or institutions involved in this competition and the instruments and strategies they mobilize in the struggle depend upon both a system of specific interests and a specifically religious authority, which each derives from elsewhere. On the one hand, this system of interests and this religious authority derive from the agent's or institution's position in the division of labour currently pertaining within the sphere of the symbolic manipulation of the laity. On the other, they result from the respective position of each in the objective structure of the relations of specifically religious authority which define the religious field. Weber consistently fails to establish a distinction between (1) direct interactions and (2) the objective structure of the relations that become established between religious agencies. The latter is crucial – even in the absence of any direct interaction; it controls the form that interactions may take (and the representations which the agents involved may have of them). Max Weber thus reduces the question of legitimacy to one of *representations of legitimacy*.

Amongst the differentiating factors connected with the religious division of labour, the most powerful is that which counterposes the *initial producers* of the principles of a (quasi-) systematic view of the world and existence, the prophets, to the agencies of reproduction (churches). The latter are organized to exercise over a prolonged period the lasting action necessary to inculcate such a vision and to invest it with the specifically religious legitimacy that is the necessary pre-condition for the exercise of that action. The prophet stands opposed to the priestly body as the *discontinuous* to the *continuous*, the extraordinary to the ordinary, the non-routine to the routine and the banal, in particular where the manner of performing his religious action is concerned (i.e. in the temporal structure of the actions of imposition and inculcation of doctrine and in the means employed in the process). (See ES, pp. 529–76.) The prophet's charismatic action basically achieves its effects by way of the prophetic word, which is exceptional and discontinuous, whilst the action of the priesthood follows a 'religious method of a rational type', which owes its most important characteristics to the fact that it is practised on a continuous basis, every day. Correspondingly, the prophet's retinue stands opposed to an administrative apparatus of the bureaucratic type such as is represented by a church, which is a body of cult functionaries equipped with a specialist training. Recruited on charismatic criteria, 'disciples' know nothing of 'career' and 'promotion', of 'appointments' and 'distinctions', of hierarchies and carefully circumscribed spheres of activity.

Prophecy cannot completely fulfil the claim that it necessarily implies, of being able to modify the lives and world-views of the laity in a deep and lasting fashion, unless it succeeds in founding a 'community'. This is in turn able to perpetuate itself in an institution capable of carrying on a lasting and continuous activity of winning acceptance for and inculcating the doctrine (this is the relationship between original prophecy and the priestly body). It is necessary for prophecy to die as prophecy, i.e. as a message breaking with routine and contesting the accepted order, for it to survive in the priesthood's doctrinal corpus, where it becomes the daily small-change of the original rich fund of charisma (ES, pp. 452–6, 464–7).

The material or symbolic force that the different agencies (social agents or institutions) can mobilize in the struggles for a monopoly of the legitimate exercise of religious power varies significantly. It is a function, at each stage in the development of the 'religious field', of their position in the objective structure of specifically religious relations of authority. It depends greatly on the authority and force they have previously acquired in that struggle.

Religious legitimacy at any given time is nothing other than the state of the specifically religious power relations at that moment; that is, it is the result of past struggles for the monopoly of the accepted exercise of religious power. The *type of religious legitimacy* a religious agency may invoke is a function of the position it occupies within the system of

127

religious power relations at a particular stage. It also depends on the degree to which that position has control over the material and symbolic weapons (such as the prophet's *anathema* or the priest's *excommunication*) of religious violence that the competing actors may bring to bear.

Whilst the authority of the prophet – an *auctor* whose *auctoritas* has continually to be won and re-won – depends on the relationship that exists at any moment between the supply of religion and the public's demand for it, the priest enjoys an *authority deriving from his very function*, which relieves him of the burden of continually having to win and consolidate his authority, and even shields him from the consequences of the failure of his religious action: 'The priest, in clear contrast [with the prophet], dispenses salvation by virtue of his office. Even in cases in which personal charisma may be involved, it is the hierarchical office that confers legitimate authority upon the priest as a member of an organized enterprise of salvation' (ES, p. 440).

Of all the practices and representations of the various religious agents that ensue from this opposition, particularly telling are the very different effects that the failure of a religious act (in the broad sense) may have. This depends on the position in the prevailing religious power relations of the agent concerned:

> In the event of failure, the magician possibly paid with his life. On the other hand, priests have enjoyed the contrasting advantage of being able to deflect the blame for failure away from themselves and on to their god. Yet even the priest's prestige is in danger of falling with that of their gods. However priests may find ways of interpreting failures in such a manner that responsibility falls, not upon the god, but upon the behaviour of the god's worshippers. There might even arise from such interpretation, the idea of worshipping the god, as distinct from coercing him. (ES, pp. 427–8)

The great oppositions into which the supernatural powers are divided, and the power relations that form between them, express in a distinctively religious logic the oppositions between the different types of religious action (which themselves correspond to different positions in the structure of the religious field) and the state of power relations in the religious field. The opposition between demons and gods reproduces that between sorcery as 'magical coercion' and religion as 'divine worship':

> The relationship of men to supernatural forces which take the forms of prayer, sacrifice and worship may be termed '*cult*' (*kultus*) and '*religion*', as distinct from '*sorcery*', which is magical coercion. Correspondingly, those beings that are worshipped and entreated religiously may be termed '*gods*', by contrast with '*demons*', which are magically coerced and charmed. (ES, p. 424, italics in original)

Similarly, the history of the gods themselves reflects the fluctuations in the history of their servants: 'The historical emergence of this differentiation [between religion and magic] is often attributable to the fact that the suppression of a cult, by a priestly or secular body, in favour of a new religion, reduced the old gods to the status of "demons"' (ES, p. 424). Or, to take another illustration of this phenomenon, where the priests have the power to deflect responsibility for failure on to the god without thereby damaging their own standing – a feat achieved by attributing the responsibility to the lay worshippers – it may turn out that 'Even renewed and increased worship of the god is of no avail . . . since the gods of the adversaries remain more powerful' (ES, p. 428).

Competition for Lay Followers

Religious power is then the product of a *transaction* between religious agents and lay people in which the systems of interests peculiar to each category of religious agents and to each category of lay people have to find satisfaction. All the power that the various religious agents hold over the lay people and all the authority they possess in the relations of competition that develop amongst them can be explained in terms of the structure of the relations of symbolic power between religious agents and the various categories of lay people over whom that power is exercised.[5] The prophet's power rests upon the force of the group he can mobilize. This depends on his ability to give symbolic expression – in an exemplary form of conduct and/or in a (quasi-) systematic discourse – to the specifically religious interests of lay people occupying a determinate position in the social structure.

As well as occasionally succumbing to the naïve representation of charisma as a mysterious quality inherent in a person or as a gift of nature ('charismatic power subsists by virtue of an affective submission to the person of the master and to his gift of grace (charisma), magical qualities, revelations or heroism, mental powers or powers of oratory'), even in his most rigorous writings Max Weber never proposes anything other than a psycho-sociological theory of charisma, a theory that regards it as the *lived* relation of a public to the charismatic personality: 'The term "charisma" will be applied to a certain quality of an individual personality by virtue of which he is considered extraordinary and treated as endowed with supernatural, superhuman, or at least specifically exceptional powers or qualities' (ES, p. 241). Charismatic legitimacy, as we see here, is grounded solely in an act of 'recognition'. To break with this definition, we must consider the relation between the prophet and the lay disciples as a particular case of the relation that, according to Durkheim, forms

129

between a group and its religious symbols. For him, such symbols ('the emblem') are not mere signs expressing 'the sense that society has of itself; they 'constitute' that sense.

Like the emblem, the word and person of the prophet symbolize collective representation that, by virtue of the creative nature of symbolization, they contribute to constituting. The prophet embodies in exemplary conduct, or gives discursive expression to, representations, feelings and aspirations that existed before his arrival – albeit in an implicit, semi-conscious, or unconscious state. In this sense, he brings about, in both his discourse and his person, the meeting of a signifier and a pre-existing signified ('You would not have sought me if you had not already found me'). Thus the prophet – that isolated individual, a man without a past, lacking any authority other than himself ('So it is written . . . but I say unto you') – may act as an organizing, mobilizing force.[6] It is, therefore, only by conceiving the prophet in his relationship with the laity (a relationship that is obviously inseparable from his relationship with the priestly body whose authority he is contesting) that one may resolve the problem of the *initial accumulation of the capital of symbolic power* (Max Weber resolved this by invoking Nature, a solution that involved him in a paradox).

However, we can be justified in bringing this question of the success of prophecy down to a question of communication between the prophet and the laity, and to the specific effect of the prophet's role in giving expression to what was previously implicit, only on condition that we also ask ourselves under what economic and social conditions this particular type of communication arises and proves effective. As a critical discourse that can find a *justification* for its claim to contest the authority of the agencies which hold the monopoly of the legitimate exercise of symbolic power only in the invocation of charismatic inspiration, prophetic discourse is more likely to appear in periods of open or latent crisis which befall either entire societies or certain classes. Prophetic discourse is thus more likely to gain success in periods in which economic or morphological transformations determine the collapse, decline, or obsolescence of traditions or value-systems that provided the principles of a world-view and a mode of life. As Marcel Mauss observed:

famines and wars give rise to prophets and heresies: violent clashes have far-reaching effects even on such things as the distribution and the nature of populations; interbreeding of whole societies (which happens in the case of colonization) necessarily stimulates the appearance of just such new ideas and new traditions . . . These collective, organic causes must not be confused with the actions of individuals, who are the *interpreters* of such phenomena rather than their masters. There are therefore no grounds for opposing individual invention to collective routine. *Continuity and routine may be the product of individual action, and innovation and revolution may be the work of groups*, sub-groups, sects or individuals acting through and for groups.

(Mauss, 1969, pp. 333–4, italics added)

Let us then dispose once and for all of the notion of charisma as a property attaching to the nature of a single individual, and examine instead, in each particular case, sociologically pertinent characteristics of an individual biography. The aim in this context is to explain why a particular individual finds himself *socially* predisposed to live out and express with particular cogency and coherence, ethical or political dispositions that are already present in a latent state amongst all the members of the class or group of his addressees.

By virtue of the fact that prophetic discourse is produced in and for a direct transaction with lay people, the (quasi-) systematization of its effects is 'dominated not by demands for logical coherence, but by *evaluations of a practical nature*'. In assembling a collection of practices and representations into a (quasi-) system endowed with and itself bestowing meaning, prophecy plays an organizing and legitimating role. Such practices and representations have in common only that they have been engendered by the same *habitus* (specific to a group or class). Thus they may be perceived in the life experience of the group as neither continuous nor unified. Prophecy can play such a role only because it has as its own generative and unifying principle a *habitus* objectively attuned to that of its addressees. The ambiguity that, as has often been noted, characterizes the message of the prophet is found in every form of discourse that, even when addressed more directly to a socially specified audience, aims at making recruits. The allusions and ellipses found in such forms of discourse are designed to promote a grasp of the message in the form of a misunderstanding or as a deciphering of a concealed message; or, to put it another way, to promote those reinterpretive perceptions that invest the message with the expectations of the hearers.

The outcome of the struggle between the body of priests and the competing prophet (with his lay disciples) depends not only on the specifically symbolic force of the prophet's message (on the mobilizing and critical effect of the new revelation – its 'de-banalizing effect'), but also on the respective strengths of the groups mobilized by the two competing agencies within the sphere of extra-religious power relations. As Weber points out, the way in which the tension between the prophet and his disciples, on the one hand, and the priestly body, on the other, is resolved is a 'question of force' (ES, p. 456). All outcomes are possible, from the physical suppression of the prophet to the annexation of the prophecy, with a whole range of possible compromise solutions in between.

The systematization to which the priests subject the original message is the resultant of the *external forces* with which the priestly body must reckon (the traditionalist or intellectualist demands of the laity; the competition between the prophet and the magician), which take on different weightings in different historical conjunctures, and of the *internal tendencies*, which have to do with the position of the priestly body in the religious division of labour and with the particular structure of the church. The church is a more or less permanent institution laying claim – more or less successfully – to a monopoly of the administration of the rewards of salvation (*extra ecclesiam nulla salus*). It presents itself as a bureaucracy of functionaries claiming 'a monopoly of legitimate hierocratic coercion', whose task it is to organize, at particular times and in particular places, the worship of the god (through prayer and sacrifice, by contrast with magical coercion), together with preaching and the care of souls. In other words, Weber's argument is, roughly, that one may speak of the existence of a church when there is, firstly, a body of professionals who are distinct from 'worldly life' (priests) and bureaucratically organized in matters of career, remuneration, professional duties and way of life outside the sphere of those duties; secondly, when dogmas and forms of worship are rationalized and laid down in sacred books, when commentaries are produced on those books and the teaching of the sacred texts takes the form of a systematic education and not merely that of a technical preparation; thirdly and lastly, when all these tasks are carried out within an institutionalized community. And the principle of this institutionalization consists, for Weber, in the process whereby charisma detaches itself from the person of the prophet to attach itself to the institution and, more precisely, to a specific *function*: 'the process of transferring the sacredness which derives from charisma to the institution as such ... is characteristic of all processes of Church-formation and constitutes their specific essence'. It follows that the church, as a body possessing and administering a charisma that is attached to a particular function (or to the institution in general), stands opposed to the sect, understood as a 'community of persons whose holiness derives from a charisma each possesses on a purely individual basis'.[7] It also follows that the bureaucratic salvation-enterprise is unconditionally hostile to 'personal' (that is, prophetic, mystical, or ecstatic) charisma, which claims to point an original path towards God: 'Whoever performs miracles on his own [in the charismatic mode], without an office, is suspect as a heretic or a magician' (ES, p. 1165). To the extent that it is a product of the progressive bureaucratization of religious administration or, rather, of 'the transformation of charisma into everyday practice', the 'banalization'

(*Veralltäglichung*) of charisma,[8] the church displays all the characteristics of 'everyday' institutions. It comprises thus 'an office hierarchy with de-limited jurisdictions, regular channels, *réglementation*, fees, benefices, a disciplinary order, rationalization of doctrine and of office-holding as a "vocation"' (ES, p. 1166).

Priestly practice and also the message the priesthood imposes and incul-cates always owe most of their characteristics to the continual *transactions* between the church and the laity. The church as a *permanent* dispenser of grace (sacraments) enjoys the corresponding coercive power of being able to accord or refuse 'holy goods' to the laity over whom it intends to exer-cise religious leadership. Yet it is from the laity that the church hopes to derive its power (temporal as well as spiritual). In this vein, Weber writes: 'The more the priesthood aimed to regulate the behaviour pattern of the laity in accordance with the will of god, and especially to aggrandize its status and income by so doing, the more it had to compromise with the traditional views of the laity in formulating patterns of doctrine and behaviour' (ES, p. 466). He then goes on to comment: 'As the masses increasingly become the object of the priests' influence and the foundation of their power, the priestly labors of systematization concerned them-selves more and more with the most traditional, and hence magical, forms of religious notions and practices' (ES, p. 466). In the general form that I have given it, this proposition defines the form of the relation that arises between the activity of the priest and the 'target public' of this activity, be that public popular or bourgeois, peasant or urban.

The nearer the body of priests is to holding *de facto* monopoly of the administration of the goods of salvation in a class-divided society, the more divergent, indeed contradictory, are the religious interests to which its preaching and pastoral activities must respond and the more those acti-vities and the agents charged with carrying them out tend to become diversified (a diversification that may range from mystical fideism to magical ritualism and from the court chaplain to the country priest). At the same time a religious message develops that owes its characteristics – in particular its ambiguity – to the fact of being the product of the search for a lowest common religious denominator among the different cate-gories of audience. The ambiguity of the initial prophecy leaves it open to the conscious or unconscious reinterpretations that successive users of the prophecy will produce, each being inclined to read the original message 'through the spectacles of their own attitude', as Max Weber puts it when speaking of Luther. Those professional interpreters, the priests, contri-bute greatly to this ceaseless work of adaptation and assimilation, which allows contact to be established between the religious message and ever new recipients of it, who may be profoundly different both in religious interests and world-view from the original audience.

133

In order to counter the attacks made by prophets or intellectualist criticism from within the laity, the priesthood has to 'assume the obligation of codifying . . . doctrine . . . and delimiting what must and what must not be regarded as sacred' (ES, p. 457). In short, it must equip itself with weapons of symbolic struggle that are at once homogeneous, coherent and distinctive; it must do this in the sphere of ritual as much as in the sphere of dogma (doctrinal corpus). The elements required to mount a defence against competing prophecies and against lay intellectualism contribute towards stimulating the production of 'banalized' instruments of religious practice; this is borne out by the fact that the production of canonical scriptures is accelerated whenever the content of the tradition is in peril (ES, p. 459). Also, the concern to define the specificity of the community with regard to competing doctrines leads to a foregrounding of distinctive criteria and differential doctrines or practices, both in the struggle against religious indifference and in efforts to make the switching of allegiance to a competing religion difficult (ES, p. 460).

Competition from the *magician*, a small independent entrepreneur hired by private individuals on an *ad hoc* basis and exercising his office outside any recognized institution, most often in a clandestine manner, contributes to imposing both the 'ritualization' of religious practice and the annexing of magical beliefs on the body of priests (e.g. as in the cult of saints or in maraboutism).

The 'casuistico-rational systematization' and 'banalization' that the priests impose on the original prophecy on the basis of 'an ultimate and integrated value-position' occur as a response to a number of converging exigencies. These include, first, the typically bureaucratic pursuit of an *economy of charisma*, which leads to confiding the exercise of the activities of preaching and pastoral care – necessarily banal and 'banalized' activities, because they are of a routine, repetitive nature – to *interchangeable* functionaries of the cult; all of the latter are equipped with homogeneous professional qualifications, acquired by a prescribed form of training, and with homogeneous instruments, designed to sustain an homogeneous and homogenizing activity oriented towards the production of a religious *habitus*. Second is the attempt to adapt to lay interests that are encountered directly in pastoral care; this is the priestly activity *'par excellence'* and the priests' real instrument of power.[9] Thirdly and lastly, we must also include the struggle against competing religions.

'Casuistico-rational systematization' and 'banalization' constitute the basic conditions of the working of a bureaucracy engaged in the manipulation of 'goods of salvation'. These conditions permit agents *of any kind whatever*, agents who can therefore be substituted one for another, to exercise the activities of the priesthood on a sustained basis, by providing them with the practical instruments – canonical scriptures, breviaries, collections of sermons, catechisms and so forth. The latter are indispensable to them if they are to carry out their functions at the least cost (to themselves) in terms of charisma, and at the least possible risk (to the institution), especially when they need to 'take an attitude toward the numerous problems which had not been settled in the revelation itself (ES, p. 465). The breviary and the collection of sermons have thus the dual role of being both 'cribs' and effective safety-barriers; they are intended both to prescribe particular forms for improvisation and also, in fact, to proscribe it.

Notes

This chapter is a slightly modified version of an article that appeared in *Archives européennes de sociologie*, vol. XII, (1971), pp. 3–21.

1 This analysis is based primarily on two texts written between 1911 and 1913, the chapter VI of ES expressly devoted to religion (ES, pp. 399–634) and chapter XV of the 'Sociology of Domination' (ES, pp. 1158–211), entitled 'Political Domination and Hierocratic Domination'. It also takes into account texts written after 1918, such as section 8 of chapter I, entitled 'The Concept of Conflict' (ES, pp. 38–40) or section 17 of the same chapter, 'Political and Hierocratic Organization' (ES, pp. 54–6).
2 According to the terms of the promise made to those who honour their parents: ES, p. 399.
3 Section 7, 'Status Groups, Classes and Religion' addresses itself to this question (ES, pp. 468–517). There is also another analysis of the differences between the religious interests of the peasantry and those of the urban petit bourgeoisie in the chapter, 'Hierocratic Domination and Political Domination' (ES, pp. 1178–80).
4 'Since every need for salvation is an expression of some distress, social or economic oppression is an effective source of salvation beliefs, though by no means the exclusive source' (ES, p. 491).
5 This description of the relationship between clergy and laity as a transaction appears inadequate to me today. I now (in 1985) believe that only the logic of the structural homology between positions occupied within the field of 'professionals' and positions occupied in the social field is capable of accounting for intersections of supply and demand that owe nothing – or at least very little – to calculations, whether of a more or less cynical nature, or to transaction understood as a conscious adjustment to demand.
6 On the 'charisma of rhetoric' and its effects in different social contexts, in particular in electoral democracy, see ES, p. 1129.
7 Conversely, the sect 'rejects institutional grace and charisma deriving from an institution'. It holds to the principles of 'lay preaching' and a 'universal calling to priesthood' (which 'any logically coherent Church forbids'), of 'direct democratic administration' carried out by the community itself (ecclesiastical functionaries being considered 'servants' of the community) and of 'freedom

of conscience', which a church with universalist pretentions cannot allow (ES, pp. 1207–10).

8 The neologism 'banalization' translates the two aspects of the Weberian concept of *Veralltäglichung* with anything resembling exactitude only if it is understood both as 'a process consisting in becoming banal, everyday and ordinary' by contrast with the extraordinary, the non-everyday (*Ausseralltäglichkeit*) and as 'the effects occasioned by the process of becoming banal, everyday and ordinary'.

9 ES, p. 464, Weber observes that the importance accorded to preaching (by contrast with pastoral care) varies in inverse proportion to the introduction of magical elements into religious practice and representations (as is shown by the example of Protestantism).

6

Rationality and the Characterization of Modern Society

BARRY HINDESS

In his review of Brentano's book, *The Development of Value Theory*, Weber argues that economic theory is concerned with working out the consequences of the assumption of economic rationality on the part of economic agents. He does this in purely analytic terms and independently of any psychological laws or assumptions. He goes on to suggest that the theory gives only an approximation to reality because, of course, the assumption that actors always act rationally does not hold. Nevertheless:

> the historical peculiarity of the capitalistic epoch, and thereby also the significance of marginal utility theory (as of every economic theory of value) for the understanding of this epoch, rests on the circumstance that – while the economic history of some epochs in the past has not without reason been designated as 'history of non-economic conditions' – under today's conditions of existence the approximation of reality to the theoretical propositions of economics has been a *constantly increasing* one. It is an approximation to reality that has implicated the destiny of ever-wider layers of humanity. And it will hold more and more broadly, as far as our horizons allow us to see.
>
> (Weber, 1975, p. 33, italics in original)

Here, as so often in his work, Weber characterizes the modern West as dominated by the secular growth of instrumental rationality. It is a theme that has been echoed by numerous subsequent writers. This chapter questions not so much the empirical adequacy of that characterization but rather its conceptual foundations. Weber's account of the rationality of the modern West depends on a specific model of the actor as a human individual, analysed in terms of concepts of interests, values, a need for meaning and a potential for rational calculation. The relations and oppositions between these concepts are central to Weber's typologies of

137

action and of the forms of legitimate domination, and to his discussions of the tensions between formal and substantive rationality. Closely related models of the actor can be found in rational choice theories in economics, political science and sociology, and in much of the social science literature on 'rationality'.

Weber's model of the actor operates with a limited and inadequate account of the conditions of action, and especially of the discursive conditions in which actors reach and formulate decisions. Similar problems arise in rational choice theories and other social scientific discussion of 'rationality'. Critical discussion of the relations between actors and the discursive and other conditions of action undermines these models of the actor and Weber's methodological individualism. I argue that social life is strictly irreducible to the constitutive actions of actors, and there are actors other than human individuals. Following a discussion of Weber's model of the actor in the first section, the remaining sections of this chapter consider problems first with his characterization of the modern West as dominated by the growth of instrumental rationality, and secondly with his treatment of rationality as an intrinsic, if sometimes inhibited, feature of the human actor. The chapter ends with a short concluding summary.

Weber's Model of the Actor

In an earlier paper (Hindess, 1977) I argued that Weber's definitions of sociology and social action represent a humanist version of the rationalist conception of action. In this conception action always involves, first, a realm of ideas (values, meanings, representations), secondly, a realm of nature and, thirdly, a mechanism of the realization of ideas in the realm of nature, namely, human action. The mechanism may be defined at the level of the individual human subject, as in Weber's methodological writings, or at some supra-individual or social level, as in much of the work of Durkheim and Parsons. But, however such a mechanism may be thought to operate, the effect of its operations is to constitute some part of the world as the product of both natural and extra-natural, or ideal, determinations. While the first are the proper objects of natural scientific investigation, the second should be objects of understanding. Social or cultural phenomena, in other words, must be analysed in terms of the ideas (values, meanings, etc.) they express.

Weber's methodological protocols clearly present a rationalism in this sense. 'We shall speak of "action" in so far as the acting individual attaches a subjective meaning to his behaviour – be it overt or covert, omission or acquiescence' (ES, p. 4). Action and behaviour are both events in nature,

138

but action is also something more. It is the expression of a meaning, which is not itself part of nature. Weber's concept of action therefore postulates a realm of ideas (called meanings or ultimate values), a realm of nature and the will and consciousness of the human individual as the mechanism of realization of ideas in nature. It is a humanism in the sense that the mechanism is supposed to operate solely at the level of the individual human subject. Weber insists that social relationships and social collectivities are always in principle reducible to the actions of individuals. They 'must be treated as solely the resultants and modes of organization of the particular acts of individual persons, since these alone can be treated as agents in a course of subjectively understandable action' (ES, p. 13).

It is well known, of course, that Weber's attempts to conceptualize forms of social action are not always consistent with this methodological individualism. But in his definitions of sociology and his explicit methodological protocols the mechanism of realization of meanings and values is always the human individual: on the one hand subject to physiological and psychological determinations, and on the other a free agent, a subject of will and consciousness. Because action involves both natural and ideal determinations, the line between action and behaviour is often very difficult to draw. Indeed, Weber insists that a large and sociologically significant part of human behaviour is 'marginal between the two' (ES, p. 4). This notion of action bordering on mere behaviour plays a central part in Weber's sociology. For example, in his preliminary outline of the fundamental concepts of sociology in *Economy and Society* he distinguishes four basic types of social action according to their mode of orientation. Two are rational: instrumentally rational (*zweckrational*), defined in relation to a system of discrete individual ends and the rational estimation of means available for their attainment; and value-rational (*wertrational*), involving a conscious belief in an absolute value and its implementation independently of the prospects for its successful realization. The others, traditional and affectual orientations, are explicitly conceived as on 'the borderline of what can justifiably be called meaningfully oriented action, and indeed often on the other side' (ES, p. 25). This suggests that 'action' should be seen as intrinsically rational: that is, it deviates from rationality to the extent that it is the product of merely natural (i.e. not specifically human) determinations. While theoretical humanism must imply the possibility of borderline cases, it is clearly impossible to derive the specific categories of traditional and affectual action in this way.

Human behaviour is rational to the extent that it conforms to meanings and values, and non-rational to the extent that it does not. It is partly for this reason that Weber insists on the construction of *rational* ideal types. If

139

we start from the presumption of rationality in our attempts to make sense of human actions, then the place of other, non-rational elements in behaviour may then be seen 'as accounting for the observed deviations from this hypothetical course' (ES, p. 6). A similar methodological presumption of rationality is one of the foundations of rational choice theories in the social sciences (cf. Hindess, 1984). Here departures from rationality are to be understood as resulting from the interference of affectual, physiological, or other elements at the level of the individual actor. We shall see shortly that a different kind of reason may also be advanced as to why action in some conditions may be more rational than action in others.

Action is the attempted realization of meanings or purposes. But what of the meanings or purposes themselves? In his final revision of the 'Introduction' to his studies of 'The Economic Ethics of the World Religions' Weber added the following passage.

> Not ideas, but material and ideal interests, directly govern men's conduct. Yet very frequently the world images that have been created by 'ideas' have, like switchmen, determined the tracks along which action has been pushed by the dynamics of interest.
>
> (FMW, p. 280)

I return below to the second sentence. For the moment consider the distinction between material and ideal interests. The first is a matter of the distribution of material goods, and more generally of whatever concerns the health, happiness and well-being of human individuals. The second concerns their search for 'meaning'. Meanings are not a function of physiological or psychological needs alone, they also refer to something beyond the material realm, to ultimate values. In Weber's model of the actor these values must be conceived as ultimate givens; they are not derived from a knowledge of material conditions and they are not determined by material interests (although Weber does not deny that there may be an important 'elective affinity' between world views and material interests: MSS, p. 56). The realm of values is a source of irreconcilable antagonism and conflict in human affairs:

> [We] must recognise that general views of life and the universe can never be the products of increasing empirical knowledge, and that the highest ideals, which move us most forcefully, are always formed only in the struggle with other ideals which are just as sacred to others as ours are to us.
>
> (MSS, p. 57)

In effect, then, we have a model of the actor as a human individual, a biological and psychological organism endowed with a potential for rational calculation and acting in terms of both material and ideal

140

interests. This actor and its orientations provide Weber with the means of characterizing the modern world in terms of the spread of instrumental rationality, bureaucracy and rational-legal domination.

I argue in the section below on 'rationality and the concept of actor' that Weber's model of the actor gives a limited and inadequate account of the conditions of action in general and of what he conceives as rational action in particular. Elsewhere I have proposed (Hindess, 1984; 1985a) that actors should be conceived simply as loci of decision and action. Actors do things as a consequence of decisions. These are called actions, and the actors' decisions play an important part in their explanation. Actors may also do things that are not consequences of decisions, and their explanation takes a rather different form. This approach has the advantage of reducing to an absolute minimum the assumptions that are built into the basic concept of actor. Actors have reasons for at least some of the things they do. Any further significant attributes that actors may be thought to possess (for example, the various 'cognitive interests' that Habermas (1977) presents as constitutive of knowledge) must therefore be seen as contingent on discursive and other conditions, as posing issues for further investigation rather than as constitutive of actors as such. In particular, actors' interests, the decisions they make and their reasons for making them are dependent on the discursive conditions which make it possible for them to be formulated. Of course, Weber recognizes that much human action is not rational, and that rationality is therefore subject to conditions. But those conditions are conceived in terms of the absence of irrational interferences with the otherwise intrinsic rationality of the actor. In effect, the assumptions built into Weber's model of the actor leave little space for questions concerning the discursive conditions in which actors reach and formulate decisions.

An important consequence of this argument is that a typology of actors' orientations, of the kind that Weber offers, is not a satisfactory starting-point for the analysis of social conditions. Indeed, there are points where Weber might seem to be on the verge of recognizing this problem. Consider, for example, the second sentence quoted above from his revised 'Introduction' to his studies on the world religions: 'Yet very frequently the world images that have been created by "ideas" have, like switchmen, determined the tracks along which action has been pushed by the dynamics of interest.' As Schluchter notes in his commentary on this passage (1981, p. 25 ff.), it suggests the need for a level of analysis (of world-views and their institutionalization) that goes beyond that of actors and their orientations.

In Weber's methodological writings action is said to depart from rationality to the extent that it is subject to behavioural (psychological or physiological) determinations. But there is in Weber's works another kind of reason why action may be less than fully rational. Consider the case of modern capitalism. In the 'Author's Introduction' published in Parsons's translation of *The Protestant Ethic* Weber tells us that rational capitalistic economic action involves calculations in terms of capital: 'an actual adaptation of economic action to a comparison of money income with money expenses takes place, no matter how primitive the form' (PESC, p. 19). Rational capitalistic economic action presupposes the existence of money, that is, it depends on conditions that cannot be defined solely at the level of the acting individual.

In the case of specifically *modern* capitalism a great deal more than this is required: the rational capitalist organization of formally free labour, the separation of the business from the household, rational book-keeping and rational structures of law and administration. '[M]odern rational capitalism has need, not only of the technical means of production, but of a calculable legal system and of administration in terms of formal rules'; otherwise there can be 'no rational enterprise under individual initiative' (PESC, p. 25). In other words, the rationality of the individual modern capitalist is inconceivable without 'the specific and peculiar rationalism of modern culture' (PESC, p. 26). What Weber represents as the most rational form of economic action depends on the prior elaboration of specific discursive forms (for example, in law and accountancy) and, more generally, on the realization of a rationality in the institutional organization of society itself. Here the rationality of the individual actor is a function of a pre-existing rationality at the supra-individual level of society. By the same token, the absence of rationality at the level of society reduces the scope for rationality at the level of the individual. With the best (i.e. most rational) will in the world, medieval capitalists could not hope to attain the level of economic rationality that is thought to be possible in the modern West. Here again, analysis of the conditions of rational action necessarily takes us beyond the level of individual actors and their orientations.

This necessity for a level of analysis beyond that of actors and their orientations is, of course, widely recognized in the literature. For example, Parsons brings a rather Weberian analysis of the unit act into a tense and perpetually uneasy relationship with a further level of analysis in terms of systems of action (Savage, 1981). Or again, Schluchter attempts a systematic reconstruction of Weber's developmental history, making use of Habermas's notion of an infrastructure of action systems. In these terms the human ability to communicate and act is the subjective correlate of an objective infrastructure. The problem with these analyses can be clearly seen in one of Habermas's commentaries on the limitations of Weber's treatment of rationality. Habermas criticizes Weber for his elision of two levels of analysis of rationality, one at the level of the actor

142

and the other at the level of systems of action. Weber, together with Marx, Horkheimer and Adorno, identifies 'societal rationalization with the growth of the instrumental and strategic rationality of action complexes; on the other hand they implicitly have in mind a more comprehensive societal rationality' (Habermas, 1979, p. 192).

So far, perhaps, so good. Unfortunately, he proceeds to locate what is missing from Weber's analyses at the level of actors' orientations. In distinguishing degrees of rationality of action 'Weber does not take the social relationship as his point of departure. He considers only the ends-means relationship of a teleologically conceived, monological action to be capable of rationalization' (1979, p. 194). Habermas offers the concept of '"communicative action" in order to bring out those aspects of the rationality of action that were neglected in Weber's actions theory' (ibid.).

Weber's treatment of social relationships in terms of actors' orientations is undoubtedly a weak point in his arguments. Actors' orientations are not generally a fruitful starting-point for the analysis of social relationships. The trouble with Habermas's proposed remedy is that it merely takes up a different aspect of actors' orientations – and in this respect it hardly advances beyond the terms of Weber's own position. For all their emphasis on the need for a further level of analysis – for example, in terms of systems and their exigencies – many of these attempts to go beyond the limits of Weber nevertheless take actors and their orientations as an essential starting-point for their constructions.

In what follows I argue that actors' orientations are not in general an appropriate starting-point for the analysis of those aspects of social life that go beyond the level of the individual actor. Weber's analysis of rationalization is therefore problematic not only because it involves a level of structural analysis that is inconsistent with his explicit methodological individualism, but also because it is a form of characterization of social conditions based on actors' orientations. This chapter is primarily concerned with the second of these issues. I consider first the 'structural' question of the characterization of social conditions in terms of rationality (or any other orientation) before proceeding to Weber's concept of rationality itself.

The Institutionalization of Purposive Rationality in the Modern West

A product of modern European civilization, studying any problem of universal history, is bound to ask himself to what combination of circumstances the fact should be attributed that in Western civilization, and in Western civilization only, cultural phenonema have appeared which (as we like to think) lie in a line of development having universal significance and value.   (PESC, p. 13)

It is always tempting to read Weber as proposing a conception of history as the progressive realization of the purposive rationality that he presents as characteristic of the modern West. The point is not that Weber proposes a necessary developmental tendency in history. His reference above to 'combinations of circumstances' suggests otherwise. Rather the problem is that he appears to operate with a hierarchical principle of ranking in terms of which other societies or cultures may be analysed according to the extent to which they realize or depart from the rationalization said to be characteristic of the modern West. Weber certainly insists that modern rational capitalism presupposes definite social conditions of existence, but these often seem little more than expressions of rationality in other spheres – the rational organization of formally free labour, rational book-keeping, rational systems of law and administration, and so on.

If modern Western civilization appears as the realization of an essential rationality then other civilizations may be conceived in terms of their departure from it. It is no surprise then that the decisive obstacle to the development of modern capitalism in the great civilizations of India and China turns out to be that the Eastern civilizations embodied a spirit alien to that of modern rational capitalism. The difficulty with this position is simply that it combines two incompatible principles of analysis. On the one hand a society or culture is the expression of an inner principle, and on the other it is subject to numerous and distinct conditions of existence (Hindess, 1977). A similar principle of ranking appears in Weber's discussion of the types of social action. Some pages after his insistence on the construction of *rational* ideal types, he goes on to suggest that mechanical and instinctive factors are completely predominant 'in the early stages even of human development' (ES, p. 17). Here, as in the review quoted at the beginning of this chapter, Weber suggests that the theoretical tools of the social scientist are more nearly applicable the closer we approach the societies of the modern West.

It would not be difficult, in response to this interpretation, to cite numerous passages in which Weber explicitly rejects any teleological account of history (especially, but not only, in his comments on Marxism). But what is at issue in those passages is teleology as an explanatory mechanism. The denial of teleology is part and parcel of Weber's rejection of single-factor explanations. For example, Weber's treatment of developmental processes within the major world religions appears to involve an inherent rationalizing tendency (cf. Roth and

Schluchter, 1979, ch. 1). But he insists that this is not the only mechanism in operation, and its significance is always seen as strictly limited in relation to other factors.

Again, the interpretation of the modern world in terms of the realization of a purposive rationality seems to be incompatible both with Weber's methodological individualism (but then any supra-individual level of analysis is problematic in those terms) and with his understanding of social life as involving irreconcilable interests and value-conflicts. On the second point, consider Weber's treatment of the formal and substantive aspects of rationality. The former refers to the calculability of means and procedures, whatever the end pursued, while the latter refers to the assessment of outcomes in terms of a particular value standpoint. The rationalization of the modern West involves the spread of formal rationality, which goes along with a considerable diversity of substantive ends. The demands of substantive rationality are invariably frustrated – if only by the actions of others (or oneself) towards alternative substantive ends. If the world is shaped by struggles around competing substantive objectives then it can hardly be analysed in terms of the realization of an inner principle. As for the tensions between formal and substantive rationality, what makes this such an issue in Weber's account of the modern world is not the fact that the demands of substantive rationality are frustrated, since that must always be the case. Rather it is that the modern West is supposed to be dominated by the world-view of formal rationality, which insists on seeing the world primarily as the field of implementation of human purposes (unlike the world-views of magic and the great religions). It is in terms of that world-view that the frustration of the demands of any substantive rationality appears so problematic.

But this point returns us yet again to the realization thesis; the tension between formal and substantive rationality is supposed to be peculiarly characteristic of the modern period precisely because it is dominated by the world-view of formal rationality. If the modern West is not to be understood in terms of such a realization thesis, then it is difficult to see why Weber (and all too many others) should make such a fuss about the rationalization of the world and its alleged consequences. If the societies of the modern West involve other significant developments, not themselves reducible to effects of rationalization, then no general propositions (or problems) concerning the character of life in the modern West follow from the extension of formal rationality. In other words, short of conceiving of the modern West in teleological mode as approximating towards the expression or realization of a world-view of formal rationality, the consequences of any extension of formal rationality will always depend on the conditions in which that extension takes place – and these cannot be expected to operate uniformly throughout the various social milieux of the societies of the modern West.

Thus, even if we were to admit that Western societies have experienced a massive extension of what, for the sake of the present argument, we might call formal rationality, that would amount merely to one distinctive feature of those societies amongst others. Neither cultures nor societies are expressions of world-views, and the consequences of whatever world-views or other cultural features may be found within them will always depend on an irreducible variety of other conditions. I have presented the argument against the analysis of societies or cultures as the expressions of some predominant world-view in a general and abstract form. It is reinforced if we consider how limited and uninformative such a characterization may be. In the context of the present argument this point can be made most forcefully by returning to the concept of actor. First, actors' orientations do not suffice to define or constitute the relationships in which they are involved. Paul Hirst has given a particularly clear demonstration of this point in his discussion of Althusser's attempt to account for the reproduction of relations of production by means of the ideological constitution of subjects (Hirst and Woolley, 1979) – but the argument applies generally to all attempts to reduce social relations to actors' orientations (Hindess, 1985a). Their rationality or otherwise may tell us something about the relationships between actors, but it cannot tell us very much.

Secondly, I have indicated above why Weber's model of the actor, as a human individual characterized by a potential for rational calculation and acting in terms of material and ideal interests, should be replaced by a more general model of the actor as locus of decision and action. This is important in the present context for two reasons. First, where formal rationality is thought to be a socially widespread feature of the way actors evaluate their situation and act within it, this raises problems of explanation that cannot be adequately posed on the basis of Weber's model. I return to this point below. Secondly, once the concept of actor is freed from Weber's indefensible theoretical humanism, then it is possible to take note of actors other than human individuals (Hindess, 1985a).

An actor is a locus of decision and action where action is, at least in part, a consequence of that actor's decisions. Human individuals are certainly actors in this sense but they are by no means the only things that reach decisions and attempt to act on them. State agencies, capitalist enterprises, churches, trades unions, political parties are all examples of actors other than human individuals. They all have means of reaching decisions and of acting on some of them. Serious problems arise, of course, if the concept of actor is extended to entities that have no identifiable means of formulating decisions, let alone of acting on them. Classes, societies, men as a collectivity subordinating women as another collectivity are all spurious actors that are sometimes invoked in political or social scientific discourse. I have discussed some of the problems with the invocation of such spurious actors elsewhere (Hindess, 1985a). For present purposes it is sufficient to note that if the concept of actor is restricted to entities capable of reaching and acting on decisions, then there are numerous significant actors in the modern world other than human individuals. It will be convenient to refer to these as social actors. Any approach to the analysis of modern societies that admits only human individuals as effective actors must be regarded as seriously incomplete.

It is often said, by Weber amongst many others, that all social actors are themselves reducible to human individuals. But that is to mistake the significance of one important difference between human individuals and other actors. Human individuals are the only actors whose actions do not invariably involve the actions of others. The actions of capitalist enterprises, for example, always depend on those of other actors (executives, managerial, supervisory and other employees, legal representatives) and therefore on the specific character of the relationships between the enterprise and these other actors. The actions of human individuals do not always depend on the actions of others in this way. This shows that there may be important differences between the conditions of action of human individuals and those of other actors. It does not show that all social actors are equivalent (except in this one important respect) or that one kind of actor is reducible to the other.

The actions of social actors are critically dependent on the modes of assessment of their situation that they deploy in reaching decisions, and on the specific sets of social relations in which they are implicated. In both respects, the characterization of their conditions of action in terms of rationality is, to say the least, not very informative. To take the modes of assessment first, consider the case of capitalist enterprises. Even if we were to accept, for the sake of argument, that capitalist enterprises were rational in their assessments, that would tell us remarkably little about how they might be expected to act. It is often suggested, by Marxist and neo-classical economists alike, that a uniquely defined mode of assessment aimed at profit maximization is imposed on enterprises by the rigours of the market. In fact it is easy to show that several distinct modes of assessment are employed by firms operating within a single national economy, to say nothing of differences between national economies themselves. There is no uniquely defined mode of assessment given by the assumption of rationality and by such rigours as the market-place may impose (cf. the discussions in Hindess, 1984; Cutler *et al.*, 1978, pt 11; Williams *et al.*, 1984). The assumption of rationality, in other words, gives a misleading impression of uniformity, and it tells us little

147

about the particular modes of assessment employed by a firm in any given case.

Similar points could be made about the relationships between enterprises (or other social actors) and the actors involved in their decisions and actions. Bureaucracy, in something like Weber's ideal-typical form, is often supposed to characterize the distinctively modern pattern of such relationships. It is distinctively modern, first, as the embodiment of instrumental rationality as a principle of organization, and secondly, in its dependence on that wider rationalization of social life in the modern world which allows for appointment on the basis of ability, the separation of home from office, payment in money rather than in kind, and so on. In fact, as Turner and Factor have noted, much of the literature on complex organizations 'has been devoted to the criticism of the rigidity and limited applicability of Weber's conception even to those organizations that aspire to maximal efficiency and rationality' (1984b, p. 52). In this case too the notion of rationality gives at best a misleading impression of uniformity in the organizational structures of capitalist enterprises, state agencies, or other social actors. There may perhaps be a sense in which instrumental rationality is an index of certain gross differences between our own and distinctively other civilizations. But it would nevertheless tell us remarkably little about the modes of assessment employed by actors in the modern world and the diverse ways in which their capacities for action may or may not depend on other actors, and still less about the sets of more or less stable relationships that may obtain between actors.

Rationality and the Concept of Actor

The argument so far has suggested that the massive extension of formal rationality into many areas of social life (such as might be supposed to have characterized the development of the modern West) merely indicates one distinctive feature of modern societies amongst others. Short of a teleological analysis of these societies as (approaching towards) the realization of an essential inner principle, it is difficult to draw any general conclusion from that feature alone. What its consequences are in any particular case will depend on other features of the society or culture in question, and these cannot be derived from the extension of formal rationality itself. Talk of the rationalization of life in the modern world is therefore less informative than has often been supposed.

This section moves on to a different order of problems by reconsidering the links between rationality and the actor it is often said to characterize. I have already suggested the need for a different and in certain respects more general model of the actor, as locus of decision and action. This formulation might appear to suggest that Weber's model of the actor could be regarded as a special case, and therefore as perfectly legitimate within limits. Unfortunately the problems with Weber's model are more serious than a simple limitation in the range of cases to which it may be applied. The effect of treating rationality and other attributes as intrinsic features of the human actor is to foreclose serious questions of the discursive conditions of action, to impose a restrictive and unnecessary psychic unity on to the conception of actor, and to misrepresent the location of what might be called rationalizing tendencies in the modern world. To establish these points we need to reconsider the ways in which rationality (or other attributes) might be considered relevant to the conceptualization of actors and their actions.

We may begin by noting that concepts of the person differ from one culture to another, and over time within cultures or civilizations. The modern Western conception of the person is not a human universal, a natural and given datum of human experience. 'Forms of specification of individuals exist in all societies but', as Hirst and Woolley (1982, p. 118) point out, 'they are not necessarily specified as individual subjects, as unique entities coincident with a distinct consciousness and will.' Within the general Western conceptualization of the person, those variants that insist on the propensity of the actor to act in accordance with a rational assessment of material and ideal interests have long occupied a predominant place in (amongst others) the discourses of politics and economics.

It is not difficult to show that the model of rational economic man is descriptively inadequate. Indeed, Weber himself makes that point. He insists that we start from the presumption of rationality in our attempts to analyse human behaviour, so that the place of non-rational elements in behaviour might be seen 'as accounting for the observed deviations from this hypothetical course' (ES, p. 6). I have argued elsewhere that there are severe problems with such a starting-point. In particular, it forecloses serious questions concerning the forms of discourse available to actors and employed by them in assessing their situation and deciding on some course of action (Hindess, 1984).

But it is necessary to go further to indicate how such inadequate conceptualizations of the actor can nevertheless play such an important part in the modern world. The first point to notice here is that the significance of the model of rational economic man and related conceptions of the person is not a matter of 'realism', in the sense of approximating to an accurate description of how people behave. These models do not have their origin in careful observation of human behaviour in the developing capitalist societies of the West. They will not disappear merely because they can be shown to be inadequate in the face both of theoretical argument and of evidence accumulated in anthropology, history, psychoanalysis and numerous experimental and fieldwork studies in our own societies. The test of falsifiability is not a significant element in the life of such doctrines. What is at stake here is not just a matter of economic or political theory, of the more or less elaborate constructions based on rational economic man and 'his' (*sic*) close relations. It is also a matter of concepts of the person that are 'implicated to a greater or lesser degree in our legal system, in our conceptions of contract and the wage labour relationship, in many of our assumptions about education, and so on' (Hirst and Woolley, 1982, p. 131).

If realism is not necessarily to be expected of these concepts of the person, they must nevertheless have a certain plausibility. It must be possible to represent the relevant aspects of human behaviour in terms of the actions of such persons, and to have some means of accounting for actions that fail to conform – for example, through categories of mental illness, affectual and other non-rational sources of motivation, and so on. The doctrine of revealed preference in contemporary neo-classical economics allows, for example, much of consumer behaviour to be analysed in these terms. A similar function is performed by the proposals of Weber and many rational choice theorists that we construct models of rational action, introducing affectual and other non-rational elements only when strictly necessary to account for deviations – and again, at a rather different level, by the normalizing discourses of psychiatry, penology and the like. In *Discipline and Punish* Foucault has shown how the discourse of the prison can find reinforcement in the very failures of the prison system (1975).

What is required then for these discourses, of rational economic man and his relations, to be implicated in significant areas of social life is that there should not appear to be too many departures from the norm, and that the departures can be explained away. In general this means that actors must appear to incorporate something approaching the appropriate model in their own assessments and decisions. It must be possible, for example, to assimilate the decision-making process in most capitalist enterprises more or less closely to the model of rational economic actor. This requirement will, of course, be relaxed for the very young, the senile and others judged to have departed considerably from the rational norm. For the rest, models of rational action are implicated in significant areas of social life to the extent that relevant actors incorporate such models into their own assessments and decisions.

Does this mean that Weber's model of the actor, or something very like it, can be saved after all – at least with regard to the societies of the modern West? Fortunately not. One reason is that the location of rationality as an intrinsic, if sometimes inhibited, property of the actor forecloses serious questions concerning the discursive conditions of decision and action:

questions of the forms of calculation available to or employed by actors, questions of the social conditions on which they depend and questions of how their availability to actors themselves depends on the actors' locations within particular sets of social relationships. I have discussed this point elsewhere (Hindess, 1984) and need not develop the argument here. But two further reasons are also worth noting. First, the presumption of rationality, as a property of the actor, implies a certain consistency or coherence across the range of the actor's behaviour, except in those cases where 'non-rational' elements intervene. If rationality is located instead in certain features of the discourses employed in the reaching and formulating of decisions, then there is no reason to assume consistency or coherence across the range of the actor's decisions. Secondly, to say that some model of rational action is incorporated in an actor's assessments is not to say that other significant elements might not also be involved. A case in point would be the self-conscious rationality displayed by actors caught up in paranoia or certain forms of compulsive behaviour. What these points show is that even if rationality were to be displayed by some actor or actors in significant areas of their activity, we should regard it as something that has to be explained by reference to the discursive conditions of action, not as an intrinsic feature of the actors themselves.

Finally, if models of rational action are indeed implicated in significant areas of social life this requires that those areas can themselves be represented as fields of instrumental action. In other words, there must be discourses in which the economy, politics, the criminal population, or whatever, can be represented as a field of potential action and effects so as to allow a 'rational' calculation of objectives and how to achieve them. The various more or less sophisticated economic discourses employed by capitalist enterprises, financial institutions and government departments would be examples. Foucault has made a similar point in his discussions of the interdependence of power and knowledge in the modern period:

> these relations of power cannot themselves be established, consolidated, or implemented without the production, accumulation, circulation and functioning of a discourse. There can be no possible exercise of power without a certain economy of discourses of truth which operates through and on the basis of this association. We are subjected to the production of truth through power and we cannot exercise power except through the production of truth.
>
> (Foucault, 1980a, p. 93)

Here the operations of power depend on the possibility of representing its field of operation in terms of a calculation of effects.

Perhaps a further attempt at rehabilitation might be suggested at this point. There is certainly a sense in which Weber is absolutely right to

151

insist that the modern period has seen a massive extension of instrumental rationality. But here too it is necessary to be wary of Weber's account. First, there is a significant element of positivism in Weber's distinction between objective and subjective rationality. In the case of the former, techniques for achieving given ends are determined in accordance with scientific knowledge. The discourses of rational action implicated in the fields of law, economic activity, or education certainly involve what Foucault calls 'regimes of truth', that is, the operation of criteria, norms and procedures for identifying or arguing about 'true' propositions in any given case. We can distinguish assessments made in terms of the appropriate regime of truth (Weber's 'objective rationality') from other assessments made by actors. Such distinctions may be important, for example, in the event that actors are required to account for their conduct – whether it should be regarded as responsible or irresponsible, careless or considered, that of a 'reasonable man' or something other, and so on. But we can register those distinctions and their ramifications without necessarily unifying the various regimes of truth in the name of science or objectivity.

Secondly, there is no reason to regard the discourses representing some part of the world as a field of instrumental action, as if they were themselves unified as just so many expressions of the one world-view or orientation. We should certainly expect to find connections between these discourses. Features of one may be incorporated in others, and some may share common features. For example, elements of the normalizing discourses of psychiatry or clinical medicine may be incorporated into criminal law. But it would be a mistake to assume an overall coherence. Examination of the connections between law and psychiatry will certainly reveal areas of incorporation, but it will also reveal considerable areas of dispute and acute tension. The trouble with Weber's position here is that the rationalization of different fields is seen in terms of an inherent unifying principle at the level of the rationality of the human individual, and of the removal of its inhibitions in the shape of spiritual and other obstacles.

Concluding Summary

I have argued against Weber's treatment of the modern West as dominated by the growth of formal rationality at two levels. First, actors' orientations are not in general an appropriate starting-point for the analysis of social relationships. In this respect, the attempts by Weber and all too many others to characterize the modern West in terms of the alleged growth of formal rationality are at best relatively uninformative, an index of gross differences between our own and other civilizations, and at worst seriously misleading. If the societies of the modern West could be regarded as just so many expressions of the one inner principle of formal rationality, then it would certainly be possible to draw general conclusions from the alleged secular growth of that orientation. But, in the absence of that indefensible teleology, it is clear that the consequences of any extension of formal rationality must depend on the conditions in which that extension takes place.

Secondly, there are serious problems with Weber's model of the actor as a human individual with a frequently inhibited potential for rational calculation and action. Not only are there actors other than human individuals, some of whose decisions have important consequences, but Weber's model gives an inadequate account of the conditions of action in general and of rational action in particular. Of course Weber recognizes that action is not always rational, and that the rationality of action is therefore dependent on definite conditions. But his methodological injunction that we should start from rational ideal types requires that those conditions be conceived as the absence of interferences with the rationality of the actor. Against that position I argue that actors' decisions and the reasons for them are dependent both on complex internal processes and on the discursive conditions that allow them to be formulated. In this sense rationality is a matter both of the discourses employed in the reaching and formulating of decisions and of their deployment by the actor. It is not an intrinsic feature of the actor as such. In this sense it is possible to pose questions of the discursive conditions of action that are foreclosed by Weber's treatment of rationality as an intrinsic, if frequently inhibited, feature of the actor. Weber's account of rationality imposes a spurious unity at the levels both of the individual actor and of such rationalizing tendencies as may be found in the modern world. There are numerous practical discourses representing parts of the world as fields of instrumental action, but the effect of treating them as so many expressions of the one world-view of instrumental rationality is to give a mistaken impression of their overall coherence and to obscure the difficult questions of the social conditions on which they depend.

7

On the Irreversibility of
Western Rationalization and
Max Weber's Alleged Fatalism

JOHANNES WEISS

Translated by Bruce Allen and Sam Whimster

A familiar objection to Weber's analyses of Western rationality holds that while they allow the negative aspects of this process to be identified, especially in regard to the further development of freedom and personality, they none the less ascribe to the process an implacable necessity and irreversibility. Two explanations have been advanced to account for this so-called 'fatalistic' position. First, it is maintained that an individualistic theory of social action is in *principle* incapable of encompassing socio-historical developments in a critical and open manner. Such a theory of social action, it is alleged, can deal only with derived states of affairs that operate at the subjective or phenomenological level alone, and its concepts and explanations do not have the theoretical power to reveal the underlying forces that determine the social totality. I do not propose to pursue this objection in its basic form. Rather I want to respond to a second version, which is more concrete in its treatment. In this it is maintained that Weber was forced to draw fatalistic conclusions about the development of society precisely because he did interpret this process (even down to its oppressive, alienating and freedom-endangering effects) as a universal historical process of rationalization (Bader, Berger 1976 *et al.*, p. 484).

The Processes of Rationalization as Pluralistic and Conflictual

In countering the criticism of Weber's alleged belief in such a rationalization process, it is first of all appropriate to recall how varied were the forms and directions that rationalization took, even indeed within the Western course of rationalization. This alone should suffice to show that the process of rationalization is characterized by deep, internal tensions and contradictions and that the Weberian theory of rationalization – and this marks it off from the unreflective conceptions of progress of the Enlightenment – has no place for a one-dimensional, unilinear and so ineluctable developmental process.

> Naturally it is possible to cite passages in Weber, where he describes the 'disenchantment of the world' in just this fashion; but such quotations torn out of context merely yield caricatures. What emerges rather from a study of the Weberian corpus as a whole is that for the author the ambiguity and hence questionability of rationalization is itself an integral part of the whole development. (Bendix, 1972, p. 53)

Thus what is involved is not so much the simple question of the reversibility or irreversibility of the process as a whole, nor a zero-sum game of 'rationality versus irrationality'; rather it is a matter of recognizing the conflicting developments, including frequent reversals, within the complex process of rationalization. Weber's attitude to the concept of rationalization is well summed up in what the philosopher R. Spaemann has recently said of the concept of progress:

> If we cling to the concept of progress in the singular, then presumably the Bomb really is the end result. We must learn, as a matter of principle, to think in the plural when we talk of progress. Progress always occurs in respect of this and that, and we always need to know whether we are not perhaps paying for this or that step forward with this or that step backwards. The concept of progress in the singular is quite an unreasonable idea. (Spaemann, 1985)

In reply to this argument it might be said that the assumption of irreversibility, attributed to Weber, is in fact closely bound up with Weber's own refusal to say anything about progress within the context of empirical knowledge, except in regard to the progress of science and technological rationalization. Because of this reduction of progress to rationalization in a technological and cognitive sense, the social process is then excluded from all possibility of evaluative judgement, and so from free and rational human praxis, and subordinated to objective laws of substantive reality (*Sachgesetzen*). Precisely because of his rejection of the traditional, value-rational concept of progress, it is then argued that Weber is forced to assert the irreversibility of the historical process.

Despite the fact that this argument may have achieved a wide currency and wear the air of the obvious, it is none the less inadequate. Admittedly it is correctly observed that any development in the cultural, social and material sphere can be described as 'objective' progress only to the extent that it leads or contributes to some improvement in cognitive or technological instrumentality (for the attainment of pre-set goals). This results in

155

the concept of progress losing any absolute or self-legitimating meaning. Its very use is relative and calls for an exact grounding in the particular case. It is thus an empirical matter to determine whether something counts as progress in a technological sense; but whether the dominant cultural ideals (intellectual, political, moral, or aesthetic, etc.) are superior to others, and hence to be accorded preference, can be debated with more or less good reasons but cannot be determined once and for all in complete clarity on the basis of an objective calculus of progress and regress.

It is precisely this last assumption that should most clearly set Weber's view of history apart from that of Marx's. The 'cast-iron laws' that for Marx govern the historical process owe much of their force and irresistibility because they concern the laws of motion of the 'material base'; they thus pertain to a layer of reality that for the most part is inaccessible to human grasp and consciousness. In this respect the dynamics of technological rationality are accorded a much more central, systematic importance in the Marxian theory of history and society than is the case with Weber.[1]

All in all it seems to me unfruitful and false in the extreme to attribute to Weber the idea that the history of modern Western society conforms to a uniform, all-pervasive and irreversible law of (technological) rationalization. It becomes apparent from a careful reading of his work that Weber was very much concerned to show the tensions that existed in the relations between the processes of rationalization as they existed, and still continue to do so, in the different socio-cultural areas; moreover to do this within Western history. What is involved is more than a conflict between formal or technological and material rationality, and between instrumental and value rationality; as, for example, the conflict between the progressive rationalization of the law and the administration of the state on the one hand, and on the other the progressive radicalization and universalization of the moral and political postulates of human and civil rights. Rather it is the case that formal or material rationalization within a particular sphere of action and meaning (the spheres of art, science, religion, the erotic, the economic and politics) raises the tension between one sphere of action and the others to the extent of complete incompatibility.

Hence when we talk about the rationalization process and society we have to provide a precise specification of those dimensions of social action in which the rationalization process takes place. The 'dialectics' of these processes lend themselves to such empirical analysis. For instance, a 'purely business relationship', which is characterized by a high degree of predictability, turns out to be ethically irrational because it rejects an interpretation and understanding on the basis of individual will and personal relationships (ES, p. 585). Having said this, the fact that the progress of 'social differentiation and rationalization' brings with it an

increasing degree of irrationality does not necessarily signify a contradiction because the social actors involved are less and less capable of
comprehending the rational basis of this progress.

> The progress of social differentiation and rationalization therefore
> usually – though not absolutely always – means a wholesale widening
> and separation of those practically affected by rational techniques and
> rules from the rational foundation of those rules, which, on the whole,
> is likely to be more mysterious to those affected than the meaning of the
> sorcerer's magical procedures is to the 'primitive'.
>
> (Weber, 1981, p. 178)

The 'communicative capabilities', to use a term of Luhmann's, of social
actors increase progressively as a result of rationalization; but this
capability is purely of a technical kind if it is not sustained through the
universalization of knowledge about the conditions and interrelationships
of communal social action (Weber, 1981, p. 178). What the end result of
this process may mean for the exclusion of emotional life from the
predominating relations of social action and thereby the reduction of
'communicability' (that is, the possibility of reaching a differentiated
inter-subjective understanding) is something that has been realized and
described by poets a long time before sociologists.

Freedom as a Function of Irreversibility

The considerations advanced so far, while possessing a certain plausibility, fall short in two respects. First, they offer an insufficient clarification
of the concept of 'irreversibility' to the extent that this concept is drawn
on in the theoretical analyses of history and society. Second, they leave the
question unanswered as to how one accounts for Weber's statements on
the inevitability of rationalization, if at the same time he allowed an
open-ended and multi-dimensional perspective. If the processes of
rationalization operated at more than one level and were characterized by
tension, why is the process as a whole inevitable and beyond the control of
even instrumental rationality?

With regard to the general presuppositions and implications of the
irreversibility thesis in the historical and social sciences, I would like to
advance an argument made by Karl Popper. In *The Poverty of Historicism*
(1957, p. 116) Popper objects in principle to the generalization of the
irreversibility of historical processes. In this he is opposing, among
others, Toynbee, who has gone on record with the following statement:
'Civilizations are not static conditions of societies but dynamic
movements of an evolutionary kind. They not only cannot stand still, but

they cannot reverse their direction without breaking their own laws of motion' (Toynbee, 1934, p. 176). In Popper's opinion theses of this kind commonly confuse (observable) trends with laws (that allegedly determine the historical process as a whole).

There is little doubt that the habit of confusing trends with laws, together with the intuitive observation of trends (such as technical progress), inspired the central doctrine of evolutionism and historicism – the doctrine of the inexorable laws of biological evolution and the irreversible laws of motion of society.   (Popper, 1957, p. 116)

In quite a different way and, at first sight, in an exactly contradictory way, the concept of irreversibility has been taken up by certain branches of the philosophy of science. In particular Prigogine and his school argue that the perception of the irreversibility of processes in nature leads to a fundamental 'metamorphosis of science' thereby arriving at a wholly new synthesis of the natural and human sciences (Prigogine and Stengers, 1979/1984; Prigogine, 1980). I cannot comment in any detail on these extremely demanding and naturally also very controversial matters at this point. However, of importance for this discussion is the fact that Prigogine draws a basic contrast between the idea of the irreversibility and the idea that prevails in classical physics of universal, deterministic laws of nature. For the classical idea implies not only a closed and static view of the world, but also the notion of the reversibility in principle of *all* processes. In such a world there is no place for spontaneity, singularity and, most of all, effective innovation. In his own research at the interface between physics and biology (rewarded with a Nobel prize), Prigogine was able to discover 'processes of spontaneous organization and dissipative structures', thereby acquiring the insight 'that irreversibility in nature plays a constitutive role, since it permits processes of spontaneous organization' (Prigogine and Stengers, 1979, p. 18).

The opposition between Popper's and Prigogine's approaches is not so much intrinsic but rather lies (from the point of view of the ramifications for the social and historical sciences at any rate) in the different reference contexts in which the concept of irreversibility is employed. Popper objects to the irreversibility assumption in the social sciences, because such an assumption does not square with the openness and indeterminacy of social development. But the same intention leads Prigogine to come out in favour of the existence of irreversibility in the historical and social sciences on the basis of his discovery of irreversibility in nature (Prigogine and Stengers, 1984, p. 208). Popper charges that the concept of irreversibility of a process is underpinned by unconditionally obligatory laws, that the lawfulness sets the process on a determined path of development and that this can all be ascertained with reliability. In contrast irreversibility

158

for Prigogine is an entirely opposite state of affairs: that neither determinism nor an unambiguous directionality underlies the concept of irreversibility.

It is only an apparent paradox that the clarification of Weber's conception of rationalization and the question of its irreversibility proceed by way of embracing both Popper's and Prigogine's arguments. From what has already been said it must be apparent that Weber does not fall foul of Popper's critique of the assumptions of irreversibility. Weber does not conflate laws and trends; on the contrary he always threw the utmost doubt on the belief that deterministic and universally valid laws were to be found in history and that they could be used for the purposes of explanation. When Weber refers to those features of the Western process of rationalization that he regarded as particularly predominant, namely, bureaucratization at the institutional level and the disenchantment of the world at the cultural level, in no sense did he draw on the assumption that these developments were law-like phenomena existing without limit and not subject to alteration. The fact that Weber did, especially at the end of *The Protestant Ethic*, make predictions that the trends of rationalization, for all their competing and countervailing tendencies, would neither weaken nor reverse themselves in the foreseeable future is *not* an infringement of his rejection of all nomothetic theories of history. Indeed it sounds extraordinarily apodictic when he speaks in the well-known passage of 'that powerful modern economic world, bound to the technical and economic conditions of mechanical production, which today shapes the way of life of all who are born into it with overwhelming pressure, and will perhaps continue to do so until the last hundredweight of fossil fuel has been burned to ashes' (WS, p. 170). The impression that Weber gives here of an irresistible and inescapable destiny is not decisively ameliorated when he wonders whether new prophets or, at least, a 'powerful revival of old ideas and ideals' will arise in the far distant future ('at the end of this gigantic development'), as opposed to a general 'mechanised petrification' (WS, p. 171).

Without doubt Weber was convinced that the process of progressive rationalization would lead increasingly to the restriction of the free play of action and have an obligatory character independent of the will of particular individuals on all spheres of life, and this applied above all to those spheres of life directly or indirectly related to the 'economic order'. To be sure he did not draw the conclusion of explaining freedom as an insight into – and a conscious adaptation to – the understanding of this necessity, or of regarding it as a fiction. His final conclusion held that everything depended on the idea of strengthening and furthering the freedom of action of the individual and of increasing its chances of development (GPS, p. 64). By itself this excludes the attribution to Weber of a 'fatalistic' attitude towards history.

159

For all of that Weber considered it unrealistic and hopeless to believe that this 'gigantic development' would turn about or let itself be turned about. This leads to the question: what grounds were there for the conviction and certainty of his prognosis? The question has no simple answer. I believe however that one aspect in the controversy over Weber's position has been overlooked. It seems to me that the Weberian prognosis has an affinity with the 'prophetic history' (*wahrsagender Geschichte*) of Kant, which for Kant was the only type he regarded as legitimate (in his 'Conflict of the Faculties'). Here Kant remarks that we can say something about the future course of history only to the extent that we, as rational actors (in the sense of practical reason), can and will wish to collaborate in the shaping of this course.

Within the framework of such a view of history, historical developments are thus held to be irreversible, because these developments flow (by and large) from the intentions of men living now and in the future. The course of history is irreversible not on account of the efficacy of deterministic laws, which would make change or reversal impossible and even unthinkable, but instead derives from the acceptance that human beings in the light of their ideals and interests would not wish such a reversal in the course of development. It is evident that this kind of irreversibility, thus understood and qualified, comes very close to the concept defended by Prigogine, whereby the irreversibility is seen as a function of indeterminacy and spontaneity. Hence at the provisional stage of their thinking Prigogine and Stengers have arrived at the idea of an 'open world', to which we all belong and which we play an active part in constructing (1979, p. 273).

On closer examination such a viewpoint would not appear to be incompatible with Weber's pronounced accentuation of the compulsory and unfree nature of the rationalization process in the West. In this regard it is of great importance that Weber did not explain the obligatoriness and irresistibility of this process by reference to the power of blind, objective laws, nor did he explain it as a result of an immanent logic of its own dynamic. It is indeed pertinent that a good part of the rationalization occurs 'behind the back' of social actors and wholly independent of their conscious motivation and decision. The decisive point, however, is that the dynamic of rationalization is never placed in doubt, or superseded or reversed, when it becomes the subject of the thinking of actors. It is precisely when acting human beings, conscious of their freedom of action, confirm their position and their capacity to act within the process of rationalization that the idea of its unalterability is particularly cogent. This may in the final analysis, as Luhmann conceives of it, touch on the fact that the self-description of a social system in social action terms is related to the temporal asymmetry of social relations; that is, again considered in principle, there is a connection between the 'irreversibility of time and the genesis of meaning as a form of information processing' (Luhmann, 1985, pp. 71, 232, 609 *passim*). This to be sure takes us beyond irreversibility as processes of change to a level of abstraction that concerns the most general (so to speak, transcendental) presuppositions of irreversibility.

More concretely, when considering the notion of the irreversibility of a course of history in a particular situation, the realization dawns that at a given state of knowledge there is no intellectually convincing or practically realizable alternative.[2] Crucially important here is that the 'state of knowledge' concerned in no way applies merely to the field of causal-analytic and technological knowledge. Thus it would be perfectly conceivable, and also possible in practice, to arrest the degree of rationality and also to reverse it in the sphere of industrial production or in the sphere of social communication facilitated by technology. What opposes this is not only, and in the long run not even primarily, the interests of the status quo, economic groups and prestige; but rather rationalization processes of this kind correspond to very strong postulates of substantive rationality of material processes – particularly to the extent that these postulates involve an optimal and just provision of material and cultural goods for more and more people (ultimately everybody).[3] The realization of these moral and political goals basically requires not a lesser but rather a greater amount of technological rationality in the production and distribution of these goods.

The same point applies to the demand, which is growing in intensity, to put a stop to the progressive exploitation and destruction of natural resources. Things being the way they are, this demand can be acceded to only through more rationality – namely, through deeper scientific insights into complex causal connections, through more refined and efficient technologies and, not least of all, through a more differentiated and efficient organizational apparatus (for the control over the requisite behaviour). Were this to be followed, the 'cage of servitude' that might conceivably be waiting at the end of this development would not be explained, at least not primarily, as the product of a technological rationality blindly following its own dynamic. And should the cage of servitude come about, it would do so because it had become the instrument for the enforcement of the most radical ideas of material rationality; this would not be contradictory but on the contrary highly consistent with the fanatical theorists of equality (from Saint-Just down to some of the dogmatic communist theoreticians of the present like Wolfgang Harich) who have expressly demanded the establishment of the cage of servitude and have worked for such a possibility.

Finally, in the sense of the intellectual and cultural rationalization (by which is meant the more restricted concept of disenchantment) it would appear, at least for the time being, that the weight of evidence tends to favour accepting his version of irreversibility.

> Magic and religion have been dispossessed by science and logic, and it is no more plausible to suppose that the process will go historically into reverse and the workers of the research laboratories of Frankfurt, Princeton and Leningrad come to share the beliefs of the Azande about witchcraft than that the results of their researches will suffer an epistemological collapse and the atomic structure of a protein molecule turn out to look incomprehensibly different tomorrow from what it is agreed from China to Peru to be today.   (Runciman, 1984)

Though we might certainly wish for a 're-enchantment of the world', and indeed actively imagine it,[4] the real question is whether – with due regard to the obligations of intellectual honesty – we seriously strive to attain it or ever could.

Similar doubts are called for in regard to the development of moral reasoning on the one hand, and the intellectualization of *aesthetic* experience on the other – even assuming that one has to be very much more cautious with the concept of 'progress' in these fields than in the case of science and technology.[5] One does not need to be a supporter of the stage theory of evolution of moral consciousness to maintain that there is no plausible way back from the moral-philosophical insights and postulates of the Enlightenment.[6] Concerning art, if I may cite the crisp formulation of H. M. Enzensberger, 'The path being taken by modern art is not reversible. Others, if they wish to, may entertain hopes about the end of the modern era, about new beginnings or a repetition of the old: I do not' (1962, p. 315). This may have a decree-like tone about it, and anyway is by no means generally accepted and complied with. But does not the Romantic movement in art – this great ambitious attempt to overcome the 'disenchantment of the world' – does not this movement tend to show that such an attempt (once again assuming intellectual honesty) leads not to a new naïveté and immediacy but instead to a condition of ironic enfeeblement?

Therefore we have every reason to consider the disenchantment of the world as irreversible in the foreseeable future, since this alone corresponds to our intellectual aspirations and requirements. This certainly does not mean that we are inexorably creeping closer to a condition of intellectual 'entropy', and that we are threatened with a dissolution of all intellectual tensions and challenges and their replacement by a uniform and diffuse medium dubbed 'rationality'. What we have to suppose rather, as I have attempted to explain in the foregoing, is that masquerading under the headings of 'rationalization' and 'disenchantment' are conflicts that are both intellectual and practical, both social and political, and that stretch to the limits what we can bear in our capacity as individuals and as members of groups and societies.

Notes

1 This perfectly unambiguous matter is persistently overlooked by Marxist critics of Weber, as for instance by Bologh (1985, pp. 35 ff.). On the argument against Marcuse, see Weiß (1981, pp. 146 ff.).
2 These remarks, all too obviously, do not deny that technical developments in different fields often follow a very narrow, blind and often self-destructive logic of perfectionism. The train of thought pursued here does not in the least bit take up the matter of the desirability or unavoidability of actual kinds of rationalization, because these questions can naturally be decided and explained only in the individual instance.
3 On Weber's views on the relation of democracy and bureaucracy see Roth (1980, pp. 121 ff.). For de Tocqueville the thesis of the inevitability of the process of democratization, including the transformation of the state into a near omnipotent power of tutelage, follows from the insight that there is no convincing moral and political argument against the creation of the equality of condition of everyone (Tocqueville, 1972, Vol. 1, pp. 6, 14; Vol. 2, pp. 318, 332–3).
4 It is a fact that such ideas are even being heard from within the citadels of serious philosophy of science: cf. Prigogine (Prigogine and Stengers, 1984, pp. 291 ff.) and M. Berman (1983).
5 A remark also echoed by Toynbee: 'The cumulative progress of science and technology has no counterpart in the ethical sphere' (Toynbee and Ikeda, 1976, p. 325).
6 This could be demonstrated, for example, by showing the inadequacies and contradictions of Arnold Gehlen's treatment of this question (Gehlen, 1969). Compare the interesting critique by Habermas (1983b). Schluchter emphasizes the impossibility of returning to a religiously determined ethic from a non-religious ethic of personality (Roth and Schluchter, 1979, pp. 48 ff.).

8

The Application of the Weberian Concept of Rationalization to Contemporary Conditions

MARTIN ALBROW

Developing the Rationalization Thesis

There is no contradiction involved in saying that Weber's theory of rationalization has enormous relevance to contemporary conditions and has even proved prophetic, and, at the same time, that it is undeveloped as a theory. It remained in his work at a relatively low level of abstraction, amply illustrated at a concrete level with examples of a comparative and historical kind. In consequence it is entirely feasible to illustrate it in a modern society such as Britain and produce an indefinite amount of evidence in support, and at the same time to remain unsatisfied at a more fundamental level as to our understanding of the underlying mechanisms. It is as if we were to analyse Britain under Thatcher in the same mode as *The Class Struggles in France* and be without the theoretical developments that were to be laid in *Capital*. It could of course be done, and convincingly at an intuitive level; and if Marx had died at an early age, we might have had to be content with that. But it would have been necessary for others to develop the theory of labour and capital, the tendency of the rate of profit to fall and the growing concentration of capital. The underlying forces would have remained relatively unclarified at the level of the *Grundrisse*.

But if Weber had lived longer would he have written the equivalent of *Capital* for the rationalization thesis? There are two counter-indications. The first is that Weber shared Nietzsche's hostility to the creation of intellectual systems. Nourished though he was like all German intellectuals in the thought of the greatest of all the system builders, Immanuel Kant, and working with the concept that was generative of systemic thought, namely, rationality, in close contact with colleagues like Rickert and Simmel who laid the foundations for systematic sociology, Weber, none the less sided with the hammer of the philosophers, the greatest iconoclast of the modern period. 'I mistrust all systematizers and avoid them. The will to a system is a lack of integrity', was Nietzsche's view in 'Maxims and Arrows', No. 26 (1968a). 'A systematic science of culture, even only in the sense of a definitive, objectively valid, systematic fixation of the problems which it should treat, would be senseless in itself', was the frequently quoted view Weber expressed in his essay on 'Objectivity' (MSS, p. 84). The Nietzschean allusion is clear enough when one takes into account that, immediately before, Weber rejects a 'Chinese ossification of intellectual life'. (For Nietzsche, Kant was 'the Chinaman of Königsberg'.) But it was characteristic of the strenuous efforts that Weber made to mediate between Kant and Nietzsche that much of his intellectual work was systematic to a high degree. The basic concepts of sociology are only the most brilliant example of a formidable drive to consistency and comprehensiveness.

The other counter-indication to the promise of theoretical development cut short by Weber's early death is hinted at in that citation from the 'Objectivity' essay. Marx's *Capital* offered a logical analysis of economic relations in the spirit of positive science. Weber acknowledged the possibility of a purely rational economic science, in the sense of a model of activity calculatedly chosen to maximize economic ends, and it was one of the inspirations of his thinking about the methods of social science. But he never developed the idea that similar models might be extended to the sciences of human action in general and more particularly to culture. We can only speculate about what he would have made of the development of linguistics, semiotics, conversational analysis, ethnomethodology, structuralism, or systems theory in general as applied to human social relations. He might have taken them on board in the same spirit as he accepted axiomatic sciences such as jurisprudence or ethics, but any elaborated theory of rationalization would have been bound to take on a different quality from a positivistically conceived economic science.

Weber's thesis was very much a historical one, backed up by a theory of motivation that was adequate at the level of meaning to explain how it was that human beings sought salvation through ascetic inner-worldly activity. The evidence of rationality in the West was there for any student to see without any need to devote special attention to the concept. Of course there was the difficulty that what was rational from one point of view might not be from another but, looked at in the round, the growth of rationality was as obvious as the growth of industry or the rise of the modern state. It had a philosophical basis in the Enlightenment; through the advance of science it was successful in pushing back the influence of religion; and through the twin disciplines of market rationality and bureaucracy the rational mode of everyday life became all-pervasive. This was the very characteristic quality of the modern world and could be illustrated in whatever sector one chose, in music, or sex, or architecture.

It is the historical specificity of his analysis coupled with the taken-for-granted nature of the concept of rationality that makes it difficult to sum up Weber's rationalization thesis. But recently Weber scholars have been able to benefit from the best analysis yet, contained in Jürgen Habermas's *Theorie des kommunikativen Handelns* (1981b). He adopts a three-way division of the rationalization process into the societal, cultural and personality. At the societal level modernization involves the independent development of the capitalist economy and the modern state. At the cultural level rationalization involves the growth and application of science but also the autonomous development guided by their own principles of art, law and morality. At the personality level a methodical life-style originally founded in the religious beliefs of the Protestants becomes dominant.

But what is the rationality that extends its influence into all these life-spheres? Habermas suggests that there are five stages within Weber's idea of practical rationality. They are:

(1) Rational technique: the calculated use of means.
(2) Technical progress: the use of more effective means.
(3) Rational choice of ends: choice on the basis of knowledge and precise calculation (as in formally rational economic activity).
(4) Life-guiding principles: action guided by generalized value-principles.
(5) Rational-methodical life-style: the unification of the previous four rational steps in a fifth in which they are balanced and their joint success is ensured.

These five points taken together make up Weber's view of practical rationality according to Habermas, but they do not exhaust the rationalization concept since Weber does not confine the idea of rationality to action, but applies it also to symbolic systems. There are then two further elements:

(6) The formal structuring of symbolic systems: both professional systems of knowledge and the systematization of beliefs about the world.
(7) Value-intensification: the increasing elaboration of knowledge and value-spheres such as art, law and morality.

(1981b, Vol. I, pp. 225–61)

Habermas's account is of course embedded within a major project that is designed to promote a fundamental shift in the focus of social theory from technically rational action towards full and free communication within social relationships. This is undoubtedly a project with long-term importance, and this is not the place to engage in a detailed examination of it. There is every reason to think that the elaboration of the idea of communicative action takes us beyond Weber's conceptualization of action with its renowned four types of purpose-rationality, value-rationality, affectual and traditional action. But Habermas's intentions do lead him to emphasize along with many others that Weber's account 'investigates the rationalization of action systems solely from the aspect of purpose rationality' (1981b, Vol. II, p. 449). This judgement sits rather uneasily next to Habermas's account, which we have already set out, with its mention of value-principles and the formalization of symbolic systems. If we look a little more closely at how this judgement of Habermas and many others comes about we will gain a better idea of the inner structure of Weber's idea of rationality. This will aid us with the purpose of this section, namely, advancing the rationalization thesis.

There is no doubt that purposive-rationality had the central place in Weber's thinking about rationality, but it would be wrong to conclude that he accorded it some metaphysical primacy. Weber had his own methodological reasons for emphasizing action in pursuit of specific goals as the most important source of ideal types in the social sciences. Economics provided him with the obvious exemplar for this way of thinking. But the essay in which he could speak of this form of action as 'rational', and equally the way in which Habermas and the rest of us go along with this usage, requires explanation if we are to understand how 'rational purposive action' and all the other elements of rationality could be taken to belong together.

In fact there was a set of assumptions underlying Weber's usage of which he was quite aware, which he did not have to spell out and which has largely been hidden from our view. The idea of rationality that he drew on had been elaborated in the eighteenth century above all by Kant. In the notion of human reason he brought together both scientific knowledge and moral rules, each governed by the idea of law. The most succinct statement of this outlook was possibly contained in *The Foundations of the Metaphysics of Morals* (1785). What a profound confidence, a sense of stating the undisputed nature of the way things are, is contained in this assertion:

Everything in nature works according to laws. Only a rational being has the capacity of acting according to the conception of laws, i.e. according to principles. This capacity is will. Since reason is required

167

for the derivation of actions from laws, will is nothing else than practical reason. (Kant, 1949, p. 72)

Kant's critiques established reason as the unifying factor between nature and humanity, and made the understanding of both dependent on transcendental ideas such as universal causality and perfect freedom. The reason the tag 'rational' could be applied by Weber so easily to action where means were chosen to achieve purposes was that for Kant reason was exhibited in two related respects. Knowledge of means involves knowledge of laws, 'how nature works', and that knowledge is advanced by science, which is governed by transcendental ideas. It is a faculty of the human mind that permits the discovery of laws in nature. Secondly, the employment of those laws for an end of whatever kind is an objective principle valid for every rational being. 'Whoever wills the end, so far as reason has decisive influence on his action, wills also the indispensably necessary means to it that lie in his power' (Kant, 1949, p. 76). This is the basic principle of Kant's famous hypothetical imperative.

Now this terminology and way of thinking are entirely familiar to Weber, as to his generation as a whole in so far as they had received a high-school education. It is therefore no coincidence that we find Kant's doctrine of the hypothetical imperative virtually restated in his essay of 1917 on value-freedom. There he outlined the fundamentally non-evaluative nature of scientific propositions in economics, stating that 'in order to attain the end x under the conditions b^1, b^2, and b^3, y^1, y^2, and y^3 are the only or most effective means' is the simple inversion of the causal proposition 'x is produced, under conditions b^1, b^2, and b^3 by y^1, y^2 and y^3'. 'For these say exactly the same thing, and the "man of action" can derive his prescriptions from them quite easily' (MSS, p. 45). Both Kant and Weber term this a purely 'technical' problem.

As I have acknowledged there is good reason for saying that Weber gave technical imperatives or what Kant also termed principles of skill a prime place in his ordering of science and his understanding of the world. But it would be altogether wrong to suggest that he ignored or was uninfluenced by the other side of Kant's doctrine of practical reason, the principles of morality summed up in the idea of the categorical imperative. What one misses in Habermas's account is a sense for the generative factors underlying Weber's idea of value-rationality. For the way Weber applied the tag 'rational' to action that adhered to values is fully comprehensible only within the framework of Kantian philosophy. Anglo-Saxon empiricism and utilitarianism always have difficulty with this idea. It is symptomatic that Weber says about value-rational action that it always involves 'commands' or 'demands' (ES, p. 25). Action is being measured against a rule that it is expected to express. Habermas does point to 'direction by principles' (1981b, Vol. I, p. 244) in this context and recognizes that the combination of *Zweckrationalität* and *Wertrationalität* forms part of the rational–methodical life-style of the ascetic Protestant, but he does not go on to accord 'following rules' the key place it has within the Weberian idea of rationality.

For Kant the supreme product of human reason was the idea of the undetermined human subject freely following the rules of duty or moral obligation. The human personality developed through that free choice of adhering to principles. The subject was also the transcendental premise of understanding nature through laws. Reason, borne by the subject, provided the unity of the moral and natural worlds. Weber's two types of action are 'rational' because they are derived directly from this Kantian idea of reason. They are almost direct parallels to the hypothetical and categorical imperatives. There is ample indication in Weber's work that this heritage of Kantian thinking was taken for granted, not so much as a doctrine but as a mode of discourse. Following rules was rational in itself and needed no explanation. 'Bureaucratic authority is specifically rational in the sense of being bound to intellectually analysable rules; while charismatic authority is specifically irrational in the sense of being foreign to all rules' (ES, p. 244), says Weber at one point. As I have pointed out elsewhere (Albrow, 1970, pp. 61–6), a neglect of this facet of Weber's understanding of rationality led Anglo-Saxon theorists in particular to believe that he was advancing a theory of organizational efficiency when he set out his ideal type of bureaucracy. It is clear that Weber adhered firmly to the Kantian theory of personality too with its emphasis on freedom through self-imposed rules. That position was set out firmly in his rejection of Knies's view that human personality introduced unpredictability into history (WL, p. 132).

Laws of nature and principles of action are at the heart of the Weberian idea of rationality. Each permit logical inference to be drawn about the relation of particular acts to a rule; and rules themselves, being part of discourse, may be brought into logical relations with each other. But that idea of rationality was not worked out by Weber from first principles. Rather it was a complex notion handed down over generations, an elaborate frame of thought, most fully expounded, although not by any means exclusively, by Kant, on which Weber could draw without embarrassment, without the need to forge systematic relations because he could take it for granted that they were already there. It is not therefore some special frailty of Weber's thought that the ideas of rationality and rationalization present themselves in a wide variety of contexts and formulations. Those were all sides of the multi-faceted idea of rationality as it presented itself to him in the culture of his time. This is not to say that those formulations are unsystematically related, but only that if the system that was there is to be revealed then some archaeological work has to be done on the idea. Weber was drawing on a cultural resource, not inventing a new theory. He never claimed to be a philosopher, but he was drawing upon the product of philosophy.

If we attend to the roots of Weber's idea of rationality we are able to resolve the puzzlement that sometimes arises when rationality is found to inhere both in practical action and also in symbolic systems. The obvious but fundamental and often ignored point is that reason belongs to the world of thought and that action becomes rational in so far as it is governed by that world. To be rational the act must be regulated by values, clearly conceived purposes, oriented to knowledge. Rationality is conferred on the act by its location within the symbolic systems. On the Kantian account rationality belongs without question to the ideal world, and it is that world which it systematizes first of all.

> Reason is impelled by a tendency of its nature to go out beyond the field of its empirical employment, and to venture in a pure employment, by means of ideas alone, to the utmost limits of all knowledge, and not to be satisfied save through a completion of its course in a self-subsistent systematic whole.   (Kant, 1787, A797, B825)

Reason was bound to tend towards systematic unity, which is 'what first raises ordinary knowledge to the rank of science' (1787, A832, B860). Reason is the 'higher faculty of knowledge', the rational as opposed to the empirical or historical (1787, A835, B863). Only in the most artificial way, therefore, can one talk of the isolated act of purposive rationality. For to accord rationality to an act is to recognize its place within a framework of knowledge and belief.

While the Kantian foundations of Weber's thinking about rationality have been inadequately exposed, it is some testimony to their strength that what has happened in the subsequent development of Weberian ideas is that the systematic underpinnings have been developed afresh. In particular the examination of *Zweckrationalität* has led to the demand that the systematic relations of that concept with rational systems of action as a whole should be analysed and that rationality as a regulative idea in social systems should be given full recognition. In fact this illustrates very well that inherent drive towards expansion and unity which Kant attributed to rationality. The quests for universality, comprehensive laws, inclusive theories and exhaustive categorizations may all be seen as part of what he called the architechtonic of pure reason, and they have been pursued relentlessly to this day.

Instead therefore of delving into the archaeology of Weber's rationalization thesis as contained in the Kantian and idealist tradition, it is equally possible for us to act as architects on it, to develop and improve it, to

170

construct a theoretical edifice adequate for the vastly increased scope, power and comprehensiveness of the rationalized society of our own time. We can, in other words, engage in what Weber called *Wertsteigerung*, or value-intensification, which is what he understood to happen in the modern world as value standpoints became increasingly explicit, their implications developed and made more rational. The rationalization process in general may indeed be seen as the intensification of rationality, in the generic cognitive value of which all particular value-intensifications shared.

This chapter can only begin to indicate what might be involved in a theoretical statement of rationality-intensification that would be adequate for the world sixty-five years after Weber's death. It is, however, helped by the fact that considerable progress in this direction has been made through the prodigious efforts of Niklas Luhmann. In his work we can discover a highly elaborated argument for locating rationality in social systems rather than in individual purposes. He draws on the Parsonian analysis of the relations between the individual actor and action systems and combines that with the decision-making perspectives of organization theory. The outcome is a general theory of system rationality in which the uncertainties and complexity, which would attach to individual purposive action were the environment and other people to be unpredictable, are replaced by institutionalized expectations of behaviour that are stabilized over time, objects and people. The actions in which people engage then become part of the wider system, and their rationality is attributed not on the basis of hidden motives but on their relation to the durable and consistent set of normative expectations.

Luhmann's examination of trust provides a good example of his treatment of rationality. It would be wrong, he says, to see this ubiquitous social phenomenon as simply 'a means that can be chosen for particular ends, much less an end/means structure capable of being optimized'; he calls for a more widely conceived sociological theory of rationalization, such as yet does not exist where 'the evaluation "rational" could follow from functional analysis' (Luhmann, 1979, p. 88). Trust and its alternative, mistrust, serve to stabilize a system order that is suited to the capacities of human beings for action. It is like learning, symbolizing and controlling in that it structures the processing of experience. 'Systems are rational to the extent that they can encompass and reduce complexity' (1979, p. 93). The point is not that trust is *per se* rational but that it is one of the mechanisms available within systems of action that permit human beings to proceed about their daily lives, fulfilling their purposes and coping with the complexity of the world around. It is the system as a whole that is rational.

It is not my intention to offer a detailed application of Luhmann's system rationality concept to modern conditions. He says that the 'prevailing empirical-descriptive orientation of sociological research' does not provide the necessary preparatory work for this more widely conceived theory of rationalization (1979, p. 88). It is unfortunately also the case that his own theory is not in the kind of codified form that makes it easy to apply. He is surely pointing in the direction in which an intensification of rationalization can be more effectively interpreted by moving away from the individual actor to the system. But it is difficult to avoid the impression that he has moved too far and at too fast a pace in two respects at least. The first is that the systemic character of human action is, in any individual instance, as problematic as the rational character of an individual action. The specification of the dimensions of administrative rationality, for instance, has taken place in the context of innumerable case studies, which show the shifting nature of criteria and boundaries.

Secondly, Luhmann is so anxious to attach rationality to social, rather than to individual, action systems that he tends to miss a much more obvious reason for stressing the systemic nature of the concept. Reason belongs to the realm of thought. Not only does it belong to that realm, it is the very principle that provides systematic unity to human ideas. I suspect that Kant would have regarded modern definitions of system as 'any set of interrelated units' as fundamentally defective. 'By a system', he said, 'I understand the unity of the manifold modes of knowledge under one idea. This idea is the concept provided by reason' (1787, A832, B860).

The philosophical and mathematical knowledge arising out of reason was for Kant the intrinsically rational, and in so far as that rational knowledge was applied to human behaviour, so far could one call it rational. That rational knowledge is, however, fundamentally systemic, binding individuals together, carried through human history, stored in institutions. Mathematics, logic, the natural and social sciences, law, the systems of religion, administration, and the skills and technology of everyday life make up that total accumulation of knowledge which one can call human rationality.

This train of thought must lead to the conclusion that we are able to address the issue of rationalization of the modern world rather more directly than Luhmann would suggest. We ought to be able to examine contemporary forms of life and ask ourselves, how far do they exhibit more advanced forms of rationality? In what sectors do we identify the intensification of rationality? Can we find more powerful calculation in production whether for needs or demands? Are the modes of interrelation between the sectors of society more highly co-ordinated? We are a long way from confining rationality to technical action and we are able to recognize the rationality of social systems when the case arises. But we do need to preserve a greater distance between the idea of rationality and the degree of rationalization that society exhibits, if only to ensure that an advance in our knowledge of the one can enhance our understanding of the other.

Two Contemporary Cases of Rationalization

What is being proposed here is a much more open-ended approach to rationality and rationalization than either offering illustrations of Weberian points in 1985 or alternatively developing an updated concept of rationality for the modern world and then applying it. The first can readily be done, as my paper on Britain showed (1982). The second is a major undertaking, as Luhmann's work demonstrates, and runs the danger of going beyond adequate empirical specification. In the following two cases an alternative procedure will be adopted. In the same spirit as Weber I am going to take a sector of social life that manifestly exhibits rationality in the Kantian sense of being guided by ideas of reason, logic, mathematics, regularity, calculability, coherence, systematic interconnectedness and so on. No attempt will be made to provide an inventory, let alone a general theoretical account of those ideas. They are all included within what Kant meant by reason, but they have been developed far beyond his own formulations. Moreover the development of reason in institutional form has gone beyond any general theory of rationality. That indeed is the justification for the approach being offered here. It is simultaneously empirical and analytical. It analyses cases to permit the gradual eliciting of a concept of rationality as already embedded in the institutional life of the modern world.

Apart from the rational organization of economic life, bureaucracy was for Weber the most pervasive expression of institutionalized rationality. It operated on the basis of both rules and knowledge, decisions being made by qualified people on the basis of systematically gathered information and legal-rational rules. In Weber's words: 'the only decisive point for us is that in principle a system of rationally debatable "reasons" stands behind every act of bureaucratic administration, namely, either subsumption under norms, or a weighing of ends and means' (ES, p. 979). There could not be a better expression of the Kantian origins of Weber's thought. One facet of bureaucracy was the accumulation of knowledge, not only technical, but also in the form of a store of documentary information gathered in the course of routine administration. Factors such as the development of modern means of communication and the development of the office and files as the focus for work were also intimately connected with the rise of bureaucracy. We do not have to look far in

173

modern bureaucracy to see the onward march of rationalization. In particular methods of processing information have developed at an astonishing rate with the development of the computer and the replacement of the filing cabinet with the disc storage of data. The first case of contemporary rationalization I wish to examine relates to data storage.

The modern computer not only makes it possible for state, commercial and other organizations to store enormously increased amounts of information about individuals. It also permits collation of data on a vastly increased scale. There has been a widespread response to this potential in the form of alarm that it could be used to supply information by the collation of data from several sources to damage individuals. Already a convention of countries within the Council of Europe has tried to set standards for the processing of data, and national legislation has been passed. In Britain this has taken the form of the Data Protection Act 1984 (United Kingdom, 1984). This Act sets out data protection principles, establishes a system for the registration and supervision of data users and computer bureaux, accords rights to data subjects and allows for exemptions from all or part of the Act.

By a series of preliminary definitions the Act provides for an enormously extended scope for state interest in computerized information. It defines data as 'information recorded in a form in which it can be processed by equipment operating automatically in response to instructions given for that purpose'. Personal data is defined as 'information which relates to a living individual', the data subject, and the data user 'controls the contents and use of data' that is to be processed automatically. The Act goes on to prohibit the holding of personal data unless the data user has registered with the Data Protection Registrar and has described the data, their sources and proposed use, providing for access to the data to all data subjects.

The Act is designed to enforce the implementation of a set of principles to be observed by data users. In brief these provide

(1)   for the fair and lawful obtaining and processing of data;
(2)   that data should be held for specific purposes only;
(3)   for disclosure of data only in accord with those purposes;
(4)   that data should be adequate and not excessive to the purposes;
(5)   that data should be accurate and up to date;
(6)   that data should not be retained longer than necessary;
(7)   that data subjects should have access and rights to amend inaccuracies.

Additionally computer bureaux are obliged to take appropriate security measures against improper access, damage, or loss of data.

These principles provide an impressive instance of the development of institutionalized rationality. They enshrine specificity of purpose as a state-imposed principle on data users whether or not the data user is gathering data for the state. It is not a particular purpose or set of purposes for which legislation is being passed, but the general category of specific purposes. Principles (2)–(6) all provide at the most abstract level for the rationalization of information-gathering and -processing by anyone for any purpose, provided the data relate to individuals and are machine processed. The European Convention to which the United Kingdom is a signatory allows for the extension of the principles to data about companies and manually held data. Were these extensions implemented then the framework for a comprehensive information system for the social life of a nation state would be largely complete. As it is the state has provided a major impetus to rationalizing the information systems of all collective and individual systems of action by providing a sanctioned set of principles: specificity; relevance; adequacy; accuracy; and temporality. These were not set out explicitly by Weber as principles of rationality, but they are clearly an elaboration on the concept as he understood it. What has happened is that the technical progress represented by the modern computer, when harnessed to considerations of the rights of individuals, generates argument and reflection leading to the elaboration of the idea of rationality. In other words, rationality does not develop in the abstract as some ideal force, but is the ongoing outcome of an interplay between technical progress and reasoned argument. In the institutions of society the outcomes of that interplay are recorded and provide the premises for the next stage of the argument.

The Data Protection Act provides not only for a system of registration for data users, but also a regulating agency in the person of the Data Protection Registrar with the power to appoint staff and a Data Protection Tribunal to hear appeals against the Registrar's decisions. Provision is therefore made for the continuous monitoring and control of an institutionalized set of rational principles. In Britain at present all bodies concerned with computerized information about individuals are engaged, or ought to be engaged, in identifying their own data protection officers, preparing to justify their holdings of data, checking their security and providing new instructions for staff. The impact of the Act is pervasive and can be far-reaching. Yet as one commentator notes, 'the number of cases of reported misuse is very small, and in most of those the misuse could have occurred equally well with manual files' (Elbra, 1984, p. 9). Indeed the significance of the Act may well be in respect of the established machinery and the consequences this has for constituting practices rather than in respect of reinforcing individual rights. In fact the Act itself establishes a range of exceptions to the non-disclosure principles that

175

makes sense only in terms of interests of state which are enhanced through the new machinery. A law to protect individual rights simultaneously increases state power, and we shall need to look at this in reviewing that other facet of Weber's rationalization thesis, the loss of meaning and freedom for the individual.

The second instance of the intensification of rationality in the modern world that I wish to examine briefly involves a response to the penetration of science into an area that in Weber's time had not yet been subjected to extensive rationalization. Research into the transmission of inherited characteristics was something Weber acknowledged was possible but had as yet produced nothing to substantiate the wild racial hypotheses that were current. He did not consider the possibility of human intervention in the genetic material of the human race. But in our own time this possibility exists and has been put into practice in a small way in the treatment of infertility in married couples. The use of frozen semen either from the husband or from another donor has been practised freely in Britain and elsewhere. In 1982 the Royal College of Obstetricians and Gynaecologists knew of more than 1,000 pregnancies where a donor other than the husband was involved. A more recent development known as *in vitro* fertilization (IVF) permits fertilization to take place outside the womb and for the embryo produced to be transferred back to the womb for further development. This technique can be used so that a woman may bear a child who is the product of another woman's egg and her own husband's semen. Or further a woman may bear a child who is the product entirely of another couple's genetic material. The capacity to produce human embryos in a test-tube opens up a chain of research possibilities that include genetic engineering, the production of genetically identical human beings (cloning), the use of other species for gestation, the use of embryos for testing drugs and the production of hybrids with other species. Public anxiety about these actual and potential developments led to a recent government report in Britain by the Committee of Inquiry into Human Fertilization and Embryology, chaired by the philosopher Mary Warnock (Warnock, 1984).

The recommendations of the Warnock Committee are that a new licensing authority should be established to regulate all infertility services and related research. Principles for the provision of services are set out including anonymity of the donor, limitation on the number of embryos to be produced from any one donor's semen or eggs, limitations on the storage time for embryos and the creation of a donor register. Research should also be regulated by placing limitations on the use of the embryo, prohibiting its sale and purchase and in general ensuring that all research is subject to restrictions imposed by the licensing authority. It was further proposed that legislation should be introduced to, among other things, make legitimate any child born by donor insemination and to make the woman giving birth and her husband the legal parents of the child, to outlaw surrogate motherhood agreements and to allow the storage authority to use or dispose of eggs, semen, or embryos under certain circumstances without donor permission.

However far the subject-matter goes beyond what Weber envisaged, he would have had no difficulty in recognizing the character of the argument with which the report was prefaced. In spite of the high feelings associated with the subject the foreword argues that moral reasoning has an important place, although 'matters of ultimate value are not susceptible of proof' (Warnock, 1984, p. 2). That reasoning is held to produce principles that establish the barriers or limits beyond which people may not go. While there might be argument about the precise nature of those limits it is held that everyone accepts that limits there must be. It is in general an argument for value-rationality, an exposition of basic principles constituting moral life. But that argument is advanced at two levels. One is that the principles enunciated do correspond with the sentiments of at least some people. The other is that it is better for some principles to be advanced rather than none at all and that incorporated in legislation they can provide a broad framework for action. In Weber's terms a general need for 'legitimate order' is being postulated, in Luhmann's it is system-rationality, the provision of clear premises for individual decision-making. Whether the law corresponds to the individual's moral sentiments or not, at least it provides a calculable answer to the problem of what is allowed.

'Some principles or other', 'some barrier', 'some limits' would indeed appear to be the preferred basis for the committee's proposals. To the question of 'where do you draw the line?' the answer tends to be 'it does not matter where, as long as it is somewhere'. That clearly is the case in respect of the date beyond which experiments may not be conducted on a live human embryo. The time limit proposed is fourteen days, one day before the formation of the primitive streak in the embryonic disc. This is justified as the 'beginning of individual development of the embryo' (Warnock, 1984, p. 66), but different bodies suggested different limits, and it is difficult to detect convincing arguments for one rather than the other. Similarly, limits of five years for the review of egg and semen stores are proposed and ten years for embryo storage, without any convincing arguments for those limits rather than others. Public alarm was caused by reports of the possibility of producing hybrids of human and other animal species, and the report recommends making such production a criminal offence. One may suggest that the barrier proposed here corresponds to a much more primitive barrier in human culture and to an anxiety with roots in the myths of many cultures, which have imagined such combinations as man and goat, man and bull, woman and fish.

The conclusion of the report provides the best warrant for saying that it is system-rationality that is the main concern. The licensing authority is the linchpin of the whole set of proposals. 'None of our other recommendations can have any practical impact until such a body is set up' (Warnock, 1984, p. 79). The tasks of the new body would essentially be to provide guidance on good practice in the infertility field and to issue licences to provide infertility treatment or to undertake research on human semen, eggs, or embryos. The body should consider setting up a central register of children born as a result of the new techniques and in the case of applicants for research licences it should satisfy itself on their suitability to carry out such research, with the applicant being 'obliged to indicate clearly the objectives of the research' (1984, p. 78). In other words, we are dealing with both the technical and the ethical rationalization of scientific research at the level of the society as a whole. In part the proposals are couched in the language of the rights of individuals, to be legitimately born, to have children in their own name, but the measures proposed create a social mechanism that vastly increases the potential for state control. As with the case of data protection this needs to be evaluated in the light of Weber's fears for individual freedom.

The two cases I have taken provide interesting leads as to the directions in which Weber's rationalization thesis can be developed. In the first place they provide evidence for the extension of rationality into spheres far beyond the experience of his time. A computerized information system covering all individuals in a nation state and the regulation of the scientific control of human genetic material extend the frontiers of rationalization considerably beyond anything Weber conceived. At the same time an intensification of rationality is implemented through the establishment of the rational monitoring and control of rationalization. Rationality is not merely a principle constituting legislative enactment, providing grounds for any particular law. It has now become the very topic of legislation. That was envisaged by Weber in the context of the codification of legal rules. But in the cases we have taken, rationality assumes an even more dynamic aspect.

In the case of the Data Protection Act there is provision for establishing the routine reproduction of specificity of purpose through the agency of the Data Protection Registrar. Additionally the Act permits the responsible minister to modify or add to the eight basic principles of data protection. In the case of the Warnock Committee recommendations, the concern is primarily with providing a regulating machinery, which can then develop its own procedures, and ultimately for arguing the case for some regulation of whatever kind. In both cases one can say that at the most basic level the concern is for establishing an agency and rational procedures that will guarantee the rationalization of conduct as a continuing process, whether on a normative or an expediential basis.

In both cases rationality is being worked through on the most general level possible. At that level certain themes such as purposiveness or monitoring recur. These do not appear in codified form, but one may infer from their recurrence that a theory of rationality appropriate for the institutionalized forms of the modern period would put them in a definite relationship with each other. It may be useful to offer the following preliminary listing:

(1) Definition of the set of system units: even with data and embryos ultimately these are brought into relation with a definite set of living individuals.

(2) Generation of principles: provision is made for the ongoing generation of normative or cognitive principles.

(3) Production of purposiveness: aimless or alien activity has no place in the system, and purposiveness becomes a requirement.

(4) Enforcing specificity: at every level anything that would make precise calculation difficult is eliminated as far as it can be.

(5) Regulation of conduct: human conduct is made regular through regulation and sanctions.

(6) Monitoring of performance: provision is made for gathering information to evaluate the effectiveness of the regulation.

(7) Reproduction of the system: whether for data or for embryos provision is made for producing new material and destroying the old.

I would argue that this set of seven themes represents an intensification of the idea of rationality as it was to be found in both Kant's and later Weber's formulations. In conclusion I will turn briefly to some of the wider issues involved in the rationalization thesis, the question of the loss of meaning, the decline of freedom and the place of irrationality. For these are the questions that finally delimit the theoretical scope of the rationalization thesis.

The Bounds of Rationality

In Weber's view bureaucratic organization was the animate machine that corresponded to the inanimate machine of the factory and fabricated the shell of bondage encasing the modern worker. Since his time the animate machine has been harnessed even more tightly to the inanimate through the application of the computer to administrative settings. Both kinds of machine Weber termed 'objectified mind' (*geronnener Geist*). Both were constituted by human rationality and, in that, their eventual convergence was an ever present possibility. His own evaluation of this situation shared the prevailing pessimism of German intellectuals in the latter part of the nineteenth century. For Kant the growth of reason meant the enhancement of human freedom; for Weber rules meant bondage, work for purposes that the individual had not set under conditions not freely chosen. Sometimes this is viewed as Weber taking over Marx's theory of alienation. It is fairer to see them both sharing the intellectual's distrust of the products of an intellectualized society, where rationality had been harnessed to the production of social life.

If the intensification of rationalization in social life corresponds to Weber's anticipation in so many respects it is none the less the case that we ought to treat the idea of a concomitant loss of meaning in social life with the utmost caution. Purposiveness and normative regulation must on any analysis be prime elements in endowing individual lives with meaning. Both functionalist and phenomenological approaches to this issue will lead to suggesting that individual purposiveness derives its strength from the social production of meaning. One might indeed suggest that so institutionalized is purposiveness in modern social life that if anything there is an over-production of meaning. The Warnock Committee took evidence from organizations interested in human fertilization as diverse as the Royal College of Surgeons, the Mothers' Union, the International Planned Parenthood Federation, Action for Lesbian Parents and the Catholic Marriage Advisory Council. More than 200 organizations and nearly 700 individuals made submissions to the committee. The issues associated with the unborn child are in fact capable of mobilizing mass support in opposing directions and impinge directly on political life in many Western societies. But that is only one issue, and the proliferation of interest groups each with their own causes, large numbers of which adopt rationalized methods of administration, that mass of cross-cutting affiliations for the individual in modern society, has not begun to be documented.

Even if we accept that the employing organization is the most significant association for framing an individual's activities in modern society, it is by no means established that the modern employee is alienated from work. It was William Whyte (1956) who pointed out that the social ethic had replaced the Protestant ethic for the large organization. There is no need to repeat here the numerous ways in which Weberian notions of formal organization or Taylor-type scientific management have been supplanted in both theory and practice. What may be conceded is that employment and the life cycle have been dissociated in the modern world, and Weber placed great emphasis on providing a meaning for death in life.

That issue does need far more analysis. There are paradoxes here, for the organization is successful in managing the entry and exit of members and in providing a framework of purposive activity that outlives them. Death may have become irrelevant in the modern organization but only because its purposes outlive people.

Equally problematical is the issue of the loss of freedom. The Data Protection Act provides an example of the contingent way that issue may be related to rationality. The Act provides for a range of exceptions to its provisions. A minister may exempt people from the provisions and safeguards of the Act on the grounds of national security, while the prevention or detection of crime provides exemption from both subject-access and non-disclosure provisions. There are different ways in which these exemptions can be evaluated. From one point of view, if the Act is seen as providing new rights and safeguards then the exemptions do no more than leave the situation of the individual as it was in those respects. But to judge the situation in this way is to neglect the fact that the machinery for the registration of personal data, created to ensure the rights, remains in existence for the exemptions. The capacity has been created for a national personal data system, and the effect of the Act is to allow this new machinery to be used for security and law-and-order purposes. How it will be used will depend on factors outside the definitions of the Act. In a similar way the creating of a licensing and registration authority for infertility research and services with rights in the storage and use of genetic material opens the way for the state control of genetic engineering.

In my paper on rationalization in Britain (1982) I argued that the relations of rationality and freedom in the case of individuals depended upon the organization of control and access to positions of control, in particular through educational provision. Making institutions more rational opens up the possibility of universal understanding, provided there is universal access to the means of obtaining that understanding. It is not reasonable to reject the possibility that rational administration does genuinely provide a predictable environment for individual decision-making and therefore enhance the scope for individual action on the part of the citizen. But access to appropriate education is greatly differentiated, and, linked with that as both condition and result, the material means for making use of the freedom provided by the rationalized state are distributed in unequal fashion. Any attempt to resolve the argument about rationality and freedom that isolates this formal issue from the material facts of the ownership and control of property runs the risk of lapsing into either Enlightenment optimism or Weberian pessimism. The prospects for individual freedom in the light of continuing rationalization and the issue of the relative power enjoyed by different groups and classes in society should not be analysed in artificial isolation from each other.

181

Of course Weber did not ignore countervailing and contradictory factors in the rationalization process. Conflicts between groups are in part taken up in his account of the conflict of value-spheres. The rationalization of different life-spheres may on his account result in their growing contradictions, as in the classic example of the nation state and the market economy, which he addressed in his inaugural lecture. However far the rationalization of social systems proceeds there will be material irrationalities. Population trends, resource limitations, health factors, the outcomes of market processes and of other conflicts, the shifts in public moods, all provide either the boundaries or the material for rational action but are outside the prescriptive rules of rationality. Just as at the individual level the capacities and strength that reason can mould provide limits to action, so at the societal level it is not possible for system-rationality to provide a closed and eternally predictable environment. Indeed as formal rationality grows there is good reason to think that material irrationalities increase equivalently. Any attempt to develop the theory of rationalization will need equally to theorize the irrationalities of the modern world. It would be a fatal mistake to imagine that the one is an alternative, much less a conclusive negation, of the other. So long as human culture survives, rationality and irrationality are locked in a dialectical embrace.

PART THREE

Problems of Modernity

9

The Dialectic of Individuation and Domination: Weber's Rationalization Theory and Beyond

JEFFREY C. ALEXANDER

Social theory not only explains the world but reflects upon it. Committed to empirical standards of truth, it is tied, as well, to the metaphysical demand for reflective equilibrium (Rawls, 1971). While, more than any other modern theorist, Max Weber insisted that scientific social theory be absolved of metaphysical ambition, he was obsessed, more than any other, with the meaning of modern life. This paradox was far from accidental. We will see that it reflected Weber's understanding of the fate of meaning in a secular world. I will argue, indeed, that Weber's empirical sociology establishes the criteria – the fundamental boundary conditions – for rational reflection about the fate and possibilities of the modern age.

Like most of the other great theorists of his time, Weber began his intellectual life with beliefs firmly rooted in the nineteenth century. Though more bellicose in his nationalism than some, he shared the general intellectual faith in the progress that lay open for Western societies. He felt that the rational transformation of nature and the rational organization of society were positive developments well within man's reach, and he linked these political and economic changes to increasing freedom for modern man.

In 1897 Weber suffered a nervous breakdown, and when he emerged from this period of emotional and intellectual mortification he was not only a different person but a chastened thinker. He was prepared, in a way he had not been before, to reflect on the dark side of the twentieth century. While this new perspective is clearly evident from the appearance of *The Protestant Ethic and the Spirit of Capitalism* in 1904, like many others in his generation Weber expressed such sentiments most pointedly in his reactions to the First World War, an event that seemed to sum up the

185

prospects of the new age. 'Not summer's bloom lies ahead of us,' he told students in his now famous lecture on science as a vocation, 'but rather a polar night of icy darkness and hardness (FMW, p. 128).

Weber explicitly linked this despair about the future course of the twentieth century to his disillusionment with the social theory of the nineteenth. In his companion lecture on science as a vocation he scorned 'the naïve optimism' according to which science 'has been celebrated as the way to happiness'. To interpret in this way what is, after all, a mere 'technique of mastering life' is a sign of immaturity. 'Who believes in this,' he asked the students rhetorically, 'aside from a few big children in university chairs or editorial offices?' (FMW, p. 143).

Weber is suggesting here that a mature thinker must sever the link between cognitive explanation and existential salvation. To assume such a link belies, according to Weber, the dire predicament of the twentieth century, and, indeed, he traces the establishment of the connection back to the time when religion still dominated human thought. He had discovered an effort to establish just this kind of relationship in his work on Puritanism. Asking his students to recall Swammerdam's exaltation – 'Here I bring you the proof of God's providence in the anatomy of a louse' – Weber suggested they should see in this statement 'what the scientific worker, influenced (indirectly) by Protestantism and Puritanism, conceived to be his task: to show the path to God' (FMW, p. 142). For a man of that earlier period, such a connection was understandable. For the man of today it is a regressive and intellectually immature, for it fails to come to terms with what, in Weber's view, is the necessarily naturalistic character of explanation in the secular age.

'An empirical explanation has to eliminate as causal factors', Weber insisted, all 'supernatural interventions' (FMW, p. 147). To accept a supernatural cause is to accept the teleological notion that natural events have occurred for some higher purpose, that their cause is neither efficient nor mechanical but derives from their ethical goal. Since modern science was first promoted by religious men, it is not surprising that in the beginning even naturalistic explanations were squeezed into this teleological frame. But once the full implications of science are understood, its effect must inevitably be exactly the opposite. 'If these natural sciences lead to anything,' Weber suggests, 'they are apt to make the belief that there is such a thing as the "meaning" of the universe die out at its very roots' (FMW, p. 142). Not to understand this is, once again, to reveal a disturbing lack of inner strength. 'Who – aside from certain big children who are indeed found in the natural sciences – still believes that the findings of astronomy, biology, physics, or chemistry could teach us anything about the *meaning* of the world?' (italics in original).

Science, then, has contributed to the icy darkness that lies ahead. A world where the very hope for meaning has died out at its roots is not a happy or reassuring prospect. Yet Weber clearly wants to suggest another, quite different implication of science as well. By separating causal explanation and existential evaluation, science offers the potential for individual autonomy. Science offers a mundane technique of calculation that is available to every man. Weber describes the goal of scientific training in just this way; it is 'to present scientific problems in such a manner that an untutored but receptive mind can understand them and – *what for us is alone decisive* – can come to think about them independently' (FMW, p. 134, italics added). This second implication must not be denied if Weber's sociology is to be properly understood.[1]

Weber's sociology is defined and also, I will suggest, limited by the dilemma he has just described. On the one hand, there is disillusionment and an existential despair that psychological maturity and cultural integrity cannot be sustained. On the other, there is real evidence of the increasing autonomy and strength of the individual. These poles embody the paradox of the twentieth century. After he recovered from his nervous breakdown, Weber devoted the rest of his life to understanding how both could be true.

How have we come to a condition of 'icy darkness and hardness', which threatens to extinguish human life and is at the same time a condition in which for the first time human freedom is finally possible? It was, I believe, to answer just this question that Weber suggested his master concept of rationalization. Rationalization is at once enervating disenchantment and enlightening empowerment. It has led to increased freedom and at the same time facilitated internal and external domination on an unprecedented scale. This ambiguity is intended. Rationalization is at once a terrible condition, the worst evil, and the only human path for liberation.

Rationalization as Individuation

Those who have recognized the critical thrust of Weber's rationalization concept (e.g. Mitzman, 1970) have, not surprisingly, failed to appreciate that it also implies the increasing freedom of man from the tyranny of forced belief.[2] 'Increasing intellectualization and rationalization', Weber acknowledges, does not mean that there has actually been increased knowledge about the 'conditions under which one lives'. This would limit rationalization to a cognitive force. Weber wants to get at something else, and something more – to the individual autonomy that makes such increased cognitive knowledge possible.

It means something else, namely, the knowledge or belief that if one but wished one *could* learn it at any time. Hence, it means that

187

principally there are no mysterious incalculable forces that come into play, but rather that one can, in principle, master all things by calculation. This means that the world is disenchanted. One need no longer have recourse to magical means in order to master or implore the spirits, as did the savage, for whom such mysterious powers existed. Technical means and calculations perform the service. This above all is what intellectualization means.

(FMW, p. 139, italics in original)

World-mastery, or at least the potential for it, has come to man through rationalization. Humans have replaced God as the masters of their destiny. Modern people are governed, or at least would like to think of themselves as being governed, by institutions that are man-made, that have been constructed for their effectiveness in achieving human goals. In principle, leaders are held accountable for the way these institutions work.

If this sounds suspiciously like the nineteenth-century outlook that Weber designed his theory to replace, this is because a crucial qualification has been left out; in no sense did Weber conceive this rationality to be natural or inherent. The point of his life's work is to show that the very opposite is the case. Intellectualization, he believed, rested upon the most unnatural motivation, led to the most abstracted orientation and inspired the most dessicated organization that the world had ever known. Far from rationality being inherent, it must be understood as the result of a long and complicated evolution of irrational, religious belief. The anti-religious nature of the modern world has a religious base. This appears to mark an inconsistency, but it would be considered so only for nineteenth-century thought. Weber holds that only if the irrational basis of rationality is accepted can the tortuous development of rationality properly be understood and the precarious condition of individual autonomy really be appreciated.

To understand what modern rationalization entails, what it allows and what it proscribes, one must understand from what it has emerged. The religious world we have lost addressed the meaning of life in a particular way; it harnessed all the different elements of life to the ethical goal incarnated in the godhead. This single goal sits atop a cultural hierarchy. It is the telos towards which every other dimension of culture is oriented. Artistic expression, understanding of the truth, love between human beings, material success, or political power – all are conceived of as serving this ethical end. Even more, all are conceived of as expressions of this ultimate goal.

Weber usually turned to Tolstoy as the modern who best articulated this anti-rationalistic spirit, and, indeed, his later works display just the kind of radical spiritualization that Weber is trying to describe. Tolstoy is not content to let events 'simply happen' in a mechanistic way; he is bent on avoiding the naturalistic conclusions to which his literary realism would seem logically to lead. The humiliation of Anna Karenina and the death of Ivan Ilyich are both turned into events that 'reveal' a higher meaning. Tolstoy places each event in a teleological framework, suggesting that it was somehow right for each to turn out as it did.

Though Weber is enormously sympathetic to this Tolstoyan point of view, he rejects it as a defensible standpoint for modern man. In the first place, this position is wrong because, quite simply, it 'presupposes that the world does have a meaning' (FMW, p. 153). By meaning, Weber is referring here not to the existential effort of individual interpretation but to a conception of teleological purpose in the cosmological sense. It is to this he objects, and he does so because it depends upon an empirical acceptance of God. The religious world-view presupposes 'that certain "revelations" are facts ... and as such make possible a meaningful conduct of life'. What Weber objects to, in sum, is the notion that certain presuppositions 'simply must be accepted', that is, accepted without any rational argument (FMW, p. 154). This is the 'intellectual sacrifice' that religion demands as its price for providing a meaningful world.

Weber asks how we have moved from a 'meaningful' world to this disenchanted one of rational choice. The answer is his religious sociology. While the existential need for meaning is constant, the intellectual approach to meaning varies. Religious interpretation emerges before nature or society can be rationally explained. It is a way of explaining the 'inexplicable' problems of suffering and unfairness. This origin in inexplicability is what leads religions to centre on the problem of salvation. It is because empirical explanation is impossible that there emerges the postulate of God. Because God has created the world, our suffering must be according to his design, and we will be saved in so far as we meet his demands.

Weber created the cross-cutting ideal types of his religious sociology in order to explain the approaches to salvation – the theodices – that had evolved in the course of world history. With the typologies mysticism/asceticism and this-worldly/other-worldly, Weber sought to describe the degree of emotionality as opposed to control that theodicies allowed, and the degree to which the religious organization of thought and emotion was directed towards world transformation or away from it.

In analysing the sociology of religion, we must never forget that Weber developed a theory of religious evolution in order to explain religion's self-destruction, that is, the movement from religion to empiricist, naturalistic rationality. What is at issue is whether religion forces man to become a tool of divine will rather than a vessel, an issue that will become central to understanding domination as well as individuation. Mystic religions, because they make salvation dependent upon possessing – becoming a vessel of – the spirit of God, encourage emotional expression and experience rather than self-control. Ascetic religions insist that man is a tool, that he must submit to God's will by following certain rules of good conduct. In this way asceticism encourages self-control and calculation.

Religious history presents a long march away from mystical to ascetic forms of the search for meaning. For the Australian aborigines the gods were easily available, and the goal of religious life was an experience of oneness through ritual participation. With the development of monotheism, religion is simplified and abstracted. God withdraws from the world, and humans know him less through experience than through written texts. The Jews were the 'people of the book'; they could not even know God's name. This thrust towards asceticism constitutes one of the fundamental causes of the rationalization of religious life. It promotes depersonalization, an outward rather than an inward orientation, and discipline of the self. Though the teleological structure of meaning remains intact, within its confines there has been significant rationalization.

The movement beyond the religious world-view cannot be understood without following out the implications of Weber's second typology. Early mysticism was almost entirely this-worldly, but later mysticism, Hinduism for example, had a strikingly other-worldly component. For their part, the major ascetic religions had been, until the Reformation, almost entirely other-worldly. They placed their great virtuosi outside the world – for example, in the monasteries of Buddhist and Christian monks. In this earlier period of religious history, renunciation could occur only if ascetics were physically separated from the world. This constituted a tremendous barrier against the spread of rationality.

With the Reformation, all this changed. Ascetic religion, and the rationalizing characteristics it represented, was brought deeply into the world. To achieve salvation one had to organize the world in accord with the impersonal word of God. This required tremendous depersonalization and self-control. Everything in the world of nature, self and society had now to be transformed in accordance with God's will. But for this transformation to happen, the whys and the whats would have to be strictly and accurately calculated. Feelings must be renounced in order to estimate God's will in a rational way. Indeed, given the awesome abstraction of God, the Puritan could know his calculation had been rational only if the transformation of this world has actually occurred. The Puritan would be known by his works. His calling was to master the world.

The stage was now set for the transition to the modern era. This-worldly asceticism continued to permeate the world, but its religious content faded away. The great Protestant scientists – Newton, for example – did not secularize nature in a literal sense. Still, their commitment to seeing in nature the manifestation of God's will and to acting upon it through calculation of its laws was but a small step. Puritan emphasis on the reason of nature and its accessibility to human calculation led directly to the notion of natural law. Natural law allowed causality to be assessed in purely mechanical terms. True, such anti-metaphysical explanation remained in the service of teleology, but it was but one short step to the idea that no force outside of nature – nothing metaphysical – could govern what was contained within it. Science, and modern rationality more generally, represents the Puritan obsession with calculation, impersonal rules and self-discipline without the Puritan belief in their divine origin. It is Puritan epistemology without Puritan ontology.

When a calculating and ascetic consciousness comes to dominate the world without being anchored in metaphysics, the result is a sense of meaninglessness. Once the anchor has been dispensed with, human existence seems disorderly, tossed this way and that. Weber (FMW, p. 140) writes that the post-religious understanding of life can be only 'provisional, not definitive'. Rational truth is still pursued, but it becomes cognitively specialized, separated from ultimate values and from other significances. For the Greeks, the exact opposite was the case. They occupied a transitional niche between religion and secular thought, much as the Puritans. Greek science, it was widely believed at the time, could give guidance in all the essentials of life.

> If one only found the right concept of the beautiful, the good, or, for instance of bravery, of the soul, one would also grasp its true being. And this, in turn, seemed to open the way for knowing and for teaching how to act rightly in life and, above all, how to act as a citizen of the state. (FMW, p. 141)

But once science has become separated from metaphysics, rationality can describe only what is, not what ought to be. In this sense it is meaningless, for it cannot answer 'the only question important to us', writes Weber, quoting Tolstoy: '"What shall we do and how shall we live?"' This is true, moreover, not only for natural science, but for every form of knowledge that seeks to be rational. Consider aesthetics. 'The fact that there are works of art is given for aesthetics,' Weber argues. 'While it seeks to find out under what conditions this fact exists . . . it does not raise the question whether or not the realm of art is perhaps a realm of diabolical grandeur.' Aesthetics does not, in other words, ask the normative question, 'should there be works of art?' (FMW, p. 144). Or take jurisprudence. 'It establishes what is valid according to the rules of juristic thought', but it never asks 'whether there should be law and whether one should establish just these rules'. To do the latter would be to assume the meaningfulness of law in a teleological way. The same goes for the historical and cultural sciences. They teach us how to understand and interpret, but 'they give us no answer to the question, whether the existence of these cultural phenomena have been and are worth while' (FMW, p. 145).

This compartmentalization of rationality has fragmented the once integrated universe. Where once there was security and direction, there is now a metaphysical disorder that gives little solace. 'So long as life remains immanent and is interpreted in its own terms,' Weber believes, 'it knows only of an unceasing struggle of these gods with one another' (FMW, p. 152). Though he senses keenly what has been lost, Weber does not wish that the religious cosmologies could be reconstructed again. He accepts its loss as the price of freedom. This-worldly asceticism has produced a fragmented world without any metaphysical integration, but it is precisely this lack of metaphysical anchorage that throws the individual back upon himself. Once God directed man; now man chooses his gods: 'You serve this god and you offend the other god when you decide to adhere to [a] position' (FMW, p. 151).

Rationalization as Domination

Yet while Weber revered the hard-won autonomy of the modern individual, he did not see individualism as the single defining trait of the twentieth century. Metaphysical nostalgia was far from the only threat to individuality. Against the individual stood barriers of much more material shape. These were the 'hard and cold' institutions of the modern world. Even while rationalization had stripped illusions from men's minds and created the possibility for active and mastering behaviour, it had created the psychological and cultural basis for an extension of institutional coercion that threatened to make this potential for freedom a bitter joke. The very forces that free man allow him to become dominated in turn. This is the ominous insight with which Weber chose to conclude *The Protestant Ethic and the Spirit of Capitalism*. 'The Puritan wanted to work in a calling', he rued (PESC, p. 181), 'we are forced to do so.'

Weber's emphasis in this famous sentence on the voluntariness of the Puritan calling is ambiguous. Referring to the individuating effects of Protestant self-control on the one hand, it points to how asceticism facilitates spiritual and material domination on the other. Hence the sentence that follows: 'For when asceticism was carried out of monastic cells into everyday life, and began to dominate worldly morality, it did its part in building the tremendous cosmos of the modern economic order' (PESC, p. 181). Demands for large-scale organization have, of course, existed from the beginning of time. Efficiency creates functional reasons for the development of such organization, and the trans-historical human desire for domination creates the psychological fuel. But the culture and psychology of this-worldly asceticism have allowed such 'natural' factors to be rationalized in an unprecedented way.

Theoretical blind spots in Weber's work made it virtually impossible for him to carry out this 'other side' of his religious-evolution argument in a consistent way. Weber showed a persistent inability to relate his historical political sociology to the cultural analysis of his religious work (Alexander, 1983a), and this is precisely what would have been necessary if this 'other side' were to have been revealed in a systematic way. For us to do so here, moreover, would be highly digressive, for it would involve the systematic incorporation of other theoretical traditions.[3] Yet while this other side is never spelled out, the main outlines of what such an argument would be like seem clear enough. The manner in which Weber constructed his historical sociology, the very nature of the categories he chose, convinces us that the outline for this other side was there – in his head, so to speak – even if he was unable to make it explicit or, much less, systematically to carry it out. What follows, then, is a *post hoc* reconstruction of what I would take this theory to be.

Weber believed that this-worldly asceticism made it possible not only to master the world but to master other human beings. Depersonalization and self-discipline promoted autonomy in part because they allowed the actor to distance his ego from emotions that represented dependency. But this rejection of one's own dependency needs forced one to reject the needs of others as well. The capacity to make a 'tool' out of oneself, therefore, also allowed one to depersonalize and objectify others. Domination could become ruthless only when the personal and idiosyncratic qualities of the other were eliminated. Just as the self became a tool for God, so would others be used for his greater glory. The god of the first great monotheistic religion – the Israelite God Yahweh – was also its god of war, and the very notion of a 'just' and crusading war emerged only with Western Judaeo-Christianity.

Bureaucracy is the most obvious institutional manifestation of the 'other side' of this abstracted, mastering spirit. The Christian Church was the world's first large-scale, successful bureaucracy. The discipline and rationality developed by the monks were important in rationalizing this bureaucracy further, and it was this form of political organization, not only the economic form of capitalism, that later became institutionalized in the world when the metaphysical content of this-worldly asceticism was removed. But economic coercion should not be neglected. Because

193

the Puritans made themselves into tools they were able to organize others in depersonalized struggle and work. The Puritan objectification of the spirit promoted, in this way, not only economic individualism but the subjective conditions for methodical domination in business and factory.

Politics was transformed in much the same way. Activism and individuality were certainly fundamental to democratization, and Weber himself wrote that religious 'election' could be viewed as an incipient form of democracy. Yet as Weber demonstrated at great length in 'Politics as a Vocation', the discipline that underlay modernity would much more likely have the effect of turning political parties, the vehicles for mass political participation, into organizations resembling machines. To produce votes, citizens in a mass society are tools, and modern politics comes to embody the domination and depersonalized motivation left over from asceticized religious life. Even the universities and the enterprises of modern science, institutions that embody more than any other the rational promise of secularizing change, were subject, in Weber's mind, to this transvaluation of values. Chance rather than merit now governs academic advancement (FMW, pp. 131–2), and the centralization of research is proletarianizing the scientist, turning him into a mere cog in the scientific machine.

Even when he indicated this other side of religious rationalization Weber did not entirely ignore the benefits that were promoted along the way. Economic growth and political efficiency were not to be sneezed at, nor was the most important benefit of all, namely, equality. The objectification that made men into tools of God's will made them all equally so. The domination of impersonal rules reduced all men to the same status. Citizenship was the other face of depersonalized domination. Weber demonstrated this in *The City*, but at very few places outside of this historical essay did he suggest that the cultural and psychological capacity for citizenship would lead to political activism and democratic change. He was much more concerned to show how citizenship allowed the mass organization of individuals for demogogic ends.

There is a wide-ranging discussion in Weber's work of the material causes for these developments in relations of domination. In *Economy and Society*, for example, he conceptualizes the sequence from patriarchal estate to patrimonial/prebendary domination, and he outlines the economic and political exigencies that then lead on to modern bureaucratization. The problem with this whole line of discussion, however (Alexander, 1983a; 1983b), is that Weber fails to bring into it the theory of the objectification of the spirit I have just described.

That he knew such a connection existed there seems little doubt. Only the intention to establish such a link can explain the brief, condensed discussion of the relation between charisma and discipline in *Economy and*

Society. Weberian interpretation (with the exception of Mitzman, 1970) has neatly confined charisma to Weber's typology of political legitimacy and his technical accounts of religious and political innovation. Given Weber's own ambiguity on this point, this is understandable. But it is not correct. There is evidence in his work that he tried to utilize the charisma concept in a much broader form. It was to be the opening by which Weber could outline the dark side of spiritual rationalization.

He begins this short segment of *Economy and Society* (ES, pp. 1148–52) with a general, non-historical statement about charisma and discipline: 'It is the fate of charisma to recede before the powers of tradition or of rational association after it has entered the permanent structures of social action.' This is simply a restatement of the typology of legitimate domination. What follows, however, shows that Weber has something very different in mind. 'The waning of charisma', he writes, 'generally indicates the diminishing importance of individual action.' Now according to the more positive side of his rationalization theory – the side that illuminates the development of individuation – rational socialization should promote individual action, not diminish it. What can explain the dramatic change in Weber's point of view?

The answer seems to be that in this essay Weber wants to point to the fact that rational ideas can work against individualism as well. He stresses that charisma can be the carrier of different kinds of idea, that it must be treated in an historical way. Of all those powers that lessen the importance of individual action, he writes, 'the most irresistible force is rational discipline'. In other words, while the waning of charisma always undermines individuality, it does so variably. When it is the carrier of rationalizing ideas, it does so very forcefully indeed.

Weber goes on to connect increasing discipline not only to rationalizing charisma, but to another key element of religious evolution, namely, to increased equality. It 'eradicates not only personal charisma', he writes, 'but also stratification by status groups'. And in the next sentence he makes the link between subjugation and rationalization as explicit as it could possibly be: 'The content of discipline is nothing but the consistently rationalized, methodically prepared and exact execution of the received order, in which all personal criticism is unconditionally suspended and the actor is unswervingly and exclusively set for carrying out the command.'

Weber can now discuss the darker side of Puritan development, for he can show how the religious rationalization it entailed led to increased discipline and not just greater autonomy. 'Insofar as discipline appeals to firm ethical motives,' Weber suggests, 'it presupposes a sense of duty and conscientiousness', and in a parenthetical aside he contrasts 'men of conscience' and '"men of honor"', in Cromwell's terms'. Rather than

195

entrepreneurial activity, Weber makes war the secular outgrowth of the Protestant ethic. He writes that it was 'the sober and rational Puritan discipline [that] made Cromwell's victories possible', and goes on to elaborate the contrasting military styles in technical terms. When Weber talks about routinization in this discussion he is referring not to the economic patterns that result from active religious commitment but to the discipline that remains. What is left after the charismatic phase of Puritanism is the habit of strict obedience.

Weber has added, then, a fundamentally new and quite different twist to his famous Protestant-ethic thesis about the relation between religious development and modern society. Yet there are strong indications in this essay that he intended to go much further. He refers, for example, to the 'disciplinary aspect' of every sphere and every historical period, without specifically tying this aspect to the development of this-worldly asceticism. He talks about 'the varying impact of discipline on the conduct of war' and argues that it has had 'even greater effects upon the political and social order'. Discipline, as the basis of warfare, gave birth to 'patriarchal kingship among the Zulus ... Similarly, discipline gave birth to the Hellenic *polis* with its *gymnasia* ... Military discipline was also the basis of Swiss democracy' (ES, p. 1152).

In other words, key elements in ancient, pre-Judaeo-Christian societies and modern post-Reformation ones alike can be causally linked to this charismatically generated subjection: 'Military discipline was also instrumental in establishing the rule of the Roman patriciate and, finally, the bureaucratic states of Egypt, Assyria and modern Europe.' Weber goes on pointedly to suggest that 'the warrior is the perfect counterpart to the monk'; the disciplinary aspect in cultural evolution promoted monasteries just as it promoted war. 'The garrisoned and communistic life in the monastery', Weber writes, 'serves the purpose of disciplining [the monk] in the service of his other-worldly master'; and, just in case his point is not yet understood, he adds that a direct result of such service might well be subjection of the monk to 'his this-worldly master' as well.

The cultural development of discipline is presented here as an independent variable in human history, a cultural push just as important as the evolution towards individuation. Weber can write, for example, that 'the emancipation of the warrior community from the unlimited power of the overlord, as evidenced in Sparta through the institution of the Ephors, has proceeded only so far as the interest in discipline has permitted'. This essay, indeed, marks the only point in Weber's entire corpus where he explicitly suggests a subjective side for his explanation of bureaucracy. He calls bureaucracy the 'most rational offspring' of discipline.

Weber emphasizes not only that cultural discipline – the 'other side' of religious rationalization – creates the desire for voluntary subjection, but that it provides a tool for extra-individual domination as well. While the existence of discipline certainly precedes any particular leader's drive for power, its existence clearly helps a power-hungry leader to achieve his ends. Would-be demagogues seize on discipline and learn how to turn it to their particular purpose; they can make good use of 'the rationally calculated optimum of the physical and psychic preparedness of the uniformly conditioned masses'. Acknowledging that enthusiasm and voluntary devotion continue to mediate even the most disciplined subjection, Weber insists that 'the sociologically decisive points' in such relationships must be connected to the historical rise of discipline and the way it facilitates external domination rather than voluntary legitimation. First, the rise of disciplined domination means that 'these seemingly imponderable and irrational emotional factors', i.e. enthusiasm and devotion, are 'in principle, at least, calculated in the same manner as one calculates the yield of coal and iron deposits'. Second, the followers' enthusiasm assumes a rationalized form, which makes them much more open to discipline: 'Devotion is normally impersonal, oriented toward a purpose, a common cause, a rationally intended goal, not a person as such, however personally tinged devotion may be in the case of a fascinating leader.'

When Weber writes that 'discipline inexorably takes over ever larger areas as the satisfaction of political and economic needs is increasingly rationalized', and that 'this universal phenomenon more and more restricts the importance of charisma and of individually differentiated conduct', his intention could not be more clear. He is arguing that rationalization results not only in increased autonomy but in the spread of impersonal domination through every sphere of life. The increased capacity for this-worldly calculation sustains individuation, it is true. But it simultaneously facilitates subjection and domination.

Weber invented the concept of rationalization to explain the seemingly irreconcilable qualities of the twentieth century. Once he succeeded in developing his theory of the paradox of rationalization, he had accomplished his goal. It is not simply the technical growth of military and industrial power, Weber now understands, that explains the horrors of our time. This depressing situation is also the outcome, quite simply, of the increasing inhumanity of man to man. This inhumanity is a subjective capacity, which has developed alongside the capacity for objectification. It is generated by the same capacity for depersonalization of self and other. It promotes discipline and subjection on the one hand, and mastery and autonomy on the other. With this new understanding Weber has translated his personal meditation on the human condition into a profound sociology of modern life.[4]

197

Flights from Rationalization

Too often in the secondary literature (e.g. Schluchter, 1979) Weber is presented as having stopped with the simple demonstration that this paradoxical structure exists. I want to suggest that this is far from the case. His personal protestation to the contrary, Weber's social theory addresses, as closely as any modern science can, the question 'How should we live?' Though Weber never reflects consciously on this strategy, this concern led him to concretize the paradox of rationalization in what are clearly existentialist terms. Like Sartre's reflections in *Being and Nothingness*, the pathos of Weber's account derives from the fact that he starts with an individual who has the capacity for freedom, though Weber describes this capacity as resulting from historical conditions rather than from human ontology.

Let us remind ourselves of Sartre's trenchant account of human existence. Outside of his self, Sartre believes, the individual faces an inert world. Inside of the self, he faces his own cowardly cravings for objectification and release. Both forces threaten to turn the 'existing' individual into a thing. When this happens, the self-consciousness that allows freedom and action turns into the self-objectification that converts contingency into determinism and consciousness into being.

Weber's understanding is remarkably similar. His actor, of course, is already objectified. Weber sees this as the basis of freedom; his historical understanding allowed him to see that individuality is sociology not just ontology. Yet the structures that exist outside Weber's 'self' are just as inert – they form the iron cage of depersonalized domination. And the dangers that exist inside of Weber's 'self' are just as real. The ego which Weber describes as the proud product of rationalization must contend, he insists, with its own capacity for self-mortification and its puerile desire to submit to discipline. For Weber, too, therefore, this dangerous and unstable situation marks the existential condition of the modern world.

What can an individual do? Like Sartre, Weber precedes this question with another. He asks, what is the individual *likely* to do? Sartre believes that the pressures of existence push the individual towards some 'mode of flight'. One way or another, most people find ways to deny their freedom. They may give up the anguish of being a free person for the horror of viewing themselves as a determined one, constituting their selves as enslaved to external, inhuman force. Or they may engage in a kind of play-acting, which wraps them in a sentimental fantasy and denies the threatening qualities of the world. Both responses are acts of bad faith; both are escapes from freedom.

Weber, too, explores 'flights from the world' at great length, though he characterizes them, more historically than ontologically, as escapes peculiar to a modern society. He, too, analyses such flights in terms of whether they refer to pressures from without or within. Though never elaborated as an explicit theory, from Weber's reflections on modernity in the last years of his life an explicit typology of world-flights can be fairly reconstructed. On the basis of this model, moreover, a clear account can be given of Weber's moral prescription for 'modern man'.

On the one hand, Weber describes the constant tendency for cynical adaptation to the demands of the day. Here is the bureaucrat who obediently follows his orders; the practical politician who pleads his helplessness before interest-group demands and the pressures of the moment; the scientist who becomes a cog in the research machine. In this mode of flight the individual becomes a mere tool of the disciplined spirit; he is no more than a means for some other determinate power or end. On the other hand, flight from the world can take an internal form. Rather than accepting the 'reality' of his objectified position, the individual tries to recreate some sense of oneness with the world, the cosmological experience of pre-modern man. This internal flight can take two forms. It might involve the attempt to re-divinize the world. In this situation the individual tries to replace the warring gods with a single, all-powerful one that can provide a firm, all-encompassing meaning for the world. Here is the idealist, reality-denying politician of 'conviction'; the professor who pretends that science can discover the meaning of life and manipulates his position of scientific authority to impart this meaning to his students; the believer who thinks he has heard the clarion call of modern-day prophecy.

Yet the recreation of oneness need not take on this kind of metaphysical hue. It can express itself completely on the psychological level, as a commitment to 'experientialism' (see e.g. FMW, pp. 340–58). The person aims here to deny the status of 'tool' bequeathed by asceticism, and to recover the status of 'vessel' allowed by mysticism (see Schluchter, Chapter 4). Eroticism is one major escape of this kind. Sex is pursued for the sake of physical gratification alone, and sexual satisfaction becomes the principal meaning of life. Aestheticism is another mystical form of escape, in which the experience of art is pursued for itself, for its form, quite separated from the ethical or intellectual meaning that marks art's content.

Sartre's analysis of flight was abstract and philosophical. Weber's is historical and concrete. With it he typified the most terrible and unrelenting pathologies of modern times, from the destructive addictions and fantasies of private life to the totalitarian temptations and murderous dictatorships that have marked the public world. He has developed a typology of the horrors of the twentieth century which is systematically related to a vast reconstruction of its institutional and cultural history. Perhaps because Weber's world-historical theory of discipline was so little developed, the far-reaching quality of his 'flight' theory has never been fully appreciated. In my view, however, it constitutes his most important meditation on modern subjectivity.

But Weber is still not satisfied even with this. Just as Sartre insists that the omnipresence of bad faith cannot obliterate the freedom that is at the ontological base of the human condition, so Weber rejects the notion that world-flight is inevitable. He is morally repulsed by world-flight and he wants to lay out an alternative. For Sartre, one must accept the anguish of freedom. Weber's answer is not different, but it is more sociological; one must find a vocation.

Existential Courage and 'Vocation'

With the notion of 'vocation', elaborated primarily in the two essays bearing that title written towards the end of his life, Weber recalls a central theme from his analysis of cultural development in the pre-secular age. It was Luther who first emphasized the *Beruf*, and the Puritans who first made the 'calling' central to religious salvation. The Puritans' vocation represented the first and most important result of the turn towards this-worldly asceticism, the religious movement that so decisively supported the development of rationality and individuation even while it ushered in the forces that threatened to overwhelm both reason and the individual.

To practise a vocation as the Puritans did means to be disciplined by a moral spirit that facilitates the realization of the self. In the first place, therefore, it is to avoid the mystical experientialism that represents a major flight from reality in the modern world. Vocational commitment also prevents the cynical adaptation to external conditions that self-objectification and material domination are likely to beget. Finally, the Puritan vocation, while definitely a conviction, was not an idealistic commitment in the utopian sense of world-flight. Vocational conviction accepts the limits of the division of labour and institutional rationalization, in the sense that its moral discipline is narrowed to the requirements of a specific task.

In all these ways, I believe, Weber was convinced that the ancient vocation of the Puritans and the contemporary vocation of modern man are the same. It seems clear to me, however, that Weber saw an enormous difference as well.[5] The Puritan maintained his vocation in the service of God, his conviction and his work serving to maintain the fabric of cosmological meaning. In Weber's view, the modern vocation cannot allow this intellectual sacrifice. The fruits of rationalization must be maintained. Once this-worldly asceticism escaped from the cosmological net it allowed a radically new form of autonomy and self-control. This-worldly religious asceticism created the first opportunity for vocation, but only in post-religious secular society can the vocational commitment achieve a liberating, existentialist form. Weber believes that vocational morality allows the modern person to maintain his autonomy in the face of the objective pressures of the iron cage.

The language Weber uses to describe 'vocation' in contemporary society, it seems to me, makes this link between Puritan and modern vocation unmistakably clear. The similarity in discourse demonstrates that secular vocations can allow some of the same psychological and cultural satisfactions as religious life. Science, Weber writes, can become an '*inward* calling' (FMW, p. 134, italics in original) whose significance for the practitioner touches the most profound issues of existence: 'Whoever lacks the capacity to . . . come up to the idea that the fate of his soul depends upon whether or not he makes the correct conjecture at this passage of this manuscript may as well stay away from science' (FMW, p. 135). Vocations, then, are concerned with salvation in the deepest sense of the word. What they have done is to connect the 'soul' of modern man – which evidently Weber thinks still exists – to rationalized tasks in the modern world. The experience of a vocation can even be mystical in a thoroughly secular way, though the passion it inspires and the 'strange intoxication' it affords may be 'ridiculed by outsiders'. Vocational commitment allows, for example, the experience of perfection associated with being a mystical vessel of God: 'The individual can acquire the sure consciousness of achieving something truly perfect in the field of science' (FMW, p. 134). To have such a calling is to realize the great humanistic ideals, 'for nothing is worthy of man as man unless he can pursue it with passionate devotion' (FMW, p. 135).

The same possibility for maintaining 'rational religion' is held out in Weber's politics essay. Here, too, Weber wants to suggest that the result of this-worldly asceticism need not be self-mortification and the crushing discipline of external force. Here, too, he presents this argument by using religious language in a secular way. Politics, of course, is intimately associated with violence. At first this association was mitigated by the degree to which politicians could live 'for' politics, maintaining, thereby, some sense of individual responsibility and control. But with mass democracy, the need develops to organize and discipline the masses, and the mass politician learns to live 'off' politics. The ideal type of this new politician, the man without a vocation for politics, is the boss, the 'absolutely sober man' (FMW, p. 109) who embodies the flight from rationalization typified as cynical adaptation to the demands of the day.

It is the rudderless man without the calling for politics who produces the 'soullessness' of modern politics. But this situation is not inevitable.

201

There remains the possibility for 'innerly "called"' leaders (FMW, p. 79). To have a calling the politician must subject himself to the discipline of a moral cause – 'the serving of a cause must not be absent if action is to have inner strength' (FMW, p. 117). The exact nature of the cause is a matter of individual choice, but 'some kind of faith must always exist'. But commitment to a cause must remain 'secular'; it must not reflect the search for re-divinization that represents another kind of flight from the world. If the politician were to submit to such an essentially religious point of view he would be committed not to a vocation but to an ethic of ultimate ends, to the 'politics of conviction'. What Weber advocates instead is the 'ethic of responsibility'.

Responsible, vocational political ethics can be achieved only if moral commitment is disciplined by rational assessment of the realistic possibilities of gaining one's ideals. 'One has to give an account of the foreseeable results of one's action' (FMW, p. 120). Faith, then, need not be eliminated from modern politics, but it must be disciplined by rationality. 'It takes both passion and perspective,' Weber writes (FMW, p. 128). 'What is decisive', he insists, is not only idealistic commitment but 'the trained relentlessness in viewing the realities of life' (FMW, pp. 126–7). Adding such scientific realism to faith, of course, is precisely what pushes this-worldly asceticism to individuation rather than cosmology, and it is this demand for 'rational accounting' that makes the pressure on the post-cosmological individual so much more intense. What becomes decisive in achieving such individuation is 'the ability to face such realities and to measure up to them inwardly' (FMW, p. 127). Only if this strength is achieved can a person have a calling for politics. Anyone 'who is not spiritually dead' must realize that this possibility does exist.

It is certainly not correct, then, to say, as so many of Weber's interpreters have, that Weber saw no escape from the iron cage other than the pursuit of irrational, charismatic politics. It is no more correct, indeed, than to describe Weber's sociology, as so many others have, as a paean to the realization of individuality in its various forms.[6] Rationalization is a movement towards individuation, but it allows for the conditions of individuality rather than individuality as such. For rationalization also creates the psychological needs and the cultural codes that sustain antiindividualistic institutional coercion in turn. Faced with such destructive, depersonalizing forces, the individual either flees from them and gives up his independence, or confronts them and maintains it.

Weber presents this confrontation as an existential choice, with all the arbitrariness that such a position implies. Sartre is quite right to insist that there is nothing that can explain or predict whether an actor has the courage to accept the anguish of freedom. Weber expresses exactly the same sentiment when he suggests that vocational commitment depends on 'the ability to face these realities and to measure up to them inwardly'. Sartre is convinced that such courage is rarely to be found, and Weber entirely agrees. From *The Protestant Ethic* on, Weber emphasizes just how unlikely vocational behaviour in the modern world will be. 'The idea of duty in one's calling', he writes, 'prowls about in our lives like the ghost of dead religious beliefs' (PESC, p. 182). When occupational behaviour is disconnected from religious direction or direct economic necessity, he suggests – he is clearly referring to conditions that develop in the twentieth century – it will rarely be elevated to a calling: 'Where the fulfilment of the calling cannot directly be related to the highest spiritual and cultural values, or when, on the other hand, it need not be felt simply as economic compulsion, the individual generally abandons the attempt to justify it at all.'

Beyond Rationalization Theory: towards a Fuller Dialectic

This sociology of modern life, I want to suggest, leaves us in a rather uncomfortable position. Weber has described an extraordinary dialectic of individuality and domination, and he has shown how from this crucible there emerges the flights from reality and the courageous assertions of freedom that are such characteristic markers of our time. Secularization has made freedom a possibility that personal courage can achieve, and from the standpoint of any particular individual actor it is impossible to predict whether individuality in this sense will ever be realized. Depersonalization, too, is an undeniable, profoundly disturbing fact of modern life. The twentieth century is strewn with societies brutalized by technology, choked by totalitarianism and sapped by existential flight.

Yet for all its breathtaking illumination – and Weber achieved more clarity about the dangers of modernity than any theorist has before or since – this theory does not seem entirely satisfactory.

The course of modernity has, indeed, been marked by dreadful self-enslavement,[7] but it has also been the site of extraordinary break-throughs in the rational understanding of mental life and the democratic support of individual rights, breakthroughs that have bolstered the self in turn.[8] While every society has been weakened by individual and group flights from reality and crippled in significant ways by hierarchical domination, several important societies have managed acute crises and chronic strains in ways that have allowed them to sustain reasonable patterns of life. Even those societies that succumbed to the horrors of modernity contained movements and institutions of a more rational and responsive bent. The new forms of organization that emerged from the destruction of these societies often demonstrate, moreover, that 'rational learning' can take place on a societal scale.

Weber's sociology indicates that in modernity such moments have been overcome, but it does not allow us to explain how such experiences have actually been achieved. They have not been random, and they have not depended on the contingency of individual courage alone. They have occurred for structural reasons which can be sociologically explained.

It is true that most of the great theorists of the twentieth century have been extraordinarily pessimistic. But there has been a small number of theorists who have taken a more optimistic path. Parsons is certainly the most significant example, and it is not an accident that among the great social theorists he is the only American. While he acknowledged, particularly in his early work, that modernization might lead to aggression and polarization, he devoted most of his life to elaborating a theory of how this reaction could be avoided. Piaget allowed him to transform psychoanalysis into an account of how socialization could create lifelong reservoirs of individual strength and rationality. On the social and cultural level Parsons argued that differentiation, depersonalization and secularization can lead to flexibility and adaptiveness rather than to discipline and rigid control.

While Weber argued that scientific rationality and ethical values should coexist, he did not identify the conditions under which such a coexistence might be achieved. Durkheim did just that. In the first place, he produced a systematic argument for the continuing 'religious' needs of human beings. He went on from there to analyse the social processes by which such needs could be met by secular symbol systems which transformed them at the same time. Durkheim knew that it was not simply individual courage and existential contingency that would permit modern actors to go beyond the purely rationalistic stance of science. Actors were bound to be dissatisfied, and he considered it inevitable that rational knowledge would be experienced as radically incomplete. The 'irrational' search for meaning that results, however, was not considered by Durkheim to be something which could be conducted in an entirely individualistic way.

Not only flights from reality but attempts to confront it ethically are sustained, according to Durkheimian sociology, by supra-individual, group process. Even science, Durkheim came to believe, must be viewed in such group terms. Science is accepted to the degree that the value of critical rationality becomes part of both the structures of modern societies and the belief systems of human beings. Modern social systems, Durkheim believed, can be organized so that irrationality is continually challenged by social movements that embody rational, emancipatory values, and so that domination is confronted by differentiated structures that institutionalize individual autonomy.

I am not suggesting that Weber was blind to the possibility that such positive developments might ever exist. It was he, after all, who wrote about vocational, professional commitments. He acknowledged that the profession of law might allow some politicians to live for politics rather than off it, and in an important early essay (Weber, 1985; Alexander and Loader, 1985) he suggested that participatory democracy could be maintained in nations that had experienced sect rather than church religion. Weber outlined a theory of citizenship for the early modern period, and he acknowledged that the formal abstractions of modern law could be abrogated by oppressed groups seeking substantive rationality.

What I am suggesting, however, is that theoretical blind spots in Weber's work, on the one hand, and his ideological sensibility, on the other, made it impossible for him to convert these insights into systematic sociological theory. Weber saw that religious evolution had freed the individual in modern societies, but he described this modern individual as isolated and culturally abandoned. Weber described how depersonalization had changed institutional structures in a positive way, but he viewed the institutional residue of the twentieth century as coercive and its socialized motivation as dependent.

These insights represent the strengths of his sociology as surely as they represent its limits. As this great and terrible century draws to a close, we must reclaim Weber's dialectic of individuation and domination as our theoretical legacy. We must also compel ourselves to surpass it in turn.

Notes

I would like to thank Sam Whimster and Scott Lash for their comments on an earlier draft of this chapter.

1 This point is made decisively in the important essay by Seidman (1983), which insists that Weber does not view the post-cosmological world in purely negative terms.
2 The only major exception is Löwith (1982), who differentiated Weber's rationalization theory from Marx's precisely in these terms, i.e. that Weber tied this development to the increased opportunities for existence in modern life (a point reiterated by Seidman, 1983). I take up this existential theme at some length later in the chapter.
3 The darker side of rationalization has, of course, been pursued by Marxism, and the specifically Weberian understanding of this development has been elaborated within the Marxist tradition by 'critical theory' as, for example, Habermas (1984) has recently shown. This tradition, however, has been unable to bring to their account of moral and social decline Weber's phenomenological thrust, particularly his commitment to understanding the role

independently constituted symbolic systems played in producing this darker side. The other traditions I have more in mind, therefore, are not Marxist ones but rather those of Elias and Foucault. Even these traditions, however, over-emphasize the power-mediating qualities of cultural texts.

4   This discussion of discipline demonstrates that there are fundamental connections between one tendency in Weber's sociology, at least, and the theory of modernity produced by Foucault (e.g., most directly Foucault, 1975). Yet while Foucault certainly draws out the nature and ramifications of anti-individualistic discipline to an extent Weber might only have imagined, he also does it in a manner that Weber would not have entirely approved. In the first place, Foucault focused only on one side of the dialectic of domination and individuality; he did not see that the expanding domination he described was intimately tied up with the extension of individuality. In the second place, Foucault is, compared with Weber, quite anti-historical in his explanation for disciplinary expansion, both in his insistence on a relatively recent 'epistemological break' as its source and in his failure to develop a comparative understanding of this phenomenon in non-Western civilizations. For both of these reasons, Foucault is able to appreciate neither the fact of the continuing – if not continuous – vitality of human responsibility in the modern world nor its sociological foundations. Much the same can be said for many other leading contemporary cultural critics, for example MacIntyre (1981) and Bell (1976). See note 6, below.

5   Here my interpretation departs sharply from the 'neo-religious' tack taken by Shils (1975) and other conservatives.

6   Mitzman (1970) is not the only interpreter to make the former charge, i.e. that Weber saw irrational, charismatic politics as the only way out. Loewenstein (1966) and Mommsen (1974), for example, have made much the same point. Parsons and Bendix, of course, are the major figures associated with the identification of Weber as a progressive liberal who saw freedom as the emerging product of world history. Though Schluchter's interpretation of Weber is more nuanced (1981), he has likewise seriously underplayed the apocalyptic, darker side of Weber's work. Habermas (1984) extends these three liberal interpreters in a similar way, though he is much more critical of Weber's failure to spell out the prerequisities even of a liberal and democratic society (a criticism that I will echo below). Yet Habermas differs by trying also to focus on the negative side of the dialectic. As I mentioned earlier, however, Habermas fails to illuminate this side of Weber's work fully because he conflates it with the anti-normative instrumentalism of critical theory (see Alexander, 1985).

7   Weber's extremism in this regard has inspired social theorists who, ignoring the subtleties of his argument, describe the modern condition as a choice between chaotic freedom and conservative regulation. Thus, drawing on Weber, MacIntyre (1981) claims one must choose between Nietzsche and Aristotle, and he chooses the teleological, hierarchalized value-framework of the latter. Neo-conservatives like Bell (1976) pose a similar choice and reject the fragmentation of modernity for religious revival (see Lash, Chapter 17). In doing so, such theorists are succumbing to what I earlier called 'metaphysical nostalgia', which is one intellectual form of world-flight.

8   See Levine (1981) for a strong argument that Weber failed to develop the kind of motivational theory that could account for such significant 'rational' movements in modernity as psychotherapy.

10

Nietzsche and Weber: Two 'Prophets' of the Modern World[1]

RALPH SCHROEDER

Nietzsche's and Weber's views of modernity are similar in at least two respects. One is their pessimism about the vacuum left in the modern world due to the decline of religious ideals; the second lies in their advocacy of powerful leaders as a possible remedy against this decline. These similarities have been noted in several commentaries on Weber.[2] Yet although there are few direct references to Nietzsche in Weber's writings, it must often seem that the affinity between them is much deeper. There is, for example, a well-known passage at the end of Weber's *Protestant Ethic* which describes the predicament of the individual in the modern disenchanted world: 'For of the last stage of this cultural development, it might well be truly said: "Specialists without spirit, sensualists without heart; this nullity imagines that it has attained a level of civilisation never before achieved"' (PESC, p. 182). Pronouncements such as these inevitably recall the Nietzschean background against which Weber was writing. They suggest that there are links not only between their views of the decline of religion and of leadership, but also between their respective assessments of the modern condition in general. More-over, in light of this close affinity beween their outlooks on the modern world, the question arises as to whether there might not be a more fundamental connection between the overall themes of their writings. Such deeper links can be found particularly in their analyses of the impact of religion and in their views of the historical development of this impact.

Nietzsche and Weber are well known for their descriptions of the transition from an age dominated by religion to the secular modern world. In fact, they were both concerned not with one great transition but two; the first was the transition from primitive religion to the universalist religions, and the second from Protestantism to the secular modern world. Both transitions are important because Nietzsche and Weber share

207

the view that the modern world is in some ways similar to the world of the primitive religions and in other ways like the world of the universalist religions. Once the parallels between their conceptions of the two great transitions have been spelled out, therefore, the close links between their outlooks on the modern world may also be seen in a new light.

From Primitive to Universalist Religion

In Nietzsche's and Weber's writings on religion there is a fundamental – if not always explicitly stated – contrast between the nature and impact of primitive and universalist religions. For the present purpose, this difference needs to be examined only in terms of the contrast between primitive religion and Judaeo-Christianity, since we will ultimately be concerned with their outlook on the modern *Western* world. In actuality, the distinction in their writings is between primitive religion, on the one hand, and all of the universalist religions – including Hinduism, Buddhism, Confucianism and Islam – on the other.

For Nietzsche, the advent of Judaeo-Christianity constituted the first of two great 'transvaluations of all values'. Yet what had preceded the first great transition? Nietzsche occasionally refers to the period before the rise of the universalist religions as having been man's 'prehistory' (*Urzeit* or *Vorgeschichte*; see Nietzsche, 1969, pp. 81, 89). He claims that during this prehistory, and thus in the absence of the Christian slave-morality, a more unfettered expression of man's will could take place. In this period, there had been an aristocracy of those who are 'by nature' more powerful. In the absence of an all-pervasive Christian conscience of good and evil, this prehistory was marked by the more authentic pursuit of a variety of human goals. This accounts, too, for the fact that there was a pluralism of values and world-views which, since they had not yet been subsumed under an all-encompassing religious and ethical system, existed in a 'natural' state of struggle or conflict.

In Nietzsche's view, Judaeo-Christian belief completely transforms this picture. In the place of an unfettered expression of man's will, his strongest aims are now denied and projected on to God (Nietzsche, 1973, p. 63). A 'natural' aristocracy can no longer exist since the disprivileged are placed at the top of the religious order of merit. The priesthood also gains in this new rank order since it acquires a monopoly over doctrinal and ethical matters. Hence the priesthood is able to displace the original, more 'natural' holders of power (Nietzsche, 1973, p. 61). In addition, a universal religious and ethical system takes the place of a pluralism of conflicting values. The competition between world-views is replaced by monotheism and by an ethic of brotherly love. Judaeo-

Christianity thus stands the previous religious and moral system on its head.

A similar break is evident in Weber's writings. He describes the pre-universalist religion as different forms of magic. All types of magic, however, are characterized by the fact that the believer seeks to achieve worldly ends through the direct manipulation or coercion of the gods (ES, pp. 399–439). The charismatic magician, for example, possesses the ability to achieve this manipulation on the basis of a 'natural' endowment with extraordinary powers. Hence, rather than reorienting his behaviour towards an other-worldly goal, as does the Christian who strives for other-worldly salvation, at the stage of magic the believer tries to coerce worldly forces in order to achieve a multitude of concrete ends. Again, since there is not yet an all-embracing system of religious values, the various supernatural forces and conflicting religious ends coexist as an unsystematic or 'natural' plurality.

The transition to universalist religion is as radical in Weber's writings as in Nietzsche's. In the first place, Judaeo-Christianity is seen as creating an all-encompassing world-view that accounts for suffering and injustice in the world – a theodicy.[3] Accordingly, the religious end must be achieved through the believer's inward transformation, rather than through the direct coercion of the gods. The moral precepts established within the Judaeo-Christian tradition dictate how this inner reorientation towards the world must take place. Another feature of Judaeo-Christianity, apart from this inner reorientation, is the emergence of an ethic of brotherly love. Also, the supernatural endowment of the magician is replaced by a hierarchy between priestly mediators, who have special access to the divine, and the ordinary believer. Thus the transition from the primitive or magical form of religiosity to Judaeo-Christianity means that there is a completely different orientation on the part of the believer and a different type of belief system; universalist religions demand an inner reorientation on the part of the believer towards a transcendent goal, whereas previous forms of religiosity left the believer's many discrete ends intact. In addition, the world of a plurality of magical forces is now replaced by an all-encompassing conception of the divine, codified and administered by the priestly élite.

The two accounts of the transition from primitive to universalist religion are therefore similar in so far as primitive religion consists of a natural or direct expression of man's aims, whereas Judaeo-Christianity demands an inner reorientation towards a transcendent goal. Secondly, both characterize the world prior to the world religions as being made up of a multitude of competing powers. The 'natural' plurality of man's aims and world-views is left intact at this stage. With the rise of the universalist religions, however, this plurality is replaced by a single, all-embracing system of values.

From Christian Asceticism to Soulless Pragmatism

The transition from primitive to universalist religion has mainly been described in terms of the contrasting features of two *systems* of belief. The most important aspect of the transition from Christian (in Weber's case mainly Protestant) asceticism to the secular world, on the other hand, lies in the transformation that occurs within the individual. Nietzsche and Weber both describe the Christian's attitude as one of attempting to transcend the given world through his other-worldly striving. This is contrasted with the modern individual who accommodates himself to the world as it is, due to a complete lack of anchoring in transcendent values. Both the adherent to an other-worldly orientation and the rootless modern individual attempt to transform the world from within. Yet the ability to do this is increasingly being eroded with the decline of the religious demand for such an attitude.

In Nietzsche, this transformation is sketched by means of sweeping psychological generalizations. While Weber is concerned to give a detailed historical account of the effect of Protestant asceticism on economic life, Nietzsche described the same impact in a much broader sense. He thought that Christian religiosity resulted in a sublimation of the self, or a self-overcoming of the individual. This was seen as being partly due to the devaluation of the given world in favour of an inward ideal. Hence Nietzsche also speaks of the '*internalization* of man' (1969, p. 84, italics in original). The effects of this self-overcoming were wide-ranging. Nietzsche thought, for example, that the origin of science, as well as the modern pursuit of knowledge in general, could be partly traced back to an ascetic ideal (Nietzsche, 1969, p. 154).

Although this orientation is still dominant in the modern world, its original religious motivation is no longer present. Indeed, much of Nietzsche's positive philosophical programme can be understood as an attempt to create a new set of values which might reinvigorate the desire for mastery over the world in the face of its ongoing decline. Nietzsche also realized that, in spite of the fact that the desire to transform the world still exists in the modern world, its whole basis has changed. So he says, for example: 'The means employed by the lust for power have changed, but the same volcano continues to glow ... and what one did formerly "for the sake of God" one now does for the sake of money, that is to say, for that which *now* gives the highest feeling of power and good conscience' (Nietzsche, 1982, p. 123, italics in original).

Weber has a similar view of the transformation of religious attitudes into modern secular ones. At the end of *The Protestant Ethic*, describing the 'iron cage', he says: 'The Puritan wanted to work in a calling, we are forced to do so' (PESC, p. 181). He, too, conceives of Protestant asceticism as a kind of self-overcoming or sublimation. Thus he describes 'ascetic conduct' as a 'rational planning of one's whole life in accordance with God's will' (PESC, p. 153). At the same time, he notes the 'entirely negative attitude of Puritanism to all the sensuous and emotional elements in culture and religion' (PESC, p. 105). Again, this ascetic attitude of world-mastery continues into the modern day, despite the fact that the original source of psychological pressure – the Protestant dogmas of predestination and of election to one's 'calling' – have vanished. The striving for mastery over the world continues to dominate modern life, yet it is nowadays completely devoid of its former religious and ethical significance. In the modern world, as we shall see, such striving can therefore only lead to what Weber calls an 'ethic of "adaptation" to the possible' (MSS, p. 24).

The Death of God and the Iron Cage

Nietzsche's and Weber's accounts of the modern world are marked by their similarities both to the age of primitive religion and to the period before the demise of universalist religion. Modernity is akin to the age of primitive religion in so far as a system of conflicting powers and world-views re-emerges. Since there is no longer an all-embracing religious and ethical order of the world, Nietzsche and Weber perceive a renewed conflict between competing value-systems. Although to some degree such conflict obviously exists at all times, the distinctiveness of the modern age lies in the increasing intensification of this conflict.

At the same time, the modern age is seen as a continuation of the age of universalist religions in so far as man's desire to transform the world from within still persists. What Nietzsche and Weber both try to do is to reinforce this desire to reshape the world on the basis of far-reaching ideals – in spite of the fact that they thought they were witnessing the inevitable decline of this impulse.

Before going on to spell out this vision of the modern world in more detail, it is necessary briefly to meet one objection to the schema outlined here. One response to this three-stage schema – primitive religion, universalist religion, secular modernity – might be to say: 'Of course the primitive and the modern worlds share the characteristic that there is a multitude of conflicting world-views and that there is no universal belief system imposed from the outside. This is true almost by virtue of the definition of a world religion, but why should it be important?'

The answer is that, apart from explaining the similarities between the two thinkers, this schema also differs in important ways from the major rival explanations of belief systems. Marx and Durkheim, for example,

211

for whom belief is basically an emanation of social circumstances, could not possibly share the theory that in terms of the impact of belief, the primitive and the modern worlds are fundamentally different from the age of the universalist religions. Far from being merely obvious, Nietzsche's and Weber's tripartite schema is in fact what sets them apart from the other major types of explanation of belief.

Nietzsche saw himself as the prophet of the 'death of God', or of the second great 'transvaluation of all values'. In this new age, the monism of previous religious and metaphysical systems would be replaced by a pluralism of values which harkens back to pre-Christian times. With the end of religion and its all-embracing moral system, values would once again have to be created by a few select individuals, instead of being imposed from the outside by Christian religion. Hence, in J. P. Stern's words, the 'task of the new age – the age which follows "on the destruction of Christian dogma and morality by Christian truthfulness" – is to preserve the spiritual energy which past ages had invested in transcendence, and to re-direct this energy toward an immanent world' (Stern, 1979, p. 148).

This task is made especially urgent as the decline of religion brings with it 'the virtual end . . . of all idealism' (Stern, 1979, p. 143). In spite of his attacks on Christianity, Nietzsche was none the less willing to acknowledge the importance of its impact. It is only, he says, 'on the soil of this essentially *dangerous* form of existence, the priestly form, that man first became *an interesting animal*' (Nietzsche, 1969, p. 33, italics in original). The effect of Christianity was to orient believers towards a transcendent goal and to further an ascetic mastery of the world. With the loss of this driving force, the modern world is bound to become ossified. Nietzsche thought that this tendency was taking shape in the form of an increase of materialism and utilitarianism, resulting in a replacement of other-worldly goals by more immediate worldly desires.

Weber, similarly, believes that the declining impact of religion will bring about the re-emergence of a pluralism of values. At the end of *The Protestant Ethic*, he foresees that the plurality of gods which had existed in the pre-Christian age would re-emerge and the struggle among them recommence: 'Many old gods ascend from their graves; they are disenchanted and hence take the form of impersonal forces. They strive to gain power over our lives and again they resume their eternal struggle with one another' (FMW, p. 149).

The absence of all-embracing religious and metaphysical world-views is not the only result of the decline of religious idealism. Weber also predicts, in Mommsen's words, that 'routinization and rationalization [will] pave the way for the rise of a new human species – namely, the fully adjusted men of a bureaucratic age who no longer strive for goals which lie beyond their intellectual horizons, which is in any case likely to be dominated by their most immediate material needs' (1974, p. 20). Like Nietzsche, he thought that this lack of idealism manifested itself in the increasing predominance of materialist and utilitarian attitudes.

Nietzsche and Weber thus have very similar views about the emergence of a struggle among value-systems in the modern world and the increasing accommodation of man to his everyday, routine needs. The difference between them is not so much in content as in the terms in which it is expressed. Nietzsche couches his pessimistic outlook in terms of individual psychology and cultural life, whereas Weber is more concerned with the ethic of modern life and its social and political ramifications.

Reason and its Discontents

So far the similarities between Nietzsche and Weber have been described in relation to their conceptions of primitive religion, of the universalist religions and of modernity. Yet there is also another way of describing these similarities which has been mentioned only in passing, namely, by showing the affinity their notions of the self and the realization of its ideals. Nietzsche and Weber both believe that the individuality of the person can be realized only through an adherence to convictions that are set apart from everyday, practical considerations. Or, to put it differently, authentic individuality exists only in so far as the adjustment to mundane necessity is surmounted.

This conception of selfhood is therefore not merely described by reference to the individual, but it is defined against the backdrop of an everyday world from which one must set oneself apart. The inward self, in Nietzsche's and Weber's view, tries to forge an autonomous life against an outside world which hampers this autonomy. The external world tends to do this because it demands that the individual's beliefs should be adjusted to a world that consists mainly of routine necessity. In this respect there is a difference in emphasis between Nietzsche and Weber; Nietzsche thinks that it is the remnants of former religious ideals and the levelling influence of the masses which constitute the reality from which the autonomous self must free itself. Weber, on the other hand, is more concerned with the fact that the bureaucratic and disenchanted nature of modern life makes for a world which imposes purely practical aims upon the individual. Both of them would agree, however, that the realization of the individual's autonomous convictions stands in opposition to a routine world of everyday demands.

These similar conceptions of individual self-realization have their roots in Nietzsche's and Weber's views of the springs of human action. For

Nietzsche, the ultimate source of a person's actions lies in the irrationality of the will; there is an instinctual striving for power in human beings which shapes both their morality and their relations with other people. This inherent desire is irrational in so far as it is not subject to conscious or rational control. A fundamental incoherence of Nietzsche's philosophy results from this psychological insight. On the one hand, the instinctual drive for power is supposedly the motivating force for all of our actions. Yet at the same time, the ideal of the Superman is of someone who is able to transfigure (and thus to control) his will in order to overcome the world and create new ideals for humanity. While Nietzsche thus wants to ascribe the ultimate source of our actions to an irrational drive, at the same time the creation of a new and 'higher' morality relies on the ability to forge or shape this selfsame will. Nietzsche's project of building a new morality therefore seems incoherent, given his conception of the irrationality of the will.

The idea of the irrationality of human behaviour has a different place in Weber's writings. For him, it is important that the individual's values should counteract the impersonal and disenchanted modern world. Yet what kind of values should they be? Weber's sociological and political writings offer no answer to this question. In his view, *any* far-reaching aims which are not merely pragmatic and are promoted by the modern individual (or the political leader) may stem the course of routinization. His only requirement is that a certain 'distance' should be maintained that allows for a realistic appraisal of the degree to which it is possible to surmount the routine, everyday world (FMW, p. 115). The pure subjectivity of these values is precisely what allows them to work against the grain of bureaucratization and disenchantment. This subjectivity or arbitrariness in Weber's view of the individual in the modern world (and particularly of the charismatic leader) has led to the charge that he is a 'decisionist' – the idea that the values of the political leader cannot be grounded in anything but a purely subjective choice (Habermas, 1971, p. 63). Indeed, it is true that'Weber's account of these choices is irrational in the sense that no objective grounds or systematic underpinning for these values can be advanced.

Nevertheless, there is a clear difference between Nietzsche and Weber with regard to the claims of unreason. Weber's advocacy of a charismatic leader is embedded within a generally pessimistic view of the possibility of re-enchanting a cold and impersonal world. Unlike Nietzsche's self-defeating attempt to establish a 'new' morality on the basis of an irrational will, Weber's subjectivism is more of a statement of the problem of self-expression in a world dominated by the ongoing disenchantment and bureaucratization of modern life. He did not, however, attempt to build a systematic moral and political theory on this basis. Furthermore, his admonition that the individual should be clear about the difficulties of converting his personal vision into practical reality constitutes a recognition that such an expression of individuality is likely to fail in the face of the increasing rationalization of the world. Whereas Nietzsche thought that the Superman's will should become imprinted on modern life, Weber's subjectivism can be seen as a statement of the problem of authentic selfhood against the backdrop of his vision of a cold and impersonal public realm.

Between Two Laws[4]

The similarities between Nietzsche's and Weber's views of the type of action demanded by the modern world can be highlighted in another way. Both define the standpoint that they see as being characteristically modern in deliberate contrast with what they consider to be the essence of the Christian ethic. Nietzsche thinks of this ethical attitude as being embodied in the life of Christ:

> Only Christian *practice*, a life such as he who died on the cross *lived*, is Christian ... Even today *such* a life is possible, for *certain* men even necessary: genuine, primitive Christianity will be possible at all times ... *Not* a belief but a doing, above all a *not*-doing of many things, a different *being*.   (1968a, p. 151, italics in original)

Only this practice of an absolute ethic can truly claim to be Christian, whereas the doctrines that were subsequently developed negated or led away from this original standpoint. Weber calls it an 'ethic of ultimate ends' which demands that 'one must live like Jesus' (FMW, pp. 119–20). Such an absolute ethic may be possible in the modern world, but it entails that actions are judged only by the intentions with which they are carried out – without regard to the consequences.

Nietzsche and Weber respect such a standpoint, yet the ideal which they advance stands in complete contrast to it. For Nietzsche, the actions of the Superman (*Übermensch*) are not judged by reference to an absolute ethic, but in terms of the success of the individual's self-affirmation. This ideal is put forward in the notion of the 'will to power': 'What is good? – All that heightens the feeling of power, the will to power, power itself in man' (1968a, p. 115).

Weber's 'ethic of responsibility' dictates that the political leader should be responsible for the consequences of his actions (FMW, p. 120). Yet this also means that 'morally dubious means or at least dangerous ones' may be necessary in order to achieve these goals (FMW, p. 120). Rather than passively accepting any consequences that may arise from an absolute ethic, Weber's politician must be prepared resolutely to partake in the violent struggle among contending world-views. In this struggle for self-affirmation, it is the pragmatic orientation towards success, rather than the purity of intentions, that should guide the efforts of the politician.

Superman and Charismatic Leader

Given their pessimistic outlook on the modern world and their assessment of the choices facing the individual within it, we can now examine the affinities between Nietzsche's and Weber's *remedies* for the modern predicament. This affinity exists despite the fact that Nietzsche's attempt to overcome materialism and nihilism, unlike Weber's, focuses mainly on the individual rather than on society.

Nietzsche's notion of the Superman (*Übermensch*) is intended to counteract the levelling of far-reaching goals through an ideal of self-overcoming. This ideal is established in deliberate contrast with religious ideals, but it is also at the same time reminiscent of them. The distinctively modern aspect of the Nietzschean concept of the Superman is that he should struggle to adhere to values he has created himself. Hence he strives for a more authentic kind of selfhood than has hitherto been possible under the influence of religion. Nietzsche's notion of the will to power may therefore be described as the attempt at an authentic expression of selfhood through the adherence to a rigoristic ethical ideal, or as the sublimation and spiritualization of the individual's drives in order to transcend the world as it is (Kaufmann, 1968, chs. 7, 8). In this way the ideal of self-overcoming is also similar to the religious ideal of asceticism which Nietzsche himself criticizes in the third part of the *Genealogy of Morals*, though with very different – namely self-created – aims. Thus Nietzsche tries to create an image of modern man as being able to resist the decline of spirit in the modern world through self-overcoming.

Although this ideal has political ramifications, Nietzsche never systematically spells them out. Or, to put it another way, although Nietzsche does venture into the realms of national and international politics, his recommendations in these areas are much less coherent than his ideal of the Superman. His writings seem to be aimed mainly at a few select individuals. Moreover, his ideal is such that it is independent of society by its very definition. Georg Simmel has summed up Nietzsche's programme in this way:

The basis on which Nietzsche imposes a system of values upon his philosophy of history may be formulated as follows . . . that he recognized values in the life of humanity only in so far as these values are – in principle as well as in their significance – independent of how humanity is shaped by social forces, despite the fact that they can, of course, only be realized within a socially formed existence.

(Simmel, 1920, pp. 207–8)

This summary of Nietzsche's position could equally describe Weber's outlook on the modern world, except that Weber's ideal also has clear political implications – apart from this individual dimension. Like Nietzsche, Weber thought that the modern individual should try to develop an autonomous selfhood through the adherence to his own far-reaching values. Such a 'personality' (*Persönlichkeit*) with a constancy in relation to ultimate values would be able to transcend the routine world of his immediate material ends (WL, p. 132). Again, this personal ethic is at once reminiscent of – and yet different from – Weber's description of the Protestant ethic. It is similar in so far as it prescribes an ascetic mastery over the world, and yet different since only authentic personal values should provide the goals of this attitude.

Weber goes beyond Nietzsche's notion of the Superman and translates this individual ethic into the political sphere. His idea of a 'plebiscitary leader democracy' is designed to allow the individual political leader as much freedom to realize his personal vision as possible – within the strictures of a democratic state (Mommsen, 1974, pp. 83 ff.). Weber wants to enhance the powers of the charismatic leader so that his ideals can have as large an impact as possible in the political realm. This impact is intended to counteract the tendency towards the increasing bureaucratization and routinization of modern society. The cultural ideals promoted by the political leader can thus create a dynamic against modern materialism and utilitarianism.

The counterpart to this advocacy of charismatic leadership on the level of the nation state can be found in Weber's description of the struggle for cultural supremacy among nations. He thinks that the competition among modern nations will take place not only in the political or economic arenas, but also in terms of the prestige or honour of a national culture. In this struggle, Weber's yardstick of success seems to be the dynamic assertion of political ideals, while nations which are 'dominated by an uncontrolled [bureaucratic] officialdom' would do better to stay out of this struggle (GPS, p. 13).

Nietzsche and Weber thus share the hope for the vigorous promotion of powerful and original ideals. Yet while Nietzsche focuses mainly on the 'higher man' who should bring about a transformation within himself, Weber is concerned with the social impact of these ideals and therefore applies them to political leadership as well as to the nation state.

217

Objectivity and the Aims of Science

Apart from these important parallels between their outlooks on the modern world, there are also major differences between Nietzsche's and Weber's standpoints. The most significant difference is between their approaches to truth and value. In spite of the unsystematic and sometimes contradictory nature of Nietzsche's remarks on this subject, he nevertheless inclined towards a pragmatist position. Truth, Nietzsche thinks, is in some way subservient to the will to power, or to the propagation of his ideal of a higher species of modern man. Or, in Danto's words, the single criterion of truth in Nietzsche's epistemology is 'always and only whether any of the structures which science exemplified enhanced and facilitated life' (Danto, 1965, p. 71). In the essay 'On the Uses and Disadvantages of History for Life' he extends this view of truth as serving the enhancement of life to historical understanding (Nietzsche, 1984, part II).

Despite the fact that Weber was acutely aware of the problem of values in social science, he tried to overcome the Nietzschean position in his methodology. He argued that sociology must attempt to exclude personal values and the perspective of a particular time. His aim was to establish an objective or value-free social science. Although this objectivity may be limited by the fact that a given socio-cultural period will be bound to ask certain questions about the past rather than others, it should none the less be the aim of the social scientist to distance himself as much as possible from his own standpoint and from the perspective of his time. Weber's attempt to establish a value-free social science allows only that, when certain aims are *given*, social science may help to find the best means to achieve them (FMW, p. 151). The social scientist should not, however, try to promote his own values or his own world-view in his work. Weber's efforts to exclude all values from social science and to achieve objectivity in our knowledge of history and society thus clearly distance him from Nietzsche's pragmatist view.

Another difference between Nietzsche's and Weber's positions is between their views of the relation between truth and reality. Nietzsche's view of this relation is again far from clear. He denounced all metaphysical theories which tried to give an account of reality as a whole. This idea was partly the result of his belief that modernity is characterized by an irreconcilable struggle between conflicting world-views. At the same time, he himself is willing to subsume all truth under the criterion of whether or not it enhances a superior life. His own position can therefore be seen as the very holism or monism for which he criticizes others. On other occasions, however, Nietzsche embraces a different position which he sometimes refers to as 'perspectivism' (Nietzsche, 1968b, pp. 493–507). This view is expressed, for example, in the following well-known aphorism in *The Will to Power*: 'Against positivism, which halts at phenomena – "There are only *facts*" – I would say: No, facts are precisely what there are not, only interpretations' (Nietzsche, 1968b, p. 481, italics in original).

Despite the ambiguity of Nietzsche's position, it is again clear that Weber's standpoint is different since he rejects both holism *and* perspectivism. In the first place, Weber denies the validity of any holistic or all-encompassing social theories. For Weber, reality is always more complex than any theory. At the same time, he maintains that the systematic growth of objective knowledge about society is possible. There is, according to Weber, only a 'hair-thin line which separates faith and science' (WL, p. 212). None the less, it is precisely this crucial distinction between mere interpretation and objective knowledge which he tried to uphold in his methodological writings. His various methodological devices – such as the ideal type, causal explanation and the comparative study – are all aimed at gaining an increasingly objective understanding of society. On this issue, too, Weber's standpoint is radically at odds with Nietzsche's.[5]

These important differences between their epistemological and methodological views should not obscure the fact that Nietzsche's criticisms of the Enlightenment faith in science account for Weber's most explicit references to his writings. Weber invokes Nietzsche in order to criticize the optimistic view that an increasing technical mastery over life is bound to lead to an increase in happiness for mankind (FMW, p. 143). Instead, they both thought that the growth of the scientific understanding of the world – or, in Weber's phrase, the disenchantment of the world – would bring about a restriction of the sphere of human values. Nietzsche claims, for example, that 'in the same measure as the sense for causality increases, the extent of the domain of morality decreases' (Nietzsche, 1982, p. 12). In a similar vein, Weber thinks that due to the ongoing rationalization and disenchantment of the world, 'precisely the ultimate and most sublime values have retreated from public life either into the transcendental realm of mystical life or into the brotherliness of direct and personal relations' (FMW, p. 155).

Conclusion

Apart from the direct influences of Nietzsche on Weber's writings, there are thus clear parallels between their views of the modern world and how they arrived at them. They both foresaw the re-emergence of some features of the age of primitive religion as well as the continuation of a Christian orientation within a secular world. Both were basically pessimistic about the modern world; they thought that the decline of religious ideals would inevitably lead to the routinization or ossification of social life. In spite of these pessimistic outlooks, their standpoints were ambiguous. Nietzsche expressed the hope that this age of nihilism might be followed by an epoch which held a great renewal in store for man. In *The Will to Power*, for example, he says: 'This time of great noon, of the most terrible clearing up: my type of pessimism – great point of departure' (Nietzsche, 1968, p. 134). Weber expressed similar long-term hopes. Although the thoroughgoing routinization and bureaucratization of society were likely to continue, at the end of this period a new dynamic of ideas might none the less be created: 'No one knows who will live in this cage in the future, or whether at the end of this tremendous development entirely new prophets will arise, or there will be a great rebirth of old ideas and ideals, or if neither, mechanized petrification, embellished with a sort of convulsive self-importance' (PESC, p. 182).

In terms of his pessimistic view of modern society, Weber was thus closer to Nietzsche than to any other thinker. Yet the differences between them remain. Nietzsche provides us with penetrating psychological insights, yet his inability to formulate a systematic and objective account of modern society and his ambiguous philosophical position make it difficult to build upon his approach. Weber's conception of the disenchantment and bureaucratization of the modern world, on the other hand, still retains much of its explanatory force. It is only the Nietzschean background to Weber's view of modernity, however, which allows us to appreciate the pathos of his vision.

Notes

1 The idea for the title has been taken from a chapter heading in Stern (1979). I would like to thank Sam Whimster for his helpful criticisms of my ideas about Max Weber.

2 The relation between Nietzsche and Weber has been discussed by Robert Eden (1983), Eugene Fleischmann (1964), Wilhelm Hennis (1985), Wolfgang Mommsen (1974) and Bryan Turner (1982c).

3 With regard to the similarity between Nietzsche's and Weber's conception of theodicy, see Bryan Turner (1981, p. 157).

4 This heading is the title of one of Weber's political essays in his collected political writings (GPS, pp. 142–5).

5 It is important to keep these differences in mind in order to avoid the temptation to assimilate Weber's and Nietzsche's positions too closely. Hennis maintains that the central – and Nietzschean – question of Weberian social science is to consider the conditions under which a certain type of human being (*Typus Mensch*) may flourish (Hennis, 1985). He bases this assertion on a passage in the methodological writings (WL, p. 517). Yet this, according to Weber, is only one of the possible aims of social science. It should not,

however, be a central presupposition which prejudices social science as a whole – as it predisposes Nietzsche's view of truth. For Weber, there can be no such all-encompassing and value-laden presuppositions. Eden goes even further. He thinks that Weber's view of social science is a defence against Nietzsche's scientific 'immoralism' (Eden, 1983, p. 143). Thus he has Weber advocating a 'moralism in matters of method' and his social science providing a 'moral service' (Eden, 1983, pp. 141, 144). Yet Weber's aim is specifically to eliminate morals from social science. This, after all, is why he is at pains to point out in 'Science as a Vocation' that the value of social science cannot be justified by reference to any moral aims whatsoever (FMW, pp. 143–5). In this respect at least, it seems that Nietzsche's and Weber's views diverge sharply.

11

The Rationalization of the Body: Reflections on Modernity and Discipline

BRYAN S. TURNER

Introduction

Although the thematic unity of the works of Max Weber has been much disputed (Tenbruck, 1980) there is at least some agreement that the process of rationalization is central to an understanding of Weber's project (Löwith, 1982). The nature of rationalization arises as a crucial issue in Weber's sociology of modern societies at every point of his sociological investigation. While there is broad agreement as to the centrality of rationality and rationalization in the thought of Weber, it is curious that this feature of his work has not received extensive and systematic scrutiny (Schluchter, 1981; Brubaker, 1984). Existing studies of Weber's treatment of rationality typically draw attention to the paradoxical nature of rationalization in human societies, especially in capitalism. There are a number of dimensions to this paradoxical quality of rationality. The process of Western rationality has to some extent a major origin in the irrationality of the Protestant quest for salvation. There is furthermore a contradictory relationship between formal and substantive rationality where substantive questions of value are subordinated to formal questions of logic. There is the further paradox that the outcome of rationalization is a world that is essentially meaningless, lacking in moral direction and dominated by a bureaucratic structure. These contradictions were summarized in Weber's metaphor of the iron cage, and the contradictory relationship between formal reason and substantive irrationality was well captured in Herbert Marcuse's famous essay 'Industrialisation and Capitalism in Max Weber' (Marcuse, 1968).

While Weber's analysis of the relationship between Protestant asceticism and capitalism has received an extensive and possible excessive commentary, *The Protestant Ethic and the Spirit of Capitalism*, contains the essential core of Weber's view of the origins, nature and effects of rationalization. The Calvinistic quest for salvational security gives rise by a process of unintended consequences to a culture that emphasized reason, stability, coherence, discipline and world-mastery. Protestantism broke the umbilical cord that had traditionally united the individual to the institutions of the church and thus generated a new form of possessive individualism, which had the effect of legitimating money and creating a culture dedicated to work and the transformation of the human environment. Protestantism undermined the particularistic relations of the family and the kin group by generating a new conception of the political system. Having isolated the individual and purified the relationship with the deity, Protestantism denied the magical efficacy of the sacraments and created a culture sympathetic to natural science and intellectual inquiry. Furthermore Protestant doctrine relating to the household undermined the traditional authority of the priest as confessor and placed greater obligations on parents as educators of sinful children (Hepworth and Turner, 1982).

The Reformation was thus a major catalyst in the transformation of Western urban culture that stimulated a new form of rationality characteristic of the urban bourgeoisie, a rational culture spreading ultimately to all classes and groups within Western civilization. Although there is considerable disagreement with Weber's view of this process and the place of religion in the transformation of the West, there is overlap between the work of Marxist historians and Weberian sociologists. Illustrations could be found in the work of such disparate writers as Lucian Goldmann (1968), Groethuysen (1968) and Benjamin Nelson (Huff, 1981).

Max Weber's studies of the Protestant sects can be seen in fact as a history of 'mentalities', that is, the history of the emergence of a modern form of consciousness that is set within a rational tradition. However, what I shall argue is that, alongside this history of mentalities, there is the history of the rationalization of the body (see Turner, 1982a; 1982b). I shall suggest that Weber's discussion of rationalization as an historical process can be seen as a discussion of both the emergence of a particular form of consciousness and as the analysis of the emergence of new forms of discipline that regulated and organized the energies of the human body.

One major feature of traditional asceticism was the restraint and regulation of the passions, which were seen to have their seat in the inner body. In both Christianity and Galenic medicine, the moral stability of the individual was bound inextricably to the equilibrium of the body. Weber's comparative soteriology of the great religions can be seen as a contribution to the historical analysis of these regulations of the passions through various systems of ritual and rite. In Protestantism, and ultimately Freudianism, this regulation and discipline involve an imposition

223

of consciousness over physiology, where the body is conceived as an energy field. This reconceptualization of the mind/body relations is an important aspect of Weber's contribution to the cultural analysis of secularization.

In *The Protestant Ethic and the Spirit of Capitalism* Weber argued that people do not 'by nature' want to earn more and more, but seek instead to reproduce the conventional conditions of existence in order to survive without surplus production. Under such circumstances it would be irrational to produce a surplus where no market or demand existed for such additional commodities. Weber's Protestant-ethic thesis sought to understand the two central conditions whereby this natural reproduction was extended. These two conditions were the separation of the peasantry from the means of production by various forms of enclosure and secondly the development of an ascetic calling in the world to dominate and master the environment. These two conditions made labour both necessary and honorific. These changes in the means of production and values had the effect of subordinating and regulating instinctual gratification.

My argument is that there is an implicit philosophical anthropology in Weber's account of rationalization, and this anthropology is not entirely unlike the anthropology that we know to be significant in the work of Karl Marx (Schmidt, 1971; Markus, 1978). Weber sees history in a way like Marx views the development of capitalism as involving tearing mankind out of the natural communal environment. In this natural environment human beings are naïve in the sense that their self-consciousness of reality is not reflexive and is largely underdeveloped. Their needs are somewhat restricted to immediate gratification and production. There is so to speak a natural relationship between need and the economy where both are kept at a minimum. There is therefore a form of distinction in Weber between use-values in this natural economy and exchange-values in a capitalist system. The rationalization of the body in terms of a disciplining of energies and an amplification of needs is thus an underlying theme of Weber's narrative of capitalist development.

In general terms we can see this secularization and rationalization of the body as a process from internal religious restraints on the passions to external secular amplifications and displays of desire. That is, bodies in pre-capitalist societies are enveloped in a religious system of meaning and ritual where the main target of control was the internal structure of emotion. In modern societies the order of control and significance is lodged on the outer surfaces of the body conceived in a secular framework as the sources of desirable feeling and personal significance. For Weber modern disciplines had their origins in two separate institutional orders; these were the monastery and the army. It was in the monastic orders of medieval Europe that the initial diets and regularities emerged to subordinate passion to the will and to liberate the soul from the cloying significance of the body as flesh. As Goffman (1961) has noted, the monastery provided a total environment of control and a culture of restraint that was devoted to the regularization of human sexual emotion. Weber's Protestant-ethic thesis suggested that this discourse of restraint within the monastic environment was transferred to the everyday life of the household via the Protestant concept of the calling to dominate reality. The Reformation transferred the monk from the monastic cell to the intimate chambers of the modern household in early capitalism. There is also the theme in Weber's military sociology that the army was the original focus of social discipline whereby large bodies of men were moulded into a disciplined unit by personal discipline and bureaucratic demand systems. When religion and militarism were combined in a single context, the consequences for the development of discipline were intensified. Thus Weber claimed that 'belief in predestination often produced ethical rigorism, legalism and rationally planned procedures for the patterning of life. Discipline acquired during wars of religion was the source of the invincibility of both the Islamic and Cromwellian cavalries' (ES, p. 573).

In both religion and war, human bodies need to be trained, restrained and disciplined by diet, drill, exercise and grooming. Entry into both realms requires initiation, fire, rituals of degradation whereby bodies are cleaned, hair is cut and individual marks of identity are obliterated (Garfinkel, 1956). In these Weberian accounts of the organization of bodily functions, we find the presence of a debate about the relationship between Apollonian form and Dionysian energy, a contrast that is dear to social theorists from Gouldner (1967) to modern structuralists. Weber's discussion of this contradiction was taken directly from Nietzsche in the debate Weber conducted over the role of resentment in the explanation of religious belief and practice (Turner, 1981). We can thus see the growth of Protestant discipline at least by analogy as a version of the imposition of Apollonian disciplines on Dionysian forces.

Weber's sociology of capitalism provides a general and systematic framework for the analysis of rationalization processes in modern society and a framework for specifically understanding the transformation of the position of the human body in society from feudalism to capitalism. Weber provided much of the detailed analysis of knowledge, power and discipline that is necessary as a perspective on the transformation of European society under the impact of modern capitalism. He was primarily concerned with changes in knowledge and consciousness, but his perspective can be extended and adapted to the analysis of the regulation of the body and of populations. There appears to be a general process whereby the body ceases to be a feature of religious culture and is incorporated via medicalization into a topic within a scientific discourse. Furthermore, the internal restraints on the body as a system of controlling the mind appear to shift to the outside of the body, which becomes the symbol of worth and prestige in contemporary societies. Briefly, to look good is to be good. Hence there is an increasing role for cosmetics and body management in a society given to overt displays of personal status within a competitive society where narcissism is a predominant feature.

From Ritual to Discipline

We can consider the secularization of the body as a feature of rationalization from a number of vantage-points and in terms of a variety of illustrations. For example, there is the transformation of dance and gesture towards a science of exercise with the growth of gymnastics and the science of sport. In his historical account of the emergence of physical education Broekhoff (1972) provided a stimulating account of the reification of the human body with the impact of Swedish techniques of exercise on European views of body training. He correctly notes that this history involves the conversion of the body from a ritual context of communal dance as a social expression to a reified phenomenon that can be drilled by scientific practices and modern assumptions. Gymnastics are admired not as expressing fundamental religious values relating society to nature but as illustrations of human drive and efficiency in the context of individualized sport and achievement. Whereas Puritans had condemned dance as a provocation of sexual appetite they recognized the educational value for young people in mild forms of exercise and exertion. The Puritanical acceptance of exercise as a suitable component of education may have created the framework for an acceptance of sport and training as valuable aspects of character-formation. Dance in the twentieth century has once more assumed an oppositional form as the youthful expression of sexuality under the impact of modern US music from the jive and the jitterbug to rock and reggae.

Further illustrations of these rationalizing and secularizing processes with respect to the human body could be illustrated in some depth from the histories of art with special reference to the representation of the body. Unlike Islamic cultures, Christianity had no objection in principle to the representation of the human form in art provided that representation was aimed at devotional and educational goals. However, it was also the case that there was considerable conflict between art and Christianity, as Weber fully recognized in his sociology of religion. He recognized an intimate relationship between religion and art where art gave expression to religious values. However, where art became institutionally separated from religion and developed values of its own, as an autonomous form of salvation, there was inevitably a strong conflict between religion and artistic values. Thus Weber noted that all

> ethical religions as well as true mysticisms regarded with hostility any such salvation from the ethical irrationalities of the world. The climax of this conflict between art and religion is reached in authentic asceticism, which views any surrender to aesthetic values as a serious breach in the rational systematization of the conduct of life.
>
> (ES, p. 608)

In Weber's view this tension was increased with the growth of intellectualism, that is, with the growth of rationalization. There is an intimate connection between the historical emergence of the nude as a feature of art, the growth of individualism and the secularization of Western culture. The increasing individualization of people as represented through their distinctive bodies was a feature of the emergence of capitalist society and the growth of a bourgeois market for representational art, especially with the medium of oil paint (Berger, 1972). The emergence of the personal portrait representing distinctive human beings was thus a movement parallel to the growth of the novel and the autobiography as literary forms (Watt, 1957).

This process of secularization is pre-eminently illustrated in the transformation of diet from a religious practice to a form of moral medicine in a secular garb in the twentieth century (Turner, 1984). The word 'diet' comes from the Greek *diaita*, which means a total mode of life. In Greek medicine the diet was an importat aspect of medical therapeutics in which the body was seen as a natural system of equilibrium governed by four humours; here diet was a method of balancing humours that were maladjusted. Diet in this sense also included moral prescriptions about exercise, sexuality, sleeping and social relationships. There is a second feature of diet, connected to the Latin word *dies* or 'day', where political diets met on certain days; in this way political life was regulated by a calendar. Combining these two features of diet, we can define dietary regimen as a total regulation of the individual body and a government of the body politic. Diet has historically been a central feature of the medical regimen of the sick in a moral economy where illness is a disorder of the political system just as disease represents literally the absence of ease in the human body. This interpenetration of medical and political metaphors is incorporated once more in the very notion of a medical regimen. The term 'regimen' is from Latin *regere* or 'rule', and as a medical notion indicates any system of therapy prescribed by a physician including, especially, a regulated diet. However, regimen also carries another meaning, namely, a system of government, which permits us naturally to speak about 'a government of the body' (Turner, 1982a). We might also note that an important element of diet was the ration in which food was distributed according to a rational system of prescriptions. Thus a ration involves both the limitation of an activity and the reckoning of elements of a diet so that rations entail knowledge and power over bodies, thus representing a crucial feature of disciplines (Aronson, 1984).

In Christianity diet was a feature of monastic practice that sought to regulate the soul through the discipline of the body. In traditional Christianity there was in fact relatively little separation of spirituality and the body. Thus the central metaphors of Christianity are focused on body functions, a set of metaphors organized essentially around the crucifixion of Christ. Although Christianity specifically rejected the body as flesh, we find numerous occasions where the notion of religious truth is bound up crucially with pain; the relationship between physical pain and truthfulness was part of the sacrament of penance especially in the institution of the confession (Hepworth and Turner, 1982; Asad, 1983). Before the Reformation these religious dietary schemes had begun to penetrate the court and secular aristocracy of Italian and French society. For example, Luigi Cornaro's *Discourses on a Sober and Temperate Life* (translated in 1776 into English) and Leonard Lessius' *Hygiasticon* (translated in 1634 into English) were influential in Italian society, where diet came to be associated with religious orthodoxy, moral virtue and citizenship. Cornaro felt it was appropriate for men of good manners to adhere to a regular diet in order to avoid melancholy and other violent passions. These European works came eventually to influence writers like George Herbert, George Cheyne and John Wesley (Turner, 1982b). Thus the growth of a methodical way of life in dietary matters was a development that was parallel to the spread of the Methodist sects of the eighteenth and nineteenth centuries.

Whereas these early dietary schemes were typically associated with religious and moral values, in the nineteenth century there was an increasing scientific literature of diet with the emergence of nutritional sciences and the application of scientific diets to such subordinate populations as prisoners and army recruits. Nutritional sciences began to measure the potential energy of food in relationship to human labour outputs in terms of calories, which were the same unit that thermodynamic students were employing in the measurement of mechanical work (Aronson, 1984). At the same time nutritional criteria were being employed by social reformers like Charles Booth and Seebohm Rowntree as measurements of poverty levels in the larger British cities; these surveys came eventually to provide the basis of British social policy in the early years of the twentieth century.

There appeared to be three important causes for the development of these scientific schemes of diet. These were (1) the need to mobilize large numbers of men in the mass wars of the late nineteenth century; (2) an increasing awareness of the dangers of poor sanitation and water supply for general health (these anxieties were combined with a new reforming movement in the schools, where there was an attempt to improve the diet of the working class); (3) economic pressures to reduce the costs of supporting large numbers of long-term inmates in the army, the prisons and the asylums. This long-term transformation of the place of diet in social relations provides a strong illustration of the general process of secularization in European societies. It should be noted, however, that medical practices in the twentieth century often retain a moral and religious content. The stigmatization of obesity, for example, under-scores how contemporary notions of purity continue to colour a world that is allegedly largely secular (Kallen and Sussman, 1984).

The Rationalization of the Body and the Individuation of Persons

There is an underlying assumption in much recent social analysis that feelings and passions in pre-modern societies were more exuberant, naïve, direct, intense and communal. There is the assumption that people expressed their emotions more directly and in a collective way without the restraints of modern individualistic and bourgeois culture. Passions in pre-modern times were untrained, untrammeled and unkempt, because they were not disciplined by the requirements of a modern individualistic culture. The strength and vitality of peasant culture were dominated by the metaphors of the body, especially those connected with eating. The festival in peasant culture expressed these communal emotional senti-ments so that individual bodies were as it were submerged within the collective body in a process reminiscent of Durkheimian ritual. This collective expression of embodiment was ultimately replaced by an individualistic culture organized more around bourgeois and mercantile consumption.

There is a strong connection between these developments in peasant culture and the transformation of court society, as Norbert Elias has shown in his studies of the civilizing process (Elias, 1976; 1982). While this ceremonial ritual of etiquette was being formulated there was also a transformation of emotion and affect so that the individual was expected to control his or her bodily behaviour through courtly norms that implied a new consciousness. We might express this in words uncharacteristic of Elias himself by suggesting that the civilization process involves a transformation of violent bodies into restrained bodies, and a process of individualization allowing private emotions and refined feeling to emerge within the court setting. At the court people no longer ate from a communal bowl with their hands but rather received their food on separate plates, and they consumed this privatized meal with the individual implements of the knife, fork and spoon. The growth of restrictions on spitting at the table and blowing one's nose was indicative of this new individualized ethic of good conduct, which was calculated not to bring offence to one's companion in a public arena. This process involved a taming of emotion and a reduction of collective excitement in the interests of a centralized court; here new moral standards emerged, giving emphasis to individual distinction and sophisticated physical actions, which were condensed into a ritual of trained bodies. The civilizing process was crucially about forms of bodily activity in a social setting where feudal knights had been disarmed and organization was focused around the centralized court of the French kings. As Elias indicates, this transformation of manners corresponded to a new architectural dispersion of bodies within the central court itself; outside the court there began to emerge a new culture organized around the bourgeois home, where new manners of physical conduct and conformity were developing along parallel lines.

The rationalization of the body develops alongside the cultivation of consciousness and the emergence of an individualistic culture that regarded strong emotion as indicative of an absence of culture and education. Rationalization involves a channelling of emotion into acceptable public expression, the ritualization of meeting in public places, the diminution of strong passions as insignia of moral worth and the emergence of a culture of detailed movement and individualized behaviour. The expression of strong passions and the collective experience of emotion were downgraded in favour of a restrained urban culture that took its lead from the aristocratic manners of the centralized absolutist courts. In short, the rationalization of culture involved the control of Dionysus by Apollo, through the mechanism of the etiquette of the table and the ceremony of the court. While these developments were originally confined to the court, they spread outward ultimately through the bourgeoisie into a wider community of capitalist urban culture.

Another feature of European society was the long-term emergence of a series of natural sciences – whose object was the human body and human population – that expressed a more detailed and differentiated treatment of the body as one component of a process of cultural rationalization. As Foucault has noted, man emerged as the product of a new set of discourses of the body and populations, the latter themselves a consequence of the French Revolution and the urbanization of Western societies towards the end of the eighteenth and the beginning of the nineteenth centuries. These human sciences were features of an expanding knowledge of man that focused on problems of labour, language and exchange (Foucault, 1970).

The clearest expression of these disciplines was in panopticism, which sought a total control of the human environment through the new forms of knowledge made possible by penology, criminology, demography and social medicine (Foucault, 1975). The centre-piece of such new institutions was the scientifically managed penitentiary based upon notions of total surveillance, efficiency and the utility of the correctly managed human body. These systems of corporal control were also the instruments of mental re-education via the total discipline of the body in a scientifically managed architectural space. We could argue that these principles of institutional development and reform sought a re-education of the mind via the discipline and organization of bodies in a regime that sought to maximize efficiency and surveillance through the application of new forms of knowledge and belief.

The new stage in this science of man has been reached in the twentieth century with radical developments in biochemistry, genetic engineering and microbiology. Now the science of the body promised to deliver life itself into the hands of today's technology of the gene whereby societies could achieve total mastery of production and reproduction through the creation of sperm and plasma banks under the centralized surveillance and control of the state. Such an achievement would be the logical outcome of Weber's view of rationalization, since man would achieve dominance over life at precisely that point where life became trivial and meaningless. It is also the end-product of Foucault's new discourse of man whereby the bio-politics of life comes to occupy the central feature of the political stage (Foucault, 1979a). This eventuality would conform perfectly to the narrative structure of Weber's sociology, in which the hero in search of excellence must unwittingly undermine the conditions that make heroism possible. Thus the Protestant in search of salvation produces an iron cage incompatible with moral discourse and personal religious status. In Foucault's archaeology, liberal knowledge in search of objective truths produces a world where power ultimately obliterates the capitalist subject himself as the author of scientific history. Both of these narrative themes in fact give perfect evidence to an argument proposed by Nietzsche in *The Geneology of Morals*, namely, that 'all great things perish by their own agency, by an act of self-cancellation'. The contradictory relationship between intention in science and outcome is at the same time a perfect illustration of the overriding fatalistic theme in Weber's sociology (Turner, 1981).

The Convergence between Weber and Foucault

A number of commentators have drawn attention to a relationship between Weber's view on rationalization and bureaucracy, and Foucault's emphasis on disciplines and panopticism. Both Foucault and Weber see modern rational practices emerging from the monastery and the army and spreading outwards towards the factory, the hospital and the home. At least superficially, Weber and Foucault appear to share a common interest in the impact of religious practices on long-term secular arrangements. At a more fundamental level Weber was, as is well known, influenced by Nietzsche in important respects (Eden, 1983; Schroeder, Chapter 10); and Foucault too has acknowledged, although briefly, the profound influence of Nietzsche on his own development (Foucault, 1977). The two theorists, further, share a common pessimism about the alleged benefits of rational reform and scientific development that underlies the theme of rationalization in both bodies of social theory. Foucault and Weber have rejected the idea of a mono-causal explanation of historical development, favouring instead a contingent view of historical outcomes as the consequence of struggles and resistance. There is also the underlying opposition, at least thematically, between the principle of emotion and sexuality under the general heading of Dionysianism versus the form-shaping rationality of the Apollonian. While this dependence on Nietzsche is significant, the relationship between Nietzsche and Weber has been inadequately explored (Fleischmann, 1964; Turner, 1982c); in general the impact of Nietzsche on contemporary literary analysis and social theory has also been somewhat neglected (Lash, 1984b). To summarize these comments, we could say that Weber's notion of the iron cage as the metaphor of contemporary bureaucratic capitalism anticipates, on the one hand, the notion of the 'administered society' in the social theories of Theodor Adorno and, on the other, Foucault's concern for the impact of rational practices and discourse on the organization of the body and populations in modern societies. It was only towards the end of his life that Foucault acknowledged the parallel between his study of the carceral society of modern capitalism and Adorno's views on the 'administered world' (Jay, 1984, p. 22).

The relationship between Weber and Foucault has been addressed directly by Barry Smart (1983); here the author recognizes the similarities between the discussion of the carceral society and Weber's notions on the bureaucratic iron cage, but denies that there is a fundamental relationship underneath this apparent convergence. Smart notices that Weber's view of rationalization is a global theory that implies an inevitable development of rational culture and further implies that no resistance to these processes is possible; therefore the appropriate orientation to the regime of rationality is one of fatalistic resignation. By contrast he suggests that Foucault is talking about rationalities in the plural rather than about a singular process of rational discourse; that Foucault sees the history of disciplines as an open-ended, contingent possibility; and that

Foucault insists upon the ever present feature of resistance in society. While Smart's characterization of Weber is justified, we should note that Weber consistently denied that it was possible to talk about general laws of social development. Thus in so far as he saw rationalization as an inevitable evolutionary development in society, Weber's position lacked internal consistency.

By contrast it can be argued that while Foucault constantly refers to resistance, he fails to provide an adequate theory of such practices and forms of knowledge. In addition, most of his illustrations of resistance tend to be the struggles of pathetic individuals who are, in practice, dominated by the discourses that produce them. For example, there is the anti-hero Pierre Rivière who, having slaughtered his mother, sister and brother, resists authority by presenting his own interpretation of events against the official discourse of madness and legal incompetence (Foucault, 1978). There is a similar anti-hero in Foucault's study of nineteenth-century French hermaphrodites where Herculine Barbin finds his/her sexuality determined by a bureaucratic discourse of sexual classification (Foucault, 1980b). Further, throughout Foucault's analysis of the prison, the medical clinic and the asylum he provides relatively little or no substantial evidence of resistance to discourse; and nowhere does he provide an analytically coherent approach to resistance. Thus in practice Foucault's position is very similar to that adopted by structuralism generally; namely, that it is the discourse which produces human experience and belief rather than human experience producing the discourse. It is the language that speaks the subject just as it is the book that reads the audience. Two related criticisms are possible in this context. The first is that Foucault, despite protest, appears to be firmly within a deterministic structuralist position whereby the knowledgeability and agency of individuals are firmly denied and systematically precluded. Secondly, there is the problem that Foucault has never satisfactorily sorted out the relationship between discursive and non-discursive practices and institutions. The weaknesses of Foucault's position are in fact an exact parallel to the weaknesses present in Max Weber's interpretive sociology.

Towards a Critique of Weber and Foucault

For Weber the roots of rationality and the process of rationalization lie deep in Western cultural history. For example, Weber gave a special emphasis to the role of the city in Western society in undermining the particularistic ties of kinship and allowing the emergence of a universalistic category of political membership within the urban community. He also attributed an important aspect of Western rationality to the fact that

233

patrimonial and prebendal institutions never fully developed in Western cultures, which early on were dominated by feudal forms of property and authority. Weber felt that Roman legal theory enabled the formation of a formal legal system in the West, whose universality in principle renounced arbitrary forms of decision-making. Furthermore, the emphasis in Christianity on the separation of the secular and sacred enabled the development of political and intellectual forces to emerge outside the control of the church. These features of Western rationality existed centuries before the emergence of industrial capitalism; thus Weber appears to be committed to the idea that rationalization is a long-term teleological and irreversible process in Western culture. That is, Weber's is largely an 'orientalist discourse' on the uniqueness of the West, which creates an unbridgeable dichotomy between Oriental and Occidental civilizations (Turner, 1978).

Although Weber presents what appears to be a long-term argument about the emergence of rationalization, he also adheres to a short-term argument in which it is a combination of capitalism and Protestantism that gives the rationalization process a new boost in the eighteenth and nineteenth centuries. He argues that Protestantism contributed to the decline of magic and superstition by eliminating the efficacy of sacramental institutions; that Protestantism also stimulated the emergence of individualism by demoting the authority of priests and ecclesiastical authority in favour of personal consciousness, which communicates directly with God through the Bible. Such a set of propositions is tantamount to suggesting that capitalism arose contingently, as an outcome of the Reformation, in combination with a series of rather specific circumstances in Europe connected with the final collapse of feudalism and the dismantling of absolutism. There is in fact a more general ambiguity in Weber's causal explanation of rationalization. It is not clear whether rationalization is an immanent process with its own unfolding and irresistible logic; or whether it is the outcome of quite specific contingent struggles between religious, secular, political and other social groups. Such problems are of course not specific to Weberian sociology, but endemic in social science because they raise questions of the possibility of strict causal explanations as opposed to analysis in terms of contingent and particular circumstances. The matter, however, is crucial in Weber since it points towards the yet more fundamental issue of whether rationalization is inevitable and determinant; or whether the process could be reversed as a consequence of specific struggles of resistance.

These drawbacks are equally implicit in Foucault's analysis of discipline where the same ambiguity with respect to agency and structure is prominent. First, Foucault's views on explanation and methodology in the social sciences rule out formally any attempt to provide a determinant explanation of beliefs and practices along the lines suggested by theories like historical materialism. These arguments were crucial in *The Order of Things* and in *The Archaeology of Knowledge* (Foucault, 1970; 1972). Foucault rejects traditional historical and sociological explanations that seek causal determinacy and argues instead for notions of archaeology and genealogy in historical method. Foucault has objected that these traditional modes of explanation familiarize history in ways that are illegitimate and impose a questionable Cartesian framework of rationality on history that is questionable. Furthermore, Foucault rejects most of the rationalistic and positivist assumptions underlying that form of history. Foucault affirms the role of accident and contingency and rejects evolutionary models of social change just as Nietzsche rejected Darwinism as a framework for historical investigation. Secondly, Foucault has rejected the progressive and evolutionary implications of much of official history, which sees the development of modern knowledge as a triumph over repression and superstition. Foucault instead sees history as a struggle of discourses which make possible such modes of interpretation but do not provide grounds for accepting them as in some way authoritative or legitimate.

Despite these methodological disclaimers, we should note that there is in Foucault's own work an implicit evolutionary history of disciplines. For example, it is difficult to avoid the conclusion that Foucault's disciplines and surveillance become increasingly and in an evolutionary manner more detailed, more complex, more efficacious and more determinant. Discourses seem to unfold and develop in ways that are not explicable other than in terms of an immanent logic. Furthermore, Foucault has not provided an adequate explanation of how there are ruptures in dominant modes of discourse. A close examination of Foucault's discussions of the emergence of prisons, social reforms and modern legislation points to an underlying causal explanation that is largely in terms of demography; that is, these new systems of control appear to be a response to the urban demographic explosion in European society, especially in the aftermath of the reconstruction of France through the revolutionary period. The growth of penology, criminology, urban sanitation and social medicine is a response to crowding on the part of the urban middle class, which sought a greater social control and surveillance over the 'dangerous classes'. Foucault's discussion of 'the accumulation of men' also suggests such a demographic determinism (Turner, 1984). Here crowded urban conditions gave rise to the need for increasing bureaucratic surveillance of populations, and resulted in an individuation of population into separate citizens whose behaviour and beliefs could be monitored and controlled. Foucault himself has argued that sociology had its origins in social medicine as an attempt to measure, to know and thereby to have power over these complex urban populations in France (Gordon, 1980). Recent histories of the growth of prisons that have developed Foucault's own set of assumptions about this history have tended to focus upon the problem of the urban labouring class and the pressure of populations, seeing the prison as an instrument of political surveillance (Ignatieff, 1978; O'Brien, 1982).

Contemporary studies suggest that Foucault's account of the growth of the prison can be incorporated relatively easily within a fairly conventional historical explanatory framework, which would attempt to see these institutions as responsive to demographic changes in the city, the growth of the working class and the response of the middle class to both medical and political problems in the urban environment of the nineteenth century. Foucault's own account of the asylum and the prison is in practice not far removed from these forms of analysis, but he overtly refuses to attempt an approach that would resemble such a sociology of knowledge. He tends to reject reductionism but fails to eludicate and develop the implicit explanatory framework that he employs. The consequence is that he has not been able to provide an account of the relationship between discursive and non-discursive practices. In turn these problems in Foucault are indicative of a failure to provide a systematic account of resistance to the new disciplines of the carceral society.

Against Nostalgic Social Theory

Nostalgia is a disease of particular interest to the historian of ideas and to the sociologist of knowledge. Nostalgia begins its Western history as the moral and medical problem of monks who suffered from a form of melancholy variously described as 'tristitia' or 'acedia' (McNeill, 1932; Jackson, 1981). Nostalgia as a form of melancholy became associated in particular with intellectuals who suffered from dryness and withdrawal from activity. The most prominent representative in literature of nostalgic melancholy is Hamlet; and there is some evidence that Shakespeare modelled the character of Hamlet on a medical work by Timothy Bright, whose *A Treatise of Melancholie* appeared in 1586 (Wilson, 1935). Since Hamlet embodies the oedipal complex, nostalgic incapacity for coming to terms with the present and an anxiety about the reality of the world in which he lives, he is also a representative of the crisis of modernity. In particular Hamlet's uncertainty about the relationship between language and reality anticipates much of the modernist predicament following Nietzsche's representation of the collapse of values as an outcome of the crisis of language.

There is a conventional argument that sociology emerged as an intellectual response to the French and Industrial Revolutions via three separate doctrines, namely, conservatism, liberalism and radicalism (Nisbet, 1967). Sociology came to be structured theoretically around a series of contrasts that identified pre-modern aspects of social order; these contrasts were the classic divisions between *Gemeinschaft* and *Gesellschaft*, status and contract, mechanical and organic solidarity, military and industrial society, and traditional and modern associations. These contrasts typically indicated a critical or at least ambivalent attitude towards modern society by identifying a pre-modern source of authority, authenticity, or stability as the point for a critique of contemporary development. Sociology, then, could be said to be a nostalgic science of society, since implicitly it is forced to identify with the past as a source of values for the critique of the present. In Marxism this takes the form of a contrast between societies based upon use-values and those based on exchange-values, and in Marxist philosophical anthropology the form of a contrast between some form of authenticity that was possible before the division of labour and inauthentic existence of the modern world. In Durkheim there is a lurking commitment to medievalism in his overt appreciation of the guild system and his use of the notion of the *conscience collective* as a desirable form of social solidarity. In Simmel there is the nostalgic notion that somehow a system of barter avoids the fleeting instability of modern society based upon abstract forms of money. The pre-eminent expression of this nostalgic conservatism lay in the fundamental distinction between community and association in the work of Toennies and other German sociologists, who presented individualism as an artificial and mechanical form of life negating the true organic source of German culture (Freund, 1979).

Weber's narrative structure of fatalism and his dependence upon biblical, or at least religious, metaphors were also classical representations of nineteenth-century nostalgic sociology as a critique of the modern. In the narrative structure of Weber's sociological studies we find the theme that intentionality and effects are always in a negative relationship (Jameson, 1973). Weber was fatalistic because he perceived in history the constant negation of human ethical activity. The pessimistic paradox of Weberian history is that all that is virtuous (reason, imagination and moral altruism) results in a world that stands in opposition to human creativity, because rationality lays the foundation of the iron cage. Some recent interpretations of Weber have attempted to minimize or deny this pessimistic and debilitating theme in Weber's backward-looking glance at pre-modernism (Roth and Schluchter, 1979; Scaff, 1984; Thomas, 1984). These interpretations require a rejection of Weber's fatalism in favour of an ethical programme that, while realistic, creates some space for engagement in reality. The genuine source of Weber's world-view, however, seems to lie more in the 'inner loneliness' of Calvinism than in Stoicism. The parable of self-cancellation is the parable of the Tree of Knowledge; our wisdom and our transgression disqualify us from the paradise of naïveté and block our entry into the modern world without nostalgia and anxiety. To this Old Testament picture of our condition Weber adds the more modern parable of Nietzsche's madman who claimed that he could smell the carcass of the dead divinity. The world in which we are imprisoned as a consequence of eating the rational apple is also utterly devoid of significance. We cannot return to paradise because we see the world through rational spectacles and cannot apprehend it without presuppositions; thus we are no longer capable of direct naïve experience free of rationalizing scepticism. Like Hamlet we are forced to say of the world that it is mere 'words, words, words'.

Towards an Evaluation of Modernity

Critical theory, Weberian sociology and the structuralism of Foucault share much in common with such nostalgic positions. We can identify four components here. First they are uni-dimensional in failing to provide a perspective on the contradictory dynamic of the modernizing process, which is simultaneously one of incorporation and liberation. Specifically they fail to grasp the positive and emancipating element of contemporary culture. Secondly there is a puritanical streak within the anti-modernist critique which tends to see all leisure pursuits, mass culture and modern conveniences as forms of human subordination via a new hedonistic ethic. They fail to theorize the element of liberation involved in a consumer culture; thus the critique of exchange-values, and the fetishism of commodities often looks like an updated version of the puritanical critique of all pleasure. Thirdly, there is as a consequence of an élitist element in the nostalgic social theory which elevates high culture to a position of absolute privilege, denigrating all forms of popular culture. Fourthly, there is a perspective on working-class culture that is predominantly incorporationist because it sees the whole consequence of modern consumerism as one of political subordination bringing about the stability of capitalism through either a dominant ideology or a dominant form of life-style.

These components of the critique of modernity have a special relationship to the problem of the body in modern society; here closer examination reveals an altogether more complex state of affairs. Although the joint development of capitalism and rationalization brought about a greater surveillance and control of urban populations (in particular the urban working class), the growth of social medicine and improvements in the urban environment were also significant factors in the improvement of health, the decline of infantile mortality, the elimination of infectious diseases and the increase in life expectancy. These improvements in the physical condition on the working class were, not only consequences of greater control, but also outcomes of popular struggles and especially of trade-union politics to achieve more substantial rights of social and economic citizenship. There is a contradictory and paradoxical relationship between, on the one hand, the growth of a state bureaucracy to survey and control populations and, on the other, the enhancement of health and physique as a consequence of popular politics for a greater distribution of wealth. Thus in the area of health reform there should be at least some recognition of the role of popular movements for better health, education and styles of living. To deny these developments is to ignore the need for bureaucracy to provide an egalitarian distribution of resources. The long-term improvement in infantile mortality rates in European societies is one rather obvious indicator of social advancement that is difficult to reconcile with such pessimistic analyses of the history of bodies and populations.

Secondly, the critique of modernity is equally puritanical and élitist in adopting an aristocratic or at least high-bourgeois attitude towards mass culture, mass society and mass consumption. The dilemmas of this position were well illustrated in Herbert Marcuse's analysis of sexuality in modern American capitalist society (Marcuse, 1955). While Marcuse wished to welcome sexuality as an oppositional force against the traditional asceticism of competitive capitalism, he could not ultimately incorporate sexual deviance and pornography within his own aesthetic ethic of cultivated man. As Douglas Kellner has noted, these neo-Marxist theories of commodity tend to be global in assuming uniform effects of all commodities on all recipients so that

> the commodities are alluring sirens whose symbolic qualities and exchange values seduce the consumer into purchase and consumption. There is both a Manichaeism and Puritanism in this perspective. Commodities are pictured as evil tools of class domination and a covert distinction is made between (bad) exchange values and (good) use value. (Kellner, 1983, p. 71)

Whereas critical theory has typically seen the growth of mass media, mass culture and the new society of leisure as subtle means of incorporation, it is important to have a perspective on the contradictory effects of such social developments. While jogging and cosmetic surgery may be regarded as part of the superficial culture of modern industrial communities, there are important benefits for the majority of the population as a

239

consequence of the transformations of diet, fashion and sport (Featherstone, 1983). Sport may be the modern version of the Roman circus in pacifying the population, but it also dramatically represents on occasions communal excitement and popular protest against contemporary conditions. Sport functions as a modern form of collective religious ritual in societies largely devoid of public spectacle (Dunning, 1983).

Most of these theories assert some close relationship between a component of modern culture and the continuity of capitalism. The nature of this component varies considerably but it is commonly assumed that some version of individualism, consumerism, private property, or the values of liberalism as portrayed in the mass media is a necessary feature for the continuity of capitalism. Whereas asceticism was originally felt to be a necessary component of capitalism in the discipline of labour it is now argued commonly that some version of calculating hedonism, leisure, or consumerism is necessary in late capitalism to lull the bodies of workers or rather the unemployed into an acceptance of capitalist accumulation. It is difficult to demonstrate any general and necessary relationship between components of culture (such as individualism) and the economic and political requirements of capitalism, although it is possible to demonstrate the existence of certain empirical and contingent connections between culture and the capitalistic mode of production (Abercrombie, Hill and Turner, 1980). Expressing this in a rather different framework, there seems to be in late capitalism a *dis*juncture between the logic of the cultural system and the requirements of the capitalistic economic substructure (Bell, 1976). Modern capitalism appears to survive with a variety of rather different forms of belief and practice, ranging in political terms from fascism to the Welfare State and in cultural terms from a permissive sexual ideology to a sexually punitive and conservative moral environment. In general, however, it seems to be the case that modern capitalism develops alongside a plurality of systems of belief and practice rather than with reference to one dominant ideology or, in Foucault's terms, a dominant 'episteme'. Within this framework popular culture is often the focus of opposition and protest against capitalism rather than an illustration of working-class or popular incorporation.

Thirdly, nostalgic sociology tends to be uni-dimensional and incorporationist in its view of modern culture, failing to grasp the paradoxical and dynamic processes of modern civilization where consumerism may have at least in principle an emancipatory impact. These negative and nostalgic perspectives fail to provide a positive evaluation of such elementary developments as sanitation, improvements in communication, the development of modern medical therapeutics and the availability of pain-killing drugs. These negative theories see the body as merely the effect of discourses and thereby fail to recognize that a theory of embodiment is a necessary pre-condition for the development of a notion of effective agency. Sociology is still to some extent stuck with a Cartesian separation of mind and body where mind is seen to be the causal knowledgeable agent and the body is relegated to an object or an environment that is subtly manipulated by consumerism or regulated by disciplines. Despite constant talk about resistance, Foucauldian bodies are merely objects of medical and political discourses. Neither Weber nor Foucault provided a phenomenology of the active body as an essential component of human knowledgeable agency. The development of sociological theory will have to incorporate an entirely new perspective on the nature of human embodiment in order to achieve a more dialectical grasp of the character of modernity.

12

Max Weber on Erotic Love: a Feminist Inquiry

ROSLYN WALLACH BOLOGH

This work addresses Max Weber's overlooked discussion of erotic love relationships. His discussion is admittedly brief, embedded in his 'Intermediate Reflections' (FMW, pp. 323–59). Nevertheless, the discussion is suggestive and provocative, not least from the perspective of feminism. Weber's analysis of the erotic love relationship implies a particular model of social interaction. Although he describes the joy and meaningfulness of erotic love in today's disenchanted, rationalized world, he also describes erotic love in terms of a conflict model of interactions. His analysis, surprisingly, resembles the analysis made by some modern-day radical feminists of all heterosexual relationships. The following work contrasts Weber's conflict model with an alternative conception of social relationships that is based on a model of sociability.

In his discussion, Weber examines the relationship between desire and ethics, and the religious etiology of that relationship in the modern world. Today, however, feminism, more than religion, raises questions regarding the relationship between sexual desire and ethics. Weber contrasts erotic love with brotherly love. He describes how salvation religion with its ethic of brotherly love finds itself in profound tension with sexual love (FMW, p. 343).

Erotic Love and Brotherly Love

Ethical salvation religions constitute an ascetic form of life. These religions involve the repression of natural bodily experience in favour of a sublimated spiritual experience. Erotic love, in contrast, reinterprets and glorifies (sublimates) the natural bodily experience and relationship to a particular, embodied other. Erotic love conflicts with salvation religion's rejection and repression of bodily and worldly interests and pleasures. From the perspective of ascetic religiosity, erotic love is a form of

242

self-indulgence, neither a self-effacing, undiscriminating brotherliness, nor a carrying out of the will of God. In this respect the attitude of rational active asceticism (e.g. the 'Protestant ethic') towards erotic love is similar to that towards the 'having of the mystic, the ecstatic experience of possessing and being possessed by a divine spirit'. Rational active ascetic religion, in which the individual is the instrument of God, rejects mystical experience as a form of self-indulgence.

However, in feeling himself 'vibrantly alive' in his love for a concrete other, the lover stands opposite the mystical experience in which there is no concrete other. The experience of salvation through erotic love competes with the devotion of a supra-mundane God. Similarly, it competes with mystical religion's 'bursting of individuation'. The 'bursting of individuation' refers to the feeling of detachment from one's own body, one's own physical sensations, and the achievement of mental emptiness, the absence of all mental content, all instrumental thought, or practical concerns. Bodily sensations and mental content make for individuation; they distinguish one self from another. The absence of bodily sensation and mental content makes for the mystical experience of individual self-transcendence and hence unity with the cosmos.

Erotic love, in contrast, elevates the relationship between particular, concrete, embodied individuals into something more than mere physical sensation; it elevates thought of the other into more than mere instrumental, practical interest. Eroticism then is substitutive for the mystic's union with God with its inherent transcendence over mere physical and practical interests. However, from the perspective of mysticism, no less than from the perspective of rational salvation ethics, eroticism appears as a 'slipping from the mystic realm of God into the realm of the all-too-human'. It appears to the mystic as a loss of the mystical 'having' of godliness (FMW, pp. 348–9).

Furthermore, erotic love conflicts with brotherly love because it is exclusive, particularistic, and self-indulgent as opposed to the inclusive universalism and self-abnegation of brotherly love. Also the passionate character of eroticism appears to the rational, religious ethic of brotherhood as a loss of self-control and as the loss of an orientation to the rationality and wisdom of norms willed by God. To the rational ascetic, the sublimated sexuality of eroticism is idolatry of the worst kind. According to the religious ethic, it is given to man to live according to the rational (functional, instrumental) purposes laid down by the divine order and only according to them. All elements of passion are considered residues of the Fall (FMW, p. 349).

The rationalization of everyday life that accompanies the development of Puritan salvation ethics ultimately undermines the religious ethic, leaving only a rationalized life-world. The demystification and disenchantment, together with the pressures of rationalism to eliminate or disregard any and all impulses that do not readily assimilate to, subordinate themselves to, or channel themselves through the process of rationalism, give rise to a new desire for salvation. The desire to escape from the over-rationalization of the world, with its attendant pressures, is experienced as a desire for meaningfulness and joy in life. Rationalism gives rise to the desire to subordinate rationalism to some higher purpose. With the loss of religiosity undermined by the very development of rationalism that was spawned by religiosity, alternative, non-religious sources of salvation take on great force and appeal.

One such source of salvation from instrumental, formal rationality is the erotic sphere, which Weber describes as providing a 'joyful triumph' over rationality. 'The erotic relation seems to offer the unsurpassable peak [of love] in the direct fusion of the souls of one to the other. This boundless giving of oneself is as radical as possible in its opposition to all functionality, rationality, and generality' (FMW, pp. 346–7). It is the antithesis of instrumental rationality, utilitarianism and formal rationality, the antithesis of bureaucratic rationality that treats each person as merely another case for the application of a general rule. The lover 'knows himself to be freed from the cold skeleton of rational orders, just as completely as from the banality of everyday routine' (FMW, p. 347).

However, the ethic of brotherly love conflicts with erotic love. Brotherly love raised to the level of a rational ethic constitutes a form of moral reason. But erotic love knows itself to be founded not in moral reason but in a 'mysterious destination'. 'No consummated erotic communion will know itself to be founded in any way other than through a mysterious destination for one another: fate, in this highest sense of the word. Thereby, it will know itself to be "legitimized" (in an entirely amoral sense)' (FMW, p. 348). There is no moral or ethical reason for the attachment. It is fate that brings the two souls together; they were 'meant' for each other. Because it is founded on amoral, irrational fate, and not on moral reasons, the relationship is essentially an amoral, irrational one. For salvation religion, this 'fate' is nothing but the purely fortuitous flaring up of passion. 'This established pathological obsession, idiosyncrasy and shifting of perspectives of every objective justice must appear to salvation religion as the most complete denial of all brotherly love and of bondage to God' (FMW, p. 348).

Yet, erotic love has a close connection with goodness in general:

> The euphoria of the happy lover is felt to be 'goodness'; it has a friendly urge to poeticize all the world with happy features or to bewitch all the world in a naïve enthusiasm for the diffusion of happiness. And always

it meets with the cool mockery of the genuinely religiously founded and radical ethic of brotherhood.

(FMW, p. 349)

For the goodness and good feeling towards the world that accompany erotic love are seen as merely a mood, a subjective state, rather than the rational commitment to brotherliness founded in religion. Because the subjective mood derives in good part from creaturely or bodily desires in relationship to a particular embodied other, such creaturely desires and human relationships are unstable and unreliable. The passionate lover changes; the desired other changes; and with these changes, the subjective mood of good feeling and the goodness that it generates similarly change. Furthermore, the salvation that characterizes erotic love in its antithesis and transcendence of everyday rationality and routine completes and conflicts with the equally radical rejection of everyday instrumental rationality inherent in the ethics of other-worldly salvation (asceticism or mysticism). Spiritual salvation overcomes the transience of the salvation offered by erotic love. The spirit is associated with permanence, the body with impermanence. In other-worldly salvation ethics, the triumph of the spirit means triumph over the body. Sexual life, which appears as the strongest connection with animality, is hence to be resisted and denied (FMW, p. 346).

In sum, a principled ethic of religious brotherhood is radically and antagonistically opposed to erotic love for the following reasons. Erotic love is a threat to a regulated life. If a regulated life derives from a commitment to carrying out God's will, that is, if a regulated life is a God-ordained life, a way of life commanded by God, then erotic love threatens godliness. Erotic love is an expression of self-indulgence. As such, it conflicts with brotherly love. The latter consists in subordinating self to other, not indulging the self. Erotic love orients to a particular other, as opposed to religious brotherly love, which orients in principle to any and all others. Erotic love is an affirmation of individuality. Individuality presupposes material bodily differences. Religious brotherly love suppresses human individuality, particularity and idiosyncrasy in favour of spiritual unity, universality and reason. Erotic love elevates bodily sensations, interests and relationships into a sublimated form. Brotherly love suppresses bodily feelings as distractions from spiritual love and spiritual relationships. 'Erotic love reinterprets and glorifies all the pure animality of the relation, whereas the religion of salvation assumes the character of a religion of love, brotherhood and neighbourly love' (FMW, p. 347).

Erotic love is exclusive. It does not extend its embrace to anybody and everybody, but in principle must exclude others. This contrast with

245

religious brotherly love, which in principle must include all others. Erotic love is subjective in the 'highest imaginable sense', resting on the lover's unique sensibilities. Brotherly love in contrast is objective in that it rests on an objective principle independent of individual sensibility. Because of the intensity of the lover's experience, because of the immediacy of the possessed reality and because the consciousness of the lover rests upon his own experience, the experience is by no means communicable. It is 'absolutely incommunicable' and therefore a counter-pole to all religiously oriented brotherliness. Finally we arrive at the element of erotic love that may be the most threatening to religious brotherly love. The element is the meaning attributed to the experience. Erotic love is experienced as

the unique meaning which one creature in his irrationality has for another, and only for this specific other. This meaning, and with it the value-content of the relation itself, rests upon the possibility of a communion which is felt as a complete unification, as a fading of the 'thou'. It is so overpowering that it is interpreted 'symbolically': as a sacrament. The lover realizes himself to be rooted in the kernel of the truly living, which is eternally inaccessible to any rational endeavour . . . The experience is equivalent to the 'having' of the mystic.

(FMW, p. 347)

Because of the feeling of communion, of complete unification, a 'fading of the "thou"', erotic love competes with mystical experience. The latter also involves an experience of unity, an experience in which the separateness of the individual dissolves and is replaced by a sense of oneness with the universe. However, erotic love differs from the latter because of the immediacy of the possessed reality, an immediacy due to the real, material existence of its object, in contrast to the mediated reality of a mystical experience. The latter requires the mediation of belief in a spirituality that is independent of any particular material existence. Not only mystical religion but rational, ascetic religion too opposes erotic love. Rational, active asceticism rejects the sexual as irrational (unpurposive) except as a means for procreation. Furthermore, erotic love competes with the devotion to a supra-mundane God and with the devotion to an ethically rational order of God.

The Erotic and Brutality: Weber and Radical Feminism

In addition to the above, the ethic of brotherly love conflicts with erotic love because the latter appears to the former as a form of brutality or compulsion, a relationship of conflict. Weber asserts: 'Veiled and sublimated brutality . . . have inevitably accompanied sexual love' (FMW,

p. 355); 'the more sublimated it [the erotic love] is, the more brutal' (FMW, p. 348). This analysis of sexual love as involving sublimated brutality links Weber to contemporary feminism.

Weber talks of sublimated brutality and sublimated erotic love. By sublimated brutality he means that the brutality is raised from the base material level of physical violence to a higher level of spiritual violence. By sublimated erotic love he means that erotic desire is raised from the base material level of sexual desire or lust to a higher level of idealization or symbolization in which the other is desired and appreciated as embodying (symbolizing) some idea that is valued as the good – hence as embodying some ideal. Thus, base material lust is made sublime, and the other is idealized. The other ceases to be a mere sexual object and becomes the embodiment of the good. Nevertheless, Weber sees the relationship as brutal and coercive, a 'relation of conflict'. He declares: 'Unavoidably, it is considered to be a relation of conflict. This conflict is not only, or even predominantly, jealousy and the will to possession, excluding the third ones. It is far more the intimate coercion of the soul of the less brutal partner' (FMW, p. 348).

Viewed from the perspective of a non-erotic, religiously inspired version of brotherly love, the erotic love relationship is described in terms of brutality, conflict and coercion. In addition to these terms, Weber also introduces the idea of the soul. Sublimation or idealization raises the lustful animal and its object to a spiritual soul. A relationship of lust may involve physical violence, but a relationship of erotic love involves spiritual violence: 'the intimate coercion of the soul of the less brutal partner'. There is a certain similarity here between Weber's description and that of some radical feminists. The relationship between brutality and sublimation involves the paradox that 'This coercion exists because it is never noticed by the partners themselves. Pretending to be the most humane devotion, it is a sophisticated enjoyment of oneself in the other' (FMW, p. 348).

A principled ethic of brotherly love does not involve any enjoyment of oneself in the other. Rather, the actor acts only out of moral commitment and not out of personal desire, except for the desire to be God's tool. There is no personal desire that is expressed and hence imposed on the other. Nevertheless, the action itself must be intended as an expression of caring about the other. Acts of brotherly love must express a desire to serve or please the other. Such acts express, however, not one's own personal desires, but an impersonal ethic motivated by desire to please God or to do good. Thus a relationship with the other becomes an occasion for expressing one's commitment to God or to an abstract moral principle; the relationship to the other is not desired for itself, something good, pleasurable, or meaningful in itself. The relationship is desired not because it is pleasing to the self, but because it is pleasing to God. With erotic love, in contrast, the act of relating to the other is pleasing to the self. It is an expression of one's own pleasure, one's own desire.

There is an ethical problem with enjoying oneself in the other. Enjoying oneself in the other implies treating the other as a means for one's own enjoyment and not as an end in itself. Desire for the other and treating the other as a means involve imposing on the other. For example, the other's presence may be intensely pleasurable. Expressing an intense desire for the other's presence may be matched by the other's desire to please. But in that case, the 'less brutal', that is to say, less imposing and therefore less coercive, partner will have been coerced. The coercion exists regardless of the rationalization that the desire for the other and the desire to please are both believed to be expressions of devotion. According to Weber, 'This coercion exists because it is never noticed by the partners themselves.' On first reading, it may seem odd, if not untenable to claim that coercion can exist without either partner noticing it and further *because* neither partner does notice it. For coercion implies the use of force or threat to gain compliance precisely because it is assumed that the other would not voluntarily comply. Is Weber changing the meaning of 'coercion'? Can the expression of desire be judged as coercive if in fact the other voluntarily concurs out of a desire to please?

Weber's judgement of coercion may not be as far-fetched as it appears on first reading, particularly in the light of recent feminist thought. Let us examine further the idea of a willingness or desire to accede to the wishes or desires of another, the desire to please. We may distinguish between action that is engaged in because it is pleasurable or desirable in itself (intrinsically meaningful) and action that is engaged in in order to please another (extrinsically meaningful). A desire to accede to the other's wishes, to please the other, seems to be an expression of willed, voluntary, desired action. Because she desires to please, the actor will see her action as voluntary. She will not necessarily see the action as compliance, but may identify the other's wishes as her own. In this way she denies her own soul; she denies that she has a soul with any self-defined desires of its own, other than the desire to please. The desirability of the specific content of the act is defined by the other. Hence precisely because neither she nor he realizes that she is denying her own soul, the love is a 'coercion of the soul'. Weber may be making a sophisticated philosophical argument that feminists have recently begun to assert in a much more concrete fashion.

Feminists have tended to make this analysis because it is women who have tended to be the ones who give in to the other out of the desire to please. Men have tended to impose their desires by making demands or expressing their preferences and expecting their women to comply out of desire to please them. Like Weber, feminists have begun to notice the coercive character of heterosexual relationships. Weber points out that the coercion exists because the partners do not notice it themselves. This would mean that if the woman or the man were aware of the coercive aspect of the relationship, then the coercion would cease. People who believe themselves to be devoted to each other would not want to hurt each other. But Weber may mean that the desire to please the other precludes the ability to see the other as coercive or to resist demands and desires expressed by the other. For Weber, the inability to resist the will of the other signals conflict. He provides the following formal definition of conflict: 'A social relationship will be referred to as "conflict" in so far as action is oriented intentionally to carrying out the actor's own will against the resistance of the other party or parties' (ES, p. 38). How would a non-coercive erotic love relationship, if conceivable, differ from a coercive one? What would be the difference in presuppositions and in consequences? These are questions that Weber does not address. He contends that conflict and coercion are integral to the erotic love relationship. Some radical feminists would agree with respect to heterosexual relationships; other feminists would not.

If, as Weber claims, the partners do not notice the coercion, what are we to make of the matter? Why is it an issue, particularly a feminist issue? If one partner, e.g. the woman, gives in to the desires of the other out of a desire to please the other, then why should this be a cause for concern? Why should this aspect of the relationship be denounced by those adhering to an ethic of brotherly love as well as by feminists? The ethic of brotherly love would denounce it, as must a rigorous philosophical analysis, on intrinsic grounds: that it is a form of coercion and as such to be deplored and rejected because it contradicts the premise of brotherly love and the premise of erotic love itself. Love, whether it be spiritual brotherly love or sexual erotic love, means a 'boundless giving of oneself' to the other. To the extent that one is demanding from, or imposing one's own will or desire on, the other, it is not a giving but the opposite.

Philosophically and religiously one may see this dimension and reject or denounce it. But on the practical level of the concrete relationship, why should men or women, e.g. feminists, denounce it? After all, if the partner willingly gives in to the desires of the other, willingly sacrifices for the other, considers it a pleasure and/or a privilege to do so, why should this be denounced rather than respected? Is the philosophical, religious and feminist position merely an expression and affirmation of a narcissistic culture, as Christopher Lasch (1979) might interpret it? Are feminists merely claiming for themselves the right to narcissistic selfishness, a right to resist or refuse the demands of their mates? Are they elevating this claim to a moral duty incumbent on women as something that must be asserted and claimed for the honour of womanhood? Is it a moral obligation for one partner to refuse, on principle, to acquiesce to any desire expressed by the other, if such compliance does not reflect a genuine, intrinsic desire on the part of the acquiescing partner? Does this not spell the end of self-sacrificing, selfless love, and is not such refusal as philosophically untenable, given the definition of love as giving, as the imposing of desire on the other?

We arrive at a paradoxical conclusion. To impose one's desire on another contradicts the essence of love as giving of oneself to the other. However, to refuse to acquiesce to the desires of the other is similarly to contradict the essence of love. Erotic love based on desire seems to be a philosophically untenable form of love. Religion responds by challenging the basis of erotic love in sexual desire. It argues that only love without desire is a true giving. Not sexual love but love for God would motivate such giving. Without desire, there would be no coercion. Similarly, the desire to acquiesce to the other, to please the other, that is motivated by sexual love for the other is not true giving; that is, despite its self-sacrificing character, it is self-serving. Only love or giving that is founded in a relationship with God, an expression of God's will and not of the individual's own desires, is free of the self-contradictory aspects that characterize erotic love. Only such principled brotherly love, as opposed to spontaneous or impulsive expressions of love, is authentic, devoid of coercion, brutality, conflict, or unbrotherly self-indulgence. Weber's presentation of the dilemma of erotic love from the perspective of religious or principled brotherly love suggests that erotic love, despite its pretensions and protestations to the contrary, is not and cannot be true love, free from the above defects. Feminist critiques of heterosexual love relationships make a similar claim, but not on the basis of abstract philosophical or religious reasoning. They base their critique on the concrete consequences that befall women who find themselves in such relationships. They cite the one-sided nature of those relationships that, despite protestations of devotion, somehow end up with women doing the serving, giving, acquiescing.

Even in relationships in which the woman is not economically dependent on the man, as witnessed by the New Left movements of the 1960s, women have been expected to be subservient. When women of the New Left initially raised the issue of the inequity in the relationship between men and women within the movement, the men responded with derision. They humiliated, ignored, rejected, or patronized the women who dared to call attention to such inequity. Other women, whose consciousness was raised by the women's movement, encountered similar resistance on the part of their husbands and lovers when they called attention to inequities in their relationships, or when they tried to express their own desires, interests, needs and opinions that were not shared by their men. Women now found that although they had willingly given to their men, and acquiesced to their wishes, their men were not so willing to do the same despite their protestations of love. This discovery led to a feminist analysis of heterosexual relations that resembles the philosophical, religious critique of erotic love presented above and referred to by Max Weber. To feminists, the problem of male privilege goes deeper than political-economic dominance.

Devotion expresses itself as desire to please the other, to fulfil the other's desires. However, to satisfy indiscriminately and unthinkingly the other's desires implies that one has no desires of one's own other than the desire to serve or please the other. This is a denial and consequently a coercion of the soul. Such self-denial on the part of the 'less brutal' one, the one who does not express and hence impose her own desires, makes for such coercion. The 'less brutal' partner in an erotic love relationship resembles the person who acts out of a religiously motivated commitment to brotherly love. There, too, the actor denies his own desires; he subordinates and devotes his soul to God. Love for God that requires a denial of one's own desires and love for the other that likewise requires a denial of one's own desires are both coercive to the soul. In the former case the reward is in knowing that one has God's grace or salvation, whereas in the latter case the reward is in knowing that one has the other's favour or goodwill. Or, rather than speak in terms of rewards, we may speak in terms of the mystical merging of one's soul with God or with the other such that one does not experience having any separate desires of one's own.

Coercion of the soul of the less brutal partner is inherent in erotic love relationships wherever the less brutal partner denies any desires of her own. By not acknowledging any separate desires, one denies having a separate self with its own soul. Hence one represses and thus coerces one's soul. This interpretation makes sense of Weber's assertion that 'This coercion exists because it is never noticed by the partners themselves.' In other words, since each desires to please the other, if it were acknowledged that one's actions or desires were an imposition that displeased the other, then they could be withdrawn, and coercion would not exist. Only by not acknowledging one's own desires, which might conflict with the desires or actions of the other, is it possible and in fact unavoidable, as Weber claims, for an erotic love relationship to be coercive. If an erotic love relationship is premised on the desire to please and be pleased, and if the less brutal partner is by definition the one who shrinks from expressing and therefore imposing her own desires or pleasures, then the less brutal partner will be left only with the desire to please. Furthermore, if the less brutal partner expresses no desires of her own for the other to serve, then the more brutal one, the one who is willing to express his desires, will be left only with the desire to be pleased by the other, as there can be no possibility of pleasing the other in any other way. He can please the other only by expressing pleasure at the other's serving of himself and his desires. One's pleasure with the other becomes, under such conditions, the pleasure one would feel at a docile and devoted pet who tries to serve and please.

Thus the inherent coerciveness that Weber attributes to erotic love relationships requires, as a condition of its possibility, one partner who desires only to please and who denies all other possible desires of her own, especially those that conflict with the desires of the other, and one partner who desires only to be pleased by the other and who denies himself the pleasure of pleasing the other. If the only desire she expresses is the desire to please him, then there is no desire of hers that he can serve. If one partner refuses to express any desires or pleasures of her own other than the desire to please the other, then the expressive, desiring other is *forced* by virtue of expressing his desires to be coercive. Hence he is coerced just as she is coerced. Coercion implies that there is an opposing will, that the unexpressive partner does have desires of her own that differ from those of the expressive partner. If, in fact, one partner had no will or desires of her own, but were merely an instrument of the other's pleasure, then we could not speak of coercion. Implicit in Weber's analysis, and in erotic love relationships, is the assumption that both parties have wills and desires of their own. The basic premise of erotic love relationships is mutual desire, an assumption that both have desires of their own, and souls of their own, that happen to correspond.

The partner who experiences desire is elated to discover that the other finds him desirable as well, that his desire corresponds to the desire of the other. Therefore, an erotic love relationship assumes that the expression of desire by one is correspondingly desired by the other. The more assertive partner therefore assumes that the other does have a separate self or soul with its own desires and pleasures. However, if one partner then exclusively identifies her own desires or pleasures with those of the other, she denies having any desires or pleasures of her own. By so doing she transforms an erotic love relationship of mutual desire into a coercive relationship. If she denies having any desires or pleasures of her own, then pleasing the other cannot be an expression of her own desire. If she is capable of having desires, but does not act on the basis of her own desires, then she is acting out of coercion.

Such self-denial transforms a relationship of mutual desire and recognition into its opposite. Without any desires or pleasures of her own, she cannot judge whether pleasing or satisfying the desires of the other is or is not pleasurable or desirable to her. A being that has desires of her own, but does not acknowledge or express them, acting only in response to others' desires and not her own, is a being that is repressed, and therefore not capable of being recognized. If she complies with the desires of the other without expressing any desires or will of her own, then she is acting in accordance within the demands or desires of the other, and hence her own spirit is suppressed and coerced. Thus the one who does not deny or suppress his own desires becomes, by virtue of the other's inability to express her own desires, coercive. The less brutal partner is in effect coercing the other, forcing him to be egocentric and coercive. It is reported that 'Weber often said that a wife *must* resist her husband, or else she is partly guilty of his brutality towards her' (Green, 1974, p. 123). Some feminist thinkers have been arguing the same and distinguishing between egoism, altruism and a third mode that is both and neither (Blum *et al.*, 1973; Held, 1973; Tormey, 1973). Other feminists have been inquiring into the conditions and presuppositions of the feminine ethic of self-sacrifice, conditions such as the dependence of women on men and the domination of women by men.

From Coercion to Sociability

Like Weber, some feminists attribute the problem to men's inherently greater propensity for brutality. If Weber is correct that the soul of the 'less brutal' partner gets coerced, and if it tends to be women's souls that get coerced, then men must constitute the more brutal sex. Other feminists reject this biological reductionism, which attributes propensity for brutality to biological sex, and suggest that the problem lies in the different socialization of men and women. They attribute to social factors the resistance of men to the acknowledgement of the problem. Men do not like to see themselves as oppressing women, particularly women for whom they profess love. They also do not want to give up the privileges to which they are accustomed as their due. For such privilege is identified with being a man. It is a source of pride, an affirmation of their worth, to be served by a woman. It is an affront to their dignity and their manliness to have that expectation called into question. Furthermore, the unwilling-ness automatically to serve the man also calls into question the woman's love for the man. If she truly loved him, she would be happy to give to him, to serve him, to please him.

If, then, a greater propensity for brutality is not inherent in the male sex – but a matter of social conditioning, resistance to loss of privilege and definition of masculinity – the question still remains whether a relation-ship of erotic love can be free of the coercive aspect noted by Weber. Or is this an inescapable feature of erotic love? Is desire inherently a coercive element in a relationship, as Weber, following the religious argument, seems to suggest? If male dominance is an essential feature of masculinity as defined by our culture, then self-consciousness of masculinity, a self-conscious critique of masculinity as male dominance, should make it theoretically possible to eliminate the coercion deriving from male privilege. But if coercion is inherent in the expression of desire itself, the imposition of one's will on another, then the problem is not even theoretically resolvable except through a self-disciplined renunciation of erotic love, a learning to discipline sexual desire as opposed to elevating it into erotic love.

The question becomes whether the expression of desire is identical to the *imposition* of desire. If I express my desire, am I imposing my desire? The answer is not as clear-cut as it might seem. One might say that there are various ways of expressing desire that theoretically ought not to involve any coercion. Yet to express oneself is to impose oneself, and to impose oneself is a form of coercion. However, we need to explore further the notion of expressing oneself. Let us think of this as communication and use the analogy with speech. Any time I attempt to speak or express myself, verbally or otherwise, I am imposing on another. My verbal sounds, physical gestures, bodily movements assault the senses of the other. The other has not invited my speech act, and if s/he has, then in so doing s/he has imposed on me, assaulted my senses. Cultures implicitly recognize in the various interactional rituals and patterns of etiquette the offensive character of self-expression, whether these be somewhat autonomous bodily expressions (such as sounds, smells, or movements) or intentionally determined expressions, such as verbal ones, gestures, etc.

The greater the familiarity allowed, the less are self-effacing rituals required. Thus apologetic phrases like 'excuse me' and 'pardon me' or a bowing of the head may precede the initiation of communication, particularly between non-intimates. Similarly they may follow unintended, involuntary bodily acts: sneeze, cough, belch, flatulence, accidental poking, jostling, stepping on a foot, etc. Any expression of self in the company of another constitutes a form of imposition or possible offence. Needless to say, however, no communication can occur without self-expression, and consequently no communication can take place without imposition. That may be why some religions require vows of silence as a humbling device for entrants into monasteries or retreats. Others allow only those expressions that are in the service of God. Hence only functional acts and talk are permissible; 'idle' acts and 'idle' talk are condemned.

In both cases, the self must be humbled and subordinated to God or the divine; the expression of self is a failure to subordinate self to the divine and hence an offence against God. Thus religions have used self-denial as a means for dealing with self-expression as imposition of self and as possible offence against the other; they have instead either treated the self as vessel of the divine or as God's tool. The latter case gives us the functional orientation to life characterizing active asceticism, whereas the former gives us contemplative possession of the holy with its flight from the world that characterizes mysticism. In both forms of salvation religion, active asceticism and world-renouncing mysticism, self-expression in general, not just as it occurs in erotic love, is seen as a form of hubris, a self-righteous or self-indulgent, offensive imposing of self on the world.

The active ascetic mode associated with a belief in predestination ends up being an unbrotherly 'blissful bigotry' (FMW, p. 326) and therefore does not resolve the ethical dilemma of social relations. The relationship between predestination and an unbrotherly lovelessness may be understood in terms of the following developmental logic. Instead of a dualism in which the omnipotence of a god is limited by the existence of a great antagonist, as in Zoroastrianism, modern religion 'restores God's sovereignty over the evil spirit who is His creature, and thereby believes that divine omnipotence is saved. But, willy-nilly, it must then sacrifice some of the divine love.' For if omniscience is maintained and God is divine love, then the creation of radical evil, and the eternity of hell's punishments for the finite sins of God's own creatures, 'simply does not correspond to divine love. In that case, only a renunciation of benevolence is consistent.'

Predestination is the belief that realizes this renunciation. 'Man's acknowledged incapacity to scrutinize the ways of God means that he renounces in a loveless clarity man's accessibility to any meaning of the world' (FMW, p. 359). This loveless clarity means the assumption of a 'providential and hence a somehow rational destination of the condemned, not only to doom but to evil, while demanding the "punishment" of the condemned' (FMW, p. 359). Thus predestination resolves the dilemma of the existence of evil within a world created by an omniscient God by making God's ways inscrutable. This solution leads to an unbrotherly lovelessness, an absolute rejection of those who are condemned. It also leads to an unbrotherly suspiciousness towards others, a searching for signs that would indicate whether the other is a member of the elect or the damned, an unbrotherly demand for the rejection and punishment of the latter. Thus the active ascetic mode with its belief in predestination sanctifies unbrotherliness in the name of some higher ethic, that of serving a mysterious and unknowable God. The unbrotherliness of this kind of religion contradicts the ethic of brotherliness. This religion, therefore, does not solve the problem of reconciling desire with ethics. It merely represses desire.

255

Mysticism does seem to solve the problem, but only at the cost of self-abnegation or absolute (internal) detachment from the body, the world and hence other human beings, a transcendence of all base material desire in a higher spiritual desire – desire for unity with the divine. The experience of spiritual unity produces a feeling of goodness and love for the world, a feeling that expresses itself in acosmic brotherly love. Religion, therefore, while articulating the problem does not offer a way of reconciling desire with ethical relations. It solves the problem by repressing desire in favour of ethics or by renouncing worldly desires in favour of the desire to be one with God.

However, as noted above, other aspects of culture too, while not providing an articulation of the problem the way that religion does, do address the same problem. Inquiry into the ways that culture ritualize interactions that contain the potential for offence, the potentially offensive and imposing character of all forms of self-expression within an interactional setting (even the expression of affection for the other can be an imposition and an offence), may offer some insight into and resolution of the problem. To begin with, the problem of coercion implicit in any self-expression that imposes on another is not limited to erotic relations, but is implicit in any form of social life. Hence all cultures must have some way of reconciling the offensive, imposing character of self-expression with the desire for social relations. This issue may be reconceptualized as the problem of sociability. We must delineate what is entailed in the phenomenon of sociability as it relates to the offensiveness of self-expression, that is, we need a phenomenology of sociability.

What constitutes a sociable relationship? Here I will focus on the structure and not the substance. Elsewhere (Bologh, 1976), building on Georg Simmel's analysis of sociability as form without substance, I analysed the playful form of sociability as the suspension of commitment to meaning (substance). That is, playfulness is the negation of substance, the employment of form without any intended meaning other than an intended display of the absence of meaning. I concluded in that analysis that playfulness establishes a sense of community based on the capacity to transcend the ordinary grounds of community: the shared commitment to some given meaning. Playfulness, like humour, shows the possibility of community even without a shared commitment to some substantive content or value.

But let us take a look now at the relationship between actors that constitutes sociability. Sociability presupposes a relationship in which the presence of one actor make a (pleasurable) difference to the other actor. This means that one party must consider the other not an object to be used or disregarded but an active subject to be responded to and whose presence is regarded with pleasure. A sociable relationship implies that the

256

actors perceive each other's presence and actions as pleasurable and therefore as desirable. In this respect sociable relationships are identical with erotic relationships. In the latter, the desire for the other includes sexual desire. In sociable relationships, both the presence of the other and the actions of the other are experienced as pleasurable and hence desirable. Furthermore, if the other is an active subject who is capable of both initiating action and responding to action, and if the response of the other to oneself and one's actions does matter or make a difference, then one must act and respond to the other with care not to evoke an undesirable response. Therefore, sociable relationships require, as a condition of their existence and continuation, caring about the effects of the actors' actions on one another.

If we think of motivated action as the expression of desire, then we may understand a sociable relationship to be made up of the expression of desire (action) that is potentially pleasing to the other and presupposes caring about the response of the other. We may conceive of the essence of sociable relationships to be desire, action, pleasing and caring. Without any of these four elements, sociable relationships deteriorate into something else, for example, the use of another to accomplish some external end. Where the other is treated as a means or as an obstruction instead of valued in itself as a source of intrinsic pleasure, then we may have an instrumental relationship but not a sociable one in the pure sense. However, since all social relationships presuppose trust that the other will not take advantage or hurt, and hence the assumption of some degree of caring, we may say that social relations and social life in general are founded on sociable relations.

If we return to the ways that cultures have devised for ritualizing social encounters or sociability, we see that they take the form of expressions of caring for the other and/or for the other's response. These expressions of concern for the other accompany the expression of self-motivated action or desire, which we called above 'self expression'. The ritualized expression of concern for the other may take the form of requesting permission, apologizing, expressing one's own subservience and/or unworthiness in relation to the other, etc. In these ways the one who engages in self-expression informs the other that s/he intends no harm or offence, that s/he would proceed only if the other is agreeable and not offended, that s/he would not dare to impose on or take advantage of the other, that s/he would willingly defer to the other, that s/he would be greatly regretful and would seek to make amends if s/he did unintentionally harm or offend the other. In other words, the initiating actor (who engages in self-expression) informs the other that s/he would subordinate her/his own desire to the sensibilities of the other. In this way the actor communicates that s/he cares about the other and the other's response

257

even more than s/he cares about realizing or expressing her/his own desire. Implicit then in sociable relationships is a receptiveness to and respect for the other. Awareness of each other's receptiveness and regard makes trust, and hence social life, possible. Social life is founded on the capacity to express both desire and self-restraint, self-expression and self-abnegation, self-indulgence and self-denial, assertion of self and caring about the other, as internal to the same act. Each act, if it is to qualify as a pure social act, a feature of a direct, unmediated sociable relationship, must be an expression of self and of caring for the other. We arrive at the notion of actors as both separate, independent and self-interested and attached, dependent and caring. Both self-interest and caring are internal to sociable action and sociable relationships.

Returning to Weber's concerns or analysis of erotic love relationships, we find that sociability presupposes that the imposing of the self on an other may itself be pleasurable to the other. The expression of one's desire may please the other. We see that imposing the self on the other is one side of sociable relations; concern for and receptiveness to the other's response is the other side. Weber sees this two-sided aspect in dualistic terms. Either one expresses and imposes one's desires and coerces, or one responds to the desires of the other and is submissive or compliant. He does not see the opposition between expressing and responding, imposing and submitting, coercing and complying as being transcended in a dialectical unity, in which each action is both and hence neither. Rather, he sees the opposition as contained in a division of labour in which one side expresses desires and the other tries to satisfy those desires, an essentially coercive relationship.

We need to inquire further of Weber's work in order to understand why he feels that this kind of coercive relationship must necessarily end up being the case. Such an inquiry must focus on Weber's conception of social life, and hence social relationships, as inherently conflictual.

13

The Secular Ethic and the Culture of Modernism

SAM WHIMSTER

The title I have given this chapter denotes one dominant idea and one subordinated tendency within his work. The ruling idea is the secular ethic: how we conduct our lives in a modern rationalized world; the subordinate idea is an expression of a more general phenomenon – namely, modernism – that receives its first showing in the field of art and culture but comes to represent a more general experience of living in the modern urbanized world. Weber effected the dominance of the secular ethic by an intellectual and personal practice that borders, as commentators have fulsomely noted, on the heroic. But at the same time he remained fascinated by the subordinated idea: the forces of modernistic affectualism that so convulsed many of the contemporary artistic, cultural and political movements in his day. Whether one calls this a fatal fascination raises a number of interesting and in some ways disturbing questions that will be addressed in the course of this chapter. It will be established that some of the ideas of modernism figure in his thought and, as I hope to show, are integral to certain of his principal concepts. In particular this chapter will examine the tensions set up by the incorporation of modernist *aperçus* within the sociology of religion. But first an outline must be given of the secular ethic and Weber's sociological justification of the necessity for this ethic.

The central idea here is how beliefs and values can be underpinned in a modern scientific world in which religion no longer provides a reconciliation between knowledge and belief. The *wrong* answer to this problem, says Weber, is to think that because science is able to explain the material world it is likewise able to furnish us with answers as to how we should conduct our lives and run our societies. Underlying this illusion is the mythic role attributed to science: that political and social and ethical problems can be adjudicated by some ultimate set of scientific values. The reason for the prevalence of this myth lies in precepts of Christian civilization that have exerted such a close, albeit troubled, association between what we know and what we believe. Once the boundary from a religiously understood world to a scientifically understood world was crossed, religious belief lost its centrality in terms of the way in which the world was seen. However, so strong were the links between cognition and belief that science was perforce made to carry a prescriptive burden, which very simply meant that there was an expectation of a scientific answer to every sort of question. In matters of ethics and belief, Weber tells us, we have to stand on our own two feet independently of any scientific crutches. At the same time this *laissez-faire* of moral beliefs should not be taken for a *laissez-aller*. Because we know the world from a scientific world-view, we have to take empirical cognizance of our actions. We are accountable for our actions because we have the ability to assess and grasp their consequences.

What is of concern here is not so much the social philosophical issues but rather how one should sustain this secular ethic in practice. Weber makes it very hard for himself and nigh impossible, in my opinion, for his audience to follow the lead he gives. He is intent on disabusing his audience, so much so that he appears at times to undermine his own position and place a correspondingly greater weight on the individual accomplishment of the ethic. To see this clearly, the sociological and psychological preconceptions of the secular ethic have to be brought out.

The sociological aspect of the secular ethic need only be dealt with briefly here, since the main propositions have been formulated elsewhere in this volume (see Introduction; and Alexander, Chapter 9). Modern society is characterized by the separation of the orders of society: the political, the economic, the intellectual or scientific, and lastly the more personal and private sphere of the aesthetic and the erotic. Each order maintains the validity and autonomy of its own values. This leads inevitably to both a pluralism of values and value-conflict. Weber is very strict about how the individual person should handle and resolve such possible conflicts of values. The sphere of the personal is a private realm and, says Weber, should not be allowed to enter into the domain of public spheres such as the economic and political. Weber's two late lectures – 'Science as a Vocation' and 'Politics as a Vocation' – contain a strong 'ought' statement: that in leading one's life in the modern world we have to recognize social reality for what it is and conduct ourselves accordingly. This means that because our life-world is fragmented between the public and private we must not intermix these separate spheres with their values and standards. So, for instance, Weber inveighs against artistic or aestheticist standards entering the political realm and its reverse, the intrusion of the political into the cultural.

While one can sympathize with Weber's demands, one would also note that they are reinforced by what might be called sociological realism. In the two late lectures Weber put forward a conceptualization of the modern world and provided a measure of empirical corroboration. But there is a major difficulty in that people living in this world may choose not to recognize this sociological realism and, for instance, conduct their business as an extension of sport, or their politics as an extension of acting. Weber is aware of these possibilities. Business as sport is one of his examples (WS, p. 171). But it is a rueful example and does not alter his contention that society is increasingly segmented into life orders. The serious challenge to this sociological vision, and by implication to the secular ethic, is the wilful refusal of people to see the nature of modern society for what it is. This brings us directly to the psychological aspect of the secular ethic and to the concept of 'personality' in Weber's work.

Recent work on Weber's notion of personality has been one of the most interesting developments in Weber studies. Professor Hennis's contribution in this volume (Chapter 2) makes 'personality' one of the key concepts of Weber's thought and in doing so relegates the more anonymous image of the social actor. Similarly Professor Tenbruck has been concerned to show that Weber's concept of man is based not on man the analytic construct of social action theory but on man as a cultural being, a person who stands for and embodies specific values (1980, pp. 345–6; 1986, pp. 13–31). What these and other studies point to is an idea of social pre-conditions of personality. As Hennis has made clear, the integrity of the complex personality requires the support of an estate society, for it is the estates that make viable the various life orders through which the individual acquires his or her identity as a cultural being.

In what follows I will pursue this social grounding of the possibility of personality. However, we also have to pursue the implications of this theory of personality into the twentieth century, and it must remain an open question whether a Weberian formulated sociology of concrete reality can develop, to use Tenbruck's words, 'the sustaining not only of the external but also the inner freedom of man in the modern world' (1986, p. 27). My concern in this chapter is to draw out some of the late-nineteenth-century presuppositions about the individual that Weber held, but also to register Weber's reactions to one of its most fundamental and enduring challenges in the twentieth century, namely the modernistic culture of an urbanized existence.

Effectively the concept of personality in Max Weber is that of a socialized person. The personality has an internal and external aspect. The internal aspect is rooted in certain psychic needs, which are met variously, depending on society and period, by magic, religion, charismatic brotherhood, artistic culture and so on. Weber does not enter into what is the nature of the individual's psychic needs; instead they are presumed to be there, and to be satisfied in various ways by external cultural and religious agencies. The internal needs of personality correspond to the provision of ideal interests. These ideal interests have to coexist with the material interests of the social, political and economic aspects of society.[1] The Weberian individual stands defined by the intersection of a material interest situation and the provision of ideal interests.

Before pursuing this issue of ideal and material interests, it should be noted that there is implicit in Weber's discussion of the personality a deeper, unexplored level, which presumes humankind has certain psychic needs and that these are not simply manufactured by external cultural agencies (see Schroeder, Chapter 10). What this deeper level of personality consists of cannot be entered into here, but since Professor Hennis recently has instructed us how to read Weber on Karl Knies it may well be the case that Weber is in agreement with Knies's view that each personality has an irrational, unique and ultimately unknowable core (Hennis, 1987). However, we do not know the extent of Weber's agreement with Knies, only that he rebuked this theory for its unwarranted emanationism (R&K, pp. 201–7).

In the 'Introduction' to 'The Economic Ethics of the World Religions' Nietzsche's psychology is counterposed to historical materialism. Weber wants to establish here that in history the content of ideas are as important as material factors. One cannot understand the ideology of the oppressed, whether an industrial proletariat or a feudal peasantry, without regard to the psychology of *ressentiment*: 'the "slave-revolt in morals" among those who are disadvantaged' (FMW, p. 270). This is one putative way of determining the psychology of the oppressed, but it in its turn is rejected by Weber. The concept of theodicy provides Weber with his explanation (see Bryan Turner, 1981, pp. 142–77). In general theological terms this refers to the metaphysical explanation of the existence of suffering and the transience of life. For Weber its sociological importance lay in its capacity to explain or rather 'rationalize' (in its Nietzschean sense) the fact that the measure of happiness, good fortune, misery and suffering are not equally shared. When related to stratification not only do the poor have to possess an account for their distress, but also the privileged for their good fortune.

The theoretical stepping-stones from Marx and Nietzsche to the theodicy problem are important because they root the problem in the content of the answers given by different sociological strata. The answers, the ideas within a theodicy, are as material as the material interests of the different strata. In this world people have material and ideal interests and can be said to possess or seek to possess material and ideal 'goods' (*Güter*). It is Weber's firm intention to regard ideal interests as equally material and decisive as external interests, such as class position (see Bourdieu, Chapter 5).

The distinction between internal and external conforms almost precisely to ideal interests (internal to the individual) and material interests (which are obviously external). The internal corresponds to a psychological need to possess explanations about the world's injustices. A simple case of this is a non-transcendental religion that justifies the superiorities of a ruling stratum:

> The fortunate is seldom satisfied with the fact of being fortunate . . . He wants to be convinced that he 'deserves' it, and above all that he deserves it in comparison with others. He wishes to be allowed the belief that the less fortunate also merely experiences his due. Good fortune thus wants to be 'legitimate' fortune. If the general term 'fortune' covers all the blessings (*Güter*) of honour, power, possession and pleasure, it is the most general formula for the service of legitimation, which religion has had to accomplish for the external and inner interests of all ruling men, the propertied, the victorious and the healthy. In short, religion provides the theodicy of good fortune for those who are fortunate. This theodicy is anchored in highly robust ('pharisaical') needs of man and is therefore understood.
>
> (FMW, p. 271)

The case of subordinated strata is more complex and often demands the assistance of a transcendental explanation. 'Almost always the theodicy of suffering has originated in the hope for salvation' (FMW, p. 273). The best known case, the salvation theodicy of Puritanism, is quite a complex variant on the 'classical' distinction between internal and external needs. Puritanism has its characteristic effects because of the coincidence of internal and external interests of the Puritan. This is the reason why the Puritan is one of history's 'bores'; the internal dimension of his psychology is entirely in synchronization with his external interests. Innerworldly asceticism is both a frame of mind and an attitude outwards to life; the Puritan literally works out his interiorized religious disposition. The more normal case allows a class derivation of the internal state from external conditions, even though Weber regards the Nietzschean and Marxian derivations as erroneous; whereas Puritanism is a peculiarity in that material and ideal interests are fully splined together, and thus theodicy has accomplished its task with no slippage. This accounts for the momentous impact of Puritanism in world-historical terms.

The model of inner psychological needs and external interests operates differently before and after those periods not preoccupied with theodicy. The era prior, which is highly relevant to any discussion of Weber's overall conceptualization of the internal and the external, to which further comment will be made below, simply does not have the need for a theodicy. Man is not so much primitive as primeval and lives in a womb-like condition not differentiating between himself and the outside world. The sociological grounds for this are an original (*urwüchsige*) community where the distinction between individual and group is not perceived. At the other end of history where the cognitive triumph of science and man's mastery of the environment have peripheralized the need for theodicy, the situation of internal needs and external interests is far more complex. Moreover Weber, for whatever reasons, is here far from clear in his utilization of the model.

One such point of complexity is the persistence of the *Beruf* mentality. The stitching together of the internal and external dimensions by the Puritan is inherited in the modern world as a kind of scar: 'the idea of "duty in one's calling" haunts our present life like the ghost of our former religious beliefs' (WS, p. 171). In Weber's sociology of modern life the interests, again both external and internal, of occupation and profession command a far greater significance than is functionally necessary in an industrialized society. This particular piece of mystification has, for better or worse, been eroded over the last three decades in Western countries. Even for Weber though, who took the idea of *Beruf* in modern life wholly seriously, there still remained the task of locating its place in the wider scheme of modern society. The pursuit of one's chosen profession or occupation is the central component in Weber's secular ethic, and was seen by Weber to be of paramount importance in Germany, towards the end of the war and in the period succeeding (Roth and Schluchter, 1979, pp. 115–16). However, the secular ethic is also about realizing the limitations of the situation one is faced with. Realism demands that one has a degree of reflexivity about one's devotion to the occupational form.

To use Merton's terminology, there cannot be a ritualist use of *Beruf*. Sociological clarity and realism demand much more. The life-world of the Puritan proceeded from an internal state that was projected on to economic life; together both subordinated any competing spheres, such as the personal, the political, or the cultural. In advanced industrial societies, these other spheres recover their independence and develop their own autonomy. The external interests of the individual person can no longer be exclusively represented by *Beruf*. The life-world is split up into competing spheres – each with its own values. The difficulty is compounded by the realization of the almost limitless possibilities of modern man's internal needs. Weber remorselessly probes the interior condition of modern man, and especially in respect to the role of science and culture, to which we now turn.

The Cultural Conditions of Modernity

Science ousts religious theodicy in modernity, rendering what previously could be seen as a rational schema of knowledge and belief as fundamentally irrational: 'religion has been shifted into the realm of the irrational' (FMW, p. 281). However, just as man's outlook was limited by the 'horizon of religion', so in Weber's day it was seen as secured by the 'horizon of science'. Weber's response to this was to say that science has no horizon. If one lives within a society that demonstrates the mastery of science and the prevalence of its conceptual habits – experimentation, hypothesizing, empiricism – one also has to realize that there is no scientific underpinning to scientific presuppositions. This is the unpalatable condition of modernity; unpalatable because there is no corresponding internal psychological input from the external pursuit of science. Weber puts this point across with a withering sarcasm that can hardly have been calculated to win him many friends or adherents.

> After Nietzsche's devastating criticism of those 'last men' who 'invented happiness', I may leave aside altogether the naïve optimism in which science – that is, the technique of mastering life which rests upon science – has been celebrated as the way to happiness. Who believes in this – aside from a few big children in university chairs or editorial offices?
> (FMW, 1948, p. 143)

Weber follows this savaging of the illusions of doing science with an equally emphatic denunciation of the misplacing of artistic and cultural values. This is a more difficult task. It is in the nature of culture to deal in illusion and not to recognize the prosaic character of social reality. Weber allows art and culture total freedom but only within their own sphere. The illusions of culture must not stray into the hard reality and clarity of politics; likewise it has to make some sort of accommodation with economic reality. Unfortunately some people do tend to transpose their artistic values into politics. Weber is brutal about this tendency. Of the poet and playwright Ernst Toller who played a leading part in the Bavarian People's State of 1919 Weber said, 'God had made Toller a politician in his wrath'. While condemning the transposition of culturalist values into politics, Weber was at the same time deeply interested in the phenomenon. When Toller was arraigned in court for treason by the re-established national government, Weber spoke in his defence to the court, arguing that because Toller was motivated by the highest artistic and ethical standards he was not able to grasp the political consequences of his actions. Toller escaped the firing-squad and lived to fight another day, using his income as a playwright to organize efforts for the Red Cross in the Spanish Civil War (see Dahlmann, 1987).

Weber's opposition to artistic and culturalist values does not stem from a cultural philistinism or lack of sympathy. The problem is entirely the reverse. Because the place of culture is so important to the conception of man, it tends to transcend its own realm and put itself forward as a

Weltanschauung for life in general. Culture can meet the inner psychological demands of the individual in a way no other set of values is able to. From the point of view of the interior dimension of man, the expectations to be derived from culture and art are maximal. Weber stands in a long tradition of humanism of an educated middle class, for whom culture and sensibility were allotted a pre-eminent place. Whatever gulfs separated the members of that stratum – whether political, academic, or religious – they were all marked by the imprint of a common upbringing and acquaintanceship with the works of literary classicism and neo-classicism. This inheritance lasted as long as the humanistic *Gymnasium* prevailed in the education system.

Weber was no more impervious to the demands of these values than were Kurt Eisner or Ernst Toller, Eduard Bernstein, György Lukács, Georg Simmel, Werner Sombart, Walter von Rathenau, Georg von Below, or some of the greatest and most accomplished products of this system at the end of the nineteenth century: Nietzsche, Stefan George and Rilke. Although they were all unreservedly rude about each other in respect to their differences (George called Weber a political rowdy (*Krakeeler*); Weber reckoned George to be a charismatic of the worst sort, an aestheticizing one), it was a rudeness that could be tolerated only through some underlying family identity. Whatever the errant direction pursued by members of this stratum it would have been pursued through a sense of high-mindedness rather than simple and unvarnished desire for wealth or power for its own sake. Weber's work is profoundly imbued with this sense of seriousness and littered with scorn for the banausic, the parvenu, the power-seeker, the philistine. This tradition of cultural humanism also obviously equipped its members with a sense of superiority and must be reckoned one of the major sources of radical élitism that so often distinguishes members of this stratum whatever their chosen field of activity – ethical anarchism, revolutionary communism, or merely *Sozialpolitik*.

In Germany neo-classicism (by which is meant the revival in Greek art and literature) overlapped, indeed merged with, Romanticism. This had enormous consequences for the concept of man and his possibilities. Romanticism signalled the psychic freedom of man in the post-religious world; it created for the first time an absence of restraint about what man can do, feel, create and achieve. This was accompanied by the drama of the inevitable over-reaching beyond man's natural capabilities, the Faustian theme of man's destiny. The major exploration of psychic freedom was the freedom to dominate one's fellow man and the tragic consequences of such a pursuit. (On the use of Romantic metaphors of action in Marx and Weber, see the stimulating essay by Scaff and Arnold, 1985, pp. 190–214.)

Max Weber's literary imagination makes a number of well-known entrances into his social scientific works. They aptly illustrate how a sociological and psychological analysis is conjoined with a literary sensibility.

The idea that modern work in a calling is ascetic in character is not, indeed, a new one. In his most profound insights, in *Wilhelm Meister's Journeyman Years* and the ending which he gave to his *Faust*, Goethe too sought to teach us that it is in the present-day world a condition of doing anything of value that one should confine oneself to specialised work, with all the renunciation of man's Faustian omnicompetence which that implies; that therefore 'doing' and 'renunciation' are today inextricably linked – which is the ascetic basis of the bourgeois style of life, if indeed it is to be a style of life and not a lack of style. For Goethe, this knowledge meant a renunciatory parting from a time of complete and beautiful humanity, which will no more be repeated in the course of our cultural development than will the flowering of ancient Athens.

(WS, p. 170)

In his conception of power Weber deploys a similar high-minded seriousness. Politics inevitably involves the pragma of power, and this attracts the 'parvenu, swaggering' power-seeker, who when faced with the direness of the exercise of power suffers 'an inner collapse'. This sort of politician 'is a product of the most shabby and superficial blasé attitude to the *meaning* of human life and which has no affinity with the knowledge of the tragic in which all action, but above all the political, is interwoven' (FMW, p. 117). As twentieth-century politicians have so manifestly shown, the burden of the tragic vision is an entirely dispensable piece of cultural baggage, and the dangers of inner collapse can be hardened by cynicism, fortified by ideology, or simply practised with a new blitheness of spirit.

This is not to suggest that Weber was some mannered cultural snob aghast at the ways of the new twentieth century, for that way leads to an anti-modernity ethic, and there is nothing in his work that would warrant such an interpretation. Instead the above passages are illustrative of a fundamental divide between internal psychological condition and external social life in his sociological analysis of modern society. Weber, because of his educational and cultural background – and it is being said that the educational and cultural are inextricably linked – points to the paramount significance of culture in a post-religious age. This operates at two levels. There is the textual level, especially in the 'Introduction', the 'Intermediate Reflections' and 'Science as a Vocation', where culture is accorded a significance competitive with redemptory ethics and also where Weber severely limits the scope of its qualities as a benison to the individual's internal psychological needs. Secondly, and in a more diffuse way, there is the level of Weber's own persona and as a spokesman of the educated and cultured middle class, where a sense of élite distinction and bourgeois outspoken dissidence continually informs what is seen as possible and at the same time not achievable.

Spelling out this second, more diffuse aspect is extremely difficult and belongs to a more ambitious project that would have to cast Weber as a representative and embodiment of a historically very singular stratum; one, moreover, that was fully aware of its own individuality and distinctiveness. Obviously I have given only the merest sketch of this distinctiveness in the above few pages. It is necessary, further, to consider how this stratum sought to come to terms with the onset of the twentieth century by looking at the differential responses of some of its members: Weber, Lukács and Simmel. But first the major textual references.

Culture and art first establish themselves alongside religion. Just as 'all religions have demanded as a specific presupposition that the course of the world be somehow meaningful, at least in so far as it touches the interests of men' (FMW, p. 353), 'cultural values', while not providing a solution to the unequal distribution of suffering, do offer a solace to the transience of life. Artistic creation produces an object that is '"timelessly" valid'. With the development of intellectualism and the rationalization of life,

> art becomes a cosmos of more and more consciously grasped intellectual values which exist in their own right. Art takes over the function of a this-worldly salvation, no matter how this may be interpreted. It provides a *salvation* from the routines of everyday life, and especially from the increasing pressures of theoretical and practical rationalism.
>
> (FMW, p. 342, italics in original)

The maximal conception is a shared value of Weber's social milieu. It is much more clearly evinced by Simmel and Lukács. These two had taken the high bourgeois concept of art and had integrated it into the vocabulary of German idealist philosophy. Individuals are 'subjects'. The artist is a subject; the artistic consumer is likewise a subject. Subjects have their own individual values. However, the creative artist objectivates his or her values into the created artistic artefact, the art object. The transference of subjective values into objective artistic values is part of the transcendent process of creation. In creating an art object the artist by his or her success produces something greater than his or her own subjectivity. The art work is no longer of the artist. Instead the artist has 'objectivated' him- or herself. As for the audience, they are shaken out of their particularity and subjectivity through the edification of beholding the art work. What the essential values of the objective art work are is a question that is answered neither platonically nor in terms of a formal aesthetic theory; rather, once created, the art work simply is. A transcendent world of objectivated artistic values exists and is taken as given; the question as to what these values consist of in formalist aesthetic terms or empirical judgements, or however else one may want to answer, is simply redundant. Presumably the content of the sublime and the beautiful cannot be penetrated, it remains a noumenal mystery.

For Simmel and the young Lukács art was regarded as the secular equivalent of a salvation belief. Artistic communities could share a universal set of objectivated values. This transcendent realm figured as a crucial release from the particularity and the distress of a normal everyday world. Simmel, of course, was an acute observer of the psychic distress that accompanies living in the modern, urbanized world. The pressures, the 'neurasthenia' of modern life, could be assuaged through a retreat to an aestheticized world. This is precisely what was created by his friend, the poet Stefan George. George had created a tonal world of poetic diction all of his own, which he and his chosen devotees inhabited. The world of modern sense impressionism, to use one of Simmel's phrases, was blotted out in an imaginary world of reverie, historical mythologization and symbolist figures. As a provision for internal psychological 'goods' it was a success; once one entered the tented folds of this fantasy, it acted as an alternative reality. Simmel, however, was also aware of its precariousness. It was a fantasy driven by a loathing of industrial civilization and instead it invoked a world of its own. This form of aestheticism was deeply impractical for an everyday conduct.

Lukács' bent lay not with the exclusive aestheticism of George but in action. None the less his position was similar to that of Simmel. Just as a community could be formed through the sharing of 'objective' artistic values, so the positing of moral and communitarian values could provide a point of attraction and aspiration for a particularized and atomized population.

The goal of artistic transcendence as analysed by Lukács and Simmel was at the same time deeply qualified. Again the language is that of German idealism, of subjective and objective worlds, but the related concepts of distance, estrangement and alienation make their appearance. If the art work represents an objective value, that which is beautiful, the social process and conditions of artistic creation and appreciation operate in such a way as to distance the art work from its creator and audience. Instead of attaining the unification of the individual subject with the transcendent, objective realm of aesthetic values, a new distance intervenes. The achievement of the 'eternally valid' now proves to be merely a transitory moment. The transcendent world can never be possessed, for being objectivated it is at the same time put beyond the subjective experience of the individual. The arguments here are manifold; partly it is a philosophical argument with alienation as the key concept – art works are produced, but the objects produced are taken away from the artist. The argument is partly sociological in that the conditions of modern life, with its extreme complexity of division of labour, throw up barriers between art work and audience. Lastly, the argument is integral to the analysis of modern culture.

The arguments concerning modern culture are decisive here. With the emergence of a post-agrarian, post-patrician world the coherence of artistic integrity was lost. What was expected of the artist, in what form it was created and how the artist was interpreted, despite undergoing change, had previously enjoyed a measure of stability and connectedness. At the start of the nineteenth century the relation between audience, artist and artistic styles suffers an increasing looseness and a play in its linkages. Lukács quotes Goethe's realization of this coming condition: 'Unfortunately some of us moderns are sometimes born poets, and we struggle and sweat . . . without rightly knowing what we are supposed to do; for specific directions should, if I am not mistaken, come from the outside, and occasion should determine talent' (Lukács, 1974, p. 81).[2] A similar observation is made by Weber in 'Science as a Vocation', where he states that Goethe was the first artist to live his life as a work of art. The coming apart of the life-world of the closed artistic community meant innumerable possibilities but also the expunging of the *habitus* of an artistic sensibility. For an artist to be free to decide on form, to be free to make personality expressive in the art work, to select new subjects and to choose whether to create something consonant or dissonant with the audience's expectations, all these are conditions that constitute the grounds for the potentialities and dissipation of modern artistic conditions.

As David Frisby and Sibylle Hübner-Funk have demonstrated, Simmel sees what is occurring in artistic modernism as emblematic of modern life in general (Frisby, 1981, pp. 68–101; Hübner-Funk, 1982). What happened in the life-world of the artistic community prefigures the fate of modern urban man. Any number of possibilities and potentialities appear attainable, but the underlying condition is a failure to achieve them because of the basic lack of symmetry between action and social forms. All that is left is an enervating experience of the multiple stimuli of city life.

The Aestheticist Ethic

Before examining where Weber stands in relation to these developments and how he differs sharply from the aesthetic viewpoint of Lukács and Simmel, who have also, quite unfairly, been bundled together, the significant issue is the commonality and continuity of this cultural background for the educated middle class. It is important to appreciate the idealism of the tradition. There is a practical realm and an aesthetic realm; there is an everyday experience and an artistic world of the highest possible values; there is a world of the possible and of what could be and a world as it actually is. The idealism here denotes not the idealization of art, or even more directly the idealization of life as art, e.g. Stefan George, but the existence of two spheres, the artistic and the real, that can never be reconciled or bridged. There existed, said Lukács, a *hiatus irrationalis* between the two spheres (which for Lukács exercised a morbid fascination). The feature of this idealism is the opposition between the world as it is and the world as it might or, even, should be. The predominating dualism for the educated middle class was the occlusion of the artistic and the ought on the one side, and the world as it was empirically known on the other. Hence the high-mindedness is a conjoint sense of the categorical imperative and the idea of the beautiful. Weber captures this when he notes that matters of ethics are now reduced to matters of taste, though, to be more exact, he has in mind the attenuation of the moral by the artistic, down which road lies decadence.

The predominating dualism in Max Weber's thought is that between science and politics, the world as it can be empirically ascertained and how we want it to be. Logically, however, one should equally seek out his position on politics and art, and science and art. The answers are not hard to find; as a good Kantian Weber insists they should remain separate, just as, of course, politics and science should be separate realms. This is not the full story, however. While Weber adhered to the radical separation between science, politics and art, events, social movements and artistic tendencies operated in a way that in practice made the separation hard to sustain. Weber's stance on these swirling currents was not one of aloofness. He stands in the midst of this turbulence propounding a degree of radicalism that must have appeared at the time as inexplicably abstract. Further, Weber seems intent on experiencing these new social movements and forces. Each time he weathers one such movement – anarchism, pacificism, expressionism, vitalism, mysticism – some part of his resistance is washed away (Marianne Weber, 1975, pp. 380, 457, 602–3, 661; Mommsen, 1984, pp. 46–7). He gives something of his own position away each time he makes a sympathetic adjustment to the movement in question. His opposition stays in place, but one is left wondering about the cost and purpose of Weber's resistance. Weber's underlying sympathy and friendship for some of these movements and their proponents, despite his implacable intellectual hostility, derive from the recognition that these people in a wholly disordered way and with wholly chaotic results are in touch with a fund of substantive values and ultimate ends by which their lives should be run.

271

If, as is maintained in this chapter, Weber belongs to a class whose world-view is *au fond* a Romantic conception of the possible allied to a sober empiricist assessment of what is, then new movements whose adherents step entirely out of the picture of this delicately sustained tension are likely – especially among the more dissident sons of the Protestant élite, e.g. Sombart, the Weber brothers, Michels – to provoke a sneaking sympathy if not an outright commitment. Max Weber found the new tensions an irresistible attraction, while others, like Lukács, Simmel and Michels, found them unbearable without a corresponding adjustment in their whole world-view.

Michels's socialism was rooted in a fundamentalist conviction ethic as to the rightness of socialist values (Mommsen, 1981, pp. 103–5; 1987), Lukács, hyped up on the mystical properties of action, attempted to hurdle the *hiatus irrationalis* between the world as it is and how it could be. Following work on his *Habilitationsschrift*, the so-called 'Heidelberg Aesthetic', the Hungarian working class were to be riveted by a transposition of cultural arguments into the field of politics. Mészáros selects the following quote as illustrative of Lukács's attitude to the political and his 'attempt at directly linking ... a particular historical situation with far-away "world-historical" perspectives' (Mészáros, 1972, p. 77):

> The true democracy – the new democracy – produces everywhere real, dialectical transitions between private and public life. The turning point in the new democracy is that now man participates in the interactions of private and public life as an *active subject* and not as a *passive object* ... The ethically emergent new phase demonstrates above all that one man's freedom is not a hindrance to another's freedom but its precondition ... we see the emergence of a unity between the individual's human self-constitution and the self-creation of mankind. *Ethics is a crucial intermediary link in this whole process.*
>
> (Quoted in Mészáros, 1972, pp. 75–7, italics in original)

When it comes to the practicalities of politics and production, it is morality that will make the revolution. During the Hungarian Revolution of 1919 Lukács confronted the fact that the 'oppressive phenomena of proletarian power – namely, scarcity of goods and high prices, of whose immediate consequences every proletarian has personal experience – are direct consequences of the slackening of labour discipline and the decline of production'. Lukács sees that 'help comes in two ways ... Either the individuals who constitute the proletariat *realise* that they can help themselves only by bringing about a voluntary strengthening of labour-discipline ... or, if they are incapable of this, *they create institutions which are capable of bringing about this necessary state of affairs*' (italics in original). Lukács is prescient enough to spot that down the second road lies not help but the Gulag. But it is the first alternative, the projection of an ethical morality on to the Hungarian workers, that attracts interest. 'It depends on the proletariat whether the real history of humanity begins, that is to say, *the power of morality over institutions and economics*' (quoted in Mészáros, 1972, pp. 35–6, italics in original).

Unfortunately we do not have documentary evidence of what Weber made of this culturalist transposition of ethics on to the hapless Hungarian workers in the same way as we do for Weber's response to Michels's own particular brand of ethical socialism. Simmel, likewise, was caught in this oscillation between a culturalist conception of the world and how it could possibly be. Intellectually this was extraordinarily creative for sociology. The refined sense of what could be gives rise to a sociology of the 'almost is'. There is no firm sociological reality for Simmel; it is the sense of social process and interchange that he captures. Reification exists only at second remove, operating as a perceived component in human social relations. 'The Tragedy of Culture' provides an analysis of the reification of the art object, such that culture can be only fleetingly experienced in its totality. Within his sociology, reification becomes a factor inherent in modern social interaction. In *The Philosophy of Money* money facilitates interaction in a complex division of labour. While money opens up new possibilities of a creative and human social inter-action – indeed does so all too successfully – it is also the token of reification in personal relations. Without money the complex life of the metropolis could not function; but social relationships that are made possible in the city – love, leisure, want-satisfaction – take on the sign of money itself. Love can become prostitution, leisure a consumer spectacle, and want-satisfaction the pursuit of profit for its own sake.

Many of these themes can also be found in Weber's sociology. The difference, however, is what concerns us. First, and it can only remain an overall generalization here, Weber is committed to a version of socio-logical realism. The social world is always one of social process and particular individuality, and the direction of trends can never be categori-cally predicted; none the less for Weber the world has an empiricist facticity that can be captured by social science. And the way in which the individual experiences the world is not one of fleeting impressionism of social relationships that *may* firm up into something concrete, as is the case with Simmel's sociology, but rather the individual is, so to speak, held in the grip of the world.

Social reality in modern life might operate through any number of sociological mediatory mechanisms that can be analysed; but this does not make social life any less real for Weber, whereas to Simmel's sensitive mind the sense of the real was always to be doubted. When one translates these differences into conduct of life they become more pronounced.

273

Individuals are faced with much starker choices. For Weber the choice is between either being overwhelmed by the world, which is the most common fate of the individual in the modern mass age, or fighting for one's own point of view and values. In the active mode one is drawing on one's own fund of substantive values and seeking to sustain them in the face of the world. In the passive mode one goes under, and presumably one's internal psychological needs give rise to *ressentiment*.

Simmel is not so forthright as to legislate on matters of life conduct. But his own personal life is of pertinence here. Simmel affected an aesthetic distance to the world and at one time was numbered as one of the George circle (Frisby, 1981, p. 22). Weber did not share this tendency, although on his visits to Berlin he was intrigued by Simmel's artistic disposition. He writes back appreciatively to Marianne after accompanying Simmel to a Beethoven concert: 'the music visibly went through his body in spirals. He is obviously very musical, and his sense of colour is also highly developed. His collection of Chinese vases of one colour is also worth seeing' (Marianne Weber, 1975, p. 496). At the outset of the war Simmel thought that all pretences would drop away and the simplified realities of 'king and country' would obtrude, though he was soon disappointed by the outcome of events. In his last years his solution was that of philosophy of life (*Lebensphilosophie*).

Expressionism and Modernism

Simmel's answer to the confrontation of the multiple stimuli of modern city life was to seek out a refined, superior-to-the masses stance in culture. Yet judging by the qualities of Simmel's critical mind, complete escape into cultural retreatism was not secure. As a literary-artistic critic Simmel grasped the imperfectibility of an aestheticist solution. If modernity gives one the social life of the metropolis, modernism in art and culture invades the traditional integrity of form and content in the art work. The artistic individual secured the tensions of the soul that derived from the flux of living by objectivating a creative part of himself into a fixed, 'eternally valid' art work. The artefact represented a timeless instance of the endless subjective flow of life (Simmel, 1911, p. 253). These conditions obtain, however, only within a traditional stable life-world of the artistic realm. Modern culture thrives and feeds on the break-up of this world. Stefan George's life and poetry are an example of this. His language broke away from a traditional poetic style; his imagery called up a private world of symbols, and it is into this private world of symbols and diction that the reader is invited. Further, the basis of this artistic communion had to be created around the charismatic personality of the poet himself. As an artistic form this is less than classic, for the intersubjective world of artistic understanding has to be entered through one person's private fashioning of language, style, image and purpose. The predilections and directions of George's own development appear to have been increasingly bizarre and demanding of the artistic credulity of his audience.

Simmel's analysis of this movement in culture and art is exceedingly astute and still repays reading as an analysis of cultural modernism. In the great cultural eras 'one particular idea can be discerned which both underlies all intellectual movements and at the same time appears to be their ultimate goal' (Simmel, 1976, p. 226). The last time this occurred in the modern world was the Enlightenment. A new form coincides with a new ideal. The emancipation of the individual, rational conduct of life and progress towards happiness and perfection occur together as a harmony of means and ideals. The present time, however, writes Simmel, sees only a *malaise* in which there are only old forms without new ideals. The result is 'life, in every imaginable sphere, rebelling against the need to contain itself within any fixed form at all' (1976, p. 225).

This is replicated in the realm of art. The unification of the subjective soul with the objective art work is rendered increasingly precarious at the point at which art seemingly liberates itself from its tutelage of patronage and its traditional audience. The emancipation of the bourgeois artist is proclaimed by the motto 'art for art's sake'. The genre that corresponds to this war-cry is in Simmel's view naturalism, occurring in European art from the 1860s and 1870s onwards. It is based, he notes, on a naïve theory of knowledge: realism. Nature is to be viewed and painted for the first time as free from any pre-given association of ideas or sentimentalities. This is naïve because the painter is not a simple means of reproducing reality. The artist's perception of reality is a crucial mediation. What is perceived will be influenced by what was significant for the artist at the moment of creation. The doctrine of art for art's sake has the consequence of interposing the artist between the picture and what is being painted in a wholly new way (Simmel, 1923, pp. 271–4).

In this respect Impressionism and Expressionism in art are the logical development of a trend set in train by naturalism. Impressionism and Expressionism display the naïve presupposition of realism. Once the artist, unconstrained by the demands of a traditional or classic style and art world, is free to decide what he sees and feels, then more of the personality and subjective state of the artist will enter the creative process. For Simmel the discontinuity in modern European art is not between naturalistic representation and the stylistic innovations of perspective, plane, coloration and the rendering of detail, but is instead part of a continuum (Simmel, 1923, p. 275). Expressionism in art is the completion of a process that starts with naturalism, even though in the course of that progress it may destroy the representational style of naturalism. 'The point of Expressionism is that the artist's inner impulse is perpetuated in the work, or to be precise, *as* the work, exactly as it is experienced. The intention is not to express or contain the impulse in a form imposed upon it by something external, either real or ideal' (Simmel, 1976, p. 229). In this way the retention of the object drawn or painted, or a resemblance to it, is 'superfluous if not actually puzzling'. At this point Simmel anticipates Abstract Expressionism *avant la lettre*.

This analysis of art was echoed in his own way of life. In his last years he came to advocate a philosophy of life in which the individual faced a stark choice between the affirmation of life independent of form, or the playing out of life within old forms. The analysis has already been replicated at the level of art, but for Simmel these were not two separate levels. Culture and social life were closely interpenetrated. Whether one takes this as a statement about how Simmel chose to live his life, or as a sociology pitched at an entirely new level, or indeed both, is a matter we have time only to note. The choice for Simmel was stark: either soul without form or mechanical reproduction of outworn forms.

Just as the artist lay at the intersection of an external form and an internal impulse of the soul, so the problem in modern philosophy and for the modern educated man is that there is a choice between the forms of metaphysics and morality on the one side and the psychological and artistic demands of the ego on the other. Simmel, in this connection, adopted the philosophy of life. The individual when faced with the forms of the world, whether social, artistic, or philosophical, can draw no certainty as to the validity of those forms. Hence, within *Lebensphilosophie*, the only surety is the affirmation of life itself. 'He [Nietzsche] found in life itself the purpose that gives it meaning which it cannot find outside itself. For the essence of life is intensification, increase, growth, of plenitude and power, strength and beauty from within itself – in relation not to any definable goal but purely to its own development' (Simmel, 1976, p. 228). The last word on this may be given to Gertrud Kantorowicz: 'Simmel does justice to expressionism by conceiving it as the will to pure dynamics, as the will to the complete documentation of inner life in its flux, in its unfalsified factuality' (Simmel, 1923, p. viii).

If Simmel is placed back into the company of his generation within the academic stratum, it can be seen that his response to the inevitable tensions of its idealist position has two components. First, the original dichotomy between art and how the world could be on the one side, and reality as it is on the other, is collapsed through the device of not admitting the philosophical sustainability of this divide. For Simmel this is accomplished in the work of Schopenhauer and Nietzsche. However, a philosophical refutation of the presuppositions of morality does not, except for philosophers, provide an existential assuaging of the tension. Modern urban life and refined artistic sensibility remain in collision. Hence the second stage, the overcoming of the artificiality of social forms, envisaged as a permanent dynamic of life and soul over forms, is necessary to complete the picture of Simmel's late attitude to the world.

The Significance of Art and Culture in Max Weber's Viewpoint

There are a large number of similarities between Max Weber's and Georg Simmel's understanding of modern culture. Before noting the most prominent, it is important to grasp a significant difference. For Simmel, culture and art always existed as a way of working out one's fate in the world, however minimal these possibilities were when compared with the 'great cultural eras'. Weber closes down even this possibility while at the same time acknowledging the pessimistic consequences of the culturalist analysis. Sharing the analysis but denying the way out makes Weber's solution much more gloomy, though I think it is a mistake to see Weber's solution as fundamentally different. As has been argued, the underlying problematic remains the same. Weber closes down one avenue, culture, but opens up another, the public realm, however unpromising and unforgiving this realm is.[3] Undoubtedly the political avenue is far more hard-headed, but it should be seen as the same problem: how to affirm one's own values (the expression of *Seele*) in the face of the external structures of the world. A crucial similarity is that Weber sees the products of mind and intellect as the fateful consequences of man's domination of the world. It is in many respects a similar analysis as that presented by Simmel in 'The Tragedy of Culture' (1911). While Simmel proposes the affirmation of life values, Weber asserts the primacy of substantive values drawn from one's inner being over, or rather in face of, the external pressures of the world. Politics – 'the slow boring of holes in hard boards' – requires a reservoir of inner convictions. (All manner of sociological presuppositions are being introduced into the argument here. Equally the cultural world may be just as unforgiving or rapturously enthusiastic. The projection of substantive values is an unresearched area; and the reason why the externalization of substantive values should be rational in one area and irrational in another – as the divide between politics and culture respectively invites us to believe – begs a host of questions.)

What then does Weber say about modern culture? We have seen that in the 'Intermediate Reflections' culture is the main competitor to a salvation religion; but in the modern era, while having credentials as a form of aesthetic redemptory values, it never really delivers. For Weber the reasons for this are mixed, and moreover the mixture is not coherent.

First, Weber's nature was far more squarely practical than Simmel's, and he was not to be persuaded of aestheticist solutions. This is partly a legacy of a stern moralism, and in particular, as Mitzmann has noted, of Weber's religious upbringing, especially the influence of his pietistic mother. When in the 'Intermediate Reflections' essay he speaks of the competition between religion and culture and of the Lutheran churches' disapproval of the painted image, some of this censure emanates from Weber himself. In this world-view non-religious art and culture can tend, unless checked, to the frivolous. *Au fond* the world of art and culture invites a complete and unashamed sensuous enjoyment of all the senses, an irresponsible indulgence (FMW, p. 342), and this is especially the case for modern culture. Modern culture cannot be disassociated from the city in advanced capitalism. Its influence is pervasive, and its attractions are ever present. One consequence of art for art's sake was the freedom not only to create new artistic forms of aesthetic enjoyment, of which Impressionism is the major example, but also to select new subject material for which the new realities of big-city life, its pleasures, its corruptions and its harshness became major themes. Weber did not remain unsusceptible to these impressions.

It is worth quoting in full a relatively neglected passage: Weber's contribution to the debate, opened by Sombart, on 'Technology and Culture' (*Technik und Kultur*) at the first meeting of the German Socio-logical Society in Frankfurt.

Obviously because of the pressure of time I can only speak provision-ally on the wholly heterogeneous subject that Sombart has mentioned, that of aesthetic evolution.

Gentlemen, Sombart has perhaps somewhat one-sidedly raised the selection of subject-matter by the artist. In addition to this he has spoken of the influence of technical conditions (*Technik*) on modern orchestral music and the like. Now the selection of subject is a very important element for the cultural-historical judgement in art history but it doesn't confront the specifically artistic. Instead the decisive question, which we have before us, would in my opinion be: to what extent do formal aesthetic values within the field of art originate from the specific technical conditions; and would the purely technical side of the situation be separated from the socio-economic? The question is highly important: what is the significance, for example, of the evolu-tion of the modern proletariat as a class for artistic development, its attempt to put itself forward culturally as a community in itself – such indeed was the nobility (*das Großartige*) of the movement? (Chairman attempts to interrupt the speaker.) '*Großartig*', just now, I openly concede, was a value-judgement, and I withdraw it. (Loud laughter.) I will say, for those of us who are interested in this movement, that it cherishes the visionary hope that it will autonomously develop and counterpose completely new values in all fields opposing those of the bourgeois world. I ask whether there are now any formal values *whatsoever* in the literary and artistic fields – not merely an extension of subject-matter – but actual formal values that have originated in this way? Gentlemen, at the moment and in a wholly provisional way I would categorically deny this question. In no case that is known to me of an artist of proletarian origin or socialist conviction does the revolutionary breakthrough in form have anything whatsoever to do with the artist's – and there are such cases – class or convictions; in most cases this is not even intelligible to those of his class. This 'naturalism' to which such artists occasionally, but by no means regularly, subscribe has brought us new subjects but not new formal values, and in literary terms the working class today stands near Schiller – when it goes well – but not modern naturalistic art. When they then present naturalism scientifically as the only acceptable, specifically revolutionary [form] – this is pure artistic non-comprehension. Since the break with prejudices in art is more easily effected by those whose natures are disposed to overcome prejudices – including class prejudices of all kinds – that is correct. However, there is certainly no sign in art of class-affiliated formal values. As already stated, this question belongs to a special, future discussion on the materialist interpretation of history, although not before a thorough and complete preparation; this belongs to the most important of the debates with which we could concern ourselves.

But today, gentlemen, we ask whether modern technology (*Technik*) does not stand in any relation to formal-aesthetic values; the answer in my opinion is undoubtedly affirmative. This is so in so far as wholly specific formal values in our modern artistic culture could only be born due to the existence of the modern city, the modern city with its tram-lines, underground, electrical and other lights, shop-windows, concert halls and restaurants, café, smoke-stacks, the expanse of walls (*Steinmassen*), the whole wild dance of tone and impressions of colour, the interwoven sensations of sexual fantasy and the experiences of variants of the psychic make-up (*seelischen Konstitution*), which affect the hungry rabble through all kinds of apparently inexhaustible possibilities of life-style (*Lebensführung*) and happiness. Partly as a protest – as a specific form of flight from this reality: the highest aesthetic abstractions or the deepest dream or most intense forms of frenzy – partly as an adaptation to it: apologists for their own imaginative intoxicating rhythms. Gentlemen, I believe a lyric poetry perhaps like that of Stefan George: a measure of which – this invulnerable defence of a pure artistic form against the tumult produced by the technology of

279

our lives – could not have been achieved without the lyric poet being shot through by the impressions (*Eindrücke*) of the modern city that smother, derange and parcellize his soul – even though he may curse it into the abyss; lyrical poetry like that of Verhaeren which emphatically affirms and in its immanent forms and unities searches out the city. Similarly I believe that wholly specific formal values of modern painting could not be perceived, since their attainment would not have been possible by people who [had not experienced] the teeming masses, the night lights and reflexes of the modern city with its means of communication – not the London of the seventeenth or eighteenth century into which a Milton could still be born and whom certainly no one thinks of as a possible product of the modern metropolis – I say, it is completely impossible in my opinion that certain formal values of modern painting could ever have been achieved without the particular impression made by the modern metropolis – a spectacle never seen before in history – powerful by day but overwhelmingly so at night. And since the visible – and this alone is of concern – of each and every modern metropolis receives its specific quality primarily not from property relations and social constellations but from modern technology, so here is the point at which technology purely as such has a very extensive significance for artistic culture.[4]

The second paragraph is remarkable, not least for its manic quality, but it is noteworthy that in the first paragraph it is established that the revolution in formal painterly values is an achievement of bourgeois art. The working class in terms of its cognitive, moral and artistic values belongs to a state of mind that is, at best, romantic. They, unlike the more aware members of the bourgeois, are unable to see the ways in which the experience of the present-day city enters not only into subject-matter (which was the theme of Sombart's contribution to the debate) but into the forms in which those sensations are captured. When Weber speaks of technology this is more than just one of many factors. It is rather the whole condition of living in the modern metropolis and its basis in modern technological conditions. This is inescapable, even for those like George who turn their back on the city. The passage is almost unsociological, for it attempts to portray a diffuse feeling of febrile excitement, of a sense of the new and of inexhaustible enjoyments, that have nothing to do with plodding sociological concepts like social constellations or property relations.

Weber also refers to the achievement of modern painters, and it is a reasonable inference to assume that he is referring to the Impressionists and Post-Impressionists. A year later, in 1911, Weber visited Paris where, says Marianne, he 'wanted to see and assimilate everything: French music, for he was thinking of a treatise on the sociology of music; modern painting and sculpture, for at some time in the future he was going to write a sociology embracing all the arts' (Marianne Weber, 1975, p. 498). Marianne reports that 'they' quickly adjusted to the masterworks of Monet, Manet, Degas and Renoir, and then turned to Cézanne, Gauguin and van Gogh. Such a report in its glibness tells us almost nothing. How did Max Weber 'adjust' to the 'impressionism' of the city and its artistic presentation? Obviously he did not remain unaffected by the blandishments of city life, as his contribution to the 'Technology and Culture' debate shows. Artistically the depiction of the city-scape set a number of trends in train. Naturalism opened up the selection of subject-matter; not only nature but increasingly street life – market, factories, pavement scenes, high life and low life and their intersections. The non-naturalistic depiction of these scenes led to a flatness of plane, a compression of perspective, a clouding of detail and a freedom of coloration. There is a correspondence between style and the sense of suggestibility, of excitement and of the shallowness of the modern city. The visual loss of depth is accompanied by a similar lack of psychic depth. Nothing stands or is signified beyond what is visually there. Wealth cohabits with poverty, beauty with ugliness; the transience and change of modern life are simply observed and set down.

The atrophy of the moral sense, that art serves some ultimate higher purpose, is epitomized in the poetry of Baudelaire, and here we do possess Weber's own interpretation. In his onslaught against the supposition that ultimate values could be underpinned by ethical, religious, artistic, or scientific premises – all of which the student audience of 'Science as a Vocation' held to be possible and valid – Weber alights on Baudelaire's *Fleurs du Mal* as a demonstration that culture no longer associates the beautiful with the good. The phenomenon that attracts Weber's attention in this work is the inversion of values. The ugly may achieve a formal beauty, and evil may be equally artistically celebrated as the good. This, as Weber observes, is a Nietzschean insight. The point we want to develop here, however, is that Weber's artistic understanding is the concomitant of Nietzsche's *The Birth of Tragedy* and not, as might seem to be more consistent, *Beyond Good and Evil*. The artistic equivalent of the latter work was transposed into philosophy of life and Expressionism, to which Weber was implacably opposed. In *The Birth of Tragedy* the dark forces that penetrated the cultic and religious life of the early Greeks – the Dionysiac frenzy and Bacchic rites – are harnessed, perfected and sublimated through artistic form, which for Nietzsche is represented by the god Apollo. Inchoate primitive energies attain the perfection of beauty through the creative powers of Apollonian form. It was art that mastered and made timeless the otherwise uncanalized passions of brute existence.

281

In *Beyond Good and Evil*, by contrast, the duality of human existence and artistic form is effaced.

The inversion of values is not the only reading of Baudelaire. Although evil receives poetic beautification, the formal qualities of beauty are not necessarily sublime. Beauty – good or evil – is simply celebrated and delighted in, and the poetry does not seek to overawe the reader. The appeal to the instinctual and the sensual takes the reader by surprise, but this is a matter of artistic artifice: the shock at finding one's desires made poetically legitimate. Behind it is a moral indifference, the facticity that both base and noble desires coexist in our imagination, and that they create a reverie to combat the boredom of everyday life. It is a poetry of desire in which the moral landscape is not so much inverted as telescoped; and the scope of imagination does not exist within a lofty artistic form, but is introverted and expressed through richly textured images and words.

Weber's interpretation recognizes but does not succumb to delights *de la boue*. The Kantian pack of art, morality and science is reshuffled to disconcerting effect but never abandoned. Art, though it might invert morality, still retains form. In philosophy of life, on the other hand, the distinctions between art, morality and even science are collapsed. The message that Weber obtains from Baudelaire is a highly charged one; the realm of art is one of 'diabolical grandeur' (FMW, p. 144). The passage about art and Baudelaire occurs at a crucial point in the argument of 'Science as a Vocation', and Weber's maximalist conception of culture is used to great effect to disabuse his audience.

So far I have spoken only of the practical reasons for avoiding the imposition of a personal point of view. Yet these are not the only ones. The impossibility of 'scientific' advocacy of a practical standpoint – except in cases which discuss the means for an already given end – derives from far deeper reasons. It is fundamentally nonsense, because the different value-orders of the world stand in irresolvable conflict with one another. Old man Mill, whose philosophy I will not otherwise praise, was exactly right on this point when he said once that if one proceeds from pure experience, one arrives at polytheism. This is shallow in its formulation and sounds paradoxical, but there is truth in it. If anything, we are even more aware of this today; not only that something can be holy although it is not beautiful, but also *because and in so far as* it is not beautiful – and one can find reference to this in Chapter 53 of the book of Isaiah and Psalm 22; we also know that something can be beautiful even though – but also *because* – it is not good. We have known this since Nietzsche and you will find it earlier presented in the *Fleurs du mal*, as Baudelaire called his volume of poems. It is a common-sense knowledge that something can be true although it is neither beautiful, nor holy, nor good. Yet these are only the most elementary cases of the struggle of the gods of the various orders and values.

(FMW, pp. 147–8; italics in original German)

Culture is invoked to deepen the analysis. The problem of conduct in the modern world is the irreconcilability between the spheres of values. But Weber does not allow what is for him a facile solution: that of accepting each value independently as a brute fact of the empiricism of life. The duality of individual choice and a set of ultimate values whose meanings and sense we can in no way penetrate is advocated by Weber against the non-dualistic vision of the elder Mill. We will leave aside the scepticism of the godson of the younger Mill as to why a philosophy should be accepted rationally if it takes an impenetrable noumenon as given. The point for Weber is that value-choice is rendered even harder when it is realized that ultimate values like good and beauty do not necessarily correspond to one another, nor do they guarantee the worth of any other ultimate value.

This passage also indicates how a modern attitude to the world can, ultimately, be sustained. The rhetoric of 'Science as a Vocation' makes this passage a point of high tension. In one sense the sustainability of conduct in the modern world is a prosaic affair. Sociologically we note that the world is increasingly divided into separate orders of life, that these each have their own values and that the personality has the freedom of choosing which values it will live by. Therefore it will experience the pull of different values as well as the difficulty of holding fast to values in the face of the complexity and the ordinariness of the world. This social philosophy, or what we have termed a secular ethic, is not of course tension-free; to be sustained it requires the necessity of value-choice and a maturity of personality. The tension management is one whose message is basically 'steady as she goes'. With patience and fortitude one can make some sense of the world and achieve a measure of control at least in one's own personal sphere.

Weber also shipwrecks this stance, however, for there are a number of pathologies that threaten it. In the most general sense Weber offers a voluntarism of choice with regard to ultimate values, but those values exist outside and beyond our choice. Man has a freedom to choose but no freedom over the choices. New values can come into existence, but this process is likewise beyond the individual's control; it belongs to the 'metanoia' of values, a subject that is philosophically and sociologically beyond scrutiny. The individual can have a sense of destiny only by abandoning him- or herself to an ultimate value. If one commits oneself to the value of a nation state, its destiny may at some point pass beyond one's

283

control and forbearance. Eduard Baumgarten emphasizes this aspect – that fate disposes over ultimate values – at the end of his study on Max Weber; it is a state of affairs beyond speech, in which the only choice left is mute acceptance, a final stance that Weber colours in as one of of feudal obedience before the lord (Baumgarten, 1964, p. 673).

The upholding of values within a single order of life can likewise prove to be extremely unstable and pathological in its consequences. Take for instance the value of artistic culture. There are four ways in which a commitment to the value of culture can destabilize. Culture is the realm of diabolical grandeur. This holds for Baudelaire as well as for the whole period of time in which culture has been religion's main rival. At bottom the artist provides a charisma of illumination (*Verklärung*), and this is not far removed from the mystic's propinquity to the oneness of the world. Apart from 'diabolical grandeur' there is a second feature: acosmic oneness with the world. The writer who clearly captures this standpoint is the early Tolstoy, and Weber's discussion places this attitude in contrast to the cosmic rigorism of salvation religion.

> The euphoria of the happy lover is felt to be 'goodness'; it has a friendly urge to poeticize all the world with happy features or to bewitch all the world in a naïve enthusiasm for the diffusion of happiness. And always it meets with the cool mockery of genuinely religiously founded and radical ethic of brotherhood. The psychologically most thorough portions of Tolstoy's early work may be cited in this connection.*
> *Especially in *War and Peace*. (FMW, pp. 348–9)

This quote occurs in the section in the 'Intermediate Reflections' on the erotic sphere of life, where culture and the erotic are contiguous spheres in Weber's analysis.

The third and fourth features are closely interrelated, and they are the 'formed' nature of culture and the pathos of culture. All artistic creation has to be realized through form, yet form under certain conditions can estrange spectator and artist from a oneness with the created object. The analysis is not dissimilar to Simmel's. But Weber links this with a Tolstoyan pessimism about the life of culture and of civilization in general.

> Civilized man, placed in the midst of the continuous enrichment of culture by ideas, knowledge and problems, may become 'tired with life' but not 'satiated with life'. He catches only the most minute part of what the life of the spirit brings forth ever anew, and what he seizes is always something provisional and not definitive, and therefore death for him is a meaningless occurrence. And because death is meaningless,

civilized life as such is meaningless; by its very 'progressiveness' it gives death the imprint of meaninglessness. Throughout his late novels one meets with this thought as the keynote of the Tolstoyan art.

(FMW, p. 140)

These themes all reoccur in the powerful concluding section of the 'Intermediate Reflections'. For Weber, complete espousal of an ultimate value is no refuge from the world. We have seen this in his condemnation of the George circle. The point being made here is that even a moderate stance, one prepared to accommodate with the world, is always prone to extreme tensions. There is the attraction of the charisma of illumination that threatens to break through to a forbidden realm – one of diabolical grandeur. Then there is the socially untenable relapse into acosmic love. Finally, in the mature 'formed' culture the timeless validity of art is taken away by the estrangement of civilized forms.

As has already been stated, Weber's notions about culture are a mixture and they are not fully consistent or coherent. He appears to operate with a kind of unexplicated mental shorthand when alluding to the pitfalls and pathologies of sustaining the secular ethic in the separate spheres. If the analysis is widened at this point to include some of the neighbouring phenomena of heroism, mysticism and eroticism as well as aestheticism, then a clearer understanding – but even then not entirely coherent – can be gained of this mental shorthand. It is also necessary to say that Weber evinces a definite resistance to a clarification of such ideas. For him the vulnerability of the psyche in its needs for the deepest internal values and their projection on to the external world is something that is often glimpsed but rarely analysed. This is partly due to Weber's espousal of a Kantian dualism that is completely disabling in a social scientific analysis of psychopathologies, and in part because his analysis of world religions is haunted by the myth of phylogenesis, which gives rise to one of the most powerful metaphors in the analysis of social life.

The Myth of Phylogenesis

The antimonies of acosmic love and charisma, on the one side, and pathos and formed life, on the other, are central to the shorthand of Weber's thinking. What original charismatic communities, acosmic love and a certain form of eroticism all have in common is an uninhibited and unconstrained sense of the world. (This same point is made by Bryan Turner in Chapter 11 of this volume, though developed in a different direction.) This state stands opposed to all developments that seek to introduce forms, whether religious, political, social, or economic, between people and between people and the world. The major stage in the move away from unconstrained relationships occurs with religion. Through magic and religion, the world, or rather people's views of the world, becomes cosmically structured. Acosmic love pre-dates this development but exists as a residual germ in all civilizations that have long since structured and formed the original sense of oneness of person with others and the world. In this sense it belongs to no period. It recalls a past innocence that is prehistorical. And this recall always exists as a possibility of yearning for a relapse into this original condition, though at the same time an extremely dangerous longing in a cosmically structured world. This is the driving-force of mysticism, of heroic communities and of eroticism at its most unformed (see Roslyn Bologh, Chapter 12, above), as well as that behind the artistic charisma of illumination.

Its mythic status resides in its atemporality. The two essential essays that depict it are the 'Introduction' to Confucianism and Taoism and the 'Intermediate Reflections', which essay links the China study and the study on Hinduism and Buddhism. The 'Intermediate Reflections' are written in a way that is extraordinarily timeless. The reader is never precisely sure whether Weber is talking about the present, even though nominally he is looking back to the world religions. Even then the discussion is remarkably uninstanced. In the more schematic 'Introduction' the period prior to religion and magic, the era of acosmic love and unconstrainedness, is beyond any empirical map of the past.

This atemporal zone can be brought into focus by playing backwards Weber's account of the rationalization process. (This does not absolve the present discussion from the question of the latent evolutionism in Weber's work, a matter that in very broad outline seems, to me at least, uncontentious.) All civilizations undergo a rationalization process, driven in its middle period – magic on one side, modernity on the other – by the need to structure the world cosmically. As Schluchter demonstrates (Chapter 4, this volume), the nature of this process and its direction are unprejudiced with regard to the particular civilizations – India, Europe, China, etc. However, the common element in this process is a movement outwards. A striking analogy to the process is given by modern astronomy. We are now accustomed to think of galaxies exploding outwards from some original core event. In Weber's idea of the social universe there is an original (*urwüchsig*) condition. History is the centripetal movement outward of forces that follow their own dynamics and thrusts. So the economic differentiates from the religious, as does the political. By the time the social scientist is privileged to cognize this process, the modern world is exploding outwards at an increasing rate, with the orders of life – culture, politics, personal life, economics and science – each proceeding according to their own drive to rationalization and the consequent conflict of orders and their values. The notion of some core event, untraceable but imputed, can be divined if one runs the rationalization process backwards. The orders of life move together, overlap and coalesce; the cosmic structuring of the world goes from the sophistication of world religions to primitive religions, until one reaches the fringes of a mythical state marked by primitive communities (*naturgegebene Sippengemeinschaften*) and the supposition of their magical practices.

Beyond this one cannot go; it is possible only to surmise. But for Weber it is a world of charismatic brotherhood, mystic oneness with the world and acosmic love. What marks history is the violent ingress of religion and its exploitation of the relations of cosmic structure (cf. Bryan Turner, Chapter 11, above). Anthropologically there is no evidence for an original unconstrained relation of people and world, although there is plenty for the production of cosmic accounts of the world. One further feature of the original state has to be mentioned and relates to the earlier discussion in this chapter of interior and exterior states. In a non-differentiated world, literally so – distinguishing neither the sense of otherness of another person nor the sense of otherness of physical reality – the tension between interior psychological need and external interests cannot exist because there is no such distinction from which the tension can be generated. Hence there is no theodicy problem.

The reasons for regarding this myth as phylogenetic are not that there is any such explicit evolutionary theory in Weber's work, as can be found, for instance, in the theory of Sigmund Freud. It is rather an implicit assumption about humankind: that there inheres in all of us a belief that at some time there existed a natural state from which the world religions have cruelly ousted us. Weber implicitly makes it the starting-point from which the processes of rationalization are set in motion. Humankind as a species, whatever its world civilizational coloration, once inhabited this blissful realm.

The myth of phylogenesis is one that also threatens and haunts the cosmic and civilizational structuring of the world. In Freud's theory this realm wells up in the unconscious as the fear of the original sins of incest, parricide and taboo. In Weber's examples the order of religion is disturbed by the acosmic brotherhood of the warrior band, in the revelation of diabolical grandeur created through the charisma of illumination of the artist, in the consuming erotic love of one for another, its rejection of religious brotherhood and its sense of itself as fated, and in acosmic mysticism. Religious and cultured humanity always has to be on its guard for such relapses. Religion and culture decide, legitimate and sanction the kind of substantive values that will fulfil and solace the internal psychological needs of humankind. But equally there is the constant threat that people will seek their own salvation, not in a heterodox religious way, but simply by conjuring up the mythical knowledge within them; that oneness with the world can be achieved without religious or cultural mediation.

It is now necessary to draw some of the strands of the argument together. Although the project of 'The Economic Ethics of the World Religions' and Weber's analysis and prescription for conduct in the modern world are two separate enterprises, it has been the intent in this chapter to demonstrate a reciprocal influence between Weber's understanding of modernity and some of the psychic needs and forces that underlie the religious studies. As a modern social philosopher, Weber endorses the analysis of the world in terms of the Kantian polarities of science, politics and art. An extremely attractive feature of this part of his work, whether one agrees with it or not, is his desire to relate these Kantian polarities to the existential problems of living and conducting one's life in the modern world. His sense of the difficulties of constructing and sustaining an adequate style of life and conduct in modernity is in part informed by his awareness of modern artistic currents and movements. Within those aspects of artistic modernism that Weber can arguably be said to be in touch with – the symbolism of George; French modernism in the guise of Baudelaire and the Impressionist and Post-Impressionist artists; Expressionism as a mode of life (*Lebensphilosophie*) – his interpretation should be seen as one proceeding from an elevated Kantian idealism typical of the broader stratum of the educated middle class. The case of Max Weber is compelling because he stands on the dissident fringe of that stratum, trying to work out solutions consistent with both his own high ethical sense of the world and at the same time the presuppositionless formulations of the modernistic outlook. The major pull of modernism, in so far as this chapter has alluded to only a segment of a very various phenomenon, is not towards a Kantian, dualistic conception of humanity. Modernist art is the result of the inward collapse of a conventional artistic life-world. Its products constitute a flattening of the moral landscape and create a completely different and new sense of the individual. The individual is not presented as in Romanticism, as having a large amount of head-room to indulge his freedom of action with its moral and tragic concomitants, but instead is more dispassionately portrayed as simply being a part in a variegated and complexly interactive world. The impressionism of modern life means, at least for the masses, a necessarily superficial world.

Max Weber is clearly aware of the sense of possibility in modernity at the psychic level of the individual, as his contribution to the 'Technology and Culture' debate so marvellously illustrates. But he also wants to impart order, the rational mastery of conduct, amidst the psychic disorder of modernity. He knows that the purities of an exclusive politics, aesthetics, or morality are non-starters. But this does not signal a collapse into a riot of sense-impressionism and the espousal of the felt enthusiasm of the moment. Instead he adopts a distinction between internal psychological needs and external interests, and he distinguishes sociologically the process of the differentiation of the various domains of the life-world and their sometimes conflicting value-realms. In this way we are in debt to his rational analysis of modernity and its psychic correlates.

However, there are also certain costs in the acceptance of this debt for the pragmatic vision of a secular ethic. Psychic needs are universal in Weber's understanding of humankind. Modern culture cannot adequately act as a replacement to the cosmically structured solution of religious theodicy. Indeed, modern culture actually exacerbates those internal psychological needs by fuelling desire and the sense of the possible. Weber is only too uncomfortably aware that internal needs, far from receding in the wake of a scientized account of the rational secular world, are left hanging and unfulfilled. Within the domain of culture the civilizational achievement of cultural forms brings with it estrangement and the feeling that culture distances us from the natural rhythms and cycle of a life's span. Against this pathos of culture is counterpoised the intemperate demand of a relapse that, in the sphere of culture, may lead to experience of the diabolical grandeur that the charisma of illumination can impart. The pathos of form – sublimation in eroticism, virtuoso technique in mysticism, routinization in charisma, in short the triumph of the cosmic over the acosmic – always carries with it the germ of its mythical origin that manifests itself as an open invitation to return.

From a social scientific viewpoint this analysis presents great difficulties, which can be faced only with a much more scrupulous and realist investigation of the psychic and social world. The major difficulty attends Weber's recognition that the source of substantive values is closely connected with humankind's internal psychological needs and that this is the case even in the modern world. For example, Cavalli, Chapter 15, demonstrates that charismatic phenomena are still an integral feature of modern politics. Yet clearly there are pathologies – at the psychological, social and political levels – and they occur pre-eminently at the intersection of external interests and internal needs. There is also a pathology of life orders, although at this point a Durkheimian sociology is probably more applicable. Recent sociological analysis would suggest contrary to Weber that the separation and differentiation of the various spheres have not proceeded outwards in an orderly manner, but that the whole process has in some way gone awry, with the specialization of domains of economic, political, cultural and personal life interpenetrating at some very peculiar angles.

The empirical investigation of the actual relations between the spheres of life in modern society may therefore indicate something other than an orderly rationalization. Certainly it would be premature to assume the pattern of the various spheres in contemporary society and to use this assumption as a so-called realistic sociological basis for advancing a secular ethic. This is one aspect of Weber's secular ethic that warrants further attention. The other aspect that commands attention is Weber's awareness of the destabilizing influences upon the upholding of the secular ethic. These influences are most in evidence in the cultural and artistic sphere and its associated personal sphere. How extensive these forces are still needs a clearer determination than has been possible in this chapter, although Weber clearly wished to keep these influences confined to the cultural and private personal sphere. Yet the connection between the destabilizing influences and the wider issue of substantive values – what are they? From where do they come? How are they transformed? Why some may be considered benign and others pathological, and the whole sociological question of their projection on to the social world – suggests that we are dealing with a central element of Weber's sociology. But how one analyses and decides which substantive values can be adequately fulfilled in the modern world and which ones go terrifyingly wrong for individual and society are questions for a project that, while being informed by Weber's profound insights, would at the least require that some of the modernist insights should rise to the surface of social scientific inquiry.

Notes

I am indebted to a number of people for having looked at this chapter and trying to counsel me away from at least some of its shortcomings – in particular Ralph Schroeder, Scott Lash, Colin Gordon and James Joll.

1 On this see the recent contribution by Stephen Kalberg: 'The role of ideal interests in Max Weber's comparative historical sociology' (1985).
2 Goethe: letter to Schiller.
3 See also J. G. Merquior, who argues for a displacement of culturalist aspirations on to a charismatic politics (1980, pp. 108–201).
4 This passage is far from clear. Weber was probably speaking too fast for the stenographer, and parts of what he said are reproduced in note form (*Verhandlungen des Ersten Deutschen Soziologentages*, 1911, pp. 95–7).

PART FOUR

Reason and
the Political Order

14

The Soul of the Citizen:
Max Weber and Michel Foucault
on Rationality and Government

COLIN GORDON

There are many respects in which one might compare Michel Foucault's work with that of Max Weber: their studies of forms of domination and techniques of discipline, their concern with what Weber called 'the power of rationality over men', their writings on methodology and intellectual ethics, their interest in Nietzsche – and the effect of that interest on the critical reception of their thought.

References to Weber in the current literature on Foucault most often relate to the themes of rationality and rationalization. Dreyfus and Rabinow (1982, p. 166) thus write that Foucault inherits from Weber 'a concern with rationalization and objectification as the essential trend of our culture and the most important problem of our time'. Sometimes the comparison is linked to a reproach. Carlo Ginzburg sees in Foucault's work a 'Weberian' vision of history which reduces everything to 'one and the same meta-anthropological and metahistorical process of rationalization'. Repudiating this characterization, Foucault (1981a, p. 8) answers:

> I don't believe one can talk in this way of 'rationalization' as something given, without on the one hand postulating an absolute value inherent in reason, and on the other taking the risk of applying the term empirically in a completely arbitrary way. I think one must confine one's use of this word to an instrumental and relative meaning.

Barry Smart (1985, pp. 138–9), like Dreyfus and Rabinow, takes this as a cue for a sharp distinction between Weber and Foucault. Weber sees rationalization as a general, global and inexorable process in the modern world, whereas Foucault insists on a much more differentiated, pluralistic, sceptical approach.

The fact, however, is that Weber is as innocent as Foucault of the so-called Weberianism that adopts a uniform, monolithic conception of

293

historical phenomena of rationalization. One can do justice to Foucault without needing to traduce Weber; moreover, a fairer understanding of Weber may offer a much more enriching way of considering the issues newly posed by Foucault. Foucault himself abstained from any direct criticism of Weber; his remarks cited above could indeed hardly be closer in spirit to Weber's own repeated, prominent and emphatic statements on the same issue: 'We have to remind ourselves that "rationalism" may mean very different things' (FMW, p. 293);

> The history of rationalism shows a development which by no means follows parallel lines in the various departments of life . . . In fact, one may – this simple proposition, which is often forgotten, should be placed at the beginning of every study which essays to deal with rationalism – rationalize life from fundamentally different basic points of view and in very different directions. Rationalism is an historical concept which covers a whole world of different things.
>
> (PESC, pp. 77–8)

Many sociologists and commentators on Weber seem to imagine that all these distinctions are, so far as Weber is concerned, flattened out by the modern advance of bureaucracy. Yet it is easy to verify that Weber actually attaches vital importance to recognition of the lasting and intrinsic differences between, notably, the style of rationality proper to the bureaucratic official and those of the entrepreneur or the politician.

This still leaves open the question of how, and how far, the question of rationalization determines the overall themes and purposes of Weber's unfinished life-work. An elaborately argued response has been constructed by Wolfgang Schluchter, who reads Weber's various comparisons between different forms and instances of rationalization as instalments towards an integrated developmental sociology of world history. Perhaps the most intractable difficulty for this proposal is suggested by the remarks by Weber that have just been quoted, if one takes them as urging not only a comparativist approach to different rationalization phenomena but also a doubt as to whether the different historical problem-fields within which questions about rationalization come to be posed can usefully be merged together under the auspices of a single overarching theory.

The latter would seem to have been Foucault's view. It appears also to be close to that taken by Wilhelm Hennis in a vigorous critique of the Schluchter version of Weber's topic as a 'universal-historical process of rationalization':

> However central the problem of rationalisation might have been for Weber, it must be placed in a far more extensive context if it is to become the key to his work – a context in which the reason for this

question being so important to Weber will become evident ... To see the process of rationalisation as Weber's fundamental theme is not incorrect. But, as is quite apparent from the state of research on Weber, it is misleading to read everything in its terms and see it everywhere.

(Hennis, 1983, p. 138)

Hennis's reading of Weber is, in its way, no less systematic, committed and single-minded than Schluchter's. His recent articles on Weber must, even if their perspective appears strange to many sociologists, surely count among the most stimulating contributions to discussion of Weber for many years. *Lebensführung*, the conduct of life, and the forms of its rationalization represent, for Hennis, *the* object of Weber's sociology.

This claim involves three interlinked propositions about Weber's work. First, some of Weber's work – for Hennis, the most important part – takes the conduct of life as its immediate and principal *topic*. Among these writings Hennis is, of course, fully justified in numbering Weber's most famous essay, *The Protestant Ethic and the Spirit of Capitalism*, with its treatment of the 'methodical conduct of life' instilled by Calvinism. More broadly, he can cite the particular interest in the 'rationalisation of *Lebensführung*' which Weber (FMW, pp. 267–301) declares in the 'Introduction' to 'The Economic Ethics of the World Religions'. Second, Hennis regards *Lebensführung* as a principle that inspires and illuminates the *methodology* of Weber's major works, particularly *Economy and Society*, where the sociological 'arena of normative and de facto powers' is envisaged and appraised in terms of the influence of these collective forces on individual life-conduct. Third, *Lebensführung* is the fundamental *ethical value-criterion* of Weber's reflections on the future of humanity (*Menschentum*). In considering the fate of modern societies, Weber's deepest concern is for the survival of a 'character' or 'personality' whose life-conduct unites pragmatic rationalism with ethical seriousness. Hennis argues passionately and with an impressive wealth of documentary evidence that the heart of Weber's sociology consists of a moral anthropology that is profoundly at variance with the positivistic tendencies of the human sciences of the present century.

From the later 1970s up to his death in 1984, Foucault's work moves in directions markedly consonant with those taken by Hennis's commentaries. The later volumes of *The History of Sexuality* are largely concerned with a description of the 'methodical *Lebensführungen*' practised in late Antiquity. Alongside the techniques of power and knowledge, Foucault now proposes a study of the 'technologies of the self', of cultural practices dedicated to the formation and transformation of the self by the self. In his earlier books the question of 'how human beings are made subjects' had been explored in terms of the heteronomous effects of power. There, subjectification was studied as subjection; here, it is studied in cultures of personal autonomy predicated on a condition of liberty (albeit the liberty of a masculine, privileged and dominant few). It is probably not coincidental that Foucault spoke, towards the end of his life, of a sense of Weber's growing contemporary importance, and that he is said to have taken a particular interest in Weber's sociology of religion; what interested him there is a topic that might repay closer study.

This was only one side of Foucault's later work. Another one is of even greater relevance for our theme. In his lectures of 1978 and 1979 Foucault began to outline a move from the previous, 'microphysical' orientation of his work, in terms of studies of particular, regional, individualizing rationalities and power structures, towards a 'macrophysics', a study of the exercise of power at the scale of whole societies and populations.[1] The rubric under which Foucault proposed to organize these new analyses was that of 'governmental rationality'. Although this work dealt mainly with modern Europe since the sixteenth century, it had important links with the concerns that were leading his studies on sexuality during the same years. Foucault points out that the growth of explicit reflection on the 'art of government' in the early modern period is accompanied by a consciously elaborated notion of the inner connectedness of the government of oneself, the conduct of individual existence, on the one hand, and the government of others, the regulation of the lives of many, on the other. The sixteenth century's neo-Stoic interest in a new culture of the self – of self-knowledge, self-mastery, self-formation – (becomes, as has been shown by Gerhard Oestreich (1983), a major constituent of the political pedagogies and techniques of the early modern state. The notion of government occupies a nodal place in Foucault's later work, for two reasons: because it designates a continuity between the micro- and the macro-levels of political analysis, and because it spans the interface between the exercise of power and the exercise of liberty.

Foucault defines 'government' as *la conduite de la conduite*, ('the conduct of conduct') – a phrase that could hardly have a more Weberian ring; it would probably be best rendered in German as *die Führung der Lebensführung*. And yet, nowhere in Weber's countless discussions of rationalism and rationalization (nor, so far as I have been able to ascertain, in any other author prior to Foucault) does one encounter the term 'governmental rationality'. Even when due allowance is made for the illusions of hindsight, this seems a surprising or at least intriguing fact. Perhaps something can be learned from an attempt to explain it.

Foucault: Governmental Rationality

Foucault's approach to governmental rationality or, in his own neologism, 'governmentality' (a term that one might also unpack, in the vocabulary of Lucien Febvre, as 'mentality of government') conjoins a set of innovations on several distinct levels. It comprises a substantive historical thesis; a distinctive perspective for research; an exposition of some relatively unfamiliar tracts of historical material; a new and more inclusive framework for his own previous studies; and, last but not least, a challenge to some contemporary habits of political reflection and criticism. I shall try here to provide a very rapid outline of each of these proposals.

(1)   Foucault's major historical thesis is that it is a distinctive trait of modern societies and the modern state to attempt the integration of two contrasted styles of collective power relation: the mode of the *polis*, structured according to principles of universality, law, citizenship and the public life, and the mode of what Foucault calls 'pastoral power', which instead accords an absolute priority to the exhaustive and individualized guidance of singular existences. The modern state is, for Foucault, a mechanism at once of individualization and of totalization. His exploration of the individualizing aspect of rationalities of government takes up themes that are often, but usually only fleetingly, evoked by Weber; it points towards systematic connections between rationality and *Lebensführung* of a kind that remain, by and large, only implicit in Weber's writings.

(2)   As we have seen, Foucault's way of handling these questions aims to extend and complement the 'microphysics of power', which he had practised in *Discipline and Punish*, by adding a 'macrophysical' analysis of practices whose focus is the administration not of individuals but of populations. Practices, rather than institutions, remain the primary objects of the inquiry. To understand what the state is, one needs first to look at the practices of government, just as the birth of the prison is to be explained by way of a history of practices of punishment and discipline. Another common trait is the attention paid to the reconstruction of explicit, reflected, articulate strategies and programmes. In his last books, Foucault reiterates this point by describing his whole work as a study of *problematizations*, that is, of the ways in which human beings conceive and address their own selves and the different aspects of their individual and collective being as problems. In this instance, Foucault's archaeological reconstructions are intended to focus attention on the historical record of problematizations of government, of the questions of how and what to govern, of how government is possible, of the essential principles of an 'art of governing'. Foucault is not saying either here or elsewhere that there is no reality but that of discourse. But he is, here as elsewhere,

insisting on the need for a certain kind of historical nominalism; economy and society, the modern objects of governing, are entities whose very intelligibility depends on ways of coding and articulating the real that have had to be invented. He is asserting that these objects of governing have particular material and conceptual pre-conditions, which depend for their existence and their operability on specific knowledges, techniques, expertises.

(3)   The field of historical data to which Foucault applies these principles of method to especially significant effect is one that, although it has certainly not been unknown to previous scholarship, has seldom been accorded the adequate strategic appraisal which is its due. This field consists of the doctrine, pedagogy and administrative practice known in early modern German-speaking Europe as Cameralism, or the 'science of police' (*Polizei-wissenschaft*). Foucault and his fellow researcher Pasquale Pasquino argue that Cameralist ideas represent the first extant form of one modern mode of political problematization whose history has too often been overshadowed (by theories of political legitimation and methods for the retention of sovereign power), namely, that of the coherent principles of a practice of governing. Cameralism is, in other words, the first explicit and systematic modern rationality of government. Reflection on reason of state was, Foucault argues, the first modern form of political thought to postulate the rationality of government as something specific, intrinsic and autonomously proper to the state; reason of state is *par excellence* a reason different and distinct from the general divine and natural ordering of the cosmos.

The science of police represents, in turn, the first attempt to endow this postulated form of knowledge with a substantive and coherent content. It identifies the state with 'the whole body of society', and links its goal, the 'happiness' of the state, to that of the 'happiness' and well-being of its individual subjects, the happiness 'of all and of each' (Foucault, 1981a; Pasquino, 1982). The strength of the state rests on the lives of its subjects and on their order, obedience and industry. Cameralism has commonly been relegated to the prehistory of economic science, its ideas supposedly consigned to archaism by the triumphs of liberalism, political economy and the market. But the advent of liberalism does not liquidate the problem of government. Liberalism indeed transforms the techniques of security inherited, in a great part of Europe, from the police state. But this history, which embraces the genealogy of the Welfare State, is traversed by continuities as well as discontinuities.

(4)   This conception of a history of rationalities of government has complex correlations and precedents in the regional histories of normalizing practices pursued in Foucault's earlier books. The *hôpitaux généraux* studied in *Madness and Civilization*, the internment institutions of the *ancien régime*, are the instrument of a police art of government. Bentham's

Panopticon, examined in *Discipline and Punish*, is a liberal theorem of political security. Here the long-standing Marxist objection that Foucault's studies preclude an investigation of the state falls to the ground; what on the contrary becomes increasingly evident is the way the impoverished and monotonous genre of what is called 'theory of the state' has obstructed any adequate consideration of *what the state does*, of the actual nature and rationale of governmental activity. One particularly important point of connection leads from this new perspective of analysis to the topic broached and formulated in *The History of Sexuality, Vol. 1* as 'biopolitics'. Biopolitics should be understood as the phenomenon whereby the individual and collective life of human populations, or even of the human species, becomes an explicit object of practices of government. Pejoratively restrictive readings of this latter theme can now be more easily resisted. What is in question here is the theme of a latent eugenic totalitarianism or state racism.

Equally implicated is the direction of mutation of welfare institutions which advance the ambitions of a kind of political economy that aspires to take into account all aspects of individual life, and not only those relating to economic activity in its narrow sense. The formation and augmentation of human capital, the cost and value of lives to individuals and to the state, become measures of political calculation. It is extremely easy in this perspective to understand why a revival of ethical discussion, an intensified public and even institutional demand for ethical expertise, has become such a striking aspect on the contemporary scene. It is easier, also, to understand in these terms why some of Max Weber's themes are attracting renewed attention.

(5) The challenge that finally emerges in a muted but increasingly telling way from this part of Foucault's work is the realization that what has appeared to be a new kind of radical politics may in some vital respects actually stand in a retarded relation to its own time. Foucault was himself celebrating this new politics, as a riposte to the modern encroachments of governmental 'biopolitics', when he wrote in the last chapter of *The History of Sexuality I*: 'No matter whether all this was Utopian: what we have here has been a very real process of struggle: life as a political object has been in a sense taken at face value and turned back against the system which was bent on controlling it' (1979a, p. 145). Why, then, have the new forces that embody this choice been of such small avail to the political Left over the past decade? A part of the answer may be that this radical theme of what might be called the self-government of the self has occurred in conjunction with a re-emergence of the theme of government *tout court*. This theme was not initiated by the Left and has found the Left intellectually unarmed and unprepared. The neo-liberal governments of Schmidt, Barre/Giscard and Thatcher have each in turn succeeded in

transforming to their own advantage the lie of the political terrain and capturing for themselves a powerful polemical initiative. They have succeeded by means of a strategy that thrusts the question of government into the centre of electoral contention, by affirming the superior serious-ness and realism of their own approach to these questions, and by coupl-ing their vision of a style of government to a corresponding model of socio-economic citizenship. Here a certain idea of the enterprise of government promotes and capitalizes on a widely disseminated concep-tion of individuality as an enterprise, of the person as an entrepreneur of the self. The theme of a capitalist *Lebensführung* reappears here not merely as an ideological stratagem but as a correlate of real modifications in institutions and practices, existences and mentalities. These phenomena are often mentioned under the rubric of a 'crisis of the Welfare State', a term that enables them conveniently to be converted into material for a habitual mode of Left critique of the state. But this style of analysis tends to misrecognize what might be more aptly grasped as a crisis, or at any rate a period of a more profound mutation in governmental rationality.

Weber: Liberal Reason of State

What would Weber have thought about all this? As we have seen, the way Foucault represents 'governmental rationality' as a distinctive object of historical study is associated with a chronological perspective that rela-tivizes the threshold between liberal and pre-liberal epochs of govern-ment, and lends a new prominence to the practices of Cameralism. From the disappointingly few references Weber makes to the latter topic there emerges an attitude that remains much closer than Foucault's to the conventional views of political economy and its historiography, as indeed to the prevalent liberal presuppositions of his time. Doubtless it is also an attitude coloured by an awareness of living in a society that retains many of the traits of the Cameralist *Polizei-* and *Obrigkeitsstaat*. Weber's view on this matter is an underdeveloped and relatively diffuse area within his overall socio-historical panorama. This may be explicable in part by a certain lack of cohesion at this point between Weber's various means of conceptualizing phenomena of rationalization, and also perhaps in part by his residual dependence in the formulation of certain aspects of this question on the official historical self-image of political economy. It is probably not coincidental that two of the occasions where Weber makes direct mention of Cameralism occur in his study of China – that is, in a context where Weber is interested in identifying varieties of rationaliza-tion that differ in kind from those of the modern West and are in some absolute sense no less 'rational' than those of the West, but are nevertheless impaired by limitations or defects disqualifying them from providing a matrix for modernity in the Western manner. Thus the writings on what Weber calls 'Chinese cameralism' in support of practices of *laissez-faire*, or on the question of the balance of trade, transpire to be illustrations of the way Chinese government 'possesses no commercial policy in the modern sense of the term' (RC, pp. 79, 136–8).

A similarly double-edged tone characterizes the discussion of (European) mercantilism in the *General Economic History*. The English mercantilism (Weber credits this term to Adam Smith) that emerges as early as the fourteenth century is called 'the first trace of a rational economic policy on the part of the prince'. But there ensues a familiar dialectic whereby the state's conscious economic rationalism, 'carrying the point of view of capitalist industry into politics', becomes the historical adversary of capitalism proper, opposing a regime of monopolies and privileges to one of market opportunities. 'Here for the last time irrational and rational capitalism faced each other in conflict' (GEH, p. 347). No doubt Weber is fundamentally at one with Adam Smith here, but there is a difference between the weighting of their respective arguments. Smith stresses the possibility and necessity of unburdening the state of its impossible task of exhaustive monitoring and anticipation of economic events in the market. Weber, on the other hand, denounces the arbitrariness and caprice inherent in an activist state policy of the mercantilist type, which frustrates market-oriented capitalism by creating unpredictable conditions for commerce, and thus negates the very benefits of predictability originally conferred by the legal rationalism of the early state (ES, pp. 848–9). Its harmonization of administrative 'clarity' with commercial 'certainty' smoothed the convergence of the state's interests with those of nascent capitalism.

Cameralism and mercantilism are then closely allied – albeit not identical doctrines. Can one conclude that Weber would have questioned the very possibility of a Cameralist 'rationality' of government? In this instance – in contradistinction to the tenor of most of Weber's observations on forms of rationality – should one infer that the irrationality of Cameralist/mercantilist policy is in his eyes the correlate of a specific intellectual shortcoming, one corresponding to the received thesis of a decisive scientific threshold dividing mercantilism from political economy?

A further indirect pointer towards this conclusion can be drawn from the China study. Weber here calls 'Confucian "reason"' a 'rationalism of order'. He glosses the Confucian meaning of the concept of *Tao* as connoting 'the external order of the universe and also the actual movement of the universe', adding that 'such an identification is frequently found in all metaphysical systems whose dialectical structure has not been perfected' (RC, pp. 169, 181–3). A similar verdict might be inferred on a conception of economic government that made no distinction between the regularities governing economic phenomena and the actual state of order maintained by the policies of the state. This conception is, precisely, the Cameralist one. As Pasquale Pasquino has put it, Cameralism acknowledges the *specificity* of the economy as an object of government, but not its *autonomy* from the state or from the activity of governing. We may recall here Weber's stricture in the opening pages of *The City*, on a prevalent usage of the historical concept of a 'city economy' (*Stadtwirtschaft*) such that 'categories relevant to measures of economic *policy* are fused with purely economic categories'. Weber objects to this that 'this economic *policy* does not represent a universal stage in the development of the *economy*' (ES, pp. 1218, 1220, italics in original). The intensely regulated guild regimes of the free imperial cities of late medieval Germany, which provided the outstanding historic models of the 'city economy', have also been identified as forerunners and prototypes of the Cameralist regulatory policies elaborated in the German princely states after the end of the Thirty Years' War; policies in which the economy and its regulation are indeed treated as one and the same reality (Oestreich, 1983, p. 161).

Weber, like Marx, promised a treatise on the state that he never lived to write; one may suspect, however, that the omission is hardly fortuitous. Weber may indeed have given a subtle account of the specific points of historical convergence between the careers of modern state and modern capitalism; he may have insisted on the inevitable technical interdependence in a developed industrial society of capitalistic and bureaucratic structures; he may have identified such extensive analogies between these structures so that, 'sociologically speaking, the modern state is an "enterprise" just like a factory' (ES, p. 1394). But there is, nevertheless, a slight but crucial discrepancy between Weber's general viewpoint and that of the essay in which Otto Hintze proposed to replicate Weber's study of the Calvinist sources of the spirit of capitalism with a parallel treatment of the 'spirit' of the early modern Prussian state. Weber could, one might think, *almost* have written Hintze's remark that '*raison d'état* and capitalism are after all closely allied sociologically' (Hintze, 1975, p. 94). What else is capitalism than modern *raison d'économie*? *Raison d'état* and *raison d'économie* stem from the same root. One could *almost* suppose that Weber might have been prepared to attribute the intention 'to bring the world under ethical, rational mastery and control', i.e. the rational objectivity of progress, not only to the Puritan entrepreneur but also to the police state. But neither of these suppositions is really tenable. Weber does indeed repeatedly and vehemently affirm the claims of '*reason of state*', but he does not acknowledge a *spirit* of state, nor – to contrast him with another neo-Weberian scholar of the following generation – does he ever propose, in the manner of Alfred Müller-Armack (1944), to juxtapose a typology of the different 'economic styles' characteristic of members of each of the post-Reformation churches with a study of their corresponding styles of 'state-practice' (*Staatspraxis*).

To clarify these issues we need to consider the context, intentions and antagonists of Weber's thought in the Germany of his time. One reason why Weber may not have felt moved to write an explicit study of the state-practices of Cameralism may well have been a sense that such a genealogy would, in a society that retained in its mores and everyday conditions so many traces of the *Polizeistaat*, have amounted to a redundant detour. Another reason could have been, contrariwise, the fact that the implications of such traces, in Weber's world and in Weber's own thinking, by no means all led in parallel lines.

The Weber who decries the adverse consequences for capitalist development of voluntarist-statist policies of the mercantilist kind is also, we may recall, the economist who declares that 'the science of political economy is a *political* science', and that 'in this national state the ultimate standard of value for economic policy, is "reason of state"' (Weber, 1980, p. 438). The provocative tone of the inaugural lecture in which these remarks were made ought not to obstruct recognition that their substance is little more than a statement of fact about the nineteenth-century German variant of political economy of which Weber was a professional exponent, namely *Nationalökonomie*. Weber's highly explicit view of the links between economic theory and state power interests reflects the known extent to which the intellectual cleavage between Cameralist and liberal styles of thought was, most especially in the German case, far from a wholly radical or straightforward one (Tribe, 1984). His choice of terminology here may call to mind Meinecke's subsequent demonstration in *Die Idee der Staatsräson* (translation, 1957) of the continuity from the seventeenth to the twentieth centuries of German preoccupations with reason of state. Foucault pays tribute to Meinecke in the course of his own discussion of the close connections between the doctrines of reason of state and the science of police; he paraphrases these seventeenth-century theories as defining reason of state – most particularly in its economic aspects – as 'government in accordance with the State's strength'.

Weber is an heir to this tradition. But it is necessary to remember that he is also, in alliance with his brother Alfred, the vigorous polemical opponent *within* the discipline of *Nationalökonomie* of, in Roth's phrase, 'the state metaphysics of men like Gustav von Schmoller' (ES, p. lix). As Mommsen puts it, 'what Weber was really after was to put an end to the mixture of social science and conservative politics which was represented by Schmoller and his school, because social science of such a kind

303

favoured in its effects the existing semi-bureaucratic type of government in Germany' (1974, p. 93). There is no breach of continuity between the young Weber's view of reason of state as the pragmatic value-criterion of the discipline of political economy and the much later, less often cited caveat in the essay on value-freedom against the deification of the state as an eternally supreme and absolute value (MSS, p. 46). Reason of state is a criterion, not an ethos or an essence. The espousal of a reason of state in combination with a debunking attitude to the 'myth of the state' current in Wilhelmine Germany would appear, in turn, to be a point of view eminently consonant with Weber's insistence on a distinctly minimalist and nominalist characterization of the state's essential traits.

> All the way from provision of subsistence to the patronage of art, there is no conceivable end which *some* political association has not at some time pursued. And from the protection of personal security to the administration of justice, there is none which *all* have recognised.
>
> (ES, p. 55)

Schumpeter was arguing a similar thesis from a similar politico-theoretical standpoint at almost the same time in his essay 'The Crisis of the Tax State'. The very supposition of the existence of a 'state' prior to the early modern era is tendentious and anachronistic.

> We are accustomed to consider certain social functions as specific to the State and others as specifically 'private'. But there is no sharp and permanent frontier which defines in an unequivocal way what matters are the concern of the State: that in itself would be to presuppose the existence of the State. (Schumpeter, 1954, p. 11)

Foucault takes up the same theme in a slightly modified key in his lectures of 1978–9; he pleads guilty to the charge of neglecting the 'theory of the state', in so far as this activity involves a deduction of historical effects from characteristics deemed essential to the state. He justifies his abstention with two reasons. First, history is not a deductive science. Secondly, the state does not have an essence; in itself the state is nothing more than 'the mobile effect of a multiple regime of governmentality' (1984, p. 21).

Foucault then proceeds to argue that political problems concerning government and the state can in fact be more adequately analysed through an approach that eschews essentialist state-theorizing. It will be suggested below that a corresponding claim might be made, in a slightly different sense, on Weber's behalf. But Foucault's stance is in one important sense a rather less minimalist one than Weber might have been inclined to countenance, since it includes the positive proposition that the modern state is peculiarly characterized by its way of undertaking a rationalized government 'of all and of each': a practice that synthesizes and symbiotizes 'totalization' and 'individualization'.

Weber was certainly acquainted with such an idea of the state, and with its linkage to the heritage of the *Polizeistaat* and, more distantly, the tradition of Christian pastoral. In his own distinctive terms, but still unequivocally, he rejected it. Such is the implication, for example, of his refusal in the 'Intermediate Reflections' to accept the assimilation in a modern context of the 'objective pragmatism of reasons of state', which defines 'the whole course of the State's inner functions' with the technical perspective of 'all "social welfare policies"' (FMW, p. 334). 'Welfare' implies in Weber's view a commitment to criteria of substantive rationality – the appraisal of the substantive meaning of justice (or 'social justice') with respect to some unique, individual case or set of cases. This stands in contradiction to the principles of formal rationality 'without regard to the person', which Weber holds to be indispensable both to bureaucratic administration and to capitalism. The contrast between formal legal rationality and 'khadi justice' (the individualized, substantive-rationalistic evaluation of individual cases) is, of course, a major and recurring element in Weber's account of the distinctive conditions of Western economic development; his perception of a recrudescence of 'khadi justice' in the society of his own time involves, correspondingly, a premonition of the corruption or ossification of that Western dynamic (see Lash, Chapter 17).

This mobilization by Weber of his contrast between formal and substantive rationality arguably does more to dramatize than to elucidate the exact basis of his resolute refusal of the idea of an individualizing political rationality. Such a refusal has, admittedly, an honourable philosophical provenance. Foucault cites on this point the discussion in Plato's *Statesman* of the pastoral conception of kingship, or of government as the ruler's individualized care of each particular subject, a discussion concluded by the remark that only a god would be capable of governing thus. One might cite in the same vein Kant's dictum that 'Wohlfahrt hat kein Prinzip' ('welfare has no principle') – cannot, that is to say, be made into a formally valid maxim for the tasks of state (1956, p. 149).

Weber's detailed opinions on questions of welfare policy are in fact more complicated than some of his general animadversions might suggest. He endorses state accident and health insurance for workers, indeed criticizing the blinkered political calculations that limited the scope of the Bismarckian provisions in this field. Conversely, the formula he uses in conceding the essentially technical and uncontentious character of certain domains of such policy ('karitativ-polizeilicher Wohlfahrts- und Wirtschaftspflege') might almost have been chosen expressly so as to suggest the possibility of deep tacit reservations (WL, p. 153). Weber's is without question a historical sensibility acutely alert to the affinity of meanings of 'Welfare State' and 'police state' – and of the linkage of the latter's residue in the national character with servile–domineering traits of *Obrigkeit* and *Untertan*. 'Diesen Herren steckt eben die Polizei im Leibe' ('these gentlemen have police in their very bones') is a characteristically phrased Weberian sally against some authoritarian practices of German industrial management (GASS, p. 396).

I suggested earlier that Foucault's definition of government as 'conduct of conduct' might be taken as in tune with Weber's theme of *Lebensführung*. This notion must, evidently, now be heavily qualified by adding that Weber would have felt the strongest distrust of the idea of a rationality pertaining to the conduct of *others'* conduct. Indeed, if he did not make a specific study of the police state this may have been – over and above the other considerations that have already been canvassed here – because this would have amounted for him at most to a temporally bounded illustration of an absolutely universal motif of his world-historical vision; namely, the hazardous juxtaposition of certain Western attainments 'which we are pleased to think of as having a universal value' with the recurringly possible fate of either a 'domestication at the hands of the State' (FMW, p. 283) or a subjugation under the secular and pastoral powers of a religious authority. Such a dialectic is seen at work even in the golden era of the Protestant ethic.

> The ecclesiastical supervision of the life of the individual, which, as it was practised in the Calvinist State Churches, almost amounted to an inquisition, might even retard that liberation of individual powers which was conditioned by the rational ascetic pursuit of salvation, and in some cases actually did so. The mercantilistic regulations of the state might develop industries, but not, or certainly not alone, the spirit of capitalism; where they assumed such a despotic, authoritarian character, they to a large extent hindered it. Thus a similar effect might well have resulted from ecclesiastical regimentation when it became excessively despotic. (PESC, p. 152)

Part of Weber's account of the conditions of possibility of Western capitalism deals, of course, with the medieval stalemate between the separate and competing powers of the Western church and empire, whose effect was that neither institution achieved a fully 'Caesaropapist' or pastoral power over individual life. Foucault follows Weber here in signalling the permanent tension and disjunction in Western tradition between, on the one hand, the philosophy of government embodied in what Foucault calls 'pastoral power', and on the other hand what he calls the 'city game' of Athenian democratic politics, based on law, citizenship and the public space. This is as contrasted with Eastern, Orthodox culture, its fusion of state and church and its image of the Christly emperor. The difference here is, of course, that Foucault credits the modern state with the 'demonic' project of combining or superposing, within a wholly secularized polity, these two radically disparate frameworks of domination. For Weber, one might say that the central problem in social politics is the maintenance of collective conditions that nurture an active individual *Lebensführung*, while resisting the latter's subsumption into a rigid, pervasive, collective-pastoral supervision and *réglementation* of life. Foucault's approach cuts across Weber's here, but only in part; he insists on paying full due to the structural differences between the police and liberal styles of government, but insists equally that these two political epistemes share a common and fundamental interest in problematizing individual existence as a concern of state. And if one turns again in this light to Weber, one can perhaps recognize more clearly how all his work does indeed focus itself on the conduct and rationality of government, even when he is not expressly couching it in these terms. If Weber is not a noted theoretician of this topic, this may be because he is one of its most passionate and pragmatically committed exponents.

The 'Lateral Science' of Sociology and the Soul of the Citizen

One way to sharpen our understanding of this side of Weber's preoccupations is to draw upon some remarks of Foucault's about the transformation effected by classical political economy in the relationship between science and government. The 'science of police' is an archetypical example of the kind of discursive practice that Foucault termed a *savoir*, a knowledge that is also, and essentially, a 'know-how'. Economy and regulation are inseparable knowledge-objects here; in the police perspective, the knowledge of economy is identical with a know-how of administration. Political economy fractures this union. At the same time as it demonstrates the ineluctable finitude of the state's own means of knowledge concerning the processes of the economy, it also breaks in principle with the notion of an art of government that could deduce its particular actions from a science of the economy. For itself, political economy assumes the position, in Foucault's term, of a 'lateral knowledge', a body of principles that the state must needs take into account in evaluating the consequences of its own actions, but which cannot be made to serve as a universal axiomatic of policy. *Laissez-faire* is, after all, not an anodyne for every care of state; it may set limits to governmental duty, but it also leaves a profound and lasting uncertainty as to the exact criteria that will define those limits in practice.

Foucault suggests that a decisive factor in this epistemological reconfiguration is played by the introduction of a new concept of *interest*. Political economy is inspired, particularly in its quality as a reflection on the history and formation of civil society, by a new realization. This is that the population which mercantilist policy had hitherto addressed as the object of its power and knowledge is composed of individual subjects each of whom is also, to the confusion of mercantilist reasoning, a *subject of interest*. Individual subjects thus are agents governed by an autonomous rationality of preferences that are irreducible, non-transferable and – regarded from the totalizing vantage-point of state knowledge – inscrutable. It is, according to Foucault's hypothesis, the heterogeneity and incongruity of this rational texture of economic individuality with respect to the quite different logic of totalization characteristic of political jurisprudence that makes the idea of a total economic sovereignty henceforth untenable. At the same time, the 'lateral science' of the economy makes an important contribution to the resources of liberal government through its exploration of the needs and capabilities of a form of civil individuality, namely, that of the *homo economicus*, relative to which the state is obliged to relinquish all claim to direct mastery.

The conception of economic individuality subscribed to by the thinkers of the Scottish Enlightenment is, of course, by no means a reductive abstraction, but rather a theme interwoven in an extended fabric of moral, historical and political reflection on human nature and character. Some present-day commentators have regretted our subsequent loss of this dimension of connectedness of economic, sociological and philosophical discourses. Weber represents an important counter-example to this diagnosis, and indeed in this he is representative of a long-established trait of German *Nationalökonomie*. In its most general character the latter is an investigation of the socially oriented action of individuals, an extension of the economic 'point of view' to encompass a study of extra-economic conditions and dimensions of human action. No doubt it is also this special perspective that most clearly differentiates Weber's sociological project from that of a 'science of society'.[2]

Wilhelm Hennis's recent articles have placed emphasis on such a framework of Weberian problematization. Central here are the relationships between a system of formative and conditioning collective societal forces – the 'arena of normative and de facto powers' – and a focal object, the 'economy' (*die Wirtschaft*), which is also and at the same time perceived as *das Wirtschaften*, 'economic action'. As Hennis points out, this latter term, whose German connotations are somewhat palely rendered by its English translation, encapsulates the respect in which *Nationalökonomie* retains the older perspective of an *Ökonomik* (oeconomy), a 'philosophico-practical' doctrine on the conduct of the household, the individual domestic economy (Hennis, 1984, p. 34). When we read Weber's declarations on reason of state as the criterion of relevance of political economy, it may be worth recalling at the same time the connections between the older *Ökonomik* and Cameralism. As Pasquino has noted, the prince is sometimes characterized in the literature of *Polizei* as the *Wirt*, the husbandman-householder-entrepreneur of his *Wirtschaft*-state (Pasquino, 1982, p. 88). This notion accurately reflects both the blurred boundary between public sovereignty and private lordship (the position of the prince as literal proprietor of his territory and people) and the disconcerting mutation effected by this new economic government upon an older, theologically tinged tradition of pastoral power: the translation of shepherd into stock-rearer, of *Hirt* into *Wirt*.

But, finally, due appraisal of the pertinence of this heritage for an understanding of Weber must be accompanied by a clear recognition of Weber's emphatic antagonism to the worlds of pastoral and police alike. *His* treatment of *Wirtschaften* and 'the orders and powers of society' – or, following the equally expressive pairing of rubrics cited by Hennis, of *Persönlichkeit* and *Lebensordnungen*, personality and life orders – presents itself to the public field of governmental action and *raison d'état* not in the guise of a rational manual of collected *Lebensführung*. It presents itself rather, like that of the political economists, as a 'lateral science', a doctrine of necessary or probable conditions and consequences that reason of state must needs take into account in the course of its pragmatic choices of action or abstention from action.

This view of the practical pertinence of a sociology shapes Weber's discussion as a multi-levelled and multi-directional space of argument. On the one hand, Weber concerns himself, as in the East Prussian agrarian studies (whose practical recommendations are, of course, sited at the furthest remove from any simple version of *laissez-faire*), with transformations in structures of agriculture, landholding and population whose unchecked consequences Weber believes prejudicial, in terms of collective character and *Lebensführung*, to the political strength of the German nation. At the other extreme, but again with a particular emphasis on specifically German conditions, there are his analyses of the formation and deformation of the character of a national ruling class ('National Character and the Junkers'; 'Parliament and Government in a Reconstructed Germany'). What Weber himself calls in quotes a 'characterology' occupies a double role within these studies, first as a dimension of appraisal of the *effects of governmental action*, and secondly as a factor (mediated through an elaborate dialectic of collective attitudes and institutional dynamics) in the evaluation of the existing level within a given society of the *capacity to govern*. Hennis has an apt comment here on the distinctive bent of liberal thinking that Weber has in common with Tocqueville: 'What they are interested in is not so much "rights" and "freedoms" as the forms of moral constitution (*Seelenverfassung*) which correspond to them' (see above, p. 73).

Hennis draws our attention to another crucial indicator of Weber's thinking by noting his remarks on the different attitudes of Jacob Burckhardt and Anton Menger to the issues posed by the modern role of the press. Burckhardt expressed liberal disquiet about the influences upon individual conduct entailed in a public political mode of life like that of the Greek *polis*, which 'conditioned the whole existence of the Athenian citizen to its most intimate aspects'. This stands in contrast to the socialist publicist Menger's vision of the press in a future society as 'assuming the ancient role of the censor, dealing in its forum with matters that one cannot leave to the Courts'. Hennis recalls here 'the way in which the ancient institution of the censor moulded, publicly supervised, cautioned and disciplined the soul of the citizen which so fascinated Machiavelli, Rousseau and even de Tocqueville (1983, pp. 166–7). Behind Weber's own scientific reticence as to the direction of his own value-rational preference in this matter, Hennis guesses at a clear if qualified inclination towards Menger's position.

This suggestion makes a good deal of sense. It is indeed both appropriate and helpful to recognize the filiation of Weber's 'characterological' themes not only to the pre-liberal sources of *Nationalökonomie*, but also the Machiavellian *topos* of republican-civic virtue – as evidenced by Weber's evocation of the 'beautiful passage' in the *History of Florence* that praises 'those citizens who deemed the greatness of their native city higher than the salvation of their souls' (FMW, p. 126). No doubt it is here that the 'ethic of responsibility' comes closest to what might loosely be called a Weberian 'spirit of state', comparable to the 'spirit of capitalism'. Such an incipient analogy might be extended to cover Weber's perceptions of the paradoxical linkages between virtues of life-conduct and substantively irrational or even quasi-nihilistic motivations; consider the 'cold divine raison d'état' behind the world-ordering vocation of Calvinism. (ES, p. 1199). But the dilemma of 'censorship' can also be read as encapsulating the dual tension in Weber's social-political perspective which gives it its most durably suggestive value for present-day reflections on government.

In the first place, putting the point as baldly as possible, Weber is surely inclined, as Hennis supposes, towards the pursuit of active measures for the well-being of the 'soul of the citizen'. But he is equally insistent that such measures must not be permitted to assume the form of a hierocratic/ welfare/police system of totalized regimentation. Both in its form and, to a considerable extent, in its particular content, this problematic is by no means peculiar to Weber; on the contrary, it epitomizes a liberal problem of government that had been openly posed during much of the nineteenth century. It may be worth remembering that the above-cited evocation of the Roman censorship connotes, at least in its literal historical reference, a specific controlling agency distinct in its basis and personnel from the other offices of political rule. Weber, like so many liberals before him, is looking for forces, measures and processes located not within the institutions of the state but in the intermediary strata of the collectivity, which will be capable of shaping and propagating the kinds of economic and political citizenship appropriate to the conditions of an industrial society. And here, like so many other liberals, Weber finds his own way of at once respecting and transcending the governmental constraints implicit in the formal-rational principles of the administrative *Rechtsstaat*.

Disenchantment and Transitions to Modernity

The preceding pages have sought to elicit, sometimes perhaps against the apparent grain of the material, a pattern of contrasts and connections between Weber's work and Foucault's interest in governmental rationality. There now remain to be considered here some connections established through the subsequent impact of Weber's ideas, which may have a more easily demonstrable significance. But first it will be necessary to draw on the support of Foucault's arguments to set aside one outstanding obstacle to the appreciation of Weber's relevance for governmental thought in our own time. This latter problem concerns the proper understanding of what may be called the second major line of tension in Weber's world-view, the issue encapsulated in the formula: 'disenchantment of the world'. Wilhelm Hennis once again shows his sureness of intuition by the stress he lays on this point, but this time it will be necessary here to take issue with his conclusions.

Although Hennis is critical of suggestions by earlier commentators that *Entzauberung* (disenchantment) is the master-theme of Weber's work, the role that he himself assigns to it in his discussion of the topic of *Lebensführung* is a scarcely less crucial one. *Entzauberung* corresponds here to that historic threshold of modernity defined by Weber's analyses, beyond which the powers and guiding values of such analyses must themselves exhaust their explanatory pertinence. The society of bureaucracy and the market is characterized by the 'ethical uninterpretability of interpersonal social relations', the 'impossibility of ethical valorisation' of human relationships within the capitalist production process. The logical conclusion of this development is the liquidation of the ideas of 'calling' and the 'man of calling' whose delineation forms the ethical heart of Weber's sociology. Hennis sees Weber as finding himself consequently reduced to silence concerning the future and confined to the composition

311

of a Mahlerian 'farewell symphony' to the lost worlds of *Lebensführung* (Hennis, 1984, p. 26).

Hennis considers that the very meaning of this theme in Weber, and hence the essential meaning of all of his work, has been rendered inaccessible (except by way of a special effort of hermeneutical reconstruction) to the contemporary public. Such inaccessibility is here due to the effects of the moral and cultural catastrophes that divide us spiritually from Weber and the old European civilization whose dissolution Weber knowingly witnessed. The ethical connotations of Weber's theme, the possibility of a (strictly non-positivistic) cultural space of practico-philosophical, anthropological discourse, are untainted by the base technocratic philistinism of later sociological generations.

Perhaps Foucault might have been willing to subscribe to an only slightly amended variant of this conclusion, with the added proviso that a useful 'return' to Weber must require that we look in our own present for those unrecognized forms in which Weber's questions have, notwithstanding all disenchanted cultural criticism, themselves returned and renewed themselves, modifying in turn the questions that it is now most useful for us to pose to Weber.

But one might also guess that Foucault might, and with good reason, have questioned the adequacy of Hennis's propositions on the meaning of *Entzauberung* in Weber. For there are strong grounds for doubting whether Weber ever embraced the postulate of a general world-historical threshold separating a (traditional) universe of the ethical from a (modern) life without ethics or ethical meaning. One might more plausibly consider that Weber's most constant theme, unbroken by any of his confrontations with the vicissitudes of modernity, is the relation between the ethically meaningful and non-meaningful components of social action. Thus it can be seen, for example, in the research project on industrial labour that even economic phenomena that Weber may have regarded as devoid of ethical meaning in themselves aroused his intense interest with regard to their possible ethical *consequences*. Elsewhere, and even more obviously, it can be noted that the supposed disappearance from the modern world of the man of calling admits of exceptions in respect of at least two callings of major interest to Weber, namely, those of science and politics, not to mention his supplementary vignette of the vocation of journalism.

Much has been made of Weber's intense empathetic feeling for the distresses provoked by the rationalization of life, sometimes rather to the neglect of his own considered responses to these challenges. There seems in general to be little basis for attributing to Weber the belief that the disenchantment of the world was a threshold of mutation that could be negotiated only at the price of unbearable moral sacrifices. What he appears to have wanted to convey was rather that different societies arrive

at that threshold – for reasons which his sociology undertakes to elucidate
– endowed with very variable levels of capability for negotiating it
successfully. It may be more dramatically satisfying to read Weber's
diagnoses of the German condition as universal cultural prophecies, the
cruel particularity of his observations on the German character being
hardly more generally palatable today than at the time of their writing;
but this reading can impose a heavy cost in mystification. The Nietzschean 'last men' lost in Parsons's translation of *The Protestant Ethic* ('this
nullity imagines it has attained a level of civilization never before
achieved') are, as in Nietzsche, first and foremost Germans. The edge of
Weber's criticism is turned not so much against the process of *Entzauberung* as such, as against the spurious and immature compensations for
Entzauberung resorted to by his fellow Germans: the mass reproduction of
the 'parvenu aristocratic' Junker personality, the eclectic epidemic of
private quests for *Erlebnis*. To deprive Weber's most immediate political
prescriptions and forebodings of their specific historical and national
context not only makes them easy game for polemical distortion, it also
does injustice to the general and durable capabilities of Weber's sociology
as a diagnostic tool. The German catastrophe certainly does not signal the
end of that sociology's viable life-span. In its largest sense, Weber's whole
approach assumes, on the contrary, the continuing temporal and regional
variability of sociological problems.

This assessment is complicated and ironically nuanced, but not radically shaken, when one turns to consider the intriguing and perhaps
inadequately studied history since Weber's own time of such vital terms in
his writings as 'life-style' (*Lebensstil*) and 'way of life' (*Lebensführung*).
Doubtless there have been phenomena of semantic banalization at work
here, which a critical theory might dwell on in melancholy, aristocratic
sarcasm. But there is also the kind of banality that attests simply to an
idea's historical success, its achieved status as a 'key-word' – 'way of life':
Western or Eastern, democratic or socialist, a motif in the theme-tune of
every aspiring world power since 1945; 'life-style': the rubric for the
cultural-commercial self-affirmation of societies of mass consumption.
Weber's Left critics went to sometimes ruthless lengths in the 1950s and
1960s to construct bridgeworks of complicity between Weber's ethics and
politics and the advent of the Third Reich. One cannot now but wonder
whether this enterprise may not have been a kind of metonymic substitute
for the recognition of a far more plausible continuity, namely, that
between Weberian ideas and the contemporary political ethos of the
Federal Republic within which these critics were writing. Perhaps
Weber's notional culpability before the fact of Nazism was only a kind of
displaced token for a deeper, never adequately reflected awareness of a
Weberian affiliation at the heart of the post war German democracy. It is,

at any rate, curious how little attention has so far been paid in the newer secondary literature to the presence of a demonstrable input from Weberian sources during the founding stages of the Federal Republic.

Weberian Neo-Liberalism

Foucault discusses, in his lectures on neo-liberal government, a group of German jurists and economists who after 1945 became known as the *Ordoliberalen*, through their common association with the journal *Ordo*: Wilhelm Röpke, Walter Eucken, Franz Böhm, Alexander Rüstow, Alfred Müller-Armack.[3] Some of its members had been taught by Alfred Weber; Müller-Armack concerned himself, as we have seen, with an explicit attempt to extend Max Weber's work. The ideas of the *Ordoliberalen* provided much of the intellectual basis for the social market principles of the post war West German polity. The core of their philosophy might be described as a vigorous revival of the Weberian theme of *das Wirtschaften* in its wide sense as glossed by Hennis. The schema of *enterprise* is presented as a model not only for the conduct of economic activity, but for the totality of human action. Individual citizens should be the entrepreneurs of themselves and their lives; individual life should be structured as a cluster of enterprises, both economic and non-economic. Rüstow describes his programme in pursuit of this goal as *Vitalpolitik* ('vital policy') and defines the inner principle of liberal democracy as *eine menschenwürdige Lebensführung* ('a conduct of life worthy of human beings') (Rüstow, 1963, pp. 36, 82). The economic market, as the space of freedom for the competitive game of enterprise, provides an acceptable rationale for the regeneration of the state as its promoter and curator: an engine of prosperity that, at the same time and *ipso facto*, recreates political order and legitimacy out of the vacuum of national destruction.

Foucault makes two interesting comments on the *Ordoliberalen*. One is to note the constructivist, anti-naturalist tenor of their thinking. The market is seen as an autonomous but not a self-sustaining order. Activist, inventive policies are called for to preserve it, and this task is to constitute the basic rationality of governmental action. His second remark concerns the anti-fatalistic character of this neo-liberalism, a version of Weberianism notably devoid of the cultural pessimism that many commentators have perceived in the Weberian theme of *Entzauberung*. Foucault presents the *Ordoliberalen* as vehement opponents of the thesis that he attributes primarily to Sombart, that the moral emptiness and disorientation of modern mass societies are a direct consequence of the liberal economic system. These phenomena are, they contend, the effects rather of the anti-liberal policies successively practised by every political regime in modern Germany.

In his book *The Social Crisis of the Present*, written in Swiss exile and published there in 1942, Wilhelm Röpke wrote: 'the author felt impelled to make a desperate effort in spiritual orientation'. These ethical and sometimes religious overtones in German neo-liberalism should not be dismissed out of hand as the philosophical window-dressing of an anti-communist restoration. More is involved, in any case, in assessing its implications than an evaluation by Weberian or other standards of the moral ambiance of Adenauer's republic. What Foucault's analysis tends to confirm is, first, that there is a real continuity of style and conviction between Weber's thought and that of the *Ordoliberalen*, and secondly that ideas such as theirs have shown a real innovative capability in the post war era, which is reflected at least to some extent in the emergence of a new collective *Lebensstil*.

These influences are legible in the governmental styles that have recently come to predominate in several Western societies: the propounding by governments to their citizens of a new ethos of responsibility, and the promotion of an 'enterprise culture' as a new model for social and economic citizenship. The political initiatives involved in these developments come largely (but not exclusively) from the Centre and Right. The same is not necessarily the case for the corresponding underlying forces of social change. The politicization of aspects of personal existence, the demand for respect or support by the state for increased demands for personal autonomy, tendencies without which neo-liberal policies could of themselves have achieved little impact, have inspired the major innovative currents in Left politics since 1968. Foucault himself has been in many ways their most representative thinker. But Foucault also suggested in 1979 that these developments had not been accompanied by an adequate reflection within the Left on the principles of a specifically socialist rationality of government, that – notwithstanding socialism's other intellectual accomplishments – there is not now and never has been such a rationality. In later years he offered a few suggestions about how this situation might be changed, by looking for ways of renewing the Welfare State that would add to its provision of basic forms of material security an equal provision of the means of individual autonomy (Burchell *et al.*, 1986; Gordon, 1986).

Both this diagnosis and this suggestion, as far as they go, may now meet with increasing agreement. In a broad sense, the political interest of Foucault's ideas about the topic of governmental rationality is the help they may offer, in the context of today's problems, towards satisfying Weber's demand for the reconciliation of an ethic of ultimate ends with an ethic of responsibility. To confront these ideas with Weber's may, as this chapter has tried to suggest, teach us something new both about Weber and about ourselves.

Notes

1 Foucault was never able to work the material of these courses into an extended version for publication. A few fragments have appeared (1979b; 1981a; 1982; 1984). On Cameralism, see also Pasquino (1978; 1982) and Tribe (1984). The latter two contain guides to the literature; important complementary material may be found in Brunner (1968) and Oestreich (1983). More generally Burchell *et al.* (1986) provide a survey and selection of related work by Foucault and others. Until shortly before his death Foucault was engaged in plans for further collective work on governmental rationalities (Gandall and Kotkin, 1985).
2 The idea of extended economics, or a generalized application to human behaviour of an 'economic approach', can be pursued in very different directions. These differences continue to structure the field of argument within which Weberian themes are debated today. Consider the distance between the projects of Gary C. Becker, on the one hand, and Albert O. Hirschman or Amartya Sen on the other. Foucault points out the marked differences between the German neo-liberalism of the *Ordoliberalen* and the United States neo-liberalism of the Chicago School; these are perhaps not without some analogy to the conflicts of Weber's time between Schmoller and the Austrian School.
3 These points are taken from Foucault's lectures of 29 March 1979 and 4 April 1979.

15

Charisma and Twentieth-Century Politics

LUCIANO CAVALLI

The Paradigm of the Charismatic Process

In *The Protestant Ethic and the Spirit of Capitalism* (1905) 'charisma' appears only once, and in the traditional Christian sense.[1] Weber's theoretical re-elaboration of the concept belongs to the second decade of the century. He developed the concept of 'charisma' as part of the framework of concepts and rules that make up his *verstehende Soziologie*: an instrument for the rational comprehension of phenomena having their roots in irrationality and emotionality. Weber recognized that his work was facilitated by the research on Christian charisma developed separately by Sohm and by Holl. In Weber's elaboration, though, one can see the influence of an important stream of Western thought, which gives exceptional men a primary role in historical development (conceived by him as being without a telos). By the use of 'charisma' Weber likewise gave a primary role to the Jewish prophets. He attributed to charismatic leaders the power to produce the most important change – that taking place *in interiore homine* (*metanoia*).

In discussing charismatic domination, Weber maintained that it was characterized by obedience to a leader charismatically qualified and, because of him, to an order revealed or created by him. Weber sketched two possible definitions of charisma. One of them, quite famous, is appropriate for the study of charismatic domination.

By 'charisma' is meant a quality of a personality which is esteemed as extraordinary (in origin . . . as magically determined), and because of which [its bearer] is considered [to be endowed] with supernatural or superhuman or at least extraordinary – not given to every man – powers or properties, or as God-sent or exemplary, and thence as 'the Leader'. How the quality in question should be evaluated in an

317

'objectively' correct way from any ethical, aesthetic or other point of view whatsoever, is naturally entirely irrelevant here.

(WuG, p. 140)

This definition and other considerations should enable us to grasp a certain type of leader–follower relationship and its peculiar dynamics in any social and historical context. Given its sketchy and unfinished character, however, this definition is not always interpreted in the same way.[2] Misunderstandings can easily arise.

The basic definition of charisma seems also to contain a *non sequitur*. It is hard to see why the possession of a given quality may induce those who consider it extraordinary, and who therefore link its bearer to the dimension of the extraordinary, to acclaim this same man as their leader. Nor is it clear why the chosen one should accept it and behave as a leader. Weber made up for these shortcomings by the introduction of two concepts, 'extraordinary situation' and 'mission', by which he analysed the sociological process connecting leader and followers. At the start of this process is placed an 'extraordinary situation'. This is frequently of an economic or political nature, but may very well be a spiritual, especially a religious situation. In such a critical situation a man with an 'extra-ordinary quality' offers both an explanation for it and a way out of it, on the condition that men follow a certain behaviour. We can deduce this from the theoretical pages of *Economy and Society* and from the only research Weber dedicated largely to charisma, that is, *Ancient Judaism*. From both works we learn also that the charismatic leader is driven by a sense of 'mission'. Indeed charisma 'constitutes a "calling" ('*Beruf*') in the emphatic sense of the word: a "mission" or an "inner duty"' (WuG, p. 142).

Both works state that possession of charisma is normally bound up with extraordinary and even pathological experiences. As to the quality evaluated as 'extraordinary', this may be of various kinds. But in *Ancient Judaism* and in 'Politics as a Vocation' Weber underscored the leader's passion for the 'cause' ('mission'), be it the cause of Yahweh or the political cause of a contemporary statesman. At times the leader's passionate dedication to his cause seems to be not only the condition of any historical accomplishment, as Hegel too believed, but also the inner strength that shines out as an 'extraordinary quality' of a personality. To become an effective leader, anyway, one has to possess specific qualities (*Führereigenschaften*), which Weber seems to consider innate.

There is no complete discussion of mass phenomena by Weber, because the charismatic process is for him simply the natural development of the vertical relationship between charismatic leader and followers. As a consequence, Weber does not systematically analyse the horizontal relationships between group members, as Freud does by means of the concept of identification. In particular, Weber's remarks on the beginning of the charismatic process – a key moment – are too hasty and even unclear. He seems to suggest that the 'extraordinary situation' determines a state of 'necessity' and 'excitement', which reminds us a little of Durkheim's 'effervescence'. As the charismatic leader enters the scene, 'hope' grows, for which he quickly becomes the embodiment, and thence 'enthusiasm', the Dionysian force active in revolutionary change.

Weber indicates a number of directions in the subsequent development of the charismatic process. Therefore we need to construct a paradigm of that process. The concept of charisma, even when elucidated and integrated, cannot suffice for empirical research. In order to decide whether a given historical fact is of a charismatic nature and might therefore be fruitfully analysed by means of the conceptual instruments shaped by Weber and his followers, one must first confront that fact with the paradigm of the charismatic process. Its construction is therefore both an important and a difficult task. Were we to adopt some secondary elements from Weber's work, erroneous conclusions would be drawn from the historical fact under consideration, and the matter is even worse if we adopt one or two of those elements as exclusive criteria.

In other writings I have developed a paradigm of elements, corresponding in my opinion to the crucial moments in the dialectics of the charismatic process, from its beginning to its end. The paradigm in its shortened form is as follows: (1) extraordinary situation; (2) 'calling' of the potential leader and his request for obedience from the potential following; (3) acknowledgement by the following and its request for a confirmation; (4) confirmation shown by the success of the leader and an act of commitment of the following; (5) structuring of the following as a leader-centred community or movement, with a leader-dependent élite ('charismatic aristocracy'); (6) the leader as the principal source of values and norms; (7) change of mind of the leader-centred group, manifest in new feelings and attitudes (feeling of togetherness, self-confidence, activism and pugnacity in the case of a movement); (8) maximum individual and collective effort for the 'cause', with positive results; (9) in the case of repeated lack of success, repudiation of the leader and possible disintegration of the following; (10) leader's death followed by succession (either the institutionalization of charisma or the disintegration of the following); (11) a new personal charisma arises in a dialectical relationship with institutionalized charisma as and when an extraordinary situation confronts it.

This paradigm is of the same nature as an ideal type. Except in a few historical cases, one should not expect to find most of these moments developed. Some are characteristically absent in Weber's own account of

319

the Jewish prophets. Moreover, according to Weber's forecasts, not all of them can develop in our rationalized society.

In studying contemporary democratic society, then, it would seem reasonable to wonder whether some moments of the charismatic process offer criteria especially relevant for empirical research. The answer is affirmative, but the choice must be far more accurate than it has generally been. For example, in a democracy the leader will not be the 'source of law' in Weber's radical sense. *Metanoia* is an overstatement of what may really happen. Religious overtones are fairly improbable.

What therefore are the minimum criteria of an initial approach that would allow us to decide the feasibility of a further investigation applying Weberian concepts, and also to decide whether a leadership qualifies as a special type demanding separate consideration? I think that such criteria are offered by the developments that occur respectively between points (3) and (4) and between (7) and (8) in the paradigm. The first development is that of the increasing 'personal trust' (this lay term is repeatedly suggested by Weber himself) accorded by the followers to the man of 'extraordinary quality' who exacts obedience. The second is the growth of the leader's psychological influence over the personality and behaviour of his followers – a development that in our rationalized society may manifest itself in already existing mass formations, such as an organized party or what we call public opinion, without a charismatic movement coming effectively into being. As already stated, this second development becomes observable through the externalization of the feeling of togetherness, self-confidence, etc., on the one hand, and positive endeavour for the 'cause', on the other. For the researcher it is important that both 'personal trust' and the psychological influence of the leader can be empirically established and even measured. For instance, the British war polls, which constantly showed a very high degree of consent for Churchill's leadership, may be considered relevant for establishing and measuring the degree of 'personal trust', though they allow no conclusive statements.

To admit the limited and lay character of charismatic phenomena in a rationalized society and the subsequent search for basic criteria in an initial analysis may, perhaps, arouse some radical doubts about using the concept of charisma in democratic politics. Do the criteria that may be drawn from the paradigm really distinguish charismatic leadership from other forms, or do they simply help to distinguish between high and low levels of the unique and ubiquitous phenomenon of leadership? A leader of high quality cannot lack a sense of being almost indispensable in a major crisis. Moreover, such a leader will soon arouse public feelings of 'personal trust', especially if he has already been 'tested' in previous moments of public difficulty. Further, it is quite understandable that public 'trust' in him as a leader affects his people's attitudes and work.

Weber's answer to these objections is that, where leadership exists, there is also charisma. Two further considerations may be added. To begin with, any leadership that demonstrably satisfies the principal criteria established by the paradigm is *re ipsa* different from ordinary leadership, and therefore it must be classified and studied separately. From this point of view the label 'charismatic' possesses both a practical and an historical justification. Secondly and more importantly, both the paradigm and the criteria derived from it have (so far) been advanced as a means to establish the feasibility of further research along the same theoretical line. Further research may reveal and explain other relevant aspects of a leadership and their dialectical relationships, which otherwise would probably have escaped scientific inquiry. Continuous reference to the paradigm may help to discover a narrow group of intimate collaborators of the leader, who might be described in Weber's words as mere instruments and 'emissaries', bound to their chief by devotion 'almost of a religious character', as one of Clemenceau's men once said; a group often of the greatest importance for the leader's success. In addition, I believe that the historical relevance of leader and following can be insufficiently appreciated by those who choose to ignore the paradigm of the charismatic process.

The concept of charisma and the paradigm I have presented carry no implication of value. They do not even allow a judgement of historical efficacy. If we want Weberian criteria for this, we must turn to 'Politics as a Vocation' (FMW, p. 103). In this lecture Weber outlines what qualities a leader with a 'calling' for politics needs to possess, in order to leave a positive imprint on historical development. He must be able to place at the service of his 'cause': passion, a sense of responsibility, far-sightedness (implying a distance from men, from events and also from himself) and power-instinct (*Machtinstinkt*). He also needs to be capable of striking a balance between an ethic of ultimate ends (*Gesinnungsethik*) and an ethic of historical responsibility (*Verantwortungsethik*); this balance also applies in the choice of means. Weber, therefore, gives pride of place to a leader's ethical and cultural qualities, in a double sense. The leader must be the true bearer and interpreter of the mature culture of his people. He must be capable of decisions based on a cultivated and specifically 'noble' reflection on history. On the basis of such criteria we must pass both political and ethical judgements on historical cases. Through them, for instance, one can immediately discern the negative characteristics, and from these it can be seen how the 'corporal dictators' of Italy and Germany followed the ways of crime and failure to the very end.

The Conditions of the Charismatic Process

Any attempt to apply the concept of charisma and the related paradigm to twentieth-century historical cases must be preceded, I believe, by some further thoughts on the 'extraordinary situation' and on the cultural and psychological prerequisities of a charismatic process.

(1)   The extraordinary situation is the point of departure for the charismatic process, and from all the references in Weber's work we gather that the situation is extraordinary from the viewpoint of the people involved in it. This is in perfect accord with the basic and constitutive principle of his interpretive sociology. In order to develop this point, though, I shall turn to the sociological contributions of Durkheim and especially of Parsons (Parsons 1949; 1951). The latter suggests that an extraordinary situation implies the pre-existence of an ordinary situation with an important group dimension. Ordinary may mean only: in accord with culturally established expectations of the people involved. On the contrary, extraordinary must mean, primarily, that such an agreement failed because of endogenous or exogenous factors, or a continuation of both. But it must also mean that the people involved are not able to re-establish a balance between the situation and expectations by the use of available cultural means. This job is then undertaken as a mission by a man of extraordinary quality. Irrespective of the merits of his project for a new balance (or order), the project could be neither understood nor accepted by the other people involved were it not formulated in terms of a common culture with specific reference to disappointed expectations. As I have said, this theoretical development is suggested by other authors, and it is also implied in Weber's pages on charisma, especially in *Ancient Judaism*. In this regard one should examine his study of the general conditions that made possible the appearance of the Jewish prophets or of Jesus on the Palestinian scene and exercised such a tremendous sway over the people. Weber's analysis makes it perfectly plain that the messages of these bearers of charisma had been given shape by the Jewish culture over decades, even centuries, and that they were anchored in established values.

A consideration of Durkheim, Parsons and Mannheim also suggests an interesting point of view on the extraordinary situation. These authors underscore that society and personality are integrated on the basis of common values and norms. Social integration goes hand in hand with personality integration, and vice versa. This is true also for collective formations inside a society. As a consequence one must expect an extraordinary situation to be characterized by disintegration at both the social and personal level. Conversely one must expect a charismatic leader in such a situation of crisis to be a man who seems to know how to

322

confront this double task. It also becomes easier to understand how an extraordinary situation may be felt so dramatically by the people involved, and how a charismatic process begins.

In principle we should now inquire whether such situations can arise in our century, but the answer appears to be obvious. Few centuries have seen changes more deep and rapid, often involving a drastic break with the past. These changes upset cultural expectations tied to vital needs, and so introduced elements of suffering and despair into the life of the contemporary masses. From such situations sprang movements and regimes to which we can apply our paradigm with success, such as the Soviet regime in Russia, the Fascist regime in Italy and the Nazi regime in Germany. In the second part of the twentieth century the Western world has not had to pass through such experiences again. In some countries, however, extraordinary situations of a political nature arose, determining the fall of the existing regime: the main case is France in 1958, where change took place with a charismatic leader, de Gaulle, at the helm.

(2)   As to the cultural prerequisites, Weber was naturally well aware of the long and ingrained charismatic tradition of the West, rooted mainly in the Judaeo-Christian religion. Nevertheless he thought that cultural conditions favourable to charismatic phenomena were dying out, and therefore those phenomena too were going to become less and less important in our era. Western rationalization was specifically responsible for that, because it gave men the conscience, or the faith, that it was sufficient to *will* in order to *be able* to know all the conditions that exercise an influence over our lives, and therefore 'no mysterious forces operated that could escape' rational analysis (FMW, p. 139). The first victim had to be religion, which was the basis for the Western charismatic tradition. But the eclipse of the 'extraordinary' dimension was a *direct* and perhaps mortal threat to charisma itself.

However, Weber's forecasts make sense only if seen over many decades. In particular, rationalization damaged traditional religions only to the advantage of secular religions, at least for a time. Weber himself had begun to analyse the growth of nationalism as a secular religion. He had gone even further in his reflection on the secularization (an aspect of rationalization) of the industrial proletariat. He remarked that among the workers traditional religion was substituted by a *Weltanschauung* giving hope of a new life in *this* world. Moreover he disclosed the need of proletarians both to think of themselves as the collective bearers of a universal 'mission' of salvation and to entrust this mission *de facto* to a 'saviour', because they were aware of their own collective inadequacy. Weber therefore came very close to conceiving of Marxism–Leninism as a popular secular religion. Weber's analysis of rationalization even gave

323

him the conceptual instruments to foresee the success of this new religion as being dependent on its paying formal homage to rationalization. Nevertheless he failed to grasp the relevance of this cultural change in the masses, and the opportunities it would give to charismatic leaders and processes. The same can be said of Weber's insight into nationalism, which *might* have helped him to anticipate the formation of totalitarian nationalist (or racist) movements and regimes. This development will be discussed below, taking the case study of Hitler and using Weberian conceptual instruments.

In recent years secularization has attacked secular religions too. Today Weber's forecasts make more sense than they did for decades after his death. But other changes make charismatic phenomena possible in a relatively weak and lay form, as is shown by the study of plebiscitary democracy (in the restricted sense I define below).

(3) With regard to psychological prerequisites, the point of departure must be, I believe, Weber's reiterated statement that the masses are 'irrational' and 'emotional'. For Weber this fact plays an important historical role, especially for the origin of the charismatic process. With the development of Western rationalization these psychological traits remain unchanged. Borrowing from Weber, one might say that rationalization for the masses is only a light mantle that can easily be thrown off. Its material attainments are enjoyed by most people without true understanding. Its ideal ambitions have no root in the soul of common man. According to Weber, in the excitement of an extraordinary situation of crisis the masses will throw off that mantle and reveal their true nature. It is only in this sense that we can speak of 'regression', with implications for the common man that are more radical than in the work of the best known psychologists who were dealing with collective phenomena at the same time, such as Le Bon and Freud. Indeed, Weber had made his own the two models of 'suggestion' elaborated by Hellpach; these he radicalized, as one can see from the examples he gives in *Economy and Society* (p. 322). These instruments served in particular to explain *metanoia*, or change of mind.

The important point is that regression is due to the extraordinary situation. The growth of irrationality and emotionality is due to a state of disorder or, in current sociological language, 'disintegration', involving both society and personality. Values and social norms appear inadequate, contradictory, ineffective, or their disregard by others is felt to be an intolerable offence. Common men become very emotional about this, but they cannot bring about a satisfactory new order, of 'integration'. Indeed they are now like monads which, having lost their harmony, can receive it back only from outside. In Weber's work the charismatic leader

324

plays this demiurgic role. I believe that this idea must be remembered in order to truly understand charismatic phenomena.

According to Weber, the charismatic leader brings about a new order, a new social and personal integration. In principle, he lifts people from a state of regression towards the dimension of the extraordinary and the divine, from where true values and norms guide both individual and social life, so endowing them with complete meaning. This is the reason for Weber's statement that the charismatic leader embodies hope, kindles dedication and enthusiasm, making men capable of their utmost efforts for the 'cause'. One aspect of the behaviour of the followers can be better explained in Freudian terms. The charismatic leader reconciles the ego and the ideal of the ego, which is felt by the individual as *the* feast of his life. Nor should we forget the extraordinary fascination of the adventure in what is 'unprecedented and new' – a feeling that charisma arouses by its irruption into the extraordinary situation at the *statu nascenti* of the future.

For Weber charisma is therefore a very positive force in the individual and social life, at least in principle. But, as history shows, there are many potential dangers of degeneration. The main one, perhaps, derives from the fact that a full charismatic leader is also the source of law, in a sense that includes the moral principles as well. He sets his followers free from any sense of guilt towards old laws and principles that he has discarded, and gives them new laws and principles, arousing a sense of obligation and of moral duty towards them. Therefore the charismatic leader bears a very great, sometimes a *total*, responsibility, which may equally serve good or evil. The danger for his followers and for humanity at large becomes tragic reality if the leader cannot balance an ethic of responsibility with one of conviction. This is not a problem of another era, that of religion and magic, but of our own time, as the case of Hitler has shown.

Charisma and its attendant problems are *always* present at least in a dormant state, even though this is largely in contrast with the outspoken forecasts of Weber that we have mentioned. Indeed extraordinary situations cannot be excluded from life and history. Only those ideologies that idolize progress can promise that. And the existential condition of man, besides and behind his psychological nature, always governs afresh the appeal of charisma to the masses.

Totalitarian Dictatorships

Following this critical reconstruction of Weber's thought it is now possible to apply the concept of charisma and its related paradigm to certain political phenomena of the twentieth century: namely, totalitarian dictatorships and plebiscitary democracy. Some Weberians would probably maintain that it is not permissible to divide the two types of regime, and that, following Weber, one should label them jointly as 'plebiscitary democracy', or perhaps as *Führer-Demokratie*. As a sociological type, plebiscitary democracy is founded on the idea of an explicit or implicit plebiscite as its 'specific means for deriving the legitimacy of domination from the trust of the masses'. Weber adds: '"Plebiscitary democracy" – the most important type of leadership democracy (*Führer-Demokratie*) – is, in its true meaning, a sort of charismatic domination which conceals itself under the form of a legitimacy supposedly deriving from the will of the governed and sustained by them only' (ES, pp. 266–7; WuG, p. 156).

In my opinion, though, a basic criterion for distinguishing the two is offered by the quality of the 'acknowledgement' given by the masses. I suggest that we speak of plebiscitary democracy when there is a free dialectic between leader's performance (success, in cultural terms) and acknowledgement (personal trust). This, for instance, was the case in de Gaulle's France, where free voting in elections and plebiscites proved the personal trust of the people in the General again and again. He left when this ceased. The manipulated vote in the plebiscites that gave power to the two Bonapartes or to Hitler, on the other hand, were not a free acknowledgement, and afterwards free elections and the conditions they require were not granted any more to the people. For these cases we can speak more properly of dictatorship and tyranny, and also of 'charismatic tyranny', when there is a relevant correspondence between an historical case and our paradigm. It is worth remembering that Weber himself in 'Politics as a Vocation' spoke of plebiscitary democracy in the sense suggested here, implicitly accepting its difference from dictatorship and tyranny.

As to modern tyranny (totalitarian dictatorship), it seems to me that the usefulness of the concept of charisma and the related paradigm can be tested, especially, in the case of Hitler (Cavalli, 1982). First, let us say that the work of Nolte (1963), Jäckel (1969) and others has demonstrated that Hitler developed a *Weltanschauung* of such consequentiality that it 'takes one's breath away' (Nolte, 1963, p. 55): a chiliastic and messianic vision of the world whose central proposition was the concept of a godlike Nature that had supposedly entrusted Hitler and his people with the mission of fulfilling its designs and, by so doing, of saving humanity. Such a *Weltanschauung* goes a long way to explaining the inner strength of the dictator, his fascination, his historical project and what he did in order to accomplish it. It must be considered a necessary condition for the strict applicability of the paradigm to the case of Hitler.

The *political* history of Hitler begins with the German defeat of 1918, which he considered an utter tragedy. The ecstatic 'vision' of Pasewalk, where a Hitler temporarily sightless had been hospitalized, constitutes the extraordinary experience that gives shape and credibility to the mission of saving Great Mother Germany. From that moment on Hitler's story unfolds according to the paradigm.

The relationship between Hitler and the Nazi Party is characterized by his evident vocation for leadership, ever since his first appearance at a meeting in September 1919. The surrender of the old party rulers and the grant to Hitler of the presidency of the party along with dictatorial powers in July 1921 are but the formal acknowledgement of a 'called' leader, to whom complete obedience is due. Hitler becomes the unquestioned Führer and the source of norms and decisions binding all party members. He is surrounded and served by a party élite that derives its authority from him alone. After the failed 1923 *putsch*, Hitler is revered and served by dedicated followers, such as Hess, in the fortress of Landsberg. Released after one year, Hitler takes control of his weakened and divided party. He rebuilds it. His re-established position of supreme *Führer* is recognized and formalized with the *Führertagung* of Bamberg and the party congress in the spring of 1926. Indeed party opposition to Hitler was never great, neither before nor after 1926. As Nyomarkay remarks, members of the opposition usually seemed to contend among themselves for Hitler's favour, rather than to endeavour to overthrow him (1967, p. 36).

It is noteworthy how Hitler exercised a sort of fascination over his followers and also over casual and, at times, biased listeners, such as those gathered in the *Bürgerbraukeller* at the beginning of the 1923 *putsch*. The assembly's sudden change of mind and its emotional adherence to Hitler's programme, after a short speech of his, help us to recognize the basic cultural condition of the Führer's oratorical spell. He voiced with absolute conviction and great strength the central values and hopes of a large part of the German people. Those values, embedded in most Germans hearts, had been firstly exalted in war, then offended and humiliated by defeat. They were the living root of strong mixed feelings, with a dominant desire for revenge and redemption. By speaking with so much love of Great Mother Germany and with such faith in revenge and redemption, he had perforce to become irresistible. To adapt Hegel's thought, we could say that Hitler's listeners, aroused by patriotic emotion in the *Bürgerbraükeller*, 'felt a power within them that is stronger than they are' and hence 'they followed' him (Hegel, 1980, p. 84–5).

The charismatic personality of Hitler together with the worsening economic crisis helps to explain the mass vote obtained by the Nazi Party and the absolute power enjoyed by Hitler, as German Chancellor, after January 1933. Again Hitler's role in the state and the relationship between the Führer, the élite and the masses continued to develop in strict conformity with the paradigm, notwithstanding the relatively high level of 'modernity' (or civilizational level attained by rationalization) already reached by the German people. Hitler was the 'supreme guide' (Neumann, 1944, p. 71), plenipotentiary, 'the sole representative of his people' (Bracher, 1973, p. 424), in the words of well-known German scholars. 'He exercised jointly the functions of supreme lawgiver, ruler and judge, leader of the party, of the army and of the people' (Neumann, 1944, p. 74). 'He could follow official norms, but he did not have to, because the will of the leadership, regardless of the form in which it is expressed . . . makes for right and changes hitherto valid laws' (Bracher, 1973, p. 425). No authority could confront his. 'There was no stable hierarchy in the party and in the state' (Haffner, 1978, p. 78). 'Nothing existed, but the Führer and his emissaries at the various levels of the system of domination' (Jäckel, 1969, p. 107). 'He could delegate power to aides, but they were and remained his unconditional subjects. He was always in complete control of the orders that they enforced' (Bracher, 1973, p. 426). The relationship between Hitler and his collaborators, even the most eminent ones such as Goering, was a relationship of absolute and at times cruel domination. To these people one can very well apply Weber's concept of *Entseelung*, in its full sense. At the same time the direct relationship between Hitler and masses developed in huge meetings characterized by the almost hypnotic spell of the Führer and by the total enraptured abandon of the masses, which amazed and puzzled detached observers. That mass attitude even verged on religious worship. The appellative 'Redemptor' sometimes applied to him can be taken as representative of this tendency to elevate the Führer and his mission to the dimensions of the extraordinary, that is, of the divine. All this corresponded with Hitler's psychological hold over the German masses, carrying with it more than temporary change of common values and attitudes, which is in accordance with our paradigm.

Obviously these developments in Germany also depended on the unscrupulous conduct of Hitler and his men, who resorted to violence, manipulation and tricks of all sorts. The legal base for Hitler's absolute rule, namely the Enabling Act of 23 March 1933, was voted in by the duped parliamentary representatives of the Catholic centre party. Because of this, the Nazis were able to destroy all democratic parties and trade unions, and to gain control over the media. The country fell into their totalitarian grasp. President Hindenburg's death allowed Hitler to unite in his hands all the powers of President, Chancellor and Supreme Commander of the *Wehrmacht*, who swore an oath of allegiance to his person. This constitutional revolution was approved by 90 per cent of the population. Coercion and manipulation had their part in that result, but reliable observers testify to widespread popular estimates that when things were going well the great majority did put their faith in Hitler (Haffner, 1978, p. 46).

One must also remember that the central mechanism of the 'confirmation' always strengthened Hitler's leadership anew. He achieved astonishing successes one after the other. By extraordinary interventions in the economy and with a sudden favourable twist in the economic trend, Hitler succeeded in starting the German engine again. The massive unemployment problem vanished in a very short time. Meanwhile law and order was – in a conventional sense – restored. In power politics, every new year brought new successes: reinstatement of compulsory military service (1935), re-militarization of the Rhineland (1936), annexation of Austria and Sudetenland (1938), protectorate of Bohemia and Moravia (1939). These successes meant fresh consent, in peacetime. When war broke out, the military victories of the early years, especially the overwhelming victory over France, strengthened public consent and trust in the person of Hitler. Only a long series of defeats and the approach of the catastrophe could at last erode the spell of the Führer over his people. Indeed General Jodl could testify: 'The force of his charisma lasted until the end of his life' (quoted in Maser, 1978, p. 476).

Altogether the example of Hitler – together with the case of Lenin (see Tucker, 1968, pp. 731–56; 1974, ch. 2) – appears to corroborate the opportuneness of using the concept of charisma and its related paradigm in the study of modern dictatorships. I would even say that without this conceptual tool it is impossible to have an exact understanding of Hitler's role and the related social developments in the Nazi Party and the German state. At the same time I would underscore that the use of these conceptual instruments has no ethical implications. The point is that the same psychological and sociological processes may also develop with leaders such as Gandhi, who from an ethical point of view must be evaluated very differently. As we should remember, the paradigm does not even allow us to foresee (or explain) the historical effectiveness of a leadership. To this end we can resort instead to the criteria given by Weber in 'Politics as a Vocation', and these condemn Hitler's leadership. Hitler especially lacked the psychological and cultural maturity that allows a balance between an ethic of responsibility and an ethic of conviction; he showed this clearly by adopting means, such as his concentration camps, that sharply contradicted the concept of humanity as shaped by Western culture. By doing so Hitler largely determined the world coalition against Germany, the rebellion of European people and the moral indictment against him and his nation, which were principal causes of the final catastrophic defeat of Germany.

It would be wrong, though, to deduce from the wickedness of the Nazi cause that mass adherence can be entirely explained by the somewhat derogatory concept of regression. In the early 1930s German society was reaching the nadir of a total crisis that threatened both social and personal integration. Hence the reintegration fostered by the Führer on the basis of values already interiorized with a high emotional investment satisfied urgent needs of survival. Given their socialization, many Germans were bound to think that Hitler's leadership was necessary for the realization of their highest values, and therefore they gave him devoted obedience and produced their utmost efforts at his command. Of course one cannot speak in the same way of the barbarous violence employed by the Germans, first against political opponents and Jews; and later, in wartime, even against the reluctant conquered nations of Europe. The Führer deliberately excited his followers to such violence, setting them free from any sense of guilt, in a way only a charismatic leader can do. In many cases behaviour that had been traditionally set apart as a transgression became a public duty and a source of merit. To these facts one can apply fruitfully the concept of collective regression, in the sense developed by the first social psychologists, such as Le Bon.

Plebiscitary Democracy

The concept of plebiscitary democracy was used by Weber in such a broad sense that it covered phenomena differing in many aspects, such as Pericles' primacy in Athens, Caesar's and Cromwell's dictatorships, the imperial power of the two Bonapartes and contemporary developments in the USA and Great Britain. While these cases possess formal elements – an explicit or implicit plebiscite – they have a substantive one in common: concentration of power in the hands of the leader trusted by the masses and his ascendancy over collective organs of democracy such as Parliament. This could vary from *de facto* dominance, as in the example of Pericles, to tyrannical forms of personal power, as in the case of Hitler and the total destruction of democratic institutions and procedures. I have consequently suggested we should distinguish between tyranny and (true) plebiscitary democracy, where democratic institutions and procedures are not abolished, and so a free dialectic between leader's performance and the trust of the masses in the person of the leader is maintained. Weber approved of plebiscitary democracy, but we have to introduce another premise into the argument lest we mistake the nature of this approval. Weber's preference certainly does not imply that he desired a democracy in which the questions of power were decided by a plebiscite in a *technical* sense, and even less – as I have just said – by a manipulated plebiscite, such as those organized by the two Bonapartes and by Fascist or Nazi chiefs. One must not forget that Weber supported this form of democracy in Germany as against another form of democracy, the *führerlose Demokratie*, characterized by the preponderance of a 'polycephalous' parliament made up of men 'without a calling' for politics, 'mean and mediocre men' with an assembly, in turn, increasingly subjected to party power. Weber sharply criticized this form of democracy, not only for its obvious unfitness for far-sighted politics at the service of country, but also for reasons of principle. Against its party oligarchical principles Weber posited the 'Magna Charta of democracy: the people's right to choose leaders directly' (GPS, p. 501). Therefore I would say that Weber applied the term 'plebiscitary' to the form of democracy he preferred – a preference that reminded him of historical occasions when the people had imposed leaders they trusted upon an oligarchy, such as Scipio Africanus and Marius. The plebiscite had been a decisive instrument for reaching this aim, and at the same time had been used to confer on these leaders adequate powers for their task, as in the case of Julius Caesar. It is significant that Weber used the concept of 'caesarism' in connection with both charisma and plebiscitary democracy. Even more meaningful, perhaps, was the fact that Weber chose the British statesman Gladstone as the typical leader of a contemporary plebiscitary democracy. Weber had in mind the 1880s election. In Ensor's words, 'Gladstone had gone behind Parliament to the people, which for the first time virtually chose its own premier' (1946, p. 66). The party leader, Hartingdon, had to make way for Gladstone, who had imposed himself as 'the dictator of the electoral battlefield' in the famous Midlothian campaign. With that, Weber added, a 'caesaristic element' had been introduced into contemporary democracy (FMW, p. 106).

Weber's preference for plebiscitary democracy after the First World War must then be explained as an aspect of his lifelong struggle to endow his country with a suitable ruling class, open to all *Führernaturen* (i.e. those possessed of leadership qualities), together with those institutional instruments that guarantee what we call 'governability'. According to him this had been at least partially achieved in the USA and Great Britain, and Germany might perhaps follow in their wake.

From Weber's political writings one gathers that the basic condition for a plebiscitary democracy is to be found in the irresistible process of democratization, especially universal suffrage, because a true *Führernatur* can be recognized only by the masses, owing to their 'irrational and emotional' character. These psychological traits of the masses are therefore at the origin of the entire process. Plebiscitary democracy, however, can develop only in a political system having the necessary prerequisites: first, a decisive concentration of power (including patronage) in the supreme political office of a democracy, such as that of the British premier or that of the US President. Secondly, the holder of this office must be directly elected by the people, and the choice must be one *between personalities*. Weber seemed to believe that in such a context the masses, given their dominant traits, are almost irresistibly attracted by great demagogic personalities ('demagogic', in the original sense, as in the example of Pericles); party machines, understanding this point, are quick to adopt a man of such a personality as a candidate for the supreme office, for this person can win elections and distribute rich rewards and prebends to the members of the machine. Weber was perhaps too optimistic. In any case, his analysis *also implied* a certain kind of party – one characterized by a relationship between mass and party. It required a party that approached Weber's ideal type of a party of patronage, also one in which the masses were not entangled in the ideology and organization of a mass party, as represented by the opposite type – a 'party based on a *Weltanschauung*'. The latter is also often a 'class party', such as the Communist parties in some parts of Europe even today.

It cannot be denied, however, that in the West, a general tendency has developed towards plebiscitary democracy in both states and parties during the second part of the twentieth century. This is the case in countries with a political system already inspired by a model of plebiscitary democracy, such as the USA; also in what used until recently to be the most typical leaderless democracy, namely, France, which adopted a model of plebiscitary democracy with the 1958–62 constitution. French parties had to adapt to this change. In the 1970s (charismatic) plebiscitary tendencies also developed in southern Europe, especially in the Socialist parties. In Greece and Spain this happened in the course of the critical change from authoritarianism to democracy with such men as Papandreou and Gonzales. In the case of Italy, the last genuine leaderless democracy, that tendency showed up in the major democratic parties as an answer to party crisis and to the failure of the political system to ensure governability. The tendency was most visible in the Socialist Party when in 1984 Snr Craxi was elected party secretary by 'acclamation'.

The fortune of (charismatic) plebiscitary tendencies in different types of democracy arouses our curiosity as to its origin, quite apart from the extraordinary situation and the personality capable of embodying those tendencies, which are patently present in all the cases I have referred to. One must start, when studying those parties that have in the last decades shifted from the model of the *Weltanschauung* and class party towards the model of the patronage party, from the conditions posited by Weber as existing both in parties and in the electorate (and so in society at large). This shift has proceeded even further in the 'catch-all party', as outlined by Kirchheimer, which may be considered as a development of Weber's model in the following respects. A corresponding development takes place in the electorate and society at large. Secularization considerably weakens traditional religions at first, and then the secular ones such as Marxism–Leninism. At the same time class structure is changed. The working class loses ground to the middle class. An individualistic and materialistic orientation becomes dominant in the course of a few years and is associated with relatively uniform life conditions and patterns.

Of course these developments in European countries did not take place at exactly the same time and in the same way, and the political effects are not, as yet, uniform. Nevertheless they have vigorously contributed to the fortune of (charismatic) plebiscitary tendencies, especially in France and Italy. For example, with the loss of its ideological and class character, the Italian Socialist Party sought a new point of reference for its unity and identity in the party secretary, Craxi, and presented him as the focal point to an electorate that itself was changing and therefore no longer responsible to the once effective party symbols. Moreover technological development in mass media contributed powerfully to the growth of (charismatic) plebiscitary tendencies. Television allows the great leader to reach a very large number of citizens directly, and to enact on them the suggestion of his exalted position and his personal spell, which is amplified by psychological and technical devices. A direct contest between significant and visible leaders (such as Kennedy and Nixon) fascinates public attention, and may become decisive in an important election. Hence the vote is given to the leader rather than to the party. In some Western countries, such as France and Italy, this tendency is strengthened by the well-rooted aversion to political parties. If the leader seems to be independent from the party, or its master, people like him the most. The vote for the leader may even become a vote against his party.

Taken together this seems to verify Weber's insight that the future growth of plebiscitary tendencies in Europe would become the modern form of the struggle to democratize democracy by expropriating the party oligarchy and of giving back to the people the essential right to choose its own leaders. This does not mean that those tendencies are going to prevail everywhere in the West, or will do so without possible regression. On the contrary, in strong contrast to this tendency stand the forces of leaderless democracy. As Weber showed in his own struggle with the myths of history, history does not possess its own telos.

Notes

1 I have developed a critical reconstruction of Weber's thought on charisma in Cavalli (1981).
2 See the English version of the definition of charisma (ES, p. 241).

16

Decisionism and Politics: Weber as Constitutional Theorist

STEPHEN TURNER and REGIS FACTOR

The National Assembly held in the Frankfurt *Paulskirche* in 1848, which opened with high hopes for the unification of Germany on parliamentary constitutional principles, was left to die a year later, in the telling phrase of Donoso Cortes, 'like a street woman in the gutter' (quoted in Valentin, 1940, p. 263). In the period of reaction that followed, during which the *Paulskirche* convention came to be described as the 'parliament of professors', one of its members, Georg Gottfried Gervinus, was accused, in a trial for high treason, of attempting to prove the historical inevitability of the supersession of monarchical forms by republican forms. This was Gervinus's second experience as a professorial martyr. In 1837 he had been one of the professors at the University of Göttingen, the 'Göttingen Seven', who protested the revocation of the Hanoverian constitution. For this he had been banished and given three days to leave the kingdom. The lesson he, and many other liberal thinkers, learned from these experiences was that the German middle classes were incapable of performing the historical role assigned to them; they lacked the political will to establish a republican order.

Both unification and parliamentarization occurred despite the political failures of liberalism. The creation of a parliamentary structure was part of the complex half-treaty, half-constitution that made unification possible, and the National Liberals became the leading party in the new parliament. The 'unpoliticality' of the middle classes that were the source of support for the party led to its slow destruction. The great division on strategy that crippled the party was a result of the dilemma created by Bismarck's attacks on the parliament that had come into being with unification, and by usurpations of its powers. The liberals were faced with the alternatives of resisting and risking diminishing what popular support they still retained, or accepting the sham parliamentarism that Bismarck allowed. Liberal politicians chose the latter, and the party gradually degenerated into an interest party without principles.

The realm of liberal thought developed differently. The combination of feeble popular support and the predominance of intellectuals made for a situation parallel to the circumstances of the members of the Frankfurt School in this century, who were forced to turn their intellectual energies from the failures of capitalism to the failure of the proletariat. Liberal thinkers made idiosyncratic accommodations in theory to the politics of power from which liberal politicians were excluded in practice. Weber grew up in this intellectual ambience of professorial liberalism. Many of its leading figures had connections to the Weber household; Gervinus himself had been the tutor of Weber's mother.

When Weber wrote on the German constitution in 1917, the political fundamentals were unchanged. Parliament was weak, and the bourgeoisie lacked political will. He proposed to strengthen parliament, but saw that the support of the bourgeoisie could not be counted on. 'One can be quite assured that the beneficiaries of the old order and of uncontrolled bureaucracy will exploit every outbreak of syndicalist putschism, no matter how insignificant, in order to scare our philistine bourgeoisie which, unfortunately, still has pretty weak nerves' (ES, p. 1461). This was the ever renewed lesson of 1848.[1] Yet fate was again to intervene on the side of reform, and Weber's constitutional proposals of the wartime period (ES, pp. 1381–469) were to have a significant influence on the Weimar constitution, in large part because they were virtually the only proposals for fuller parliamentarization in existence when President Wilson forced the dismantling of the monarchy. On the strength of his proposals, Weber became a member of a working group that drafted the proposal that, after considerable modification, became the Weimar constitution.

Weber presented no constitutional theory as such. To reconstruct the premises of his constitutional thinking we are obliged to proceed by making something of the scattered critical remarks and observations he made on the themes of the legal and historical constitutional thinkers he read, discussed and had relations with. It happens that there is a wealth of remarks of this sort, and that Weber had a close personal relationship with a figure who plays an important role in the development of German legal thinking, Gustav Radbruch (Radbruch, 1951, p. 84; Marianne Weber, 1975, pp. 452, 454). Radbruch based a full-fledged relativistic philosophy of law on premises about the rationality of value-choice that Weber shared. Weber's explicit statements do locate him in relation to his peers and immediate predecessors; he was a link in the progressive transformation of fundamental premises about constitutional order. The aim of this chapter is to show what the progression was, and how Weber contributed to it.

Ihering's The Law as a Means to an End

Weber was well aware of the great names of contemporary constitutional thinking and legal philosophy. When he entered university studies in Heidelberg, he read Ranke and Savigny, representatives of 'conservative' approaches to German legal and constitutional development. In Immanuel Bekker's course on Roman law, a subject in which Weber was ultimately to be habilitated, and which was then among the most prestigious of the academic disciplines, he was introduced to the work of Rudolph von Ihering, the polemical opponent of Savigny (Marianne Weber, 1975, p. 65; cf. Mommsen, 1984, p. 4). Later, as a student in Berlin, he attended the lectures of Gneist on German constitutional law and on Prussian administrative law (Mommsen, 1984, p. 11). The ideas of several of the legal thinkers prominent in his student days are found, transformed, at the centre of Weber's sociology; Rudolph Sohm was the source of 'charisma', Gneist of the idea of the centrality and indispensability of bureaucracy. His emphasis on the centrality to Western civilization of the 'rationality' of Roman law reflected the dispute between Romanists and Germanists, including Savigny and his successors, whose historiographic views Weber rejected as so much mysticism.

In Radbruch's textbook on the philosophy of law, he identifies Ihering as the thinker in whose mind 'all motifs of thought' of earlier philosophy of law 'were gathered and joined' to produce 'the renascence of legal philosophy' that had taken place during the time Weber was trained in the law (1950, p. 66). The general analytic thesis of Ihering's major work, *Der Zweck im Recht* (*The Element of Purpose in Law*), was that laws are analysable in terms not just of abstract concepts, the method of the then dominant 'conceptualist' school, but of ends: 'It is not', he said, 'the sense of right that has produced law, but it is law that has produced the sense of right. Law knows only one source, and that is the practical one of purpose' (translated in Stone, 1950, p. 301). The premise that laws were compromises that served practical purposes grounded a practical, historical method of analysing the ends of given laws in terms of the interests they are designed to accommodate.[2] As it happens, Ihering provides us with a direct link to liberal political philosophy, for he was the most prominent German admirer of Utilitarianism, and especially of Bentham, whose own discussion of laws provided part of the vocabulary for the historical, evolutionary approach Ihering developed.

'Acting, and acting with a purpose', Ihering said, are synonymous (1968, p. 9). Purpose, as Ihering used it, is the 'ideational form' of an interest (1968, p. 7); interest is the 'real force which moves the human will' (1968, p. 39). However, 'the will is not under the law of causality, but under the law of purpose' (1968, p. 18), which is to say that, while action is moved by interest, it is not the mechanical product of external causality (1968, p. 17). The dialectical target of these definitions was Kant, whose ethics separated ideation and will, and of whom Ihering tartly remarked that 'You might as well hope to move a loaded wagon from its place by means of a lecture on the theory of motion as the human will by means of the categorical imperative' (1968, p. 39). The attraction of Kant's theory was that it was part of a solution to a traditional problem for German liberals, the question of the relation between individual purposes and the purposes of 'higher' entities, such as the state. Gneist had supposed the existence of a mysterious harmony between the two types of purpose. Ihering gave a different solution to this problem, designed to be an improvement both on the German liberal tradition and on the Utilitarians: 'The answer is, the world exists by taking egoism into its service, by paying it the reward which it desires. The world interests egoism in its purposes, and is then assured of its co-operation' (Ihering, 1968, p. 25).

The reasoning built on Bentham. The world has two levers; the first lever is given by nature in the form of pleasure and pain (Ihering, 1968, pp. 26–7), and a second arises by *connecting one's own purpose with the other man's interest* (1968, p. 28, italics in original) and securing 'agreement of wills' between parties. Ihering was rather vague on the character of this 'subjective' or psychological 'lever', and said only that it is an 'indirect compulsion' (1968, p. 34) and that the agreement of wills, in such paradigmatic cases as commercial agreements may depend on salesmanship. The basic properties of the commercial transaction are preserved in the state. The state, as Ihering defined it, is an association that is distinguished as a type of association by its claim of an exclusive right to exercise certain forms of coercion. Ihering went beyond mere definition to inquire into the justification of the state's claim to this exclusive right. The justification he arrived at was necessity; coercion was found to be indispensable to the achievement of the purposes for which these associations were formed.

Ihering made his reputation in Germany for an argument against Utilitarianism. Identifying egoism with *individual* purposes, Ihering argued, led to a fundamental conceptual difficulty. Mill conceded the propriety of the interest of society in various regulations designed to keep an individual from acting against the interest of others, but denied the propriety of laws that have the purpose of forcing an individual to act for his own good against his will. In doing this, as Ihering pointed out, he conceded the validity of a standard of the interest of society. But Mill's attempts to draw a line between justified and unjustified intrusions into individual freedom were, Ihering showed, hopelessly *ad hoc*. Mill had said, for example, that law could forbid a person selling himself into

slavery on the grounds that freedom cannot be used for its own destruction. But *every* contract, Ihering observed, 'contains a partial renunciation
of freedom' (quoted in Stone, 1950, p. 302). Mill's difficulties were not,
as it happened, purely theoretical. In 1905 Dicey opened the published
form of his *Lectures on the Relation between Law and Public Opinion during the
Nineteenth Century* (1962, p. xx) by quoting the same passage in Mill,
with the purpose of showing how far towards a recognition of collective
interests public opinion had gone in the preceding fifty years. The
conceptual consequence of admitting the validity of collective interests is
that 'individual' interests become only one set of ends among many
interests, which may have equal or superior force.

The Evolution of Law

The source of all interests is to be found in 'egoism'. But egoistic interests
or purposes create *social* interests by virtue of the fact that the realization of
most egoistic interests is possible only through other individuals (Stone,
1950, p. 305), and in particular through 'associations' with distinct
purposes. These 'associational' interests have a degree of autonomy; for
just as a contract involves the renunciation of freedom, the subordination
of the interests of the individual in an 'association', legal or informal, that
defines a purpose is a necessity for the achievement of many purposes.
Social interests of this sort persist historically over longer periods than the
particular individual egoistic interests that compose them, but are also
subject to evolution and alteration. New circumstances and conflicts
create new coincidences of interest and new opportunities for artificially
creating coincidences of interests. In commerce the salesman secures an
'agreement in wills' by his 'ideational representations' of new purposes,
which in turn produce new circumstances under which new purposes
may be created. Similarly for law: 'One purpose of law is produced out of
the other with the same necessity with which, according to the Darwinian
theory, one animal species is developed from the other' (translated in
Stone, 1950, p. 303). This, Ihering saw, was 'a new inexorability, but
not', he thought, 'one before which men may remain passive; rather one
which requires constant struggle and conscious seeking of ends on the
part of men' (translated in Stone, 1950, p. 303).

Understanding the ends that men formerly sought to achieve through
law provided Ihering with a method of *Ideologiekritik*. Past doctrines and
laws could be understood as ideational representations of the purposes of
past associations, based on former coincidences of interest. The ideas and
practices of the past thus came to represent not 'merely the arbitrary and
the obsolete', as they had for Bentham, but 'the imperfect realisation of

the principle of utility' (Stone, 1950, p. 303). Ihering also attempted a better formulation of this principle, which took cognizance of those egoistic interests of the individual that arise from the fact that one must realize one's egoistic interests through others, a project he did not live to complete. The attempt itself presumes that 'egoistic interests' are in some sense natural or fixed, and that the collective or social purposes that are served, in different social and historical circumstances, by different laws, are themselves more or less fixed. The similarity between this premise and the doctrine of the mutability of law in Aquinas must have been pointed out to him after the first edition of *Der Zweck im Recht* appeared, for in the second he not only admitted it but chided intervening generations for having overlooked it (Stone, 1950, p. 301 n.).

Force and the State

Law is a *modus vivendi* that is recognized as binding and hence as a standard for judging individual conduct. There is one fixed interest in which it is rooted: peace. Intelligent egoism and moderation counsel peace, so it is rational to obey, and states arrange matters so that one is punished for disobedience. But such utilitarian reasons for obedience do not of course always obtain, which suggests that there are occasions when this *modus vivendi* ought not be honoured. Ihering acknowledged this: 'Law can conflict with life,' he said, and went on to add that in these conflicts 'we choose life' (Ihering, 1968, p. 189), because 'law is not the highest thing in the world, not an end in itself; but merely a means to an end, the final end being the existence of society' (1968, p. 188). The character of these special occasions is a point of some importance for Ihering's historical argument. In the normal case, individual and collective interests do coincide. Ihering stated this as a 'law' to the effect that common interests are always preponderant over individual interests, by which he meant that because of the necessity of achieving our ends through others, there are real, more or less fixed interests in a peaceful social order that are always greater than the real individual interests against any such order.

But the form that this order may take is not *strictly* determined by these interests, in part because new combinations or coincidences of interests may be conceived and articulated, and new forms of association invented. In the unusual occasion, the situation of revolution, where 'unorganized force' faces the organized force of the state, or the situation of dictatorship, where the law must be suspended to preserve society,[3] politics is replaced by force. So where we must

choose either law or life, the decision cannot be doubtful: force sacrifices law and rescues life. These are the *saving deeds* of the power of the government. At the moment when they are committed they spread fear and terror, and are branded by the advocates of law as a criminal outrage against law's sanctity; but they often need only a few years or decades, until the dust which they have raised has settled, to gain vindication by their effects.

(1968, p. 189, italics in original)

Any successful use of organized force is better than anarchy, the impotence of state force (1968, pp. 234–5). But the exceptional moments are when law is made and new orders are established. These moments are also a source of the political maturity of nations, for the experience of upheaval teaches the necessity of the state and law (1968, pp. 416–17).

The *de facto* predominance of organized power over unorganized power usually gives the state the upper hand against revolution. But the *possibility* of conflict means that vigilance in preventing 'any organization that threatens it on the part of the forces of the people' (1968, p. 237) is an essential task of the state. This 'negative task' of the state means that the state's right to coerce must be an absolute monopoly, such that other associations can coerce only with the implied but revocable consent of the state. The positive task of the state is the achievement of greater efficiency in the organization of force: 'The State organization of forces may be designated as the proper *technique of the political art*', and the state has the practical obligation to achieve 'the highest possible perfection of the organization of its own forces' (1968, p. 237, italics in original). The 'State of modern times which has understood as no other has how best to make up for the insignificance of its forces by an exemplary organization' is Prussia (1968, p. 237).

Purposes as Decisions

Much of Ihering's analytic practice was retained by Weber. Like Ihering, he assumed both that the interests of a particular historical period are more or less fixed, and that the interests articulated as the purposes of associations would in fact be largely without force if they did not coincide with pre-existent interests. Weber also retained Ihering's method of *Ideologie-kritik*; when he encountered a legal doctrine, he asked what interests or compromise between interests it articulates (e.g. ES, pp. 874–5). The seeds of Weber's destruction of Ihering's assumptions about the relative fixity of interests, and the basis for Weber's radicalization of the concept of interest, are planted in Ihering's own texts. In *Der Zweck im Recht* Ihering made, in passing, the comment that some 'rewards' are 'ideal' (1968, p. 147). In a widely read speech on the historical importance of the

340

defence of 'rights' where the cost of this defence goes beyond any benefit to immediate material interests, he used the term 'ideal interests' as a means of describing the motivation for these struggles (1915, p. 127). In Ihering's uses, the term is never drastically separated from the interests of a more tangible sort that the ideal articulates. But the usage itself laid the foundation for the transformation of the concept which is used to transform Ihering's project.

Ihering expected that human purposes could be systematically related in an impersonal hierarchy, with an order determined by the historical evolution of one collective purpose out of another – an inexorable process itself largely determined by the existence of more or less fixed 'egoistic' interests. Weber and Radbruch insisted on the irrationality of the relations between these choices. Anarchism, to choose a familiar example, becomes for Radbruch a form of individualism. He understood 'individualism' as a category of value-choice antinomic to the categories in which the values of the nation and culture fell (1950, pp. 94, 99). In place of the necessity of ordering purposes in an impersonal, 'objective' hierarchy – in which, for example, the choice of individual values over collective values can be understood as a kind of self-contradiction – they insisted on the necessity of ordering value-choices in a personal hierarchy, that is, to recognize the potential conflicts between choices and to make 'responsible decisions', conscious decisions between fully understood alternatives (MSS, p. 18; Radbruch, 1950, p. 136). They insisted on the irrationality of the relations between the array of choices present at any historical moment. Radbruch called this doctrine, whose premises Weber shared,[4] 'decisionism' or 'relativism'. When Radbruch called it 'relativism' he was careful to insist that it was not, as he puts it in one book,

> cognate to Pilate of the Gospel, in whom practical as well as theoretical reason becomes mute: 'What is truth?' It is cognate rather to Lessings' Nathan, to whom the silence of theoretical reason is the strongest appeal to practical reason: 'May each of you vie with the other then in bringing out the power of the gem in his own ring.'

> (1950, p. 58)

The philosophical basis of the doctrine was formulated repeatedly in their writings: 'Statements concerning the Ought may be established or proved only by other statements concerning the Ought. For this very reason, the ultimate statements concerning the Ought are incapable of proof, axiomatic. They may not be discerned but only professed' (Radbruch, 1950, p. 55).

Law is an arena in which persons with potentially different ultimate values may share common subordinate or intermediate values. Radbruch quoted a French jurist to this effect.

Peace, security – these are the first benefits the law is to afford us. Even if we should be in profound, irreducible disagreement on the higher ends of the law, we could nevertheless arrive at an understanding so as to make it achieve these intermediate ends in which we are all interested. (Quoted in Radbruch, 1950, p. 108 n.)

The understanding or 'agreement of wills' with respect to these common intermediate ends itself contains 'decisions' between rationally irreconcilable options (cf. Radbruch, 1950, p. 109). Radbruch argued that in law the choices were further structured by the fact of the mutual dependence of the three basic values – individuality, collectivity and community – that constituted the sphere of law. The achievement of each required, he argued, the achievement, to some extent, of the others. Radbruch was a socialist, and held to what he called a 'social view' of the law. His analysis of private property exemplifies his point: 'even the individualistic theories of ownership were never purely individualistic. They were based on the assumption of a prestabilized harmony between individualistic selfishness and the common weal' (Radbruch, 1950, p. 166). Consequently, 'even in the legal view of today, private ownership appears as an area of activity for private initiative, entrusted to the individual by the community, entrusted in the expectation of its social use, always revocable if that expectation is not fulfilled' (Radbruch, 1950, p. 167). This formulation, he thought, turned the question of nationalization into a factual question of its effects. Weber neither considered that the evidence supported such a policy nor believed in absolute rights, such as property rights. Nor did 'rights' figure in his historical analyses; the notion that the evolution of law proceeded through the struggle for rights, one of Ihering's central historical conceptions (Ihering, 1915), is absent in Weber.

Constitutional arrangements are means, or intermediate ends. As Weber put it, 'forms of State are for me techniques like any other machinery' (translated in Mayer, 1956, p. 76).[5] Ihering believed that the problem of the efficient use of force, the positive task of the state, was inherent. 'Politics as a Vocation', written at a time when constitutional issues were very much in the air, begins with an assertion of the diversity of constitutional forms:

What is a 'state'? Sociologically, the state cannot be defined in terms of its ends. There is scarcely any task that some political association has not taken in hand, and there is no task that one could say has always been exclusive and peculiar to those associations which have been the predecessors of the modern state. Ultimately [he agrees with Ihering] one can define the modern state sociologically only in terms of the specific *means* peculiar to it, as to every political association, namely, the use of physical force.

(FMW, pp. 77–8, italics in original)

When Ihering discussed the evolution in law he assumed that, in the evolution of purposes, the purposes of peace and security provided by Attila continued to be provided by regimes with higher purposes. Weber repeated this, giving it a decidedly Hobbesian twist:

> In the final analysis, in spite of all 'social welfare policies', the whole course of the state's inner political functions, of justice and administration, is repeatedly and unavoidably regulated by the objective pragmatism of 'reasons of state'. The state's absolute end is to safeguard (or to change) the external and internal distribution of power; ultimately, this end must seem meaningless to any universalist religion of salvation. This fact has held and still holds, even more so, for foreign policy. It is absolutely essential for every political association to appeal to the naked violence of coercive means in the face of outsiders as well as in the face of internal enemies. (FMW, p. 334)

Beneath the benevolent veneer of the modern Welfare State are the realities of power. But Weber did not conclude, as Ihering did, that peace was a basic purpose of law. Instead, he rejected the distinction between peace and struggle:

> 'Peace' is nothing more than a change in the form of the conflict or in the antagonists or in the objects of the conflict, or finally in the chances of selection. Obviously, absolutely nothing of a general character can be said as to whether such shifts can withstand examination according to an ethical or other value-judgement (MSS, p. 27)

Where Ihering believed that success stemmed from the use of force for the right, by which he meant the predominant collective interests, Weber said, 'The very success of force, or of the threat of force, depends ultimately upon power relations and not on ethical "right", even were one to believe it possible to discover objective criteria for such "right" . . . "reasons of state" thus follow their own external and internal laws' (FMW, p. 334).

If we read Weber's remarks as a selective repudiation of Ihering, we are faced with some questions. Ihering's philosophy of the state, for all its inadequacies, was a more or less coherent whole. How do Weber's revisions of Ihering fit together and how do they fit with those doctrines, such as interest, *raison d'état* and law as compromise, that Weber does not reject? In particular, how do they bear on the special concerns of his constitutional writings? Here the comparison with Ihering is striking, for

Weber rejected the idea of a fixed *ultima ratio* for the state that Ihering had made the basis for his own theory of state-form.

The Constitutional Decision

The rhetorical community Weber addressed in his 'political' writings on the constitution is not the community of those who share or could be made to share his particular values or interests, but a community of persons whose party and material interests Weber took as given. In his conduct on the constitutional committee, Weber's tendency to accept interests as unalterable pre-conditions, and to focus on the devices of the constitutional structure that serve to relate given institutionally articulated interests, was especially marked. He was attentive to the domestic interests given by the pre-existing federal system – the part-constitution, part-treaty of the first Reich – as well as to the class and religious interests articulated by the parties. His readiness to face up to and accept these interests had the defects of its virtue of realism; he thought solely in terms of the compromises made possible by these interests, and tended – as he did in his accounts of English and Russian constitutional history – to ignore those political ideas, public sentiments and traditions that could not be easily reduced to his formula of 'material and ideal interests'.[6]

Yet, on his own premises, one can discuss the question of forms of state as a 'technical' problem *only* by reference to ends. Weber's audience was constituted by some shared circumstances. To the extent that it shared values, they were not shared values in the sense of shared *ultimate* values, for it was an audience composed of members of parties with *opposed* interests and *opposed* ultimate values. Whether the audience could be said to share some set of subordinate values – peace, order and the like, for example – is another question. One might pursue the question of constitutional form by seeking common interests, or by proposing a compromise between interests that could become a common purpose. Weber proceeded as though in this realm of means a choice of intermediate ends remained, and the point of his primary essay, 'Parliament and Government in a Reconstructed Germany', was to define this choice.

The circumstance that limited the possibilities of choice was the inevitability of greater parliamentarization and democratization. As he correctly perceived, those who had served in, and sacrificed for, the war would not be willing to return to a political community in which their enfranchisement was partial and of doubtful effect. Weber attempted to impress this inevitability on his readers, and ridiculed those who longed for a 'German' 'integrative' state-form.

The problem that occasioned the essay was leadership. In the context of

1917, in the midst of a constitutional crisis brought on by the failures of the war, this was a *pragmatic* problem, which Weber used to turn away his readers from immediate concerns over leadership to focus on the constitutional system. He gave examples drawn from a wide range of parties and origins, of leaders and persons with leadership potential whose talents had been badly used by the system. He also gave examples of leadership failure that could not be blamed on parliamentarism but represented the failures of leadership which he blamed on the monarchy and on traditional bureaucratic élites (ES, pp. 1425–6). Elaborate examples were not necessary to make the point that stronger and better leaders were needed. The problems were evident to everyone in the face of Ludendorff's intervention into the political affairs of the Office of Chancellor, actions whose consequences were still being played out at the time Weber's articles were appearing in the *Frankfurter Zeitung*.

The air was already thick with recriminations over this episode, over the failure of peace initiatives and over the handling of naval mutinies, recriminations that were to become only more dramatic and inclusive in the postwar period. Weber assimilated these present problems to an older problem, revealed by the careers of Bismarck and his unimpressive successors. The older problem was a familiar liberal theme; the Junkers had presented themselves as the leadership class indispensable for national greatness; liberals from the time of unification and before had disputed this claim, comparing the Junkers unfavourably to the English aristocracy (cf. Gneist, 1886, vol. II, p. 392). Weber continued this polemical tradition. In 1917 he wrote that

> only one thing is indisputable: every type of social order, without exception, must, if one wishes to *evaluate* it, be examined with reference to the opportunities which it affords to *certain types of persons* to rise to positions of superiority through the operation of the various objective and subjective selective factors.
>
> (MSS, p. 27, italics in original)

In 'Wahlrecht und Demokratie', also published in 1917, Weber assailed the Junkers as a pseudo-aristocratic caste whose 'conventions and forms' were 'supported by the structure of bureaucracy' (FMW, p. 392) and whose characteristic social institutions, such as the duel corps, 'serve as a convenient way of taming men' (FMW, p. 393).

Weber's solution to the problem of creating a pool of leaders was vague in its details but simple in design. The career of Bismarck revealed a weakness within the older constitutional system, the problem of succession. The rise of a worthy successor, that is, a leader with the capacity to amass popular support for his measures despite the reluctance of the parliamentary parties, could have developed neither in the bureaucracy nor in the parliament. In Germany there was a legal obstacle that prevented parliamentary figures from holding significant posts in the administration. Thus the person with power instincts was forced to choose between bureaucratic office and its discipline and political 'responsibility' in a powerless body. In fact, Weber argued, the born leaders in Germany chose neither. Bismarck was himself largely to blame for this; he had emasculated parliament politically and rendered it hopelessly unattractive as a career for a person with the political talents that make for leadership. The manifest inadequacies of parliamentary leadership were thus the consequence, not the cause, of parliamentary impotence. 'The level of parliament depends on whether it does not merely discuss great issues but decisively influences them; in other words, its quality depends on whether what happens there matters' (ES, p. 1392).

The tactical problem of the text is to persuade his readers of the merit of a particular constitutional arrangement, in which parliament had expanded powers, but where one of its major purposes – to be a nursery for leaders – was served indirectly. The model for this is countries like England, which have proper parliaments, with ministerial responsibility and the possibility of votes of no confidence, where parliaments select the leaders, and where the leaders are accountable to parliament and must run their departments according to guidelines set by parliament (ES, p. 1408). In these systems, Weber says, one finds a particular kind of struggle.

> Every conflict in parliament involves not only a struggle over substantive issues but also a struggle for personal power. Wherever parliament is so strong that, as a rule, the monarch entrusts the government to the spokesman of a clear-cut majority, the power struggle of the parties will be a contest for this highest executive position. The fight is then carried by men who have great political power instincts and highly developed qualities of political leadership, and hence the chance to take over the top positions; for the survival of the party outside parliament, and the countless ideal, and partly very material, interests bound up with it require that capable leaders get to the top.
>
> (ES, p. 1409)

But *only* where there is real power to be had through these struggles 'can men with political temperament and talent be motivated to subject themselves to this kind of selection through competition' (ES, p. 1409).

Beneath the formal arrangements of parliamentary decision-making, Weber saw other processes. In England, Weber said,

> the broad mass of deputies functions only as a following for the leader or the few leaders who form the government, and it blindly follows them *as long as* they are successful. *This is the way it should be.* Political

346

action is always determined by the 'principle of small numbers', that means, the superior political maneuverability of small leading groups. In mass states, this caesarist element is ineradicable.

(ES, p. 1414, italics in original)

It was the caesaristic element itself that he took to be the only basis upon which high politics might be conducted. 'Since the great political decisions, even and especially in a democracy, are unavoidably made by few men, mass democracy has bought its success since Pericles' times with major concessions to the caesarist principle of selecting leaders' (ES, p. 1452).

The Selection of Intermediate Ends and Means

When he remarked that Bismarck had reduced parliament to 'nothing but the unwillingly tolerated rubber stamp of a ruling bureaucracy' (ES, p. 1392), Weber appealed to an old liberal fear. Ihering had expressed this anxiety, in the older language of the opposition between state and society, when he spoke of the danger that arises from 'applying the common means in opposition to the society and in favor of its administrators' (ES, p. 223). One might expect that the likelihood of this happening would increase as a natural consequence of the process of the concentration of force that he regarded as the positive task of the state. Ihering had no solution to this danger. Weber expressed the point in much more colourful language. The 'animated machine' of bureaucratic organization, together with the inanimate machines of industry, are, he says, 'busy fabricating the shell of bondage which men will perhaps be forced to inhabit some day, as powerless as the fellahs of ancient Egypt' (ES, p. 1402). Weber claimed that this is not an inevitability, but the result of a value-choice. The circumstances of modern society are such that 'if a technically superior administration *were to be the ultimate and sole value* in the ordering of' the affairs of state, it would certainly come to pass (ES, p. 1402, italics in original). Weber's concern was to show that another value-choice is possible and preferable.

Weber sought the rejection of bureaucratization as an intermediate value, on the ground that this intermediate value was inconsistent with the value of national greatness. For Germany to accept bureaucratic rule, he said, would be to accept the political fate of being 'condemned to remain a small and conservative country, perhaps with a fairly good public administration in purely technical respects, but at any rate a provincial people without the opportunity of counting in the arena of world politics – and also without any *moral* right to it' (ES, p. 1462, italics

347

in original). Weber, of course, did not think of 'Swissification' as a serious alternative, and he was aware that this was not what his audience wished. The real question was not of wish but of will. The challenge posed by the 'choice' was to the quality of the will of his audience – in the face of the cruel realities of politics (hence his quotation of a passage in *The History of Florence*, where Machiavelli 'has one of his heroes praise those citizens who deemed the greatness of their native city higher than the salvation of their souls': (FMW, p. 126), and in view of the necessity of a reach that exceeds the easily grasped (hence Radbruch's praise of Don Quixote: Radbruch, 1950, p. 53; cf. MSS, p. 46).

When the war was ended and the form of government changed, the parliamentary leadership proved to be as ineffective in power as the wartime chancellors had been, and Weber grew disenchanted with the prospect of a true parliamentary system. In the complex politics of the development of the Weimar constitution, he fought for a 'Strong President', elected by popular vote for a long term[7] – the closest practical equivalent that could be found to what he considered the specifically caesarist constitutional technique, the plebiscite, i.e. 'not an ordinary vote or election, but a profession of faith in the calling of him who demands these acclamations' (ES, p. 1451). The impulse behind this attempt to strengthen the office of the president is not new, as Weber's 1917 discussion of caesarism makes clear.

In Weber's original proposal, the formal rules strengthening parliament are the *de jure* means to a *de facto* constitutional order that has particular properties, of which the existence of a nursery for leaders is one. These properties, together with the underlying realities of modern politics – the indispensability of bureaucracy, the ineluctability of the principle of caesarism, the necessity of making concessions to caesarism for there to be great politics in democracies, and the inevitable rule of the few – create what might be called the 'consequential' constitution, the constitution as it really works.

When Weber discussed the level of underlying practical realities, the significance of parliament is defined by its relation to caesarism. In the course of discussing the problem of succession in a caesarist polity Weber observed that 'the rise, neutralization and elimination of a caesarist leader occur most easily without the danger of a domestic catastrophe when the effective co-domination of powerful representative bodies preserves the political continuity and the constitutional guarantees of civil order' (ES, p. 1457). Here we glimpse a particular constitutional ideal: a regime in which the leader has the fullest means of validating his popular support, but limited means to remain in power after failures and in which there is the *de facto* constraint on his power to destroy political continuity of a parliament made up of ambitious persons with an interest in maintaining a system in which they have a stake. This is the order that Weber held out as the best available means to the common intermediate end of national greatness. It is not, of course, a guarantee. Whether this end is itself to be merely professed or truly meant is a matter of will – of national will, which can be destroyed by excessive class conflict, and of the will of the individuals who make up both the masses who acclaim and the leaders, who must act with the sober strength of those truly called to politics and tested in its ways.

The parliamentary leaders who negotiated the final constitution whittle away the powers to be granted the president, against Conservative opposition, until the sole unlimited power of the president was to declare a state of exception (a state of siege), suspending the fundamental rights established elsewhere in the constitution (article 48) (Brunet, 1922, p. 165). The article required that parliament be informed immediately of such declarations and that they be revoked at its demand. The requirement could be temporarily evaded by the use of article 24, which empowered the president to dismiss parliament, by requiring a new election within sixty days. Weber apparently took no special interest in article 48 (Mommsen, 1984, p. 378), later made notorious by its role in the quasi-legal Nazi seizure of power. He could not have been oblivious to it, however, in view of the stress writers like Ihering placed on the indispensability to the state of legally arbitrary power for self-protection, and in view of his own insistence on the doctrine of *raison d'état*, and of the central place of the practice of declaring states of exception in German government from the time of unification. In the period after the war, when the empire had gone out of existence and the Weimar constitution had not been adopted, the Spartacist rebellions were suppressed on the basis of the practice and precedent of the old constitution (Koch, 1984, pp. 133–4, 254). The same powers were freely invoked by Ebert's Socialist government, with Radbruch as attorney-general (Koch, 1984, p. 254). This government's suspensions of basic legal principles, such as the principle of *nulla poena sine lege*, and its one-sided application of the Law for the Protection of the Republic, established precedents that were used in turn by the Nazis (Koch, 1984, p. 284). The persistence of these political practices puts the reliance on the doctrine of *raison d'état* in this legal tradition in a particular light. Neither were the powers abstractions nor were they curtailed by restrictive conventions. This qualifies any interpretation of Weber's caesarism. His endorsement of the principles behind the practices was itself given without qualification, and reflected his belief that the fundamental realities of politics to which the practices were a response would not change under any constitutional arrangement.[8] He must have expected leaders to use these powers, and for a responsible parliament to assent routinely to their use – the ambitious being mindful that, as leaders, they would themselves want to have these powers at their disposal.

The Realm of Necessity

'What is the spiritual basis of parliamentarism today?' When Carl Schmitt asked this question in 1923 he went to the core of the problem that Weber's transformation of the constitutional problem had created. Weber and, before him, such thinkers as Gneist had been liberals by sentiment even as they gave increasingly illiberal formulations to their fundamental political ideas. Read without these liberal sentiments, Gneist's slogan 'freedom is order, freedom is power' (quoted in Krieger, 1957, p. 358) is totalitarian mysticism, and Weber's constitutional vision of charismatic competition between aspiring caesars is a celebration of irrationalism. Schmitt, who came to this tradition of constitutional reasoning without sharing these liberal sentiments, was able to discern the contradictions behind it.

By the time Schmitt raised this question, it was evident that the Weberian constitutional formula, in which plebiscitarian parliamentary democracy was justified as a socio-technical device for producing leaders, was no longer plausible, and that the foundational question had to be asked anew. Schmitt made the point that in the times of Burke or Mill parliamentarism was linked with a belief in public discussion, but that in the time of Weber, Preuss and Naumann the conditions of mass democracy had reduced discussion to propaganda appealing to interests and passions (1979, p. 11). Schmitt traced the difficulty to the inherent conflict between liberalism and democracy, a conflict he saw embodied in the Weimar constitution itself. The democratic idea, Schmitt said, was 'the assertion of the identity of law and the will of the people' (quoted in Schwab, 1970, p. 62). The legal forms of this identity include the practices of popular initiatives, referendums and acclamation, the first of which was directly provided for in the Weimar constitution. Liberalism, in contrast, rests on the idea of public debate and the enactment of laws as the result of free parliamentary discussions, also provided for by the constitution. In fact, he observed, the condition of public debate did not obtain in Weimar politics; parliamentary discussion itself was not taken seriously; decisions were made behind closed doors by party or coalition committees (Schwab, 1970, pp. 68–9).

Schmitt's alternative returned him to the fundamental problems of modern legal and political thought, but the tools he used were for the most part the tools of the tradition of nineteenth-century legal 'positivism'. This tradition was itself defined only retrospectively, and the term, in its German applications, is best used with caution. Weber used the term to make historical observations on the development of law, as when he commented that 'legal positivism has ... advanced irresistibly' (ES, p. 874); but here he meant little more than the disappearance, in legal thinking, of the idea of natural law and its manifestations. The Hobbesian formula that *auctoritas, non veritas*, makes law, which Schmitt placed at the centre of his own legal theory, was the alternative to natural-law theory accepted by nineteenth-century positivism, and for that matter by such twentieth-century relativists as Radbruch (1950, pp. 115–17). Schmitt used it to re-emphasize the issue of authority in polemical opposition to the normativism of the twentieth-century 'positivist' Kelsen, who, he considered, had mistaken part of the law – the part that dealt with deduction from basic legal norms – for the whole.

Normativism, Schmitt argued, has a hidden presupposition; it presupposes that the normal situation obtains, and therefore cannot account for the abnormal situation. The legally paradigmatic case of 'abnormality' is the situation in which a state of exception is declared in response to 'necessity', and this case reveals a level more basic than Kelsen's *Grundnorm*; the power to decide on questions of necessity, to decide on the declaration of a state of exception, is a power that transcends the presupposition of a normalcy and thus places its holder in a position that is more fundamental than positions whose powers presupposed normalcy, such as the position of a judge. It is from this observation that Schmitt constructs his distinctive theoretical contribution, which we can best understand by returning to Ihering. For Ihering, the fundamental character of the law was determined by relatively fixed egoistic interests, such as peace. Peace is secured by the order-creating actions of the dictatorial law-giver, and is the primal basis of law: the binding of norm and force (Ihering, 1968, pp. 186–8). This was also Schmitt's conception and the conception he attributed to Hobbes when he described him as a 'decisionist'. The sovereign is the *summa auctoritas* and the *summa potestas* in one, as Schmitt put it, and the sovereign decision is an absolute beginning, which grounds the norm as well as the order (1934, pp. 27–8).[9] To show that force is indispensable to the *establishment* of order is only part of the story, of course; the achievement of normalcy, as Ihering recognized, is never final. Occasions when it is threatened by force may arise, and the primal basis of law in the binding of force and norm again becomes visible. At this primal level there is a large element of moral arbitrariness. Ihering stressed, for example, that in the entering into of alliances it is not right, but accident, that determines which alliances will enable the preservation of order (1968, p. 220).

Weber accepted these conclusions, but he varied Ihering's premises in a way that minimized the possibility of rational reconciliation of conflicts of interest through law. As we have seen, Ihering considered that ideal interests which have been historically effective have never been far removed from tangible material interests, interests of the sort that compromise may readily preserve. The ideal interests Weber identified in history, such as the other-worldly interests of Protestantism and the various ideals of which charismatic leaders have been the bearers, are not the sort that can be reconciled through compromise. They are, as Weber said, like warring gods. The plebiscitarian democratic form that he promoted as a constitutional structure served to *make* values compete by subjecting their charismatic champions to the test of public acclamation. In this ideal we see the last vestige of the liberal faith in public discussion – no longer as a faith in its rationality, but as a faith in the power of leadership appeals to command voluntary devotion.

Ihering could benignly contemplate the state of struggle that he believed history to be, because he believed that progressively better compromises would arise through struggle. Weber did not share this optimism, but he believed that the struggle between the charismatic politicians could be harnessed by a plebiscitarian democratic constitution to serve the end of national greatness. He knew that 'the fact that both [the Centre and the Social Democratic] parties dissociated themselves from the parliamentary system made parliamentary government impossible' (FMW, p. 112). He expected that the plebiscitarian presidency, in contrast to parliament, would be less weakened by the conduct of these parties. The Weimar presidency, however, was much weaker in relation to parliament than the presidency Weber desired.

During the Weimar era, Schmitt observed, some of the parties were 'totalizing'. They followed their adherents from cradle to grave, attempting to instil in them the correct *Weltanschauung*,[10] and were in a fundamental sense unwilling to engage in political debate in the sense envisioned by liberal parliamentarism. Their anti-parliamentarism went beyond 'dissociation', as practised by the parties of the old Reich. By defining its 'enemies' directly, that is not by pressing for laws through public debate, but by making these identifications the basis of their politics and often of direct action, these new parties, such as the Nazis and the Communists, undermined what Schmitt regarded as the most significant political monopoly of the state, its capacity to draw the distinction between friend and enemy (Schwab, 1970, p. 78). Schmitt saw that constitutional order could not withstand the pressures of the plural and unrestrained demands of these parties.

Schmitt discussed the problem of the legal tools for the defence of the state, notably the dictatorial means of article 48, and studied the underlying theory of dictatorship. He concluded that, in the Weimar system, it was the responsibility of the president to act in defence of the constitution.

The constitution, he held, is 'inviolable' in essence; its provisions must be interpreted in light of the necessities of the defence of the constitutional order as a whole (Bendersky, 1983, p. 97). This suggested that the president was not only obliged to use the legal means provided by the constitution for its defence but obliged by his oath to go beyond the letter of the constitution, if necessary, to preserve its essence.

Where the legal order is itself threatened, and the threat cannot be resolved by 'normal' means, it is not 'values' but what Weber calls the 'objective pragmatism of "reasons of state"' (FMW, p. 334) that governs politics. The sphere of politics reduces to the elemental problem of decision: the problem of identifying the enemy and choosing allies. Weber made no attempt to theorize the situation of necessity, or to relate it to his theory of value-choice. He simply acknowledged it. Schmitt's account of necessity served to circumscribe the place of value-choice by drawing the contrast between ordinary politics and occasions when action is a response to an autonomous and distinct 'necessity'. This step transformed the structure of political reasoning Weber developed. Necessity, which had been to Weber an unintegrated category, became for Schmitt a large and autonomous realm of the irreducibly 'situational' and unique: *necessitas non habet legem*. The enlarging of this realm, as Schmitt's critics saw, was a further step in the de-rationalization of politics.

Schmitt did not limit his constitutional thinking to the realm of necessity. He proposed eliminating parts of the constitution in order to arrive at a document accepted by all significant parts of the population, a strategy closer to Ihering's or Weber's. The range of common ground, however, had never been very large; the contradictions in the original document itself testify to that. In the end, this common ground diminished and the president, Hindenburg, who was reluctant to rule by article 48, appointed Hitler Chancellor in the hope that effective parliamentary rule could be restored. Hitler had different hopes. His aim was to change the 'essence' of the constitution, and his manner of doing so embodied an image that had become successively more central in the de-rationalizing progression from Ihering through Weber to Schmitt – of the primal bond between the order-creating law-giver and the obedient multitude.

Notes

1   For a discussion of the events of 1848, which shows the character of the proletarian and peasant threat, and suggests how it would have been seen by the bourgeoisie, see Valentin, 1940, pp. 220–46.
2   The principle gave rise to a school of *Interessenjurisprudenz*, based on the doctrine that the judges' application of the law should respect the implicit compromise between interests contained in a given law.

3 Ihering treated dictatorship in 'conditions of necessity' (1968, p. 188) as abnormal, but not as historically unusual, even for a more or less stable legal order.

> In case of necessity a dictator was named in Rome, the guarantees of civil freedom were set aside, law receded, and unlimited military power stepped into its place. Corresponding measures at the present day are the right of the government to declare a state of siege, and to issue provisional laws without the co-operation of the estates of the realm; such measures acting as safety valves, to enable a government to remove the distress by course of law. (1968, p. 188; cf. Schmitt, 1928)

4 In the early pages of his 1917 essay, 'The Meaning of "Ethical Neutrality"', Weber commented, in a footnote, that 'as to the "irreconcilability" of certain ultimate evaluations in a certain sphere of problems, cf. G. Radbruch's *Einführung in die Rechtswissenschaft*. I diverge from him on certain points but these are of no significance for the problem discussed here' (MSS, p. 11). Radbruch's views on these issues in this text were consistent with other of his works quoted in this chapter. Cf. also Chroust, 1944.

5 Weber amplifies this thought elsewhere, when he says that

> it is possible to defend quite meaningfully the view that the power of the state should be increased in order to strengthen its power to eliminate obstacles, while maintaining that the state itself has no *intrinsic* value, that it is a purely technical instrument for the realization of other values from which alone it derives its value, and that it can retain this value only as long as it does not seek to transcend this merely auxiliary status.
> (MSS, p. 47, italics in original)

6 Cf. Pipes, 1955, esp. pp. 398–9.

7 Weber's later constitutional writings, which were addressed to the day-to-day development of constitutional discussion, are analysed in Mommsen (1984, pp. 332–81).

8 Although these vast emergency powers have analogues elsewhere in western European constitutions, the sheer extent of their use in Germany may be said itself to alter the character of the office of president, especially in relation to parliament. Carl Schmitt appreciated, as Weber perhaps did not, the *constitutional* significance of these practices.

9 Ethical decisionism, the position of Weber and Radbruch, is distinct from, though not inconsistent with, this legal theory. Radbruch, indeed, suggests that what Schmitt would call decisionism could be derived from relativism (1950, pp. 116–17). Nevertheless, the passages usually cited in support of the claim that Schmitt was a nihilist, relativist, or decisionist in the ethical sense are open to a different interpretation: that, in the historical circumstance of a plurality of values, authoritative decision remains the *fons et origo* of legal order, and that even when the fundamental principles are agreed, as in the church, this fundamental necessity obtains, and takes the form of the problem of authoritative interpretation of basic principles (cf. Schwab, 1970, p. 46). Both these problems arise, Schmitt says, from the same source, the wickedness of man. 'In a good world among good people . . . only peace, security, and harmony would prevail. Priests and theologians are here just as superfluous as politicians and statesmen' (quoted in Bendersky, 1983, pp. 87–8).

10 A contemporary example of this would be the radical movements in Israel which pursue settlement policies contrary to those that the government approves.

17

Modernity or Modernism? Weber and Contemporary Social Theory

SCOTT LASH

A number of chapters in this book address – directly or indirectly – the issue of what is distinctive about *modern* social life. Here, in keeping with much of the best and predominant currents of sociological wisdom, 'the modern' is mainly understood in contradistinction to the traditional. More specifically, most of those who characterize our times, and Weber's times, in terms of the modern are speaking about *modernity*. Conventional usage has habitually spoken of modernity as an era that was ushered in via the Renaissance, rationalist philosophy and the Enlightenment, on the one hand, and the transition from the absolutist state to bourgeois democracies, on the other. What I want to argue in the pages that follow cuts somewhat strongly against the grain of this position. It is that our times and 'the modern' should be understood, not as modernity, but in terms of *modernism*. Whereas modernity was inaugurated in the sixteenth and seventeenth centuries, modern*ism* is usually taken as a paradigm change in the arts which began at the end of the nineteenth century. I wish to propose, however, that not only contemporary arts but contemporary social practices, taken more generically, can be understood in terms of modernism. Further, my claim here is that modernism registers a fundamental break with the assumptions of modernity.

My arguments to support this claim are drawn from consideration of three of today's leading social thinkers – Daniel Bell, Michel Foucault and Jürgen Habermas – on the nature of the modern. They are drawn also from consideration of one 'classical' sociological thinker, Max Weber, again on the nature of the modern. In pursuing these arguments I shall at the same time make a subsidiary argument for convergence among these four social analysts. This second claim is that each of these major social thinkers has articulated a position whose logic entails a conception of the modern which is that, not of modernity, but of modernism. Each of these

355

positions thus comprises a view of contemporary sensibility and social practices that foregrounds fundamental *departures* from the Enlightenment and the rationalizing ethos of modernity.

Since the early 1980s the long-standing inquiry into questions of modernity has been joined by widespread debate on the more specific nature and significance of modern*ism* (Giddens, 1981; Habermas, 1981a). What has remained unresolved in these controversies is whether modernism constitutes a deepening or an undermining of the Enlightenment's project of modernity. I shall argue below that to pose the question of modernism one-sidedly as a deepening of a set of processes set in train by the Enlightenment or equally one-sidedly as an undermining of such a set of processes is falsely to pose the problem. Instead, I shall maintain, aesthetic modernism and its social correlates must be understood as a fundamental *transformation* of this project that includes not only both a deepening *and* an undermining of Enlightenment rationality, but also the transmutation and renewed development of *instrumental* rationality. Modernism is thus a three-dimensional configuration. I shall discuss these three dimensions each by reference to the above-mentioned commentators. I shall look at the modern, first, as a disruption of Enlightenment rationality through consideration of Daniel Bell's concept of modernism; second, as a new departure in instrumental reason – in which former principles of unity and transcendence are replaced by principles of plurality and immanence – through fairly strict consideration of Michel Foucault's concept of 'the Modern'; third, as a deepening of Enlightenment rationality – or in terms of the development of 'substantive rationality' – through the treatment of Jürgen Habermas's notion of 'modernity'.

Then I shall turn to consideration of Max Weber. Here we shall see that Weber's classical sociology of modernity, like its contemporary sociological counterpart – indeed Bell and especially Habermas have been crucially influenced by Weber – also understands the modern in a sense consistent with modernism. The recent interpretation of Weber by Habermas (1984) and Schluchter (1981) as well as by younger writers – Brubaker (1984) and Turner and Factor (1984a) – have understood the conditions and limits of rationality pre-eminently through Weber's essays on the sociology of religion. I shall follow their lead in my treatment below, except that I shall focus instead on Weber's sociology of law. Here it is well known that Weber was a proponent of 'legal positivism'. What is less a matter of common agreement and what I shall argue for below, is the thoroughly modern*ist* nature of Weber's legal positivism and of his sociology of law.

Modernism as Anti-Rationality

Among sociologists, Daniel Bell's view of modernism in *The Cultural Contradiction of Capitalism* (1976) is closest to the standard literary-, music- and art-critical characterizations of the phenomenon. When Bell speaks of modernism, what he above all addresses is the 'modern sensibility'. The modern sensibility here is an attribute of individual social actors caught between structural changes in society, on the one hand, and culture on the other. All of these changes in the social, in culture and in the individual have been in the direction of an attack on ultimate, or even stable, 'foundations'. Modernist anti-foundationalism challenges and undercuts ultimate (or even enduring) grounds for knowledge, moral action and aesthetic judgement as well as the stability of everyday life. Modernist culture or aesthetic modernism has for Bell two major dimensions. The first he calls the 'eclipse of distance', the second the 'rage against order'. By 'eclipse of distance' Bell means the dissolution of aesthetic distance between performer and spectator, of psychic distance between author and work of art. This is exemplified in the overwhelming of the spectator through the foreshortening of perspective by expressionists like Munch; the new preoccupation with the material in painting, to the point at which brush strokes, the density of paint and texture are more important than either figure or ground. The eclipse of distance is not only spatial, but temporal, as narrative is disrupted from the succession of beginning, middle and end, through use of stream of consciousness and general repudiation of continuity (Bell, 1976, pp. xxi, 48–9). The 'rage against order' is for Bell even more basic to aesthetic modernism. What is at issue here is not just the often noted modernist war against the sacred, its original difficulty and attempt to disturb the audience, to *épater le bourgeois*; not just modernism's anti-foundationalist revolt and rage against the prevailing style. Key instead is its drive towards self-infiniti-zation; its insistence on the imperiousness of self, on 'man as the self-infinitizing creature' impelled to search for the beyond; its Faustian placement of the self in place of God (Bell, 1976, pp. xx, 47, 49–50). The self in modernism's Faustian dimension is for Bell surely not 'abstract man', or a notion of God's replacement by rationalist moralities of humanism. It is instead a Dionysian self rooted in the aesthetic–sensual conceptions of subjectivity. Not only was the formal nature and rational ordering of modernist art in its early decades rooted in a set of valuations that apotheosized the aesthetic realm, but this aestheticism was necessarily linked with an instinct-centred psychology in so far as the aesthetic justification of life meant that the 'quest for the self was to explore its relation to sensibility' (Bell, 1976, p. 52).

Bell's account of the modernist sensibility embraces also an implicit aesthetics of reception. Here the receptivity of the audience to the new art forms is conditioned by a set of social structural changes that are equally anti-foundationalist, in which – and the similarities with Marshall Berman (1983) are striking – 'all that is solid melts into air'. What Bell and Berman mean here is that sensibility is not just a question of a relationship to works of high (or even popular) culture, but that it is a relation of our senses to the sounds, images, figures, feelings, even eroticism of everyday life. Perhaps most basic here is a reordering, which is often also a disordering, of the temporal and spatial patterning of our sensations. Temporally, what this means is that with revolutions in transport we are presented not just with a new awareness of motion and speed, but with a jarring increase in the velocity of the succession of images, and a succession of much more widely *varied* images. With radio, phonographs, television, video and now digitalization, it has meant an unusual increase in the frequency of communications (Bell, 1976, p. 47), to the extent that meaning is heavily devalued in an 'overload' of communications. The paradigm-shift in our spatial logic of sensation has been even greater, not the least because, as Bell underscores, the old narrative culture has been replaced by modernism's essentially visual sensibility. A temporal organi-zation of sensation reigned at the turn of the nineteenth century in which our cultural equipment was limited to the narrative modes of theology, literature and oratory. Visual sensation is, of course, temporal and spatial. This is a matter not only of the pervasion of newer visual cultural modes of painting, cinema, architecture and television, but of the sights of the city itself; of the new spatial juxtaposition of sharply contrasting social classes, ethnicities, modes of appearance and comportment, and sheer numbers of people; of the change from the closed village structure to the impressions of urban architecture – the visual impressions of the 'man-made landscape; cityscape and roads, dams and bridges'. The point here, as Bell notes, is that the 'immediacy of the visual image does not allow for the contemplation of the written word', especially where there is a rapid succession of images (Bell, 1976, pp. 106–7).

This reordering/disordering of our spatio-temporal patterning of sounds and images is furthered in the modernist tendency to substitute for a set of ultimate values based on tradition, religion, or reason, a new belief system founded on experience, and sensation. In this sense, as Bell observes, the main source of modernist identity is experience. With the decline of the family and social class, identities are confirmed in the simultaneity of a generation. Our experience and knowledge of increas-ingly numerous others in increasingly numerous interactions, our multi-plied *self*-experience – with the modernist disjunction of person with the number of functional role he or she fulfils – make our 'sensibility open to immediacy, impact, sensation' (Bell, 1976, pp. 88–91).

Bell's cultural-contradictions argument is oriented less to the precariousness of the capitalist economy than to what he sees as the decline of Western civilization, of the civilization of modernity itself. His more embracing claim then is that modernism is undermining modernity. Bell here suggests an account for the rise and decline of Western civilization in the realms of morality and of aesthetics. In the moral sphere, the rise of Western civilization takes place along the dimension of religion-bound asceticism and later a Whig-like secularized sobriety, itself based ultimately on a theological cosmology; the downward slope traces the dimension of modernist hedonism, whose roots were already present towards the beginning of modernity in the Hobbesian psychology of limitless appetites (1986, pp. 80–3). In the aesthetic sphere, the mechanical cosmology of a rational and unified order inaugurated in the Renaissance is dissolved in the modernist cosmology of disorder, in modernism's conception of a plurality of cultural orders and of a culture-bound subjectivity, which now needed to impose order on an unregulated and chaotic reality (pp. 86, 96). The Renaissance assumption of a well-ordered universe was 'rational' in that formal mathematical principles were applied to painting to impart a geometric lawfulness to artistic space. It was rational also in its rootedness in a scientific cosmology, in which space was understood in terms of depth, time in terms of sequence; in which music was characterized by 'an ordered structure of sound intervals', and narrative by a beginning, middle and end (pp. 108–9). In literature, for example, the break with such a rationalist cosmology was instanced in the obsession in poetry and prose with the materiality of the word: with attempts to institute a musical principle of simultaneity in, for example, Flaubert, hence disrupting ordered time sequence; with the surrender of narrative control by the rational ego in Proust, in which memories of the past repeatedly incur upon the present (pp. 112–14, 117).

In his depiction of modernist sensibility, Bell has etched a notion of modernism as essentially disruptive of rationality, thus outlining one dimension of modernism as a cultural configuration. The second side of the modernist triangle describes a deepening and becoming immanent of *instrumental rationality*. To elucidate this dimension of modernism we turn to Michel Foucault.

Modernism as Instrumental Rationality

Foucault, unlike for example Toennies or Durkheim, does *not* work in terms of a contrast of tradition with modernity. In most of his writings he speaks instead of two post-traditional epochs: the Classical, which spans the Enlightenment, and the Modern. Foucault's 'Modern', I shall argue, shares many basic characteristics with modernism. His periodization should be placed in the context of French intellectual life already marked by similar models advanced by Sartre and Roland Barthes. The latter two promulgated a chronology of aesthetic forms, in which a Classical period began in the sixteenth century and a Modern in the mid-nineteenth century, the second of these corresponding to the rise of literary modernism (see Lavers, 1982, pp. 61–2). Foucault has in effect transmuted this aesthetic periodization into a chronology of theoretical discourses articulated with configurations of power. He has, in other words, changed it into a periodization of *instrumental* rationality. Here Foucault presents an account of instrumental reason in which two basic principles unite what he conceives as the Modern with aesthetic modernism. These are (1) a principle of plurality which contrasts with the Classical principle of unity and (2) immanence as counterposed to the Classical principle of transcendence. Let us address these two principles in terms of knowledge and power.

In the aesthetic realm, as we saw above, modernism departed qualitatively with the ordered unity prescribed by Alberti's Renaissance aesthetic. Foucault's analysis of a similar shift, from the unified operation of power in the Classical to the plural development of 'micro-arenas' of power in the Modern, has already been the subject of commentary (Lash, 1985). A parallel process of change in the realm of knowledge has been less widely discussed. Classical discourse, observes Foucault in *The Order of Things* (1970), was located in a homogeneous field, in which all knowledge 'proceeded to the ordering of its material by the establishment of differences and defined those differences by the establishment of an order'; an order that, he goes on to argue, held true not only for the sciences but for mathematics and philosophy as well (1970, p. 346). The unifying framework of this homogeneous and Classical episteme is what Foucault calls 'mathesis universalis' (1970, p. 349). What this presumes for Foucault is a single and universal order of *representation*. That is, the Classical episteme, which establishes an order of things through classification by smallest differences, is dependent on a relationship between the classifications and the things that is one of representation. The reader of *The Order of Things* is puzzled by the fact that Foucault offers no such single ordering principle to the Modern. The Modern episteme, in contrast, he defines by 'the retreat of mathesis'; the retreat of a view of a homogeneous epistemological space and unified ordering. Foucault's aim is to argue against those who would attribute to Modern knowledge the unifying principle that man has become the object of discourse. Instead he maintains that the epistemological basis on which the human sciences developed was unalterably plural. The appearance of the sciences of man is, for Foucault, conditioned by three new nineteenth-century departures in Modern knowledge: first, a biology whose object becomes the living organism; second, an economics that now gives priority to labour; and third, a linguistics (philology) whose new object is concrete individual languages. The human sciences are for him based on the incorporation into human subjectivity of the objects (life, labour, language) of these new Modern (non-human) sciences. The point is not only that is the homogeneous episteme of the Classical replaced by the plurality of the Modern, but that the heterogeneity of the latter underlies the putatively unified nature of man in the human sciences.

The second transformation in the development of a modernist instrumental rationality is that from the principle of transcendence to the principle of immanence. Modernist art displays immanence rather than transcendence in that it breaks with the dualist model of mimesis and the dualism of figure and ground of pre-modernist art. In addition it is self-referential in its formalistic valuation of the material, of textured layers of paint, of the word. Further, it breaks – in, for example, primitivism – with Western, transcendental and realist rationalities. Foucault in *The Order of Things* understands changes in the form of knowledge in a parallel vein, in which Classical knowledge (seventeenth and eighteenth centuries) assumes a principle of transcendence, and Modern knowledge (nineteenth and twentieth centuries) a principle of immanence. Perhaps the best way to grasp what Foucault is getting at here is via Hegel. When Hegel criticized Kant for the latter's 'abstract' idea of reason, he was criticizing a transcendental and dualist model of knowledge, in which the knowing subject and reason were radically separate from the object under consideration. The objects of knowledge here, nature and society (in *The Philosophy of Right*), should, Hegel propounded, also be understood as possessing rationality. This conjugation of reason with nature, and *eo ipso* the social, was the very crux of Hegel's dialectic (Taylor, 1975). Once nature and the social also were characterized by reason – and Weber's work too would be unthinkable without the previous existence of such a conceptual mode – then reason was no longer transcendent, but was now immanent, in the object of knowledge itself.

In Foucault's account of the Modern sciences Hegel's prescriptions seem to have come true. All Classical knowledge here is, as just mentioned, based on principles of representation and classification. This assumes a transcendental model of knowledge based on a dualism of, on the one hand, the knowing subject and, on the other, the object of knowledge. In this, the knowing subject first *represents* the object and its qualities in words (and the original French title of *The Order of Things* was *Les mots et les choses*), and then uses these words to *classify* the objects under consideration. Here, as in Hegel's characterization of abstract reason, both the subject and the words are radically distinct and separate from the object of knowledge. In contrast, Foucaldian Modern knowledge has become based on a principle of immanence, in the Hegelian sense that reason itself has become a quality of the object of knowledge. This has come to pass for Foucault in two senses. (1) Modern science is no longer classificatory, but has engaged with a set of structural interconnections interior to the object of knowledge itself; that is, science has become engaged with a rationality which is proper to its object (Foucault, 1970, p. 244). (2) In the history of Modern sciences first the 'living organism' and then man has taken the place of the object of knowledge. Previously man had been only the subject of knowledge. This Modern immanence, Foucault argues at some length, is characteristic of both natural and social (human) sciences.[1]

This new immanence of Modern knowledge is at the same time a new departure in the operation of instrumental reason. First, it is reason and the development of the human sciences through whose mobilization new forms of power and domination are possible. Second, it is reason and science that provide modes of legitimation for such domination. The point is that immanentist forms of discourse have become at the same time immanentist forms of power. That is, in the Classical, power was lodged in a transcendent juridico–discursive instance, a transcendental state. In the Modern, sovereignty is lodged in the social itself, and power circulates immanently 'in the capillaries of society'; the state is no longer above us but among us. Classical power operates negatively through the exclusion of madmen, criminals, the indigent and the idle from discourse and from citizenship. Modern power, on the other hand, operates positively; it individualizes, normativizes and mobilizes (through the *inclusion* into citizenship) bodies in the reproductive interests – both economic and military/demographic – of the social.

Classical power acts on bodies; Modern power, immanently, on souls. What this means is a shift from a coercive to a moral and therapeutic form of power. Classical madness was a matter of 'dungeons, tortures, chains', a 'continuous spectacle' (Foucault, 1967, p. 260), a matter of negative and repressive power. In the Modern asylum, however, a therapeutic model has reigned, or more accurately, as Foucault notes, a 'moral' strategy with a therapeutic source of legitimation. The moral strategy has operated through the 'soul' or 'conscience' of the madman; here the doctor 'organized guilt for the madman as consciousness of himself'; the doctor has attempted to build into the madman's consciousness an internalized categorical imperative, and thus mobilized the madman's body through his soul. Through an intricate system of observation, rewards and punishments, the madman was to come to recognize his 'guilt' and thus 'return to his awareness of himself as a free and responsible subject, and consequently to reason' (1967, p. 247). Thus 'instead of submitting to a simple negative operation that [in the Classical] loosened bonds and delivered reason's deepest nature from madness, one was in the grips of [a Modern] and positive operation that confines madness in a system of rewards and punishments, and included it in the moment of moral consciousness' (1967, p. 250).

For Modern power to act thus on souls, and through moral consciousness, entails a break with Classical juridico-discursive forms of power. This meant most of all the dissolution in the Modern of man as a rights-bearing subject. The disappearance of the transcendental state and the undermining of foundations in the Modern meant *eo ipso* the end of Classical natural-rights doctrine. For Foucault the negative character of power in the Classical left an important sphere of autonomy even to the prisoner and the madman, who in critical respects still functioned as rights-bearing subjects. Thus madness in the Classical comprises a 'symmetrical' and 'reciprocal' relation between the keeper and the madman, in which fear raged on both sides of the gates; in which autonomy was granted to the madman in that 'observation involved only the madman's monstrous surface', in which the sane man 'read in the madman . . . the imminent moment of his own downfall' (Foucault, 1967, p. 249). The Classical, Foucault observes, involved an 'abusive dialogue between reason and unreason', whose 'spectacle was the very element of the madman's liberty' (1967, p. 261). The Modern, on the other hand, entails an absence of rights, in which the madman loses 'full adult juridical status'. Rights disappear, but legislation remains and deepens, with the asylum and the doctor imparting legislation to the moral consciousness of the insane, which then, itself, becomes the legislator.[2]

One hesitation that there might be in understanding Foucault's Modern in terms of modern*ism* is that he dates the former as beginning at the end of the eighteenth century, while aesthetic modernism is a phenomenon of the last decades of the nineteenth century. But if one is consistently to understand the Modern – as I have argued Foucault does – in terms of a plural, anti-foundationalist and immanent instrumental rationality, then it would seem to me more appropriate to date it towards the end of the nineteenth century; that is, not at the beginning of capitalism but at the outset of '*organized* capitalism'. The rationalization of management and the shop-floor, the bureaucratization of the capitalist state, the rationalization of extra-institutional practices of social workers *vis-à-vis* the mad, criminal, indigent, 'idle' and otherwise deviant were phenomena contemporaneous with the birth of the Welfare State at the end of the nineteenth century. The beginnings of nationalism – hence the priority of the social – as well as the centrality of demographic concerns, and the ethos of social citizenship (cf. e.g. Kocka, 1974), as well as the birth of the human sciences themselves, came by most accounts (and even at points by Foucault's) rather at the end than at the outset of the nineteenth century. Foucault is idiosyncratic in his particular chronology because of the earlier rise of nationalism and bureaucracy in France, and because of his focus on the *origins* of Modern discourse (in Kant) instead of on its subsequent *pervasion* in the human sciences and aesthetic modernism, for which the Kantian revolution provided conditions of appearance and existence. In any event, no one has captured with such acuity the specific nature of modernist instrumental rationality, the specifically modernist forms of knowledge/power, as has Foucault. The thematic that runs implicitly throughout his work is one of a great paradox in which the Classical age, the Age of Reason, sets up an epistemology of order against a social reality of chaos, whereas the Modern(ist) age puts forth an epistemology of chaos – while at the same time creating an instrumentally rational and strait-jacketing social reality of organization and order.

Modernism as Substantive Rationality

If Bell has presented us with a portrait of modernism as the crisis of rationality and Foucault as the anti-foundationalist and immanentist deepening of instrumental rationality, then Critical Theory has traced the third segment of the triangle circumscribing the modernist cultural-ideological space and has given us a view of modernism as substantive rationality. By substantive rationality is meant a deepening of the emancipatory side of the Enlightenment's project of reason. Enlightenment reason is – in Hegel's critique – abstract, general and formal, and deals in 'abstract man' and 'abstract morality'; in modernity reason becomes concrete and substantive. It no longer deals just with man's 'surface' but enters immanently to his external, internal and social nature.

Adorno, in this context, has provided us with a modernist aesthetics of substantive rationality – that is, an aesthetics which propounds a deepening of the Enlightenment's project. This rationality is not only embodied in the systematic and formalist working through of the aesthetic material in high modernists such as Picasso and Schönberg, but also in the cognitively critical functions that Adorno assigned to art (see Bürger, 1985, p. 122; Jay, 1985, pp. 26–7; Wellmer, 1985, pp. 92–4). Let us, however, turn directly to considerations of the notion of modernity purveyed by Jürgen Habermas.

The first thing that should be noted about Habermas's conception of modernity is that it is a *post*-Enlightenment notion, and is surprisingly close to Bell and Foucault; for all three, cultural modernity is catalysed by Kant and fully crystallizes with the development of aesthetic modernism.

Habermas follows Weber and Piaget in dating the onset of the modern as not just post-Christian but post-rationalist and post-foundationalist (Habermas, 1981a; 1984, pp. xli, 163; 1985, pp. 195–6). The reality of the modern is in fact that of Weber's 'plurality of gods and demons'. Habermas's aim is, however, to save us from that very foundationless plurality by realizing the project of the Enlightenment and Greek Antiquity (1984, p. 10) on modernism's dubiously friendly terrain. In this quest Habermas goes beyond Adorno's aesthetics into an account of substantive rationality in social sciences and in everyday interaction in the 'life-world'.

In regard to aesthetics, Habermas is in agreement with Adorno's advocacy of the separation of the aesthetic sphere from the life-world (Jay, 1985, p. 129). Habermas would also seem to advocate an aesthetics of beauty and truth. But here he begins to part company with Adorno. First, the importance of works of art for Habermas lies mainly in their influence on the life-world and in their fostering of communicatively rational action. Therefore Adorno's formalism would lead to an over-emphasis on beauty as a criterion of aesthetic judgement. Habermas and writers such as Wellmer (1985, p. 109) and Bürger (1985, p. 130) instead have called for a 'semanticization' of art. This is also connected with what they see as a one-sided emphasis on artistic production in Adorno, for which the theory of communicative action (which is at the same time a theory of *inter*action) would complement with a *Rezeptionsaesthetik*. Primacy here is given to rationalizing effects on the life-world, which would be not just on 'our evaluative language ... but reach into our cognitive interpretations and normative expectations and transform the totality in which these moments are related to one another' (Habermas, 1985, p. 202).

For Habermas, the growth of rationality entails a cumulative learning process and, perhaps first and foremost, the 'discursive redemption' of (descriptive, moral and evaluative) statements. Because such criteria are not applicable without inconsistency to aesthetic statements, Habermas, unlike Adorno, refuses to speak of 'aesthetic rationalization'. Yet there is an important sense in which the logic of Habermas's theory of communicative action makes it possible to speak of truth and even of rationality of artistic production. Habermas's understanding of modernity hinges crucially on the separation of theoretical, moral-practical and aesthetic spheres in culture. This separation is mirrored by a decentring of subjectivity in the life-world in which external nature, social nature and internal nature are respectively differentiated. Here the counterpart of the normative sphere is social nature, and the counterpart of the aesthetic sphere is internal nature. Now internal nature in Habermas's life-world can be more or less rationalized. When it is rationalized it is likely that the 'expressive statements' or the expressive dimension of statements made by social actors will be rational. Statements are for Habermas rational along the expressive dimension when they are 'candid and self-critical' (1984, p. 43). Cognitive, normative, evaluative and expressive statements are for Habermas at the same time validity claims. Such claims are plausible and statements are rational when they are 'discursively redeemable'. Behind every type of statement lies, for Habermas, a 'discourse', in which the grounds for validity claims come under question. Behind expressive statements then lies 'expressive discourse', in which 'we call someone rational if he makes known a desire, intent, feeling, mood, shares a secret, confesses a deed etc. and then can reassure critics by drawing practical consequences and behaving consistently thereafter' (1984, p. 15). This is closely related to what Habermas calls 'therapeutic critique', in which 'the argument of a psychotherapist ... trains the analysand to adopt a reflective attitude toward his own expressive manifestations'. Here sincerity is crucial because 'anyone who systematically deceives himself about himself behaves irrationally' (1984, pp. 20–1). The point in this context is that Habermas speaks in the same tones about the productions of the artist. This is visible in his observations on the rationality of aesthetic discourse; here 'reasons have the peculiar function of bringing us to see a work or performance in such a way that it can be perceived as an authentic expression of an exemplary experience, in general as the embodiment of a claim to authenticity' (p. 20). Thus the rationality of an expressive statement is similar for Habermas to the validity of a work of art, and it is not inconsistent with his overarching framework to speak of aesthetic rationality.

Although Habermas states that he wants to oppose the dominance of the 'cognitive-instrumental' dimension of modernity over the moral-practical and aesthetic-expressive dimensions, he indeed seems to depreciate the aesthetic realm. He devalues the expressive-mimetic dimensions of language in favour of its communicative dimension, and is not, as Jay (1985, p. 137) observes, 'cognizant enough of the perhaps more contradictory than complementary nature of cognitive and aesthetic attitudes to nature'. At points Habermas (1981a; 1983) seems almost in agreement with Bell's diagnoses and implies that aesthetic modernity is undermining theoretical and practical rationality, although to be fair Habermas would limit this to the (many) forms of modernist art that are at odds with his own tastes. This devaluation of the aesthetic realm is entailed perhaps by the very logic of his break with Adorno's Hegelian framework. The categories of reason, reflection and consciousness in Adorno have a heavily foundationalist, even metaphysical coloration. Habermas, it is well known, breaks with such a philosophy of consciousness for a philosophy of language. But he needs very much to save a notion of reason. The only way that he can do this in a modernity that has largely broken with realist epistemologies and the metaphysics of natural rights is through understanding reason in terms of discursively redeemable validity claims. This 'seminar' model of rationality poses no problems in dealing with descriptive statement of the theoretical realm. But when it is equally brought to bear in the moral-practical and especially the aesthetic realm, as well as the communications of everyday life, it asserts an unavoidable cognitivist bias. Habermas, for example, understands what was 'reflection' for the philosophy of consciousness in terms of 'validity testing'. Adorno's Hegelian cosmology allows him to think through the 'unities-in-sublation' of reason and nature, the spiritual and the mimetic, sign and image; syntheses that despite their origin seem to have a considerable empirical fruitfulness, just as does the ultimately Hegelian concept of substantive reason. Habermas, in his very contemporary philosophy of language, cannot revert to the old metaphysics, hence he is forced to speak at best rather unconvincingly of a complementary totality of influence of aesthetic, theoretical and moral-practical cultural spheres in the life-world, and at worst in terms of the devaluation of the aesthetic and the expressive.

Despite his relegation of the aesthetic and focus on discursive redemption, Habermas is indeed a theorist of substantive rationality. In Hegel's sense, Habermas's rationalization of the life-world would be unlike Kantian abstract morality, the rationalization of ethical substance, of *Sittlichkeit*. Habermas's project is not just for the rationalization of normativity, or of social nature, but his idea of therapeutic critique mentioned above is a project for the rationalization of inner nature, of our expressive subjectivities. Such rationalization of the life-world is for Habermas the great opportunity that modernity leaves open to us. Let us once again stress here that Habermas's modernity is a post-Enlightenment, post-foundationalist view very like the moder*nism* that we discussed above in Bell and Foucault. Modernization is thus for Habermas a process of 'decomposition and differentiation', which creates a 'decentred' or 'unbound' subjectivity (1985, p. 199). But whereas for Bell this aspect of modernism fosters irrationality and a culture of desire-gratification, for Habermas this very modernist 'plurality of gods and demons' paradoxically opens up the possibility of substantive and communicative rationality (see Alexander, Chapter 9).

What Habermas is claiming here is that only in modernity is there sufficient differentiation of subjectivity that communications can take the form of discursively redeemable validity claims. And since Habermas chooses to define rationality largely in terms of such validity claims, it is modernity that promises the brightest hopes for reason. The crux of his argument here is that, prior to modernity, there was too much confusion and conflation of the (cognitive, moral-practical, evaluative, expressive and hermeneutic) dimensions of communication for the latter to be rational. Habermas cites with approval in this context Piaget's three-stage periodization of mythical-narrative, religious-metaphysical and modern world-views. In the mythical world-view of primitive society, Habermas notes, there is insufficient distinction between the natural world and the social world, between the inner world and both of the latter, and between language and states of affairs in order for there to be a rationality of communications. This absence of differentiation makes 'internal validity conditions' impossible and leads to contradictions in normative actions in tribal societies (Habermas, 1984, pp. 46–9, 57–8). Moreover, the assessment of validity claims is contingent on a developed sense of individuality that is impossible in primitive societies because of the absence of a differentiated subjective (or internal) nature; identities are hence not individualized but tied to collective knowledge in myths and rituals (1984, pp. 51–2). But insufficient differentiation for communications of discursively redeemable validity claims persists into the Age of Reason and the Enlightenment itself. Reason, while metaphysics persists, is not yet primarily a matter of rational justification and is not yet differentiated from normative orderings, such as in natural law, or from the ordering of external nature itself. This residual foundationalism makes rational critique impossible. Reason, as laid down in Alberti's aesthetics, is still not differentiated as a metaphysical ordering of art for there to be (with several significant exceptions) fully individualized works of art prior to modernism. It is only in the presence of modernist differentiation of spheres, worlds and dimensions of utterance and discourse that the type of unbound subjectivity is present that for Habermas is the necessary condition of rational critique and of substantive rationality.

I have now at some length, through treatment of three leading contemporary social theorists, put an argument for a sociological periodization. It is one that in particular creates a challenge to the classical sociological periodization of *Gemeinschaft* to *Gesellschaft*, status to contract, mechanical to organic solidarity, or, more generally, tradition to modernity. What I have argued is that after modernity, or perhaps at some point during modernity, something new came into being. This something has often been termed 'post-modernity' (e.g. Lyotard, 1984); but because the features of aesthetic modernism also describe its broad parameters, I have called it 'modernism'. I have argued that these three social analysts (through Bell's notion of 'modernism', Foucault's of 'the Modern' and

Habermas's of 'modernity') present a view of contemporary Western society which is very much that of modern*ism*.

I have proposed that these analysts have outlined the three main dimensions – anti-rationality, an immanent instrumental rationality and substantive rationality – of modernist culture. The three dimensions are, I think, intimately interwoven. Discussion of how they are interwoven is beyond the scope of this essay. However, the *plausibility* of such inter-weaving is suggested by, for example, Freudian theory. This pre-eminently modernist cultural discourse constitutes a break with Enlightenment reason in all three of the above senses. It addresses anti-rationality to the extent that it challenges the assumption that we are rational animals. It involves a deepening of instrumental rationality in so far as, for instance, asylums and social work have been influenced by its teachings. It embodies substantive rationality in so far as reason is no longer formal and abstract but penetrates into the human psyche; that is, in so far as it uses reason to understand our very irrationality. Max Weber – and it is probably no accident that classical sociological theory, Freudianism and aesthetic modernism developed at about the same time – also stands in a crucial relationship to the three dimensions of cultural modernism. It is to him that we now turn.

The Place of Weber

Unlike contemporary scholars, Weber could not write with any great self-consciousness of aesthetic modernism. Yet he wrote contempor-aneously with the rise of aesthetic modernism, and his writing shared a number of crucial themes with it. Let me touch on a few of these briefly. Modernist art's anti-representational ethos and its concern with the aesthetic material mean that it is essentially self-referential. Similarly, Weber's (and Durkheim's) epistemologies do not assume that knowledge provides a mirror for (social) nature; knowledge instead is self-referential in the sense that its categories and rules take on meaning only within the context of given forms of life.[3] Weber purveys the self-referential thematic not only in his epistemology but also in his ethics. Here, for example, the absolute ethical validity built into Kant's notions of the 'empirical will' and the 'pure practical will' (of the categorical imperative) is sociologized respectively as the instrumentally rational and value-rational social actor. To transform such ethical categories into sociological concepts is to take away their absolute character and make them self-referential categories of particular forms of social life (see Lash, 1984a, pp. 40–2).

The best confirmation of Weber's sociological modernism is to be found in the 'Intermediate Reflections' (FMW, pp. 323–59). In this he discusses the five value-spheres (economic, political, aesthetic, erotic and intellectual) which have become self-consciously differentiated in the modern. He talks about each sphere in terms of a three-stage periodization, stages that are not dissimilar to Habermas's primitive, religious-metaphysical and modern. The second of these stages includes the world religions and, by implication, mechanical and rationalist cosmologies. The third stage describes the famous modern 'plurality of gods and demons'. In the case of each value-sphere, Weber stresses the similarities of the modern with the primitive, and the dissimilarities of the modern with the religio-metaphysical stage. What the modern shares with the primitive here are also characteristics of aesthetic modernism; these are a renewed particularism – in comparison with the universalism of the religio-metaphysical – and a break with rational foundations. Thus modernist art departs sharply from the natural-science-based rationalist assumptions of mechanical cosmologies, and each of Weber's spheres becomes once again primitive in its break with the possibility of any ultimate grounding in reason or in a rational and universalist religious ethic. The very 'gods and demons' characterization of the modern recapitulated the plural theologies that preceded the world religions and should be understood in three senses: first, that as in Greek Antiquity the various value-spheres themselves would be assigned gods; second, that competing gods and demons within a sphere could find no ultimate grounds for legitimation (Brubaker, 1984, p. 73); and third – and this is given the most extensive treatment in the *Religionssoziologie* and especially in *Ancient Judaism* – that primitive and modern (but not the Gods of world religions) gods are not universalist in terms of concrete time and space but are gods of particular cities or of particular nations (Habermas, 1984, pp. 182 ff.).

In Weber's more general consideration of the value-spheres (see the Introduction to this volume) there is purveyed a notion of modernity which shares at least a dozen characteristics with aesthetic modernism (and the aesthetic modernist sensibility), which was outlined above in the discussion of Daniel Bell. These are: (1) self-referentiality; (2) anti-rationalism; (3) value-pluralism; (4) a new importance of the erotic; (5) a notion of aesthetic aura; (6) the possibility of a rationalized modernist aesthetics; (7) a convergence with the primitive; (8) a more radicalized individualism; (9) the disappearance of the sacred; (10) a renewed immanence; (11) anti-foundationalism; (12) a scepticism towards the theoretical in general and grand theory in particular. The germ of such a modernist reading is present in the interpretations of Weber inaugurated especially by Schluchter (1981) and Habermas (1981b). One area in which such a reading has been notably absent, however, is in Weber's political sociology in general, and his sociology of law in particular. Let me now argue that this pre-eminently non-cultural area can be understood in terms of modernism.

Modernism, Politics and Weber's Legal Positivism

Weber's sociology of law connects significantly with each of the three dimensions of modernism. As a *descriptive* sociology it can account for, and opens up possibilities for, each of the three dimensions. As a prescriptive doctrine of jurisprudence it excludes, I shall argue, on the one hand, substantive rationality and, on the other, anti-rationality in the more extreme forms of 'decisionism'. Also as a prescriptive doctrine, Weber's advocacy of 'legal rationality' is tantamount to – as much of the secondary literature has conventionally held – an advocacy of instrumental rationality. It is however, at the same time a great deal more.

The rationalization of law for Weber was based on two central assumptions, first of the separation of law and ethics and second that law be a deductively rational, coherent system. Thus for Weber the historical rationalization of law has consisted of (1) a series of progressive differentiations ending in the differentiation of law from ethics, and (2) a progressive process of formalization. Weber traces this rationalization across what amount to four ideal-typical stages that correspond less to chronological history than to an internal logic of rationalization. The four stages are (1) the primitive, in which the law is formal and irrational; (2) the traditional, in which law is substantive and irrational; (3) a 'transitional' stage of natural law, in which law is substantive and rational; and (4) modern law, which is formal and rational (see ES, pp. 809–15, 852–5). For Weber, then, substantive rationality in law is surely a pre-modern state of affairs.

Law that is substantive and rational is found, Weber maintains, in theocratic legal systems, in natural law and in welfare-type social justice jurisprudence. Such law is substantive in that it is based on an ultimate value. It is rational in so far as it is intellectualized and systematized, by university-trained church or legal scholars (Kronman, 1983, p. 78). The difference between the university base of rational law and the guild anchoring of irrational English common law was of importance for Weber.[4] Indeed, Weber's whole treatment of rationalization gives inordinate weight to intellectualization, in which the functionaries of the intellectual sphere, be they systematizing theologians or legal scholars (ES, pp. 883–4), play an 'imperialistic' role in bringing about the rationalization of the other spheres. Natural law jurisprudence – for Weber the 'purest form of value rationality' – effectively bridges the transition from traditional to modern law. Natural law is pre-modern in so far as ethical

371

and legal spheres have not yet been differentiated. It is also pre-modern in the sense that it assumes a set of fixed legal principles and thus the absence of a process of legal change. This is exemplified in the physiocratic doctrine that politics would be regulated by laws governing the natural order of society, the latter being made known to the monarch by enlightened public opinion (see Turner and Factor, 1984a, ch. 9). Yet natural law doctrine was intellectually rationalized. Though state law had to correspond to the laws of nature, natural law did promote the principle of enactment, and a sort of procedural legitimation by reasoned argument (Habermas, 1984, p. 264). Notwithstanding these rational characteristics, Weber was convinced – and correctly so – that the overall dominance of an ultimate value such as social justice would in the end damage legal predictability and thus legal rationality (Kronman, 1983, p. 95).

Natural law theories, and more generally substantively rational legal theories, are hence untenable for Weber in modernity. There have, however, been a number of recent attempts to resuscitate such doctrines which break with the metaphysical assumptions of Enlightenment-based natural law, and instead ground natural rights in reasoned discourse (Rawls, 1972; Dworkin, 1977). Habermas's theory of communicative action too has been commonly understood as a substantively rational ethics; it can also be seen, I have argued elsewhere, as another variant of discursively grounded natural law theory (Lash, 1985). Anthony Kronman has with special acuity argued that Weber's sociology of law advocates, at least implicitly, a similar position. For Kronman (1983, p. 21) Weber's jurisprudence rests on a guiding assumption that the creation of laws and legal events are 'posits' or acts of choice.[5] Key here (Kronman, 1983, pp. 84–5) is that events in regard to law be understood through the logical analysis of legal *meaning*, and that such juristic meaning of the legal event 'expresses or reflects human purposes or intentions'. This differs from pre-modern law, which viewed legal meaning as residing in external sense data. Modern law then for Kronman assumes the possibility for legal actors (whether legislators, judges, legal theorists, or laymen) of 'personality', of Weber's idea of meaningful life conduct. Here legal action is a question of the self-conscious realization of values. And legal actors come under the Weberian principle of *verstehen*, hence meaningfulness, rather than *erklären*, and causality. This view of legal action, as self-reflexive and logical, dovetails significantly with the new discursively grounded theories of substantively rational law. Kronman's use of Weber here opens up fascinating and desirable avenues for jurisprudence. But it is an illegitimate reading of Weber. This is so for two reasons. First, because Weber's notion of legal legitimation excludes self-reflexive behaviour on the part of lay legal actors, whose acceptance of norms is mostly due to 'habit' or 'faith'. Second, because Weber's insistence on the very separation of spheres would allow only legal elements to enter into the self-reflexivity of the legal actor, especially in the sense that Weber assumes that the meta-juristic *grounding* of modern legal *systems* is excluded from rational reflection.

Weber's relationship to the second dimension of modernism, instrumental rationality, is altogether more complex. Analysts such as Mommsen and Habermas (1984) have understood Weberian legal rationality as very much the equivalent of instrumental or purposive rationality. Mommsen's argument here was that Weber explicitly contrasted legal rationality with natural law, and further that the Weberian notion did not even presuppose a parliamentary system (Mommsen, 1984, pp. 423–4). One problem with Mommsen's (and Habermas's) interpretation of this is a lack of clarity as to what is meant by 'purposively rational' law. There are several ways in which law can be purposively rational, and these depend on two questions. (1) What entity is serving as an instrument for given interests? (2) For what interests does the instrument serve? The answer to the first question is either a given legal rule or a legal system. The answer to the second is the interests of a nation, a social class, or an individual. Now Weber's sociology of law in *Economy and Society* devotes very little discussion to legal rules or legal systems as an instrument of *any* of these interests. Most of the discussion of law and the economy is devoted not to how law serves as an instrument for economic interests but how certain legal structures function as conditions for capitalist development (see Habermas, 1984, p. 256). And even this discussion is secondary to the main theme of the *Rechtssoziologie*, which is the *formal rationalization* of law.[6] In this sense the sociology of law runs parallel to the studies of religion. Though the project of the latter is the discovery of religious pre-conditions of capitalism, most discussion is devoted to the rationalization of the world religions. In the case of law and religion, it is rationalization, and a highly intellectualist process of rationalization, that lays down the 'tracks' on which the battles of interest are fought out.

Yet law is, among other things, for Weber importantly connected to class and national interests. In effect Weber pursues two prima facie mutually contradictory notions of law. The first, as just mentioned, advocates a formally rational legal system. The second is the purposively or instrumentally rational connection of law with interests. Legal thinking that features this latter notion is known as 'sociological jurisprudence' (see Stone, 1966, pp. 502–17). This legal doctrine was first importantly developed by Rudolf Ihering (see Turner and Factor, Chapter 16), a theorist who exercised a profound influence on Weber. Ihering's idea of law in terms of the objectives of interests was fundamentally hostile to the 'legal-positivist' paradigm in which Weberian formal rationality was grounded (Hunt, 1978, p. 104). In Weber, however, there are elements of both doctrines, and I think that these seemingly contradictory conceptions are reconcilable. Although legal positivism insists *contra* natural-law theory that 'the law is the commands of the state', its seamless, rational, clear and consistent legal *system* must in the end be based on a fundamental norm. This norm cannot, as in natural-law theory, be rationally justified. And this norm – which serves as a guiding principle for the entire system of legal rules – can be such that the system effectively serves class or national interests.[7] Thus Weber's prescriptive legal doctrine, while not in the least reducible to instrumental rationality, is consistent with the latter.

These considerations invite comparison with Foucault. Weberian formal rationality of law would correspond with Foucault's pre-Modern 'juridico-discursive' forms of power. The very generality and impersonality of formally rational law, and the fact that its origins lie in the intellectual abilities of jurists to evolve a progressively more logical and consistent jurisprudence, presuppose a vision of law as transcendent to social interests. Foucault (1975, pp. 52–3) understands (and Weber is in basic agreement) such a general, impersonal and 'repressive' form of law to give greater dignity to the individual than Modern law, which is largely based on a therapeutic principle. Weberian jurisprudence, in so far as it advocates formal rationality, thus bears in our terms certain premodernist traits. In so far as it envisages *instrumental* rationality, Weber's conception would, as judged against Foucault's criteria, be fully modernist. This is because Weberian instrumental rationality entails a connection with social and/or national interests in which law loses its transcendent qualities. Foucault (1975, pp. 210–12) laid particular stress in this context on how Modern legal systems recruit and mobilize individuals in the interest of nations.[8]

To address the third and anti-rationalist dimension of modernism in Weber's sociology of law is necessarily to address the problem of 'decisionism'. Here a system of law would need to rest on ultimate norms whose choice would be a matter of ungrounded 'decision' (Turner and Factor, 1984a, pp. 43–7). What this means also is that there is no rational basis for choosing one system of law – and discussion here is usually of constitutional law – over another (Turner and Factor, Chapter 16). Weber is a decisionist in this sense, and this follows directly from his commitment to value-free social science (Strauss, 1953). If, in this context, facts (in social science) must be set free from values, then values too (in ethics and jurisprudence) must indeed be set free from facts. That is, there can be for Weber no ultimate rational grounding of ethical values. The same would then hold true for those ultimate norms in which systems of constitutional law are grounded.

The attacks on Weber as decisionist have surely involved a more serious charge than this. They have involved comparison with Carl Schmitt, Third Reich legal theorist, whose decisionism is based on his reading of Hobbes.[9] What this seems to entail is that a 'decision' has already been made as to a legal system's ultimate norm, and that this norm is *raison d'état* itself. Hence the constitutional form which a nation chooses should be a function of *raison d'état*. The comparison with Schmitt pertains, perhaps more importantly, to a further element of anti-rationality: to Schmitt's counterposition of 'legality', on the one hand, and 'legitimacy', on the other.

Schmitt largely equated legality with parliamentary rule, the representation of pure material interests, the *Rechtsstaat*, purposive rationality and interest-group pluralism in general. None of this provided a basis, according to Schmitt, for *legitimacy*, by which he meant a more thoroughgoing integration of the masses into a national order. This was to be provided through a presidential 'plebiscitary leadership democracy', which would serve national interests and constitute a 'crystallization point for a new "substantial order"' (Mommsen, 1984, p. 387). As the Weimar Republic shifted away from parliamentary sovereignty in 1930, diverse political forces drew on Schmitt's doctrine promoting a presidential defender of the 'real' German constitution, which was counterposed to the parliamentary constitution of 1919. Schmitt drew here on Weber's advocacy of a strong plebiscitary and presidential principle for the Weimar Republic and from his more general ideal type of charismatic legitimation. Weber himself was, of course, sceptical of the intrinsic value of parliamentary institutions and saw that in Germany they were likely to be little more than a space for the battles of a plurality of pure material interests (ibid., p. 452).

We should, however, not overplay the connections between Weber and Schmitt. First, Weber had more of a commitment to legality and the *Rechtsstaat* than did Schmitt. This was not so much because it would provide a principle of legitimacy to the masses but because it would enhance calculability for economic transactions and provide a certain – though surely circumscribed – space for individual rights in general. Schmitt's subordination of the legal system to a 'substantial order' was such that the violation of Weber's principle of formal rationality was inevitable, as it proved to be in the Third Reich. Moreover, Schmitt's concern for a plebiscitary presidential constitution was far more tied up with the integration and mobilization of the masses than was Weber's. Weber's view of the masses, as we noted above, was of a rather passive force. His élitist ethos did away with the centrality of the *need* for a dominant ideology in organized capitalism (cf. Abercrombie, Hill and Turner, 1980). His advocacy of a strong presidency was mainly rooted in the context of international power politics.

Concluding Remarks

I have in the above pages argued that there is a surprising convergence between the notions of the modern advanced in contemporary social thought – in Bell, Foucault and Habermas – and in Weber's classical sociological formulations. I have maintained further that the conception of the modern in each of these cases has much more in common with the modern*ism* inaugurated in the late nineteenth and early twentieth centuries than with the modern*ity* of the Renaissance and Enlightenment. I have argued that modernism must be understood not only as an undermining of Enlightenment rationality, but also and simultaneously as a process of the deepening of the latter into substantive rationality and as a process of the pervasion of a newly immanent instrumental rationality. I have contended as well, via a discussion of Weber, that modernism is not just a matter of the cultural realm, but that its ethos also extends to twentieth-century law and politics.

These considerations of 'sociological modernism' might, I hope, be cause for reflection, at least for sociologists. What we might begin to ask ourselves is, for example, should we rethink the distinction between the traditional and the modern bequeathed to us by Toennies, Durkheim and Simmel? Moreover, should sociology – which has in the past implicitly and now explicitly addressed the issue of modernism – be understood as part and parcel of the phenomenon itself? Classical sociology, as I argued above in the case of Weber, shares a number of essential constitutive characteristics with modernism. Sociology did in fact develop in contemporaneity not with modernity but with (aesthetic) modernism. To pose these questions is to assert scepticism in the face of the still generally accepted Parsonian legacy of a sociology exclusively concerned with modernizing, rationalizing and civilizing functions. It is to take seriously Hegel's 'Owl of Minerva' metaphor and to apply it reflexively to sociology itself.

Notes

I would like to thank Sam Whimster for his helpful criticisms.

1 Foucault's description of the Modern sciences in *The Order of Things* also parallels aesthetic modernism in its assumption of constant change. In contrast to the relative stability of Classical knowledge, the chronology of the Modern human sciences which Foucault narrates is one in which each succeeding discourse cuts away the foundations of its predecessors. Thus Foucault more or less idiosyncratically presents a vision in which a sociology of action is replaced by a sociology of structure; the latter is then undermined by

semiotics, itself only to be subject to critique and undercutting by psycho-analysis (Foucault, 1970, pp. 356–79).

2   Thus for Foucault the Modern asylum 'would guarantee bourgeois morality a universality of fact and permit it to be imposed as a law on all forms of insanity' (1967, p. 259). In the Modern no longer 'is unreason set outside of judgement, but it is recognized, classified and made innocent forever . . . in a perpetual judgement . . . an operation which takes place through the intermediary of the internalization by man of the juridical instance' (pp. 268–9). Modern discipline through the creation of a moral and rational consciousness in the madman, while underpinned by therapeutic legitimations, is carried out on the model of the family. Here in the asylum madness becomes childhood, where the madman is 'subject to the authority and prestige of the man of reason, who assumes for him the concrete figure of an adult'. This process becomes only worsened in psychoanalysis, in which 'the powers of the asylum become abolished and concentrated in the person of the doctor'. The moral and rational consciousness now becomes super-ego; the doctor more literally becomes parent through the transference (Foucault, 1967, p. 278). Further, 'thrusts of the instincts' are no longer just against a rational-moral consciousness, but . . . against the solidity of the family institution itself and against its most archaic symbols' (1967, p. 254).

3   Equally, for Weber, consistent with Rickert's neo-Kantian views, Western knowledge has greater validity because it operates through rationalized modern Western values. This does not entail, however, a realist epistemology, in which knowledge somehow corresponds to reality (Bürger, 1976, pp. 49–56; Schluchter, 1981, p. 144; Habermas, 1984, p. 186).

4   On the juxtaposition of different elements within English law, see the instructive analysis recently put forward by David Sugarman: *Weber, Modernity and 'The Peculiarities of the English': The Rationality and Irrationality of Law, State and Society in Modern Britain* (1986).

5   The very focus on enactment and the destruction of meta-juristic principles in Weber legal-positivist jurisprudence also are resonant with the destabilizing and continually disruptive ethos of modernism.

6   Full rationalization of the law comes about only in modern formal rationality, in which the process of intellectualization begins to question and then undercut the very rational foundations of natural law itself. Thus modern formally rational law is characterized by a separation of law and ethics, a focus on enactment in the absence of meta-juristic principles, the clear and consistent separation of general legal rules from particular legal events that can be subsumed by those rules, and an enhanced importance for the intentions of legal actors. Weber's formally rational legal positivism assumed a 'logically clear, internally consistent . . . gapless system of rules, under which . . . all conceivable fact situations must be capable of being logically subsumed' (ES, p. 656).

7   What Weber himself desired, it has been argued, was a system of civil law that favoured the interests of the bourgeoisie as a class, and a constitutional law based on a norm that promoted national interests (see Mommsen, 1984, pp. 406, 450–1).

8   The rise of sociological jurisprudence which features an instrumentally rational (i.e. interest-linked) notion of law was roughly contemporaneous with the rise of aesthetic modernism (see Dicey, 1962).

9   I am indebted for this point to Professor E. Böckenförde.

References

Abercrombie, N., Hill, S. and Turner, B. (1980), *The Dominant Ideology Thesis* (London: Allen & Unwin).

Abramowski, G. (1966), *Das Geschichtsbild Max Webers* (Stuttgart: Klett).

Albrow, M. (1970), *Bureaucracy* (London: Macmillan).

Albrow, M. (1982), 'Max Weber and the rationalization thesis: the case of modern Britain', paper prepared for the Tenth World Congress of Sociology.

Alexander, J. C. (1983a), *The Classical Attempt at Theoretical Synthesis: Max Weber*, Vol. 3 of *Theoretical Logic in Sociology* (Berkeley: University of California Press).

Alexander, J. C. (1983b), *The Modern Reconstruction of Classical Thought: Talcott Parsons*, Vol. 4 of *Theoretical Logic in Sociology* (Berkeley: University of California Press).

Alexander, J. C. (1985a), 'Habermas' new critical theory: problems and prospects', *American Journal of Sociology*, vol. 91, no. 2, pp. 400–25.

Alexander, J. C. and Loader, C. (1985), 'Max Weber on churches and sects in North America: an alternative path toward rationalization', *Sociological Theory*, vol. 3, no. 1, pp. 1–13.

Antonio, R. and Glassman, A. (eds.) (1985), *A Weber–Marx Dialogue* (Lawrence: University Press of Kansas).

Aronson, N. (1984), 'Comments on Bryan Turner's "The government of the body: medical regimens and the rationalisation of diet"', *British Journal of Sociology*, vol. 35, pp. 62–5.

Asad, T. (1983), 'Notes on body, pain and truth in medieval Christian ritual', *Economy and Society*, vol. 12, pp. 287–327.

Bader, V. M., Berger, J. *et al.* (1976), *Einführung in die Gesellschaftstheorie* (Frankfurt: Suhrkamp).

Baumgarten, E. (1964), *Max Weber, Werk und Person* (Tübingen: Mohr).

Bell, D. (1976), *The Cultural Contradictions of Capitalism* (London: Heinemann).

Below, G. von (1926), 'Zum Streit um das Wesen der Soziologie', *Jahrbücher für Nationalökonomie und Statistik*, vol. 124.

Bendersky, J. W. (1983), *Carl Schmitt: Theorist for the Reich* (Princeton University Press).

Bendix, R. (1972), 'Max Webers Soziologie heute', in D. Käsler (ed.), *Max Weber, Sein Werk und seine Wirkung* (Munich: Nymphenburger).

Bendix, R. (1984), *Force, Fate and Freedom: On Historical Sociology* (Berkeley: University of California Press).

Berger, J. (1972), *Ways of Seeing* (London: BBC/Penguin).

Berman, M. (1983), *All That is Solid Melts into Air* (London: Verso).

Berman, Morris (1981), *The Reenchantment of Work* (New York: Cornell University Press).

Blum, L., Homiak, M., Housman, J. and Scheman, N. (1973), 'Altruism and women's oppression', *The Philosophical Forum*, vol. 5, nos. 1–2, pp. 222–47.

Bologh, R. W. (1976), 'On fooling around: a phenomenological analysis of playfulness', *The Annals of Phenomenological Sociology*, vol. 1, pp. 113–26.

Bologh, R. W. (1985), 'Gegenüberstellung von Max Webers dualistischem Konzept und Karl Marx' dialektischem Konzept', in W.-D. St-Diamond and R. Homann (eds.), *Bürokratie als Schicksal* (Opladen: Westdeutscher).

Bracher, K. D. (1973), *The German Dictatorship: The Origins, Structure and Consequences of National Socialism* (Harmondsworth: Penguin).

Breuer, S. (1982), 'Max Weber und die evolutionäre Bedeutung der Antik', *Saeculum*, vol. XXXIII, pp. 174–92.

Breysig, K. (1896), 'Über Entwicklungsgeschichte', *Deutsche Zeitschrift für Geschichtswissenschaft, Monatsblätter*, Neue Folge, I: 6.

Breysig, K. (1902), *Kulturgeschichte der Neuzeit. Vergleichende Entwicklungsgeschichte der führenden Völker Europas und ihres sozialen und geistigen Lebens* (Berlin: Bondi).

Breysig, K. (1905), *Der Stufen-Bau und die Gesetze der Welt-Geschichte* (Berlin: Bondi).

Breysig, K. (1907), *Die Geschichte der Menscheit*, Vol. I: *Die Völker ewiger Urzeit. Die Amerikaner des Nordwestens und des Nordens* (Berlin: Bondi).

Breysig, K. (1962), *Aus meinen Tagen und Träumen* (Berlin: Bondi).

Brinkmann, C. (1937), *Gustav Schmoller und die Volkswirtschaftslehre* (Stuttgart: Kohlhammer).

Broekhoff, J. (1972), 'Physical education and the reification of the human body', *Gymnasion*, vol. 9, pp. 4–11.

Brubaker, R. (1984), *The Limits of Rationality: An Essay on the Social and Moral Thought of Max Weber* (London: Allen & Unwin).

Brunet, R. (1922), *The New German Constitution*, trans. J. Gollomb (New York: Knopf).

Brunner, O. (1968), *Neue Wege der Verfassungs- und Sozialgeschichte* (Göttingen: Vandenhoeck & Ruprecht).

Bücher, K. (1894), *Die Enstehung der Volkswirtschaftslehre* (Tübingen: Mohr); translated by S. M. Wickett as *Industrial Evolution* (New York: Holt, 1907).

Burchell, G., Gordon, C. and Miller, P. (1986), *The Foucault Effect: Essays on Governmental Rationality* (Brighton: Harvester).

Bürger, P. (1985), 'The decline of the modern age', *Telos*, no. 62, pp. 117–30.

Bürger, T. (1976), *Max Weber's Theory of Concept Formation* (Durham, DC: Duke University Press).

Cahnmann, E. J. (1973), *F. Toennies: A New Evaluation* (Leiden: E. J. Brill).

Cahnmann, E. J. (1981), 'Toennies and Weber: a rejoinder', *Archives Européennes de Sociologie*, vol. XXII, pp. 154–7.

Carroll, J. (1977), *Puritan, Paranoid, Remissive: A Sociology of Modern Culture* (London: Routledge & Kegan Paul).

Cavalli, L. (1981), *Il capo carismatico. Per una sociologia weberiana della leadership* (Bologna: il Mulino).

Cavalli, L. (1982), *Carisma e tirannide nel XX secolo. Il caso Hitler* (Bologna: il Mulino).

Chroust, A. (1944), 'The philosophy of law of Gustav Radbruch', *The Philosophical Review*, vol. 53, pp. 23–45.

Cutler, A. J., Hindess, B., Hirst, P. Q. and Hussain, A. (1978), *Marx's Capital and Capitalism Today*, Vol 2 (London: Routledge & Kegan Paul).

Dahlmann, D. (1987), 'Max Weber's relation to anarchism and the anarchists: the case of Ernst Toller', in W. J. Mommsen and J. Osterhammel (eds.), *Max Weber and his contemporaries* (London: Allen & Unwin).

Danto, A. (1965), *Nietzsche as Philosopher* (New York: Columbia University Press).

Derrida, J. (1978), *Writing and Difference* (London: Routledge & Kegan Paul).

Dews, P. (1984), 'Foucault's theory of subjectivity', *New Left Review*, no. 144.

Dicey, A. V. (1962), *Lectures on the Relation between Law and Public Opinion in England during the Nineteenth Century* (London: Macmillan).

Diederichs, E. (1925), *Leben und Werk* (Jena).

Dreyfus, R. and Rabinow, P. (1982), *Michel Foucault: Beyond Structuralism and Hermeneutics* (Brighton: Harvester).

Dunning, E. (1983), 'Notes on some recent contributions to the sociology of sport', *Theory, Culture and Society*, vol. 2, pp. 135–42.

Dworkin, R. (1977), *Taking Rights Seriously* (London: Duckworth).

Eden, R. (1983), *Political Leadership and Nihilism: A Study of Weber and Nietzsche* (Tampa: University Presses of Florida).

Elbra, R. A. (1984), *Guide to Data Protection* (Manchester: National Computing Centre).

Eldridge, J. E. T. (ed.) (1972), *Max Weber: The Interpretation of Social Reality* (London: Nelson).

Elias, N. (1976), *The Civilising Process, Vol. 1: The History of Manners* (Oxford: Blackwell).

Elias, N. (1982), *The Civilising Process, Vol. 2: State Formation and Civilisation* (Oxford: Blackwell).

Elias, N. (1983), *The Court Society* (Oxford: Blackwell).

Ensor, R. C. K. (1946), *England 1870–1914* (London: Oxford University Press).

Enzensberger, H. M. (1962), 'Die Aporie der Avantgarde', *Einzelheiten* (Frankfurt: Suhrkamp).

Featherstone, M. (1982), 'The body in consumer culture', *Theory, Culture and Society*, vol. 1, pp. 18–33.

Ferry, J. M. (1985), 'Modernisation et consensus', *Esprit*, Mai, pp. 13–28.

Fleischmann, E. (1964), 'De Weber à Nietzsche', *Archives Européennes de Sociologie*, vol. 5, pp. 190–238.

Foucault, M. (1967), *Madness and Civilization* (London: Tavistock).

Foucault, M. (1970), *The Order of Things: An Archaeology of the Human Sciences* (London: Tavistock).

Foucault, M. (1972), *The Archaeology of Knowledge* (London: Tavistock).

Foucault, M. (1975), *Discipline and Punish: The Birth of the Prison* (London: Allen Lane).

Foucault, M. (1977), *Language, Counter-Memory Practice: Selected Essays and Interviews* (Oxford: Blackwell).

Foucault, M. (1978), *I Pierre Rivière, Having Slaughtered My Mother, My Sister and My Brother* (London: Peregrine).

Foucault, M. (1979a), *The History of Sexuality, Vol. 1: An Introduction* (London: Allen Lane).

Foucault, M. (1979b), 'On governmentality', *Ideology and Consciousness*, no. 6, pp. 5–21.

Foucault, M. (1980a), *Power and Knowledge* (Brighton: Harvester).

Foucault, M. (1980b), *Herculine Barbin: Being the Recently Discovered Memoirs of a 19th-Century Hermaphrodite* (Brighton: Harvester).

Foucault, M. (1981a), 'Omnes et singulatim: towards a criticism of "political reason",' in S. M. McMurrin (ed.), *The Tanner Lectures on Human Values, Vol. 2* (Cambridge University Press).

Foucault, M. (1981b), 'Questions of method', *Ideology and Consciousness*, no. 8.

Foucault, M. (1982), 'The subject and power', afterword to Dreyfus and Rabinow, op. cit.

Foucault, M. (1984), 'La phobie d'état', *Libération*, 30 June.

Freund, D. (1974), 'Max Weber and Alexis de Tocqueville', *Archiv für Kulturgeschichte*, vol. 56, pp. 457–66.

Freund, J. (1979), 'German sociology in the time of Max Weber', in T. Bottomore and R. Nisbet (eds.), *A History of Sociological Analysis* (London: Heinemann).

Frisby, D. (1981), *Sociological Impressionism* (London: Methuen).

Gandall, K. and Kotkin, S. (1985), 'Governing work and social life in the USA and the USSR', *History of the Present*, no. 1 (Berkeley: Department of Anthropology, University of California).

Garfinkel, H. (1956), 'Conditions of successful degradation ceremonies', *American Journal of Sociology*, vol. 61, pp. 420–4.

Gehlen, A. (1969), *Moral und Hypermoral. Eine pluralistische Ethik* (Frankfurt/Bonn: Athenäum).

Giddens, A. (1981), 'Modernism and post-modernism', *New German Critique*, no. 22, pp. 15–18.

Giddens, A. (1985), *The Constitution of Society* (Cambridge: Polity).

Gneist, R. (1886), *The History of the English Constitution*, trans. P. A. Ashworth (New York: Putnams).

Goffman, I. (1961), *Asylums* (Garden City, NY: Anchor).

Goldmann, L. (1973), *The Philosophy of the Enlightenment: The Christian Burgess and the Enlightenment* (London: Routledge & Kegan Paul).

Goldschmidt (1891), *Handbuch des Handelsrechts*, Vol. I, Erste Abteilung: *Universalgeschichte des Handelsrechts*.

Gordon, C. (ed.) (1980), *Power/Knowledge: Selected Interviews and Other Writings, 1972–1977* (Brighton: Harvester).

Gordon, C. (1986), 'Question, ethos, event: Foucault on Kant and enlightenment', *Economy and Society*, vol. 15, no. 1.

Gouldner, A. W. (1967), *Enter Plato: Classical Greece and the Origins of Social Theory* (London: Routledge & Kegan Paul).

Green, M. (1974), *The von Richthofen Sisters* (New York: Basic Books).

Groethuysen, B. (1968), *The Bourgeois: Catholicism versus Capitalism in 18th-Century France* (London: Barrie & Rockcliffe).

Habermas, J. (1971), *Knowledge and Human Interests* (Boston: Beacon).

Habermas, J. (1973), *Towards a Rational Society* (London: Heinemann).

Habermas, J. (1979), 'Aspects of rationality of action', in Gereats (ed.), *Rationality Today* (University of Ottawa Press).

Habermas, J. (1981a), 'Modernity and postmodernity', *New German Critique*, no. 22, pp. 3–14.

Habermas, J. (1981b), *Theorie des kommunikativen Handelns* (Frankfurt: Suhrkamp).

Habermas, J. (1983a), 'Neo-conservative culture criticism in the United States and West Germany', *Telos*, no. 56, pp. 75–89.

Habermas, J. (1983b), *Philosophical–Political Profiles* (Cambridge, Mass.: MIT Press).

Habermas, J. (1984), *The Theory of Communicative Action, Vol. One* (London: Heinemann).

Habermas, J. (1985), 'Questions and counter-questions', in R. Bernstein (ed.), *Habermas and Modernity* (Cambridge: Polity).

Haffner, S. (1978), *Anmerkungen zu Hitler* (Munich: Kindler).

Hall, J. A. (1985), *Powers and Liberties: The Causes and Consequences of the Rise of the West* (London: Penguin).

Hart, H. L. A. (1961), *The Concept of Law* (Oxford: Clarendon Press).

Hegel, G. W. F. (1980), *Lectures on the Philosophy of World History* (Cambridge University Press).

Held, V. (1973), 'Marx, sex and the transformation of society', *The Philosophical Forum*, vol. 5, nos. 1–2, pp. 168–84.

Hennis, W. (1982), 'Tocquevilles "neue politische Wissenschaft"', in Stagl (ed.), *Aspekte der Kultursoziologie. Festschrift für M. Rassem* (Berlin).

Hennis, W. (1983), 'Max Weber's "central question"', *Economy and Society*, vol. 12, no. 2.

Hennis, W. (1984), 'Max Webers Thema. "Die Persönlichkeit und die Lebensordnungen"', *Zeitschrift für Politik*, vol. 31, no. 1, pp. 11–52.

Hennis, W. (1985), 'Der Typus Mensch und sein Verhängnis – Nietzsches Genius im Werk Max Webers', *Frankfurter Allgemeine Zeitung*, 7 December.

Hennis, W. (1987), 'A science of man: Max Weber and the political economy of the German historical school', in W. J. Mommsen and J. Osterhammel (eds.), *Max Weber and his Contemporaries* (London: Allen & Unwin).

Henrich, D. (1952), *Die Einheit der Wissenschaftslehre Max Webers* (Tübingen: Mohr).

Hepworth, M. and Turner, B. S. (1982), *Confessions: Studies in Deviance and Religion* (London: Routledge & Kegan Paul).

Hindess, B. (ed.) (1977), *Sociological Theories of the Economy* (London: Macmillan).

Hindess, B. (1982), 'Power, interests and the outcome of struggles', *Sociology*, vol. 16, no. 4, pp. 498–511.

Hindess, B. (1984), 'Rational choice theory and the analysis of political action', *Economy and Society*, vol. 13, pp. 255–77.

Hindess, B. (1985a), 'Actors and social relations', in S. P. Turner and M. Wardell (eds.), *Sociological Theory in Transition* (London: Allen & Unwin).

Hindess, B. (1985b), 'Interests in political analysis', in J. Law (ed.), *Power, Action and Belief* (Sociological Review Monograph).

Hintze, O. (1975), 'Calvinism and raison d'état in early seventeenth-century Brandenburg', in F. Gilbert (ed.), *The Historical Essays of Otto Hintze* (New York: Oxford University Press).

Hirst, P. Q. and Woolley, P. (1982), *On Law and Ideology* (London: Macmillan).

Hübner-Funk, S. (1982), *Georg Simmels Konzeption von Gesellschaft* (Cologne: Pahl-Rugenstein).

Huff, T. (ed.) (1981), *On the Roads to Modernity, Conscience, Science and Civilizations: Selected Writings by Benjamin Nelson* (Totowa, NJ: Rowman & Littlefield).

Hunt, A. (1978), *The Sociological Movement in Law* (London: Macmillan).

Ignatieff, M. (1978), *A Just Measure of Pain: The Penitentiary in the Industrial Revolution, 1750–1850* (London: Macmillan).

Ihering, R. von (1915), *The Struggle for Law*, trans. J. Lalor (Chicago: Callaghan).

Ihering, R. von (1968), *Law as a Means to an End*, trans. I. Hasik (South Hackensack, NJ: Rothman Reprints).

Jäckel, E. (1969), *Hitlers Weltanschauung. Entwurf einer Herrschaft* (Tübingen: Rainer Wunderlich).

Jackson, S. W. (1981), 'Acedia, the sin and its relationship to sorrow and melancholia in medieval times', *Bulletin of the History of Medicine*, vol. 55, pp. 172–85.

Jameson, F. (1973), 'The vanishing mediator: narrative structure in Max Weber', *New German Critique*, vol. 1, pp. 52–89.

Jaspers, K. (1919), *Psychologie der Weltanschauungen* (Berlin: Springer).

Jay, M. (1984), *Adorno* (London: Fontana).

Jay, M. (1985), 'Habermas and modernism', in R. Bernstein (ed.), *Habermas and Modernity* (Cambridge: Polity).

Kalberg, S. (1980), 'Max Weber's types of rationality: cornerstones for the analysis of rationalization processes in history', *American Journal of Sociology*, vol. 85, no. 5, pp. 1145–79.

Kalberg, S. (1983), 'Max Weber's universal-historical architectonic of economically-oriented action', in *Current Perspectives in Social Theory* (Westport, Conn.: Greenwood Press).

Kalberg, S. (1985), 'The role of ideal interests in Max Weber's comparative historical sociology', in Antonio and Glassman, op. cit.

Kallen, D. J. and Sussman, M. B. (eds.) (1984), *Obesity and the Family* (New York: Haworth Press).

Kant, I. (1787), *Kritik der reinen Vernunft*.

Kant, I. (1949), *Critique of Practical Reason*, trans. L. Beck (University of Chicago Press).

Kant, I. (1956), *On History*, ed. L. Beck (Indianapolis: Bobbs-Merrill).

Kaufmann, W. (1968), *Nietzsche: Philosopher, Psychologist and Antichrist* (Princeton University Press).

Kellner, D. J. (1983), 'Critical theory, commodities and the consumer society', *Theory, Culture and Society*, vol. 1, pp. 66–84.

Kelsen, H. (1949), *General Theory of Law and the State* (Cambridge, Mass.: Harvard University Press).

Kern, F. (1970), *Kingship and Law in the Middle Ages*, trans. S. B. Chrimes (New York: Harper).

Knoll, J. H. (1957), *Führungsauslese in Liberalismus und Demokratie* (Stuttgart: Kohlhammer).

Koch, H. W. (1984), *A Constitutional History of Germany in the Nineteenth and Twentieth Centuries* (London: Longman).

Kocka, J. (1974), 'Organisierter Kapitalismus oder Staatsmonopolistischer Kapitalismus', in H. Winkler (ed.), *Organisierter Kapitalismus* (Göttingen: Vandenhoeck & Ruprecht).

Krieger, L. (1957), *The German Idea of Freedom: History of a Political Tradition* (Boston: Beacon Press).

Kronman, A. (1983), *Max Weber* (Jurists: Profiles in Legal Theory), (London: Edward Arnold).

Krüger, D. (1983), *Nationalökonomen im wilhelminischen Deutschland* (Göttingen: Vandenhoeck & Ruprecht).

Lamprecht, K. (1896), 'Was ist Kulturgeschichte? Beitrag zu einer empirischen Historik', *Deutsche Zeitschrift für Geschichtswissenschaft, Vierteljahresheft 2*, vol. 1, pp. 75–150.

Landshut, S. (1929; 2nd edn 1969), *Kritik der Soziologie* (Berlin: Neuwied & Luchterhand).

Lange, V. (1983), *The Classical Age of German Literature 1740–1815* (London: Edward Arnold).

Lasch, C. (1979), *The Culture of Narcissism* (New York: Norton).

Lash, S. (1984a), *The Militant Worker, Class and Radicalism in France and America* (London: Heinemann).

Lash, S. (1984b), 'Genealogy and the body: Foucault/Deleuze/Nietzsche', *Theory, Culture and Society*, vol. 2, pp. 1–17.

Lash, S. (1985), 'Postmodernity and desire', *Theory and Society*, vol. 14, no. 7.

Lavers, A. (1982), *Roland Barthes: Structuralism and After* (London: Methuen).

Levine, D. N. (1981), 'Rationality and freedom: Weber and beyond', *Sociological Inquiry*, vol. 51, pp. 5–25.

Loewenstein, K. (1966), *Max Weber's Political Ideas in the Perspective of Our Time* (Cambridge: University of Massachusetts Press).

Löwith, K. (1982), *Max Weber and Karl Marx* (London: Allen & Unwin).

Luhmann, N. (1968), *Zweckbegriff und Systemrationalität* (Tübingen: Mohr).

Luhmann, N. (1979), *Trust and Power*, ed. T. Burns and G. Poggi (Chichester: Wiley).

Luhmann, N. (1985), *Soziale Systeme* (Frankfurt: Suhrkamp).

Lukács, G. (1974), *Soul and Form* (London: Merlin Press).

Lyotard, J. F. (1984), *The Postmodern Condition* (Manchester: Manchester University Press).

MacIntyre, A. (1981), *After Virtue* (South Bend, Ind.: Notre Dame University Press).

Marcuse, H. (1955), *Eros and Civilization: A Philosophical Inquiry into Freud* (Boston: Beacon Press).

Marcuse, H. (1968), *Negations: Essays in Critical Theory* (London: Allen Lane).

Marcuse, H. (1971), Discussion of 'Industrialization and Capitalism', in O. Stammer (ed.), *Max Weber and Sociology Today* (Oxford: Blackwell).

Markus, G. (1978), *Marxism and Anthropology* (Assen: van Gorcum).

Maser, W. (1978), *Adolf Hitler. Eine Biographie* (Munich and Berlin: Herbig).

Mauss, M. (1969), *Oeuvres, Vol. III: Cohésion sociale et divisions de la sociologie* (Paris: Editions de Minuit).

Mayer, J. P. (1956), *Max Weber and German Politics: A Study in Political Sociology* (London: Faber).

McNeill, J. T. (1932), 'Medicine for sin as prescribed in the penitentials', *Church History*, vol. 1, pp. 14–26.

Meinecke, F. (1957), *Machiavellism: The Doctrine of Raison d'Etat and its Place in Modern History* (London: Routledge & Kegan Paul).

Merquior, J. G. (1980), *Rousseau and Weber: Two Studies in the Theory of Legitimacy* (London: Routledge & Kegan Paul).

Mészáros, I. (1972), *Lukács' Concept of the Dialectic* (London: Merlin Press).

Meyer, E. (1910), *Kleine Schriften* (Halle: Niemyer).

Mitzman, A. (1970), *The Iron Cage* (New York: Knopf).

Mitzman, A. (1973), *Sociology and Estrangement. Three Sociologists of Imperial Germany* (New York: Knopf).

Mommsen, W. J. (1974), *The Age of Bureaucracy* (Oxford University Press).

Mommsen, W. J. (1981), 'Max Weber and Roberto Michels', *European Journal of Sociology*, vol. 22, no. 1.

Mommsen, W. J. (1984), *Max Weber and German Politics* (University of Chicago Press).

Mommsen, W. J. (1987), 'Robert Michels and Max Weber: moralist fundamentalism versus political pragmatism', in W. J. Mommsen and J. Osterhammel (eds.), *Max Weber and his Contemporaries* (London: Allen & Unwin).

Müller-Armack, A. (1944), *Genealogie der Wirtschaftsstile* (Stuttgart: Kohlhammer).

Munch, R. (1982), 'Talcott Parsons and the theory of action, II: the continuity of development', *American Journal of Sociology*, vol. 87, pp. 771–826.

Neumann, F. (1944), *Behemoth: The Structure and Practice of National Socialism, 1933–1944* (New York and Toronto: Oxford University Press).

Nietzsche, F. (1968a), *Twilight of the Idols* (Harmondsworth: Penguin).

Nietzsche, F. (1968b), *The Will to Power* (New York: Vintage).

Nietzsche, F. (1969), *Genealogy of Morals* (New York: Vintage).

Nietzsche, F. (1973), *Beyond Good and Evil* (Harmondsworth: Penguin).

Nietzsche, F. (1982), *Daybreak* (Cambridge University Press).

Nietzsche, F. (1984), *Untimely Meditations* (Cambridge University Press).

Nisbet, R. (1967), *The Sociological Tradition* (London: Heinemann).

Nolte, E. (1963), *Der Faschismus in seiner Epoche* (Munich: Piper).

Nyomarkay, J. (1967), *Charisma and Factionalism in the Nazi Party* (Minneapolis: University of Minnesota Press).

O'Brien, P. (1982), *The Promise of Punishment: Prisons in 19th-Century France* (Princeton University Press).

Oestreich, G. (1983), *Neo-Stoicism and the Early Modern State*, trans. D. McLintock (Cambridge University Press).

Parsons, T. (1949), *The Structure of Social Action* (New York: McGraw-Hill).

Parsons, T. (1951), *The Social System* (Glencoe, Ill.: Free Press).

Parsons, T. (1966), *Societies: Evolutionary and Comparative Perspectives* (Englewood Cliffs, NJ: Prentice-Hall).

Pasquino, P. (1978), 'Theatrum politicum. The genealogy of capital – police and the state of property', *Ideology and Consciousness*, no. 4, pp. 41–72.

Pasquino, P. (1982), 'L' "Utopia" practicabile. Governo ed economia nel Cameralismo tedesco del settecento', *Quaderni delli Fondazione G. G. Feltrinelli*, no. 20.

Pipes, R. (1955), 'Max Weber and Russia', *World Politics*, vol. 7, pp. 370–401.

Pollock, Sir F. (1961), *Jurisprudence and Legal Essays* (Westport, Conn.: Greenwood Press).

Popper, K. (1957), *The Poverty of Historicism* (London: Routledge & Kegan Paul).

Portis, E. B. (1978), 'Max Weber's theory of personality', *Sociological Inquiry*, vol. 48, pp. 113–20.

Prager, J. (1981), 'Moral integration and political inclusion: a comparison of Durkheim's and Weber's theories of democracy', *Social Forces*, vol. 59, pp. 918–50.

Prigogine, I. (1980), *From Being to Becoming: Time and Complexity in the Physical Sciences* (San Francisco: Freeman).

Prigogine, I. and Stengers, I. (1979), *La nouvelle alliance. Metamorphose de la science* (Paris: Gallimard). English translation (1984), *Order out of Chaos: Men's New Dialogue with Nature* (New York: Bantam).

Radbruch, G. (1950), 'Legal philosophy', in K. Wilk (ed. and trans.), *The Legal Philosophies of Lask, Radbruch and Dabin* (Cambridge, Mass.: Harvard University Press).

Radbruch, G. (1951), *Der innere Weg: Aufriß meines Lebens* (Stuttgart: Koehler).

Rawls, J. (1972), *A Theory of Justice* (Cambridge, Mass.: Harvard University Press).

Rendtdorff, T. (1980), *Ethik, Grundelemente, Methodologie und Konkretionen einer ethischen Theologie*, Vol. 1 (Stuttgart: Kohlhammer).

Rorty, R. (1980), *Philosophy and the Mirror of Nature* (Oxford: Blackwell).

Roth, G. (1980), 'Sociological typology and historical explanation', in R. Bendix and G. Roth (eds.), *Scholarship and Partisanship* (Berkeley: University of California Press).

Roth, G. (1984), 'Max Weber's ethics and the peace movement today', *Theory and History*, vol. 13, no. 4, pp. 491–511.

Roth, G. and Schluchter, W. (1979), *Max Weber's Vision of History: Ethics and Methods* (Berkeley: University of California Press).

Runciman, W. G. (1984), 'Congenial aspirations', review article on J. Habermas, *The Theory of Communicative Action*, Vol. I, in *London Review of Books*, 4 October.

Rüstow, A. (1963), *Rede und Antwort* (Ludwigsburg: Hoch).

Savage, S. P. (1981), *The Social Theories of Talcott Parsons* (London: Macmillan).

Scaff, L. A. (1984), 'Weber before Weberian sociology', *British Journal of Sociology*, vol. 35, pp. 190–215.

Scaff, L. A. and Arnold, T. C. (1985), 'Class and the theory of history: Marx on France and Weber on Russia', in R. Antonio and R. Glassman (eds.), *A Marx–Weber Dialogue* (Lawrence: University of Kansas Press).

Schluchter, W. (1979), 'The paradox of rationalization: on the relation of ethics to the world', in G. Roth and W. Schluchter (eds.), *Max Weber's Vision of History* (Berkeley: University of California Press).

Schluchter, W. (1981), *The Rise of Western Rationalism: Max Weber's Developmental History* (Berkeley: University of California Press).

Schluchter, W. (1984), 'Max Webers Religionssoziologie: Eine werkgeschichtliche Rekonstruktion', *Kölner Zeitschrift für Soziologie und Sozialpsychologie*, vol. 36, pp. 342 ff.

Schmidt, A. (1971), *The Concept of Nature in Marx* (London: New Left Books).

Schmitt, C. (1928), *Die Diktatur* (Munich: Duncker & Humblot).

Schmitt, C. (1930), *Hugo Preuss: sein Staatsbegriff und seine Stellung in der deutschen Staatslehre* (Tübingen: Mohr).

Schmitt, C. (1934), *Über die drei Arten des Rechtswissenschaftlichen Denkens* (Hamburg: Hanseatische Verlagsanstalt).

Schmitt, C. (1979), *Die geistesgeschichtliche Lage des heutigen Parlamentarismus* (Berlin: Duncker & Humblot).

Schmoller, G. (1900), Vol. I *Grundriß der Volkswirtschaftslehre*, Vol. II (1904), (Leipzig: Duncker & Humblot).

Schönberg, G. (1897), *Handbuch der politischen Oekonomie* (Tübingen: Mohr).

Schumpter, J. (1954), 'The crisis of the tax state', *International Economic Papers*, vol. 4, pp. 5–38.

Schwab, G. (1970), *The Challenge of the Exception: An Introduction to the Political Ideas of Carl Schmitt between 1921 and 1936* (Berlin: Duncker & Humblot).

Seidman, S. (1983), 'Modernity, meaning and cultural pessimism in Max Weber', *Sociological Analysis*, vol. 44, pp. 267–78.

Shils, E. (1975), 'Charisma, order and status', in E. Shils (ed.), *Center and Periphery: Essays in Macro-Sociology* (University of Chicago Press).

Simmel, G. (1911), 'Der Begriff und die Tragödie der Kultur', in *Philosophische Kultur: Gesammelte Essais* (Leipzig: W. Klinkhardt).

Simmel, G. (1920), *Schopenhauer und Nietzsche* (Munich: Duncker & Humblot).

Simmel, G. (1923), *Fragmente und Aufsätze – aus dem Nachlaß und Veröffentlichungen der letzten Jahre*, ed. G. Kantorowicz (Munich: Drei Masken).

Simmel, G. (1971), *Georg Simmel: On Individuality and Social Forms*, ed. D. N. Levine (University of Chicago Press).

Simmel, G. (1976), *Georg Simmel*, ed. P. Lawrence (Sunbury: Nelson).

Smart, B. (1983), *Foucault, Marxism and Critique* (London: Routledge & Kegan Paul).

Smart, B. (1985), *Michel Foucault* (London: Ellis Horwood/Tavistock).

Sombart, W. (1893), 'Studien zur Entwicklungsgeschichte des italienischen Proletariats', *Archiv für soziale Gesetzgebung und Statistik*, vol. 6, pp. 177–258.

Sombart, W. (1899), 'Die gewerbliche Arbeit und ihre Organisation', *Archiv für soziale Gesetzgebung und Statistik*, vol. 14, pp. 368–405.

Sombart, W. (1906), *Warum gibt es in den Vereinigten-Staaten keinen Sozialismus?* (Tübingen: Mohr); trans. P. Hocking and T. C. Husbands, *Why Is There No Socialism in the United States?* (White Plains: International Arts and Science Press, 1976).

Sombart, W. (1913), *Studien zur Entwicklungsgeschichte des modernen Kapitalismus* (Munich: Duncker & Humblot).

Spaemann, R. (1985), 'Fortschritt – eine ganz unvernünftige Idee', *Süd-deutsche Zeitung*, no. 92.

Stammer, O. (1971), *Max Weber and Sociology Today* (Oxford: Blackwell).

Stern, J. P. (1979), *A Study of Nietzsche* (Cambridge University Press).

Stone, J. (1950), *The Province and Function of Law: Law as Logic, Justice and Social Control* (Cambridge, Mass.: Harvard University Press).

Stone, J. (1966), *Social Dimensions of Law and Jurisprudence* (London: Stevens).

Strauss, L. (1953), *Natural Right and History* (University of Chicago Press).

Strauss, L. (1966), *The Political Philosophy of Hobbes: its Basis and Genesis*, trans. E. M. Sinclair (University of Chicago Press).

Sugarman, D. (1986), *Weber, Modernity and 'The Peculiarities of the English': The Rationality and Irrationality of Law, State and Society in Modern Britain*, Working Paper Series (Madison: University of Wisconsin Institute of Legal Studies).

Taylor, C. (1975), *Hegel* (Oxford University Press).

Tenbruck, F. (1975), 'Wie gut kennen wir Max Weber?', *Kölner Zeitschrift für Soziologie und Sozialpsychologie*, vol. 131, pp. 719 ff.

Tenbruck, F. (1980), 'The problem of thematic unity in the works of Max Weber', trans. M. S. Whimster, *British Journal of Sociology*, vol. 31, no. 3.

Tenbruck, F. (1986), 'Max Webers Werk: Methodologie und Sozialwissenschaften', *Kölner Zeitschrift für Soziologie und Sozialpsychologie*, vol. 38, no. 1.

Thomas, J. J. R. (1984), 'Weber and direct democracy', *British Journal of Sociology*, vol. 35, pp. 216–40.

Tocqueville, A. de (1972), *Democracy in America*, ed. P. Bradley (New York: Knopf).

Tormey, J. (1973), 'Exploitation, oppression and self-sacrifice', *The Philosophical Forum*, vol. 5, nos. 1–2, pp. 206–21.

Toynbee, A. (1934), *A Study of History*, Vol. I (London: Oxford University Press).

Toynbee, A. and Ikeda, D. (1976), *The Toynbee–Ikeda Dialogue: Man Himself Must Choose* (Tokyo: Kodonsha).

Tribe, K. (1984), 'Cameralism and the science of government', *Journal of Modern History*, vol. 52, no. 2, pp. 263–84.

Troeltsch, E. (1931), *The Social Teaching of the Christian Churches* (London: Allen & Unwin).

Tucker, R. C. (1968), 'The theory of charismatic leadership', *Daedulus*, vol. 97, no. 3.

Tucker, R. C. (1974), *Stalin as a Revolutionary 1879–1929: A Study in History and Personality* (New York: Norton).

Turner, B. S. (1978), *Marx and the End of Orientalism* (London: Allen & Unwin).

Turner, B. S. (1981), *For Weber: Essays on the Sociology of Fate* (London: Routledge & Kegan Paul).

Turner, B. S. (1982a), 'The government of the body: medical regimens and the rationalisation of diet', *British Journal of Sociology*, vol. 33, pp. 254–69.

Turner, B. S. (1982b), 'The discourse of diet', *Theory, Culture and Society*, vol. 1, pp. 23–32.

Turner, B. S. (1982c), 'Nietzsche, Weber and the devaluation of politics: the problem of state legitimacy', *Sociological Review*, vol. 30, pp. 367–91.

Turner, B. S. (1984), *The Body and Society: Explorations in Social Theory* (Oxford: Blackwell).

Turner, S. P. and Factor, R. A. (1984a), *Max Weber and the Dispute over Reason and Value* (London: Routledge & Kegan Paul).

Turner, S. P. and Factor, R. A. (1984b), 'Weber, the Germans and "Anglo-Saxon convention": liberalism as technique and form of life', in R. M. Glassman and V. Murvar (eds.), *Max Weber's Political Sociology* (Westport, Conn.: Greenwood Press).

United Kingdom (1984), *Data Protection Act* (London: HMSO).

Valentin, V. (1940), *1848: Chapters of German History*, trans. E. Scheffauer (London: Allen & Unwin).

Verhandlungen des Ersten Deutschen Soziologentages (1911), 'Technik und Kultur' (Tübingen: Mohr).

Walter, A. (1926), 'Max Weber als Soziologe', *Jahrbuch für Soziologie*, vol. 2, pp. 1–65.

Warnock, M. (1984), *Report of the Committee of Inquiry into Human Fertilization and Embryology* (London: HMSO, Cmnd 9314).

Watt, I. (1957), *The Rise of the Novel: Studies in Defoe, Richardson and Fielding* (Harmondsworth: Penguin).

Weber, Marianne (1975), *Max Weber: A Biography*, trans. H. Zohn (New York: Wiley).

Weber, M. (1892), 'Zur Rechtfertigung Göhres', *Die christliche Welt. Evang.-Luth. Gemeindeblatt für Gebildete aller Stände* 6. Jg, no. 48, cols. 1104–9.

Weber, M. (1894a), 'Die deutschen Landarbeiter', *Bericht über die Verhandlungen des 5. Evangelisch-sozialen Kongresses* (Berlin: Rehtwisch & Langewort).

Weber, M. (1894b), 'Was heißt Christlich-Sozial?', *Die christliche Welt. Evang.-Luth. Gemeindeblatt für Gebildete aller Stände*, 8. Jg. no. 20, cols. 472–7.

Weber, M. (1902), Review of Philipp Lotmar, *Der Arbeitsvertrag, Archiv für soziale Gesetzgebung und Statistik*, vol. 17, pp. 723–34.

Weber, M. (1961), 'The three types of legitimate rule', in A. Etzioni (ed.), *Complex Organizations* (New York: Holt).

Weber, M. (1975), 'Marginal utility theory and "the fundamental laws of psychophysics"', trans. L. Schneider, *Social Science Quarterly*, vol. 56, no. 1, pp. 24–36.

Weber, M. (1976), *The Agrarian Sociology of Ancient Civilisations* (London: New Left Books).

Weber, M. (1977), *Critique of Stammler*, ed. and trans. G. Oaks (New York: Free Press).

Weber, M. (1978), 'Anticritical last word on *The Spirit of Capitalism*', *American Journal of Sociology*, vol. 83, no. 5, pp. 1105–31.

Weber, M. (1979), 'Developmental tendencies in the situation of the East Elbian rural labourers', *Economy and Society*, vol. 8, pp. 177–205.

Weber, M. (1980), 'The national state and economic policy [Freiburg Address]', *Economy and Society*, vol. 9, no. 4, pp. 428–49.

Weber, M. (1981), 'Some categories of interpretive sociology', *Sociological Quarterly*, vol. 22, pp. 151–80.

Weber, M. (1982), *Die Protestantische Ethik II. Kritiken und Antikritiken*, ed. J. Winckelmann (Gütersloh: Gütersloher Verlagshaus).

Weber, M. (1985), 'Church and sect in North America', *Sociological Theory*, vol. 3, pp. 7–13.

Weiß, J. (1981), *Das Werk Max Webers in der marxistischen Rezeption und Kritik* (Opladen: Westdeutscher Verlag).

Wellmer, A. (1985), 'Adorno's aesthetic redemption of modernity', *Telos*, no. 62, pp. 89–115.

Whyte, W. (1956), *The Organization Man* (New York: Simon & Schuster).

Williams, K., Williams, J. and Thomas, D. (1984), *Why Are the British Bad at Manufacturing?* (London: Routledge & Kegan Paul).

Wilson, J. D. (1935), *What Happens in Hamlet?* (Cambridge University Press).

Winckelmann, J. (1952), *Legitimität und Legalität in Max Webers Herrschaftssoziologie* (Tübingen: Mohr).

Wolff, K. (ed.) (1950), *The Sociology of Georg Simmel* (New York: Free Press).

Index